SEEKING THE FAVOR OF GOD

VOLUME 1:

THE ORIGINS OF PENITENTIAL PRAYER IN SECOND TEMPLE JUDAISM

Society of Biblical Literature

Early Judaism and Its Literature

Judith H. Newman,
Series Editor

Number 21

SEEKING THE FAVOR OF GOD

VOLUME 1:

THE ORIGINS OF PENITENTIAL PRAYER
IN SECOND TEMPLE JUDAISM

SEEKING THE FAVOR OF GOD

VOLUME 1:

THE ORIGINS OF PENITENTIAL PRAYER IN SECOND TEMPLE JUDAISM

Edited by

Mark J. Boda

Daniel K. Falk

and

Rodney A. Werline

Society of Biblical Literature
Atlanta

SEEKING THE FAVOR OF GOD
Volume 1: The Origins of Penitential Prayer in Second Temple Judaism

Copyright © 2006 by the Society of Biblical Literature

All rights reserved. No part of this work may be reproduced or transmitted in any form or by any means, electronic or mechanical, including photocopying and recording, or by means of any information storage or retrieval system, except as may be expressly permitted by the 1976 Copyright Act or in writing from the publisher. Requests for permission should be addressed in writing to the Rights and Permissions Office, Society of Biblical Literature, 825 Houston Mill Road, Atlanta, GA 30329 USA.

Library of Congress Cataloging-in-Publication Data

Seeking the favor of God / edited by Mark J. Boda, Daniel K. Falk, and Rodney A. Werline.
    v. cm. — (Early Judaism and its literature ; no. 21)
Includes bibliographical references and indexes.
Contents: v. 1. The origins of penitential prayer in Second Temple Judaism
ISBN-13: 978-1-58983-261-9 (paper binding : v. 1 : alk. paper)
ISBN-10: 1-58983-261-2 (paper binding : v. 1 : alk. paper)
    1. Bible. O.T.—Prayers—History and criticism. 2. Worship in the Bible. 3. Seliḥot. 4. Apocryphal books (Old Testament)—Criticism, interpretation, etc. 5. Judaism—History—Post-exilic period, 586 B.C.–210 A.D. I. Boda, Mark J. II. Falk, Daniel K. III. Werline, Rodney Alan, 1961–.
    BS1199.P68S44 2006b
    296.4'509014—dc22   2006032390

14 13 12 11 10 09 08 07 06   5 4 3 2 1
Printed in the United States of America on acid-free, recycled paper
conforming to ANSI/NISO Z39.48-1992 (R1997) and ISO 9706:1994
standards for paper permanence.

Contents

Abbreviations vii

Preface ix

Defining Penitential Prayer
    Rodney A. Werline xiii

"I Was Ready to Be Sought Out by Those Who Did Not Ask"
    Samuel E. Balentine 1

Confession as Theological Expression: Ideological Origins of
    Penitential Prayer
    Mark J. Boda 21

Socio-Ideological *Setting* or *Settings* for Penitential Prayers?
    Dalit Rom-Shiloni 51

The Speech Act of Confession: Priestly Performative Utterance
    in Leviticus 16 and Ezra 9–10
    Jay C. Hogewood 69

Lament Regained in Trito-Isaiah's Penitential Prayer
    Richard J. Bautch 83

The Affirmation of Divine Righteousness in Early Penitential Prayers:
    A Sign of Judaism's Entry into the Axial Age
    William Morrow 101

When None Repents, Earth Laments: The Chorus of Lament in
    Jeremiah and Joel
    Katherine M. Hayes 119

"…Why Do You Let Us Stray from Your Paths…" (Isa 63:17):
    The Concept of Guilt in the Communal Lament Isa 63:7–64:11
    Judith Gärtner 145

Ezra 9:6–15: A Penitential Prayer within Its Literary Setting
    Michael W. Duggan 165

Form Criticism in Transition: Penitential Prayer and Lament, Sitz im Leben and Form
    Mark J. Boda 181

Afterword
    Samuel E. Balentine 193

Bibliography 205

Contributors 223

Ancient Sources Index 225

Hebrew Words Index 239

Modern Authors Index 241

Subject Index 247

Abbreviations

AB	Anchor Bible
ABD	*Anchor Bible Dictionary.* Edited by D. N. Freedman. 6 vols. New York: Doublday, 1992.
ATD	Das Alte Testament Deutsch
AUSS	*Andrews University Seminary Studies*
BETL	Bibliotheca Ephemeridum theologicarum Lovaniensium
Bib	*Biblica*
BibInt	*Biblical Interpretation*
BibOr	Biblica et orientalia
BKAT	Biblischer Kommentar, Altes Testament
BRev	*Bible Review*
BTB	*Biblical Theology Bulletin*
BZ	*Biblische Zeitschrift*
BZAW	Beihefte zur Zeitschrift für die alttestamentliche Wissenschaft
CBQ	*Catholic Biblical Quarterly*
CC	Continental Commentaries
DSD	*Dead Sea Discoveries*
ER	*The Encyclopedia of Religion.* Edited by Mircea Eliade. 16 vols. New York: McMillan, 1987.
EstBib	*Estudios bíblicos*
EvT	*Evangelische Theologie*
ExAud	*Ex auditu*
FAT	Forschungen zum Alten Testament
FOTL	Forms of Old Testament Literature
FRLANT	Forschungen zur Religion und Literatur des Alten und Neuen Testaments
HAR	*Hebrew Annual Review*
HBS	Herders biblische Studien
HBT	*Horizons in Biblical Theology*
HvTSt	*Hervormde teologiese studies*
HSM	Harvard Semitic Monographs
HUCA	*Hebrew Union College Annual*
IBC	Interpretation: A Bible Commentary for Teaching and Preaching
Int	*Interpretation*

JBL	*Journal of Biblical Literature*
JJS	*Journal of Jewish Studies*
JSNTSup	Journal for the Study of the New Testament Supplement Series
JSOT	*Journal for the Study of the Old Testament*
JSOTSup	Journal for the Study of the Old Testament Supplement Series
JTS	*Journal of Theological Studies*
NCB	New Century Bible
LD	Lectio Divina
NICOT	New International Commentary on the Old Testament
OBO	Orbis biblicus et orientalis
OBT	Overtures to Biblical Theology
OTL	Old Testament Library
OtSt	Oudtestamentische Studiën
RB	*Revue biblique*
RevQ	*Revue de Qumran*
RGG⁴	*Religion in Geschichte und Gegenwart.* Edited by Kurt Galling. 4th ed. 8 vols. Tübingen: Mohr Siebeck, 2001.
SAA	State Archives of Assyria
SBB	Stuttgarter biblische Beiträge
SBLAcBib	Society of Biblical Literature Academia Biblica
SBLDS	Society of Biblical Literature Dissertation Series
SBLEJL	Society of Biblical Literature Early Judaism and Its Literature
SBLMS	Society of Biblical Literature Monograph Series
SBLSP	Society of Biblical Literature Seminar Papers
SBT	Studies in Biblical Theology
SJ	Studia judaica
SJLA	Studies in Judaism and Late Antiquity
STDJ	Studies on the Texts of the Desert of Judah
TDOT	*Theological Dictionary of the Old Testament.* Edited by G. Johannes Botterweck and Helmer Ringgren. Translated by John T. Willis, Geoffrey W. Bromiley, and David E. Green. Grand Rapids: Eerdmans, 1973–.
TLOT	*Theological Lexicon of the Old Testament.* Edited by Ernst Jenni and Claus Westermann. Translated by Mark E. Biddle. 3 vols. Peabody, Mass.: Hendrickson, 1997.
TRE	*Theologische Realenzyklopädie*
USQR	*Union Seminary Quarterly Review*
VT	*Vetus Testamentum*
VTSup	Supplements to Vetus Testamentum
WBC	Word Biblical Commentary
WMANT	Wissenschaftliche Monographien zum Alten und Neuen Testament
WTJ	*Westminster Theological Journal*
WUNT	Wissenschaftliche Untersuchungen zum Neuen Testament
ZAW	*Zeitschrift für die alttestamentliche Wissenschaft*

Preface

Over the course of two years at the close of this past century (1998–99) four volumes were published in the field of Second Temple Judaism that considered in varying degrees texts and issues related to penitential prayer. Their appearance suggested that the study of this form of prayer was of interest within the academic guild, but unfortunately the simultaneous character of their publication meant that there had been little room for interaction between the works. It was this that brought together a group of five—Richard Bautch, Mark Boda, Daniel Falk, Judith Newman, and Rodney Werline—to facilitate discussion on this topic at the Annual Meeting of the Society of Biblical Literature for a three-year period from 2003 to 2005. Participation in the consultation was open to all SBL members. While papers were invited for the thematic session each year to ensure coverage of that year's focus, an open session provided opportunity for any consultation member to contribute. The hope was that the sessions would facilitate interaction over past contributions, showcase new and fresh ideas, as well as synthesize the results that had been gained thus far in the study of these prayers. It was also hoped that this would encourage dialogue between scholars working in areas related to Second Temple Judaism but isolated by other disciplinarian lines (Hebrew Bible, Qumran, Second Temple literature, New Testament, post-70 C.E. Judaism, early Christianity). Each year the consultation invited a senior scholar who had worked extensively in the field to set the recent work in the broader scholarly context, to offer a critical review, and to provide trajectories for future research.

One of the key goals of the consultation from its inception was the publication of the best of its papers, with the focus of the volumes on the themes of the three years of the consultation (origin, development, impact). The present volume concerns the origins of penitential prayer in the Babylonian and Persian periods as it investigates the earliest phase of penitential prayer literature found in the Hebrew Bible.

Immediately following this preface, readers will find Rodney Werline's paper delivered at the inaugural session of the Penitential Prayer consultation, which provided a preliminary working definition of penitential prayer for the group's work. Various contributors in this and following volumes will make reference to this paper, which was intended "as a starting point, not the final word."

This is followed by Samuel Balentine's contribution as senior scholar. He picks up where his key volume, *Prayer in the Hebrew Bible,* ended in 1993 and wisely provides a succinct historical context for the study of penitential prayer since that time. His essay identifies points of intersection and conflict between the various studies, especially in relation to their definition of penitential prayer, methodology of form criticism, conclusions on tradition history, identification of *Sitz im Leben,* and explanation of institutionalization. Balentine ends by encouraging further analysis of the traditio-historical character of the prayers, greater sensitivity to the theology of lament and penitence, closer attention to the priestly role in the development of penitential prayer, and heightened focus on Job for understanding the relationship between penitence and lament in Second Temple Judaism.

Mark Boda then provides a synthesis of the ideological traditions that were key to the origination and expression of this prayer form. Through this one can see not only how important certain theological emphases were to the development of this prayer form but also how the prayer form itself became an avenue for expressing and embracing a theological response to the demise of the state.

Dalit Rom-Shiloni is the first of a series of new voices contributing to the study of penitential prayer, this time drawing on her extensive research on exilic prophetic traditions. Rom-Shiloni reconsiders the relationship between penitential prayer and communal laments, an issue of enduring conflict within recent study of these prayer forms, and argues that penitential prayer represents a polemic against communal lament by providing an "orthodox" alternative to such protest prayer forms. She suggests that penitential prayer forms arose within "orthodox circles" (DtrH, Priestly, prophetic traditions) and the communal laments within "nonorthodox circles." In this she denies to communal laments the status of "proto-penitential prayers." Thus, similarity between communal laments and penitential prayers is related to the intent of the one to replace and/or attack the other.

Jay Hogewood provides a new perspective on the ritual-critical dimensions of penitential prayer through the lens of speech-act theory and performative utterance. He accomplishes this by leveraging the theory and methodology of John L. Austin and applying it to the study of Lev 16 (a priestly ritual text) and then to Ezra 9–10, a key text in which a penitential prayer is embedded. By this means, Hogewood establishes not only the importance of confession to penitential prayer but also the force and meaning of such confession within priestly rituals and prayers.

Focusing his attention again on the prayer found in Isa 63:7–64:11, Richard Bautch showcases an example of a prayer in which lament was retained. In this he takes aim at those who speak of the loss of lament in the "postexilic" period and argues that lament remains as a "vestigial and proximate" influence through the efforts of later redactors of the book of Isaiah. The reemergence of "lament" in Isa 63:7–64:11 serves as a device that creates tension between past and present.

In this he shows that lament serves as "the penultimate point in the theological progression toward the confession of sin" (98).

While previous works looked to developments within Judaism (and in particular within the Hebrew Bible) for the shift from lament to penitential prayer as the dominant request form, Morrow supplements this by pointing to the global theological shift (identified by Karl Jaspers as "Axial Age" ideology) attested in Second Isaiah, which envisions Yahweh as transcendent deity removed from the vicissitudes of history. Morrow focuses on the contribution of the book of Job to the question of the shift from communal lament to penitential prayer and argues that the book represents Axial Age theology, especially in Elihu's speeches, which undermine Job's right to lament against God. This view of a transcendent God can also be discerned within the penitential prayers and is emphasized further by the focus on explicit divine instructions on holiness, which reveals the failures of the community and justifies any absence or punishment by the deity.

With Katherine Hayes there is a shift to synchronic methodologies as she investigates various voices of lament and penitence in Jer 1–12 and Joel 1–2, which "appeal to and model responses for a reading audience" (143). These texts give voice to the distress of the prophet and the deity but also incorporate the voice of the mourning earth, which plays the role of a tragic chorus concerned with the indifference of the people. Hayes shows through Jer 12 how lament can play a cathartic role in acknowledging and mourning the tragedy and through Joel 1–2 how it can be used to lead the audience toward repentance and a new beginning. Subsequent consideration of the penitential prayer tradition leads Hayes to the conclusion that "grieving and lamenting are a necessary part of the process of realignment with God and a prequel to repentance" (142).

While Richard Bautch focuses mainly on the form-critical dimensions of Isa 63:7–64:11, Judith Gärtner considers the redactional significance of this prayer on the book of Isaiah as a whole. She shows how this prayer not only plays off of Isa 6 with its emphasis on the disciplinary hardening of the heart of the people but also incorporates many allusions to passages throughout the book of Isaiah, a technique that effectively summarizes the book's main themes. Gärtner thus shows the role that lament and penitential prayer can play in the shaping of a literary piece.

Michael Duggan continues the synchronic investigation undertaken by Hayes and Gärtner with his consideration of the role that the penitential prayer in Ezra 9:6–15 plays in the overall rhetoric of the book of Ezra-Nehemiah. He argues that the prayer fits admirably within its immediate literary context of Ezra 9–10, expressed in a prose style appropriate to its narrative context and functioning to transition the reader from autobiography to narrative. By identifying resonances in vocabulary and structure between the material that follows the prayer (Neh 1–13) and that which precedes (Ezra 1–8) in the book, Duggan highlights the role that a penitential prayer played in the rhetoric of a biblical book.

In the penultimate chapter, Mark Boda reflects on his past research as one of the "early" proponents of a penitential prayer genre distinct from lament and provides summary conclusions on the form-critical dimension of penitential prayer. He admits some naivety in earlier argumentation, while retaining his conclusion that penitential prayer represents a significant formal shift in the prayer tradition of Israel. He proposes greater attention to what he calls *Ausblick aufs Lebens* (outlook/perspective on life) as a supplement to the traditional focus on *Sitz im Leben* (setting in life).

The final chapter is Samuel Balentine's response to the volume as a whole, providing an assessment of the accomplishments of the present volume and areas that need to be explored further. He traces three topics through the various contributions to the volume: texts and methodologies, the relationship between lament and penitence, and theologies and ideologies. In conclusion, he identifies lingering issues and questions, including theodicy, the contribution of Job, and the role of Scripture in biblical and contemporary prayer traditions.

With his mature perspective on the topic, Balentine thus frames the volume as a whole, providing integrity and closure to the discussion, while suggesting further trajectories for reflection and research. We would like to express our special thanks to Sam for his supportive participation in the consultation as well as the volume. Furthermore, we are thankful to all of the other contributors to the present work who have been patient with the editorial team as the volume took shape.

There are others, however, outside the consultation we would like to thank for their help on this volume. John C. Reeves was the editor of the SBLEJL series in the early stages of planning for the consultation and encouraged us with his willingness to publish the results in the series. With Judith Newman now assuming the responsibilities for the series from John, we were delighted to work with someone who has been so instrumental in the development of our project.

Thanks are also due to Leigh Andersen and the Publications staff at the Society of Biblical Literature for guiding us through the editorial process. We are grateful for graduate assistance from McMaster Divinity College, especially the work of Joel Barker, David Beldman, and James D. Dvorak, all of whom helped to bring the manuscript into its final form.

Finally, we are thankful for the Society of Biblical Literature, without whom this book and the foundational consultations would have been impossible. Our hope is that these volumes will be but a springboard for further reflection and scholarship on this rich history of prayer.

Mark J. Boda, Hamilton, Ontario
Daniel K. Falk, Eugene, Oregon
Rodney A. Werline, Greensboro, North Carolina

Defining Penitential Prayer*

Rodney A. Werline

At the beginning of our investigation into penitential prayer, we should briefly consider the process of definition, propose a definition for penitential prayer, provide some explanation for the definition, and present some of the basic characteristics of the prayers. The goal of this task of definition is to begin our conversation and to move toward clarity and precision in our investigation. I do not supply this definition and exposition as the standard for our work together. Through our work over the next three years, however, perhaps we can continue to consider the issue of definition and arrive at some consensus.

As we define penitential prayer, we have the opportunity to remember what we have learned about words and their meanings over the past several decades. A word achieves its meaning by the way that a community uses the word by placing it in relationship to other words or ideas. We should remove from our minds the notion that we are defining and speaking about the idea of penitential prayer in its purest form. In our case, we are the community determining the meaning of the word for our work, a group in this setting that is primarily interested in the academic study of religion. Consequently, the definition will reflect the academy's long tradition of critical methodologies. Our definition will determine what we study, from what perspective we work, and what will become primary examples of penitential prayer and what will become secondary material.

Much of the recent literature about penitential prayer, produced by many people in this consultation, employs form and tradition criticisms when analyzing the prayers. These two methodologies that we have inherited and have used have proven valuable because of the nature of our material: the prayers are written. They immediately seem to invite some kind of literary analysis. However, this also means that we have spoken and written about these prayers primarily from

---

* This paper was presented in this form, with only minor changes, at the inaugural meeting of the Penitential Prayer Consultation (Annual Meeting of the Society of Biblical Literature, 2003). The paper has been included in this volume in its original form because several of the authors in this and subsequent volumes refer to it in their essays.

the perspective of the prayers as literary pieces with a secondary concern for the historical forces and settings that formed them as literature.[2] We tend to isolate forms and formulaic expressions and explain developments in these. Thus, the definition that follows, since my own work still remains primarily within these criticisms as well, reflects the interests of these methodologies, their questions and the answers they yield, and their limitations.

Those who originally offered such prayers probably did not first think of these prayers in literary terms and with a view toward the development of a tradition. They probably first thought of the prayers within their own experience of God, their history, their people, and themselves. If we changed our primary methodologies we might arrive at a different definition for penitential prayers. At least, our analyses would look quite different. An example of this in a different but related area of study is Samuel Balentine's *The Torah's Vision of Worship*.[3] Perhaps over the next three years other methodologies (e.g., sociology and anthropology) can be utilized in order to improve our understanding of what we define as penitential prayer and to direct us to new perspectives.

The worth of our definition is established by how well it functions in this community, this consultation within the academy. It should enhance and not inhibit our ability to speak clearly and concisely to one another, and it should assist in making distinctions and comparisons between penitential prayer and what we see as related phenomena: various psalms, hymns, liturgies, litanies, confessions, and so forth. We can offer a definition of penitential prayer as a distinct genre because a number of prayers exhibit a similar form and contain similar formulaic expressions. Despite these similar features, though, modern interpreters have concluded that prayers from the biblical and Second Temple periods were not fixed.[4] The influence of Deuteronomic thought and language on these prayers is unmistakable and helps to group them together. However, detailed investigations of individual prayers have shown significant influences from other groups and traditions.[5]

My definition of penitential prayer has not significantly changed since my monograph appeared in 1998.

---

2. Bilhah Nitzan (*Qumran Prayer and Religious Poetry* [trans. Jonathan Chipman; STDJ 12; Leiden: Brill, 1994], 4) also recognizes that much study on prayer has focused on literary analysis and that more must be done: "While these studies [past form-critical work] do in fact clarify the literary tradition of biblical prayer, the question of the use of prayer as an accompaniment to the sacrificial cult (especially during the First Temple period) remains largely unanswered."

3. Samuel Balentine, *The Torah's Vision of Worship* (OBT; Minneapolis, Fortress, 1999).

4. Rodney A. Werline, *Penitential Prayer in Second Temple Judaism: The Development of a Religious Institution* (SBLEJL 13; Atlanta: Scholars Press, 1998), 4.

5. E.g., see especially Mark J. Boda, *Praying the Tradition: The Origin and Use of Tradition in Nehemiah 9* (BZAW 277; Berlin: de Gruyter, 1999), who has demonstrated the Priestly influences on this tradition.

Penitential prayer is a direct address to God in which an individual, group, or an individual on behalf of a group confesses sins and petitions for forgiveness as an act of repentance.

My first qualification about the kind of speech found in penitential prayer, that it is a "direct address to God," springs from my more general working definition of prayer itself; prayer is a direct address to God initiated by the human. It follows, then, that the human will typically address God in the second person as "you." In this regard, I completely agree with Judith Newman's criteria for prayer.[6] As she also proposes, this excludes conversations between God and humans from the category of prayer.[7] Not all scholars or people who practice religion would agree with such a qualification for prayer.[8] Indeed, many consider reading sacred texts, lighting candles, liturgy, dance, meditation, and perhaps even life itself as prayer. However, in order to be able to distinguish between various forms of worship and to speak about them clearly, I have restricted my definition of prayer in this manner.

This first criterion for penitential prayer does not often present problems. We should not find many instances in which we wonder if what we label as penitential prayer meets the criterion of a direct address to God. Still, some problems exist. For example, we might discuss the place of the penitential poem in Isa 63:7–64:12.[9] The poem begins by addressing God in the third person. A shift to second person occurs in verse 14c and continues in the verses that follow, as the

---

6. Judith Newman, *Praying by the Book: The Scripturalization of Prayer in Second Temple Judaism* (SBLEJL 14; Atlanta: Scholars Press, 1999), 6–7.

7. Ibid., 7.

8. Broad definitions of prayer appear in some of the literature. See Jack W. Corvin, "Stylistic and Functional Study of the Prose Prayers in the Historical Narratives of the Old Testament (Ph.D. diss., Emory University, 1972), 23; Henning Graf Reventlow, *Gebet im Alten Testament* (Stuttgart: Kohlhammer, 1986), 89. Patrick D. Miller suggests that conversations with God might be considered prayer: "Use of the non-technical language for saying and speaking thus press one toward a broader rather than a narrower definition … that is, *conversation with God*. In some sense, almost any address to God functions as prayer" (italics original, see Patrick D. Miller, *They Cried to the Lord: The Form and Theology of Biblical Prayer* [Minneapolis: Fortress, 1994], 33). Similarly, in New Testament studies, John Koenig claims that cries to Jesus should be considered prayer (*Rediscovering New Testament Prayer: Boldness and Blessing in the Name of Jesus* [Harrisburg, Pa: Morehouse, 1998], 115). Bilhah Nitzan also uses a broader definition of prayer in her examination of Qumran prayer and religious poetry: "Nevertheless, the word 'prayer' will be used as a general term to designate all the types of poetry used in the worship of God" (*Qumran Prayer and Religious Poetry*, 4). However, because of the nature of the Qumran material she investigates, her definition does not raise as many problems as some of the other broad definitions of prayer.

9. For a detailed study, see Richard J. Bautch, *Developments in Genre between Post-exilic Penitential Prayers and the Psalms of Communal Lament* (SBLAcBib 7; Atlanta: Society of Biblical Literature, 2003).

text's passion also rises. Psalm 106 begins with third-person speech that refers to God, moves into second person (including the typical language of confession of sin in v. 6), and then slips back into third person. Do we speak of these texts as penitential prayers?

A different problem surfaces in 1 Kgs 8. It is not a penitential prayer per se, but it does instruct Israel about repentance and encourages God to respond in an expected way, with forgiveness and restoration, all of this in the form of a prayer. The covenant-renewal ceremony in 1QS presents its own set of issues. After the priests recite God's mighty deeds (lines 21–22a), and the Levites recount Israel's sins (lines 22b–24a), those entering the covenant "confess" (ידה) and say:

> We have committed iniquity, we have transgressed, we have sinned, we have acted wickedly, we and our ancestors before us when we walked [contrary to the statutes]. True and righteous [is God in sending] his judgment against us and against our ancestors. (lines 24–26)

This confession is cast in third-person speech in reference to God. Should this be understood as a penitential prayer? Or is this confession simply a public declaration made before the community? But is God not listening in? Nevertheless, I still maintain that the *Community Rule* has taken components found in many penitential prayers—acclamation of God's saving deeds, recitation of Israel's sins, and confession of sins—and transformed them into a liturgy. Still, we have left penitential prayer and moved into a different genre.[10]

Most penitential prayers relate to the predicaments of the community; they are communal in nature, even when offered by an individual. The individual prays on behalf of the group. Often the community in mind is the whole of the Jewish people. Deuteronomic ideology shaped this aspect of these prayers through its interest in the sin and disobedience of the people as a whole. However, in the Second Temple period, divisions among groups sometimes transform the idea of the penitent community from the people as a whole to the members of a particular group. While *The Words of the Heavenly Lights* (4Q504) surely originated before the Qumran community, since the text contains none of the usual sectarian terminology, as these daily prayers get taken up into the Qumran community they must have been subsumed into the sect's ideology. Those who are the confessing righteous have become the sectarians, not the Jewish people as a whole.

The simplest form of the confession of sin, which appears in several prayers, is "We have sinned (חטא), we have acted in iniquity (עון), and have acted wickedly (רשע)."[11] Several prayers recite the history of Israel's sins along with the

---

10. See Werline, *Penitential Prayer*, 136–37. For these three aspects of penitential prayer in other penitential prayer or related texts, see Neh 9; Pss 78; 105; 106; Isa 63:7–64:12; and 4Q504.

11. See also the forms of confession in these texts, not all of which are penitential prayers: 1 Kgs 8:47; Neh 1:6; Ps 106:6; Jer 14:7; Dan 9:5; Bar 2:12; Pr Azar 6; 1QS 1:24–25.

confession. We also frequently encounter a declaration of God's righteousness: "You are righteous, O Lord."[12] After confessing sins, the supplicants typically ask for forgiveness and petition God to remove the punishment that has come upon the people because of their sin, thoughts that are the product of Deuteronomic influence. This petitionary section sometimes begins with the rhetorical marker ועתה, "And now...."[13] Those offering the prayers believed that the prayers assisted in the process of repentance. They expected that this act, perhaps accompanied by other actions, would restore their relationship with God and that their situation would improve. The relationship of the prayers to other penitential acts is complicated. However, especially complex is the function of these prayers in relationship to the temple (or perhaps its absence) and its sacrificial institutions. Simple statements about prayer replacing sacrifice require more thought and nuance.[14]

Again, I propose this definition and brief description of penitential prayer as a starting point, not the final word. Over the next three years, we must continue to return to the issue of definition. I hope that our continued careful study and conversations and the application of new methodologies will both clarify our understanding of these prayers and broaden our perspectives.

---

12. Cf. Ezra 9:15; Dan 9:7; Bar 1:15; 2:6; Tob 3:2; Pr Azar 4–5a; *Ps. Sol.* 2:15

13. E.g., Dan 9:17; Bar 2:11.

14. A fine contribution to this problem is Daniel K. Falk, "Qumran Prayer Texts and the Temple," in *Sapiential, Liturgical and Poetic Texts from Qumran: Proceedings of the Third Meeting of the International Organization for Qumran Studies, Oslo, 1998* (ed. Daniel K. Falk, Florentino García Martínez, and Eileen M. Schuller; Leiden: Brill, 2000), 106–26.

"I Was Ready to Be Sought Out by Those Who Did Not Ask"

Samuel E. Balentine

Introduction

The title for this essay comes from the opening words of Isa 65. I confess that I chose these words without much forethought; there was a deadline for sending in the abstract, and this seemed as good a place to target for a beginning as any other! In retrospect, perhaps the muses were at work in ways I did not recognize at the time. More than ten years ago, these were the words I used to close my book, *Prayer in the Hebrew Bible*.[1] I offered nothing more than a citation; there was no discussion of the relation of these words to the preceding communal lament in Isa 63:7–64:11, no exploration of how the confession of sin in this lament may have signaled a transformation in the genre of communal lament that required further attention. Prayers of penitence were on my radar then, but my assessment was limited to texts that had long been tagged with this label (Ezra 9:6–15; Neh 1:5–11; 9:6–37; Dan 9:4–19) and mostly followed the conventional thinking of the time. A new generation of scholarship on penitential prayer has now moved texts and traditions that had been of rather marginal interest front and center, and as a result the landscape of our understanding about the "conventions" of prayer has changed in significant ways.

My assignment is to review the new work on penitential prayer and to place it in the context of previous research. Toward this end, the comments that follow address three primary matters: (1) previous scholarship on the role and function of penitential prayer within the context of biblical prayer; (2) the contributions of current research on prayer, especially its attention to the origin, development, and impact of penitential prayer within the broader context of Second Temple Judaism; and (3) an assessment of what remains to be done.

---

1. Samuel E. Balentine, *Prayer in the Hebrew Bible: The Drama of Divine-Human Dialogue* (OBT; Minneapolis: Fortress, 1993).

Previous Scholarship on Penitential Prayer

The long interpretive history of penitential prayer begins with a rather loose identification of the seven penitential psalms (Pss 6; 32; 38; 51; 102; 130; 143). The sixth century Latin father Cassiodorus (*Expositio Psalmorum*) may have the distinction of being the first to treat these psalms as a distinct group focused on repentance, but he appears to have relied on a previously established tradition, most likely originating with Augustine.[2] The reasons why these psalms first attained this label are elusive, but it is reasonable to suggest that a connection (largely confessional in nature) was made between the references to the wrath of God in certain of these psalms and Paul's use of these psalms in Romans to support the argument that God's wrath is occasioned by a failure to repent of sin.[3] A close inspection of the content of these psalms, however, suggests that the label "penitential" is more prescriptive than descriptive. Four of the seven (Pss 32; 51; 130; 143) contain no mention of God's anger; of the three that do, only Ps 38 (v. 19 [MT]) develops the connection between divine wrath and a confession of sinfulness on the part of the psalmist. We may suppose that Romans provides the hermeneutic for uniting the seven psalms under one thematic emphasis, eliding dissimilarities that might otherwise call their connection into question.

Interpretation of the penitential psalms in the medieval and Reformation periods extended this understanding, with slight modifications. For catechetical purposes, medieval commentators linked the seven penitential psalms to the "seven deadly sins," which were associated not with original sin but with specific temptations that plague everyday life (wrath: Ps 6; pride: Ps 32; gluttony: Ps 38; lechery: Ps 51; avarice: Ps 102; envy: Ps 130; sloth: Ps 143). In this way, these psalms were incorporated into a sacramental system that promoted contrition as a realizable and perfectible virtue, which moved the penitent closer to the ideal: imitation of the humility of Christ. The Reformation's use of these psalms, perhaps best exemplified by Luther, who called them the "Pauline psalms," essentially returned to the Pauline side of Augustine's interpretation.

Two hermeneutical shifts may be noted, both rooted more in the distinctive emphases of Reformation theology than in any critical assessment of the psalms themselves. First, the reformers eschewed the allegorical interpretation preferred by medieval commentators in favor of a metaphorical model that spiritualized the "sins" confessed by the psalmists as indicators of a conscience stricken by the guilt of human failure. Second, the reformers accented the impossibility, not the

---

2. See the brief survey of these matters in Harry P. Nasuti, *Defining the Sacred Songs: Genre, Tradition and the Post-Critical Interpretation of the Psalms* (JSOTSup 218; Sheffield: Sheffield Academic Press, 1999), 30–56.

3. Rom 3:4 cites Ps 51:4; Rom 3:20 refers to Ps 143:2; Rom 3:24 refers to Ps 130:7; and Rom 4:7–8 cites Ps 32:1–2.

possibility, of humans to imitate Christ because of their sinful nature. Confession requires *faith* not *works*; forgiveness is a promise sustained by God's grace, not God's reward.[4]

The form-critical approach to the Psalms pioneered by Hermann Gunkel in the nineteenth century marked a decisive change in the study of penitential prayer. Two new perspectives have particular bearing on the issues at hand. First, Gunkel's focus on *form* led him to conclude that the penitential psalms were no more than a subcategory of the larger genre of the lament, which typically accents complaint and protest, not penitence. Lament psalms insist that the burden for acknowledging and resolving whatever has gone wrong mandates God's justice and righteousness, not human contrition. Although lament psalms, especially the corporate laments, may include penitential motifs, Gunkel objected to the traditional understanding that penitence was a major characteristic of psalmic prayers. Of the seven so-called penitential psalms, he conceded the label without reservation only to Ps 51, which departs from the norm by grounding its appeal for God's intervention in the psalmist's confession and the appeal for forgiveness.[5] Second, Gunkel's concern to connect the psalms' literary forms to the social *setting* (*Sitz im Leben*) in which they functioned shifted the focus away from searching for the psalmist's personal reasons for prayer—such as the desire to confess and be forgiven for specific sins—toward institutional settings in the ongoing life of the community. Gunkel, and to a still larger degree his student Sigmund Mowinckel,[6] advocated a cultic setting for what came to be regarded (with modifications and refinements) as the five major types of psalms: hymns of praise, communal laments, individual laments, individual thanksgiving songs, and royal psalms. This form-critical classification effectively dislodged the penitential psalms from their previous place of importance. Praise, lament, and thanksgiving could be firmly anchored to the traditions and conventions of ancient Israel's cultic worship, but not penitence, at least, so Gunkel and Mowinckel hypothesized, not in any way that merited understanding it as a defining and recurring aspect of corporate piety.

Claus Westermann represents another and still more consequential shift in the study of penitential prayer. Although he continued the form-critical approach of Gunkel and Mowinckel, Westermann focused not on the institutional/cultic settings of the psalms in ancient Israel but instead on the distinctive theology the

---

4. On these hermeneutical shifts in Reformation theology, see James S. Preus, *From Shadow to Promise: Old Testament Interpretation from Augustine to the Young Luther* (Cambridge: Harvard University Press, 1969).

5. Hermann Gunkel, *Einleitung in die Psalmen: Die Gattungen der religiösen Lyrick Israels* (Göttingen: Vandenhoeck & Ruprecht, 1933), 131–32, 251–52. Of the remaining seven penitential psalms, Gunkel included Ps 130, with reservation, and the Prayer of Manasseh.

6. Sigmund Mowinckel, *Psalmenstudien* (6 vols.; Kristiana: J. Dybwad, 1921–1924); *The Psalms in Israel's Worship* (Nashville: Abingdon, 1962).

psalms conveyed and on its abiding importance for the community of faith. Two types of prayer were of principal importance, praise and lament, for "In Israel," Westermann argued, "all speaking to God moved between these two poles."[7] Westermann traced the historical development of both these genres of prayer, but it is his survey of the history of lament that provided the base line for the assessment of penitential prayers for approximately the next fifty years.[8]

Westermann tracked the historical development of lament through three stages. The first and earliest stage consists of short appeals to God that arise directly and naturally from situations in daily life. The occasion requires no cultic framework, the pray-ers no cultic mediator. These early laments are typically embedded within narrative contexts and are presented as integral and formative parts of a recounted course of events (e.g., Exod 18:10; Judg 15:18; 2 Sam 15:31). Of the formal elements that characterize the genre (address to God, lament, and petition), the lament or complaint against God, most often introduced with the question "Why?" dominates this early stage (e.g., Exod 5:22–23; 17:3; Josh 7:7–9; Judg 6:13, 22; 21:3; Num 11:11). Both individuals and the community may raise the question, but the lament of the individual is more common.

In the *second* or middle stage, these once brief, independent appeals are fused into poetic/psalmic forms. The *Sitz im Leben* is the settled community, where both the temple, which provides the center for worship, and the state, which provides political stability and social structure, create a self-evident corporate consciousness of belonging to God. The formal elements of lament are more clearly delineated in the psalms than in early prose prayers, and Westermann discerns differences in both structure and tone. The complaint against God is dominant in corporate laments, especially in the reproaching questions "Why?" and "How long?"[9] and in accusatory statements.[10] The complaint against God is also present in individual laments, but the dominant means for expressing it shifts from accusatory questions and direct statements to muted negative petitions addressed to God, for example, "Do not hide," "Do not be silent," "Do not be far from me."[11]

---

7. Claus Westermann, *Praise and Lament in the Psalms* (trans. Keith R. Crim and Richard N. Soulen; Atlanta: John Knox, 1981), 154; cf. *Elements of Old Testament Theology* (Atlanta: John Knox, 1978), 156.

8. Claus Westermann, "Struktur und Geschichte der Klage im Alten Testament," *ZAW* 66 (1954): 44–80 ("The Structure and History of Lament in the Old Testament," in *Praise and Lament*, 165–213).

9. For "Why?" questions, see, e.g., Pss 44:23–24; 74:1. For "How long?" questions, see, e.g., Pss 79:5; 80:4; 89:46; cf. Hab 1:13; Jer 14:8, 19; Isa 58:3.

10. E.g., Pss 44:9; 60:10; 89:38; 108:11; cf. Lam 3:42–45; Isa 64:12.

11. Westermann cites the following examples ("The Structure and History of Lament," 185 n. 53): "Do not hide" (Pss 27:9; 55:1; 69:17; 102:1; 143:7); "Be not silent" (Pss 28:1; 39:12; 109:1); "Forsake me not" (Pss 27:9, 12; 38:21; 71:9); "Chasten, strike me not" (Pss 6:1; 38:1; 39:10–11); "Rebuke me not" (Pss 6:1; 38:1; 39:11); and "Cast me not off" (Pss 27:9; 51:11).

Confession of sin seldom occurs in this second stage of lament;[12] instead, psalmists typically couple the complaint against God with a protest of innocence.

The *third* or late stage in the history of lament coincides with the defeat of the state and the destruction of the temple, a calamitous political and religious loss for Israel that dramatically changed the way it prays. The self-evident consciousness of belonging to a viable community of God that defined the laments of the Psalter is replaced by a "conscious and reflected belonging"[13] imposed by the trauma of exile. Absent the cult and its rituals, the language of prayer shifts from poetry to prose. The content of prayer shifts from lament and complaint that raise questions about God's justice to confession of sin that exonerates God by acknowledging human guilt. The exemplar of these transformations is the "prayer of penitence," which first appears, in Westermann's judgment, in the prose prayers of Neh 9 and Dan 9, then in the post-canonical prayers of 1 Esd (3 Ezra) 8:73–90, the Prayer of Manasseh, *Pss. Sol.* 9, and Bar 1:15–3:18.[14]

Westermann understood the shift to penitential prayer to signal the dissolution of the lament psalm as a fixed prayer form in ancient Israel. From the beginning, Israel's prayers had held in viable tension the complaint against God and the petition for redress. After the exile, the lament "was gradually pushed more and more into the background" until it was "finally excluded altogether from the prayer."[15] Praise of God becomes the norm, and this redefines the context for lament, in effect shifting the reason for addressing God from complaint about what God *had not done* to confession of sin that justifies what God *had done*. Why does the lament recede from prayer in the later stages? Westermann's explanation deserves to be quoted in full, because it is the compass by which a good deal of the current work on penitential prayer plots its course:

> How and why it [the lament] becomes silent can easily be observed. The theology of the Deuteronomic school—which declared the history of the wilderness sojourn (esp. Deut 9:7ff.) and even more the history of established Israel, to be a history of disobedience, and which sought to prove that political annihilation was the righteous judgment of God—began to formulate a way of thinking in which complaint against God was absolutely disallowed. The guilt of the Patriarchs was so earnestly and consciously taken over that, in place of the complaint against God formerly found in laments concerned with the fate of the nation, now the exact opposite appeared, viz., the justification of God's righteousness or simply praise of the righteousness of God.[16]

---

12. Westermann cites only Ps 51 as an example; see "The Structure and History of Lament," 206.
13. Westermann, *Elements of Old Testament Theology,* 156.
14. Westermann, *Praise and Lament,* 206.
15. Ibid., 206–7.
16. Ibid., 171–72.

Westermann's explanation of the shift from lament to penitence is important; indeed, his discernments found the new work under discussion in this volume, because he places penitential prayer as a literary type on a firm form-critical foundation. But before tracking this further, it is instructive to linger for a moment in order to consider the theological accents he adds to the discussion.

Westermann effectively dismissed the third stage of the history of lament, which foregrounds penitence rather than complaint, as "merely a late form of the Psalm of lament (at least in Israel)."[17] In his judgment, the displacement of lament by the prayer of penitence represents a significant theological loss, not only for ancient Israel but also for the contemporary community of faith. *For ancient Israel*, once "complaint against God is disallowed, there can be no lament in the strict sense of the word." Suffering, whatever its nature or impact, is interpreted within the nexus of sin and punishment, which means, "perforce," that the "doctrine of the righteousness of God" defines every prayer.[18] The polarity between praise and lament, which had been a staple of Israel's prayers, collapsed. In its place emerged a "kind of self-conscious piety" that is "forced to justify God's actions." As a result, "what heretofore had been an occasion for lament now becomes an occasion for praising the righteous God." The loss of lament from ancient Israel's prayers caused a similar loss for *the contemporary Christian community*. With Gunkel, Westermann argued, that this "doctrine of the righteousness of God" reinforces Paul's contention that every lamenter, every sufferer, "appears before God as one who is guilty." The result was the elimination of lament from Christian prayer. To counter this loss, Westermann issued a strong appeal for the restoration of lament to Christian worship, without which the Church is vulnerable to the charge that it considers the "guilt of sin" more important than the "sufferings of the world."[19]

With respect to the study of the Psalms, no one has taken up Westermann's challenge with more passion and influence than Walter Brueggemann. Brueggemann has argued that the psalms of lament are not only structurally central for the entire Psalter, they are also theologically and existentially central to the life of faith. The "anatomy of the lament psalm," he suggests, is a window onto the "anatomy of the soul."[20] Lament is important because it invites and enables the articulation of the universal human experience of suffering.

Brueggemann goes further, however, to argue that lament is also vital, because it keeps alive the possibility that status quo political and religious systems, as well as the divine authority that may be presumed to sustain them, can be effectively questioned and changed. Prayers of praise typically affirm the moral

---

17. Ibid., 206 n. 99.
18. Ibid., 203.
19. Ibid., 274.
20. Walter Brueggemann, *The Message of the Psalms: A Theological Commentary* (Minneapolis: Augsburg, 1984), 19.

order of the world God has created and invite individuals and community to conform to it. Prayers of penitence acknowledge disorder in God's world, but they avoid direct challenge to systemic problems that may require correction, insisting instead that humans bear the brunt of responsibility for whatever has gone. While both praise and penitence are important and necessary responses to God, neither is fully adequate. It is lament that is peculiarly suited to raise the unsettling questions that hold religious and political systems accountable to nonnegotiable aspirations for justice and righteousness. The loss of lament is therefore exceedingly "costly," Brueggemann argues, because if legitimate questions about the moral order of the world are silenced in the sanctuary, it is likely that challenges to social and political injustice will be muted outside the sanctuary as well.[21]

Westermann and Brueggemann move the discussion of lament's relationship to penitence beyond Gunkel's form-critical analysis. Both are less concerned with the *Sitz im Leben* of prayer in ancient Israel's cultic institutions than with the theological function of prayer in contemporary faith and practice. Both understand genre analysis as more than merely a descriptive task; it is also an evaluative and constructive task, which invites interpreters to judge a genre's theological importance and to conceptualize its function in the modern world. Both, especially Brueggemann, privilege lament over penitence in large measure because of its distinctive function in raising questions about the social order.

As Nasuti has suggested, it is likely that Westermann and Brueggemann's valuation of lament has less to do with refinements in the methodology of form-criticism than with changes in their own historical contexts as interpreters.[22] On this side of the Holocaust, to cite but one of the most obvious contributing factors, experiences of extreme suffering make it increasingly difficult, if not impossible, for biblical interpreters to remain within the conventional theological framework of sin and punishment, whatever its merits may be. What sin can possibly explain or justify the killing of six million Jews as the punishment of a just and righteous God? Both the extent and the inexplicability of the death and destruction that the modern world has witnessed, Nasuti plausibly suggests, invites and perhaps requires that theologians of prayer place the accent on lament and complaint, not contrition and confession.

In my judgment, Nasuti's suspicion concerning the shifting historical context for interpretation is correct. But it also seems to me that this observation both

---

21. Walter Brueggemann, "The Costly Loss of Lament," *JSOT* 36 (1984): 64. Brueggemann pursues these matters in numerous publications, e.g., "From Hurt to Joy, from Death to Life," *Int* 28 (1974): 3–19; "The Formfulness of Grief," *Int* 31 (1977): 263–75; "A Shape for Old Testament Theology II: Embrace of Pain," *CBQ* 47 (1985): 395–415; "Theodicy in a Social Dimension," *JSOT* 33 (1985): 3–25. For further discussion of lament within the context of Old Testament theology, see *Theology of the Old Testament: Testimony, Dispute, Advocacy* (Minneapolis: Fortress, 1997).

22. Nasuti, *Defining the Sacred Songs*.

clarifies and complicates our assessment of penitential prayer. Westermann surmised, as noted above, that the historical catalyst for the replacement of lament with penitence in ancient Israel's prayers was the trauma of the exile. That experience, he argued, was so devastating that Israel had no choice but to yield to the Deuteronomistic theologians, who insisted it could only be interpreted as a divine judgment on disobedience so definitive that it muted any conceivable protest of innocence. Westermann's assessment, however, only begs a further question. Do calamitous experiences for faith communities, whenever they impose themselves on the consciousness of the ancient or the modern world, invite and/or require only penitence, never complaint? In short, if Nasuti is correct in suggesting that the historical context of interpreters has a decisive bearing on the assessment of lament and penitence, why and how is what the community of faith suffered in 586 B.C.E. qualitatively different from what it faced in the aftermath of 1933–1945? How are we to understand that in one context penitence was advocated, and presumably widely accepted, as the only legitimate response to God, while in the other lament? The sociology of penitence and lament requires further inspection. I will return to this issue below.

Given the enormous influence of Westermann and Brueggemann, it is perhaps not surprising that in their wake the work on Israel's "penitential prayers" was mostly conducted on the margins, just below the radar of what they argued was of vital theological importance. In the main, four such penitential prayers continued to claim some attention: Ezra 9:6–15; Neh 1:5–11; 9:6–37; and Dan 9:4–19. Following Westermann's lead, a number of scholars noted that these late prose prayers, while similar to lament, are distinct with respect to their form and content. Their distinctiveness was summarized by W. S. Towner, who may be taken as representative of others who were mining the same fields.[23] (1) Of all prose prayers in the Old Testament, these alone contain the key word *lehitwaddeh*, "to make confession" (Ezra 10:1; Neh 1:6; 9:3; Dan 9:4, 20). The *hitpa'el* form of the verb *yādāh* occurs just ten times in the Hebrew Bible with the meaning "confess," and of these, six occur in these four prayers. (2) These prayers are considerably more elaborate than earlier prose prayers and are eclectic in their language, borrowing from earlier traditions, especially Deuteronomistic, and combining the various elements into a formal structure that moves from praise of God to confession to petition for forgiveness. (3) Each prayer is deci-

---

23. W. Sibley Towner, "Retributional Theology in the Apocalyptic Setting," *USQR* 26 (1971): 210–11; cf. Otto Plöger, "Reden und Gebete im deuteronomistichen und chronistischen Geschichtswerk," in *Festschift für Günther Dehn* (ed. Wilhelm Schneemelcher; Neukirchen-Vluyn: Kreis Moers, 1957), 39–44; Moshe Weinfeld, *Deuteronomy and the Deuteronomic School* (Oxford: Clarendon, 1972), 39–43; Henning Graf Reventlow, *Gebet im Alten Testament* (Stuttgart: Kohlhammer, 1986), 277–284; Balentine, *Prayer in the Hebrew Bible*, 103–17; Patrick D. Miller, *They Cried to the Lord: The Form and Theology of Biblical Prayer* (Minneapolis: Fortress, 1994), 244–61.

sively penitential in character, and in this respect can be linked to the penitential emphases in Solomon's temple prayer (cf. 1 Kgs 8:46–47, 49), which is a prime exemplar of the Deuteronomistic perspective. Thus in Dan 9:5 the confession "We have sinned and acted perversely and wickedly" is virtually a verbatim repetition of 1 Kgs 8:47. Similar confessions occur in the prayers of Ezra and Nehemiah (Neh 1:6–7; 9:16–18; cf. Ezra 9:6, 7, 13, 15). (4) The penitence motif is accented with a complementary emphasis on God's sovereignty, mercy, and justice. A repeating affirmation—"the great and awesome God who keeps covenant and steadfast love to those who love you and keep your commandments" (Dan 9:4; Neh 1:5; 9:32)—undergirds the summons to contrition as the only appropriate response to God, whose "righteousness" (צְדָקָה; 3x in Dan 9: vv. 7, 14, 16; cf. v. 18) is tempered with "mercy" (רַחוּם; 6x in Neh 9: vv. 17, 19, 27, 28, 31 [twice]).[24]

It is fair to say that these four characteristics of penitential prayers were generally agreed upon. Other critical issues, however, continued to be debated. The following may be singled out for brief mention, for in different ways they anticipated the work that was to come.

(1) While there was general agreement that the four texts listed above belonged to the genre of "prose prayers of penitence," a number of additional possibilities were suggested. Gunkel associated confession of sin primarily with the communal psalms of lament, where he found the motif present but not prominent. For more fully developed examples of the *Bussleider*, he looked to the prophets (e.g., Isa 59:12; 64:4, 6, 8; Jer 14:7, 20; Ezek 14:23), through whose influence, he argued, the confession of sin first came to prominence at the time of the exile. Although he did not pursue these prophetic examples in any detail, he opened the door for others who would. In a similar way, Westermann had noted, but did not explore, that the penitential motif, which first appeared in Neh 9 and Dan 9, was also present in post-canonical prayers. He cited as examples 1 Esd (3 Ezra) 8:73–90, the Prayer of Manasseh, *Pss. Sol.* 9, and Bar 1:15–3:8. Following Westermann, others noted that a still wider range of Second Temple texts might be included, e.g., Tob 3:1–6; the "Words of the Luminaries" (4Q504) 1:8–7:2; 1QS 1:24–2:1; CD 20:28:30; Prayer of Azariah; LXX Prayer of Esther; and 3 Macc 2:1–20.[25]

(2) The recognition that the penitential genre extended into the Second Temple period invited the suggestion that it may have influenced the development of prayer in the synagogue. L. Liebreich, who viewed Neh 9 as an early

---

24. Balentine, *Prayer in the Hebrew Bible*, 104, 116.
25. E.g., John J. Collins, *The Apocalyptic Vision of Daniel* (HSM 16; Missoula, Mont.: Scholars Press, 1977), 185–87.

exemplar of the synagogue liturgy, made the most forceful argument.[26] Liebreich's argument was not persuasive for all, but in view of the work that was to follow, we can say that he was not wrong to pursue the connections between penitential prayer in the biblical period and post-biblical Jewish liturgy.

(3) Gunkel and Mowinckel set in motion a search for the cultic setting of Israel's prayers. Mowinckel's suggestion that many of the psalms had their setting in an annual fall covenant renewal ceremony was particularly attractive to many, and a group of scholars emerged who argued that this was also the original setting for the penitential prayers.[27] O. Steck recognized that these penitential prayers drew upon a lively homiletic tradition that embodied the Deuteronomic view of history, and he extended the discussion by arguing that this tradition was kept alive in postexilic covenant renewal ceremonies by Levitical circles.[28] Edward Lipiński added to this suggestion by proposing a structure for a postexilic "penitential liturgy," in which prayers of confession, along with silence, fasting, and the use of sackcloth and ashes, were ritual acts for repairing covenantal breaches.[29]

(4) A consistent and primary claim with respect to penitential prayers was that they drew heavily upon the sin-punishment-repentance theology of the Deuteronomistic tradition. Alongside this claim, some scholars, as evidenced by the work of Steck and Lipiński, noted that the literary genre of penitence that emerged in the Second Temple period was a hybrid comprised of traditions rooted in both prophetic and priestly circles. Although six of the ten occurrences of the verb "to confess" (ידה, *hitpaʿel*) occur in prayers conventionally identified as "penitential" (Ezra 10:1; Neh 1:6; 9:3; Dan 9:4, 20), three of the remaining four belong to the Priestly stratum of the Pentateuch (Lev 5:5; 16:21; 26:40; Num 5:5; the fourth is 2Chr 30:22). These references, only marginally explored in the previous generation of scholarship,[30] seed the necessary discussion that has now emerged on the Priestly contribution to penitential prayer.

---

26. Leon Liebreich, "The Impact of Nehemiah 9:5–37 on the Liturgy of the Synagogue," *HUCA* 32 (1961): 227–37; cf. Yehezkel Kaufmann, *The Religion of Israel* (Chicago: University of Chicago Press, 1960), 210.

27. E.g., Gerhard von Rad, "The Form of the Hexateuch," in *The Problem of the Hexateuch and Other Essays* (Edinburgh: Oliver & Boyd, 1963), 1–78; idem, *Old Testament Theology* (New York: Harper & Row, 1962), 1:18–19, 88–89; Albrecht Alt, "The Origins of Israelite Law," in *Essays on the Old Testament and Religion* (Oxford: Blackwell, 1966), 79–132; Klaus Baltzer, *The Covenant Formulary: In Old Testament, Jewish, and Early Christian Writings* (Philadelphia: Fortress, 1971).

28. Odil H. Steck, *Israel und das gewaltsame Geschick im Alten Testament* (Neukirchen-Vluyn: Neukirchener, 1967), e.g., 134–35.

29. Edward Lipiński, *La Liturgie Pénitentielle dans la Bible* (Paris: Cerf, 1969), e.g., 37–38.

30. E.g., Andre Lacocque, "The Liturgical Prayer in Daniel 9," *HUCA* 47 (1976): 119–42.

The Contributions of Current Research on Penitential Prayer

In the last decade a new generation of scholars has focused its attention on the development of penitential prayer in Second Temple Judaism. The books of Werline, Falk, Newman, Boda, and Bautch, plus others who have contributed doctoral dissertations, articles, and essays to a steadily expanding bibliography on the subject distinguish the new research.[31] Although these works were researched in relative isolation from one another, they display a number of shared concerns, which signal several new emphases. If I may limit myself to the book-length discussions, the following points of intersection between them strike me as especially significant.

(1) The *definition of penitential prayer* appears to be a less vexing task than that which perplexed a previous generation, which struggled for clarity and precision on what constituted prayer more broadly conceived. Werline reasonably proposes a simple working definition: "A penitential prayer is a direct address to God in which an individual or group confesses sins and petitions for forgiveness."[32] Bautch amplifies the definition by identifying five distinctive features of such prayers: functional efficacy (repentance effects God's forgiveness), communal dimension (individual penitence is addressed in solidarity with a national consciousness of moral failure), structuring conventions (self-conscious use of the lament genre), ceremonial context (related, but not reducible to the cult), and intertextual character (the reuse of religious thought from earlier generations).[33] With some variations, each of the authors works within these definitional parameters.

(2) With respect to *methodology*, the new work sustains the form-critical interest in genre analysis but shifts to an increasing reliance on traditio-historical investigation. Tracking the appropriation and transformation of antecedent literary and theological traditions in penitential prayers has resulted in an emerging consensus concerning what Newman has identified as the "scripturalization" of prayer. This scripturalization process, she argues, appears prominently first in Solomon's prayer in 1 Kgs 8:23–53, then develops in Second Temple prayer in three major ways: the "retelling of history" (e.g., the prayer in Neh 9); the typological

---

31. Rodney A. Werline, *Penitential Prayer in Second Temple Judaism: The Development of a Religious Institution* (SBLEJL 13; Atlanta: Scholars Press, 1998); Daniel K. Falk, *Daily, Sabbath, and Festival Prayers in the Dead Sea Scrolls* (STDJ 27; Leiden: Brill, 1998); Judith H. Newman, *Praying by the Book: The Scripturalization of Prayer in Second Temple Judaism* (SBLEJL 14; Atlanta: Scholars Press, 1999); Mark J. Boda, *Praying the Tradition: The Origin and Use of Tradition in Nehemiah 9* (BZAW 277; Berlin: de Gruyter, 1999); Richard J. Bautch, *Developments in Genre between Post-exilic Penitential Prayers and the Psalms of Communal Lament* (SBLAcBib 7; Atlanta: Society of Biblical Literature, 2003).
32. Werline, *Penitential Prayer*, 2. See also his "Defining Penitential Prayer," in this volume.
33. Bautch, *Developments in Genre*, 1–6.

use of earlier traditions to legitimate a contemporary situation (e.g., the prayer in Jdt 9:2–14); and the use of biblical citations, allusions, and interpretations to exemplify good and bad behavior (e.g., the prayer in 3 Macc 2:2–20).

(3) With respect to the *development* or *trajectory* of the traditions that contribute to the emergence of penitential prayer as a religious institution in the exilic period and beyond, the new work displays some broad agreements. Most target Solomon's prayer in 1 Kgs 8 as being at or near the beginning point of the emergence of confession as a major motif in prayer. Similarly, there is consensus that the postexilic prayers in Ezra 9, Neh 9, and Dan 9 represent the first fully developed examples of the genre. Tracing the institutionalization of penitential prayer in the Second Temple period and in rabbinic literature has proved more difficult.[34] Bautch's conclusion, it seems to me, is an accurate assessment of where we are: although the confession of sin dominates in the Persian period, its predominance "waxes and wanes" in the Hellenistic and Roman eras.[35]

There are also significant differences in how the new work tracks the development of penitential prayer, especially in the critical transformative period between 1 Kgs 8 and the prose prayers of Ezra, Nehemiah, and Daniel. Werline and Bautch continue to stress the influence of Deuteronomic traditions on 1 Kgs 8, grounded for example in Deut 4 and 30, and the prophetic development of these traditions in texts such as Jer 29:10–14 and Isa 63:7–64:11. The latter text is critical for Bautch, who sees Third Isaiah's transformation of the communal lament psalm, specifically by highlighting confession of sin, as the crucial link in the move toward more fully developed penitential prayer forms. Boda agrees with the importance of the Deuteronomistic link, but he has argued that Deuteronomistic idioms have been decisively transformed in the early Persian period by Priestly and Ezekielian traditions. With respect to the prayer in Neh 9, he targets the shaping influence of Josh 7, Lev 26, and Ezek 18, along with Ps 106.[36]

---

34. Cf. Esther G. Chazon, "A Liturgical Document from Qumran and Its Implications: 'Words of the Luminaries' (4QDibHam)," (Ph.D. diss., Hebrew University, 1991); idem, "Prayers from Qumran: Issues and Methods," *Society of Biblical Literature 1993 Seminar Papers* (Atlanta: Scholars Press, 1993), 762–64; idem, "Prayers from Qumran and Their Historical Implications," *DSD* 1 (1994): 265–284; "4Q DibHam: Liturgy or Literature?" *RevQ* 15 (1992): 447–56; Bilhah Nitzan, *Qumran Prayer and Religious Poetry* (Leiden: Brill, 1994); Ezra Fleischer, "On the Beginnings of Obligatory Jewish Prayer" [Hebrew], *Tarbiz* 59 (1990): 397–444; Stefan Reif, *Judaism and Hebrew Prayer: New Perspectives on Jewish Liturgical History* (Cambridge: Cambridge University Press, 1993); Moshe Weinfeld, "Prayer and Liturgical Practice in the Qumran Sect," in *The Dead Sea Scrolls: Forty Years of Research* (ed. Devorah Dimant and Uriel Rappaport; Leiden: Brill, 1992), 241–58; idem, "The Prayers for Knowledge, Repentance and Forgiveness in the 'Eighteen Benedictions'—Qumran Parallels, Biblical Antecedents and Basic Characteristics" [Hebrew], *Tarbiz* 48 (1979): 186–200.

35. Bautch, *Developments in Genre*.

36. Cf. Volker Pröbstl, *Nehemia 9, Psalm 106 und Psalm 136 und die Rezeption des Pentateuchs* (Göttingen: Cuvillier, 1997).

4) The search for the missing links that explain the transition from 1 Kgs 8 to the prayers in Ezra, Nehemiah, and Daniel brings into focus another issue: the *Sitz im Leben* of penitential prayer. A critical question, as Westermann noted, is when and how did an emphasis on confession of sin come to replace lament? Westermann suggested the transition was rooted in Deuteronomic theology. This theology was kept alive, Steck argued, in postexilic covenant renewal ceremonies, which he associated with Levitical circles. Both aspects of this discernment have come under review.

Much of the new work continues to posit a covenant-renewal setting in which penitential prayer would have played an important role. The difficulty with this proposal, as often noted, is that there is little or no firm evidence that confession of sin was a characteristic component in covenant ceremonies. Werline and Bautch sustain the argument for the covenant setting by suggesting that prophetic circles transformed the Deuteronomic idiom by recasting its emphasis on sin and divine judgment in casuistic terms that explained how repentance could repair covenantal failures and reverse God's judgment. Both recognize the transformation involves the appropriation of idioms of penitence that resemble those typically associated with the Priestly tradition, but neither sees the Levitical circles as primarily responsible for the emergence of this new prayer genre. Bautch, for example, recognizes that the thematic combination of "law and liturgy" in Ezra 9 has form-critical relationships to both the communal laments and the Levitical sermon, but he concludes that at most this confirms only that the text is a mixed genre. In terms of both content and contextual features, Ezra's "penitential preaching" draws more heavily on the prophecies of misfortune in Amos, Micah, and Ezekiel.[37]

Boda has offered a detailed critique of the covenant ceremony setting and has argued that its transformation betrays close affinities with the Priestly tradition. He has shown that the only example of a *Rib-Gerichtsdoxologie* in which praise of God and confession of sin functions explicitly to silence lament is Josh 7, a text that has important links to Ezra 9–10. Although there may be Deuteronomistic influence on Josh 7, Boda recognizes that its literary setting and a decisive number of specific linguistic features confirm that it was either preserved in priestly circles before being incorporated by Deuteronomistic editors or that a priestly redactor incorporated it into the Deuteronomistic History.[38] He traces the emphasis on the declaration of God's righteousness (צַדִּיק אַתָּה), another prominent feature of penitential prayer (Ezra 9:15; Dan 9:14, 16, 18; Neh 9:8, 33), to Ezekiel's concept of righteousness and guilt (e.g., Ezek 18).[39] Here too, he argues that priestly tradents have transformed classic Deuteronomisms. As further evidence of this

---

37. Bautch, *Developments in Genre*, 80–86.
38. For a list of Priestly terms in Josh 7, see Boda, *Praying the Tradition*, 61.
39. Ibid., 62–66.

transformation, he underlines various links between the prayer in Neh 9 and prophetic texts from the early restoration period (Zech 1:1–6; 7:1–8:23; and Haggai), which also draw upon the Priestly tradition. The evidence as a whole suggests to Boda that penitential prayer emerged in Yehud in the early Persian period, before the completion of the temple and most likely just prior to the missions of Haggai and Zechariah, during a time when the lament *Gattung* was being transformed by both priestly and prophetic circles.

In sum, Boda proposes a different answer to Westermann's fundamental question about how and why confession of sin came to replace lament. His conclusion deserves to be quoted in full, for it opens the door on a significant shift in the ongoing debate about who is responsible for the emergence of penitential prayer in Second Temple Judaism:

> What tradent circles have been responsible for the transformation from lament to Penitential Prayer in the later period of Israel's worship? This investigation has affirmed previous scholarship's focus on the Dtr movement. Dtr vocabulary present in Penitential Prayers reveals their indebtedness to Dtr theology. It is essential to the justification of God and his blamelessness and forms the theological foundation for the silencing of lament. However, Priestly and Ezekielian influence cannot be overlooked, as shown by the use of vocabulary from these tradent circles. These closely related tradent circles take the Dtr call for justification of God and repentance of the people and express them in practical terms, showing the implications of Dtr theology for the *Gattung* of lament: i.e. a particular style of confession, a silencing of lament and a new mode of renewing covenant.[40]

(5) Finally, the new work has brought back to the fore the question concerning when and how penitential prayer was "institutionalized," that is, how did it become a required observance with fixed times, rites, and liturgical ceremony? Werline cites four indicators of the move toward institutionalization: (1) formulaic declarations for confession of sin and God's righteousness; (2) the establishment of specific or prescribed prayer times, either daily, Sabbath, or festival; (3) an endorsement of penitential prayer as a means for removing sin that is the functional equivalent of sacrifice; and (4) a generalized and accepted use of vocabulary and motifs that defines a community's origins and distinguishes its adherents as members of a "penitential reform movement."[41] Based on these criteria, Werline suggests that the move towards penitence as an institutionalized response to history begins with 1 Kgs 8, a Deuteronomistic text that defines the temple primarily in terms of prayer rather than sacrifice. It then becomes firmly established in the penitential prayers of Ezra-Nehemiah during the Persian

---

40. Ibid., 73.
41. Werline, *Penitential Prayer*, 3–4.

period, is adapted to new historical and political circumstances in the prayers of Dan 9 (Antiochus IV) and Bar 1:15–3:8 (Antiochus V), and is instrumental for penitential movements that produce texts like *Jub.* 1, 23; *1 Enoch* (the "Animal Apocalypse" [*1 En.* 85–90] and the "Apocalypse of Weeks" [*1 En.* 93:1–10; 91:11–17]), *T. Mos.* 3–4, 5, 7, and the Qumran scrolls.

Werline accepts the conventional understanding that the destruction of the temple precipitated, if not required, the institutionalization of prayer as a substitute for the temple cult, particularly in relationship to sacrifice. Daniel Falk has challenged this view with a reassessment of the provenance, liturgical function, and "prayer practices" in key texts from Qumran. Two pieces of his argument may be singled out as especially relevant for the topic here.

First, four fragmentary manuscripts (1Q34a; 4Q507; 4Q508; 4Q505 + 509) contain "festival prayers," which were prescribed for liturgical use on appointed times like the Day of Atonement and the Feast of Weeks. Because the Festival Prayers at Qumran display similarities with festival prayers both in the Second Temple period and in later synagogue liturgy, especially a shared emphasis on prayer as an acceptable sacrifice, it has been argued that Qumran marks a decisive stage in the move toward institutionalization. Falk interprets these similarities differently. He suggests that they are part of a "common currency," which indicates that liturgical prayer at Qumran was not a newly created institution to replace sacrifice.[42] The evidence supports the conclusion that Qumran adopted and adapted elements already established with the Temple cult as customary institutions, and shaped from them a coherent liturgy, making it natural to apply sacrificial language to them.[43]

Second, within the "common currency" of liturgical prayer at Qumran, Falk gives attention to one particular modification: the incorporation of confession in the annual covenant ceremony, which likely occurred during the Feast of Weeks. The most complete description is preserved in the *Community Rule* (1QS 1:18–2:18), which describes a ceremony comprising blessing, historical recital of God's merciful acts and the iniquities of the people, confession of sin, acknowledgment of God's just sentence, and blessings and curses. The structure and the language of the ceremony, as often noted, is comparable both to the covenant formulary of Deut 27 and to the penitential prayers of Neh 9, Dan 9, and Bar 1:15–3:8. Falk refines this judgment by noting three important dissimilarities that suggest the covenant ceremony in the *Community Rule* is unique: it contains no mention of forgiveness and renewal of covenant; it contains no petition for mercy; and instead of the petition for mercy, it includes blessing and curse.[44]

---

42. Falk, *Daily, Sabbath, and Festival Prayers*, 187.
43. Ibid., 254–55.
44. Ibid., 222.

Each of these distinctives, especially the last, Falk suggests, has important implications for understanding the role of penitence in Qumran prayers that have not been sufficiently recognized. He proposes that the covenant ceremony in 1QS adopts and adapts both Deuteronomic and priestly biblical precedents for exclusivistic reasons that have broad atoning consequences. The confession of sin functions as a self-conscious affirmation of the community's status as God's elect. As a "priestly-oriented society," they regard themselves as the faithful remnant that is justified in invoking the covenant curses of Deuteronomy on its opponents. They also understand that confession of sin sustains the promise that God will remove the curses from the land (Lev 26:40–45). Thus, covenant renewal by the faithful has an atoning efficacy for the wider community. Falk suggests that a distinctive feature of the confession of sin in 1QS is the *priestly-oriented* "scripturalization" of Deuteronomic emphases. This assessment extends Boda's conclusion concerning the priestly transformation of Deuteronomic idioms in the early Persian period.

An Assessment of the Work That Remains

Space permits little more than a few general discernments concerning where our future work on the penitential prayers may lead.

(1) The shift from form-critical to traditio-historical analysis has been productive and merits further development, especially if we are to capitalize on the distinctive characteristic of "retelling history" or the "scripturalization" of prayer in the Second Temple period. Boda's work on Neh 9, aptly titled *Praying the Tradition*, demonstrates the rewards. His careful analysis of the traditions in play in this prayer (creation, Abraham, exodus, wilderness, law, conquest, Sabbath) invites similar analyses of the other biblical exemplars of penitential prayers (Ezra 9, Neh 1, Dan 9). The broader range of texts investigated by Newman, Werline, Bautch, and Falk effectively maps the terrain that is yet to be covered, but what they gain by extending the range of Second Temple prayers that merit investigation, they have perforce limited to suggestive generalizations that await more detailed scrutiny, text by text.

(2) Both form criticism, especially as practiced by Westermann, and traditio-historical analysis as utilized by previous scholars—one thinks immediately of Gerhard von Rad—had a definite theological component. This theological component is largely missing in the work under review here. Westermann's question concerning why lament receded from the later stages of biblical prayers and why it came to be replaced by confession of sin remains critical. His answer involved a theological judgment: under the influence of Deuteronomistic theology, which interpreted all of history within a sin-punishment nexus, lament lost whatever authenticity it enjoyed. A theology of personal and corporate guilt trumped one that previously reserved a role for faithful protest and complaint against divine injustice. Westermann, Brueggemann, and others considered the substitution of

penitence for lament a theological loss, not only for ancient Israel but also for the contemporary community of faith. As Nasuti has argued, their exegesis may be criticized as being prescriptive rather than descriptive. Their theological preference for lament over penitence may be more attuned to their own historical and cultural contexts as interpreters than to the ancient texts they examined. That said, they were clearly reaching for an understanding of the ideology, sociology, and especially the theology of lament and penitence. In my judgment, this remains a task worth our investment.

The issue that requires exploration may be framed with a brief reference to two contrasting perspectives on the "theology of exile," one from within the discipline of biblical studies, the other from outside. Daniel Smith-Christopher's *A Biblical Theology of Exile* draws upon the postexilic prayers of penitence (Ezra 9; Neh 9; Dan 9) in order to explicate the social function of shame.[45] He concludes that the Deuteronomistic "politics of penitence" advocates both a sociology and a theology of shame. From the sociological perspective, it summons exilic communities to examine and reject the abuse of power exemplified by their forebears during the period of the monarchy. From the theological perspective, the theology of shame encourages exilic (diaspora) communities to "confess the sins of their ancestors." The objective should not be to seek a return to the "fantasy of power"[46] but instead to ask the question, "What must I do to be saved?" (Acts 16).[47] The only legitimate answer, according to the Deuteronomistic theologians, is repentance. "Like the Deuteronomistic editors," Smith-Christopher says, "it is part of our task as modern Christians to rethink our history and thus to engage in the critical historiography that will condemn the 'sins of our ancestors' (and relegate their advocates to lesser roles in courses in Christian history)."[48]

From another perspective, Edward Said's seminal essay, "Reflections on Exile," invites questions concerning the Deuteronomistic theology of shame. Does exile mandate a *politics of penitence* because an exiled community's leaders have abused power, or a *politics of resistance* in the face of abusive powers that impose exile on a people, thereby forcing them into a world that recognizes no transcendent court of appeal? "Exile is not, after all," Said reminds us, "a matter of choice: you are born into it or it happens to you." Then these words, on behalf of the Palestinians, for whom Said speaks, "But, provided that the exile refuses to sit on the sidelines nursing a wound, there are things to be learned: he or she must cultivate a scrupulous (not indulgent or sulky) subjectivity."[49] Elsewhere in the same col-

---

45. Daniel Smith-Christopher, *A Biblical Theology of Exile* (OBT; Minneapolis: Fortress, 2002), 105–23.
46. Ibid., 122.
47. Ibid., 200.
48. Ibid.
49. Edward W. Said, "Reflections on Exile," in *Reflections on Exile and Other Essays* (Cambridge: Harvard University Press, 2000), 184.

lection Said amplifies what he means. Drawing upon lessons he says he learned from the German-Jewish philosopher and critic Theodor Adorno, "perhaps the most rigorous example of such subjectivity," Said offers the following counsel to diaspora communities: "Reconciliation under duress is both cowardly and inauthentic: better a lost cause than a triumphant one, more satisfying a sense of the provisional and contingent—a rented house, for example, than the proprietary solidity of permanent ownership."[50]

If, as Said suggests, exile is fundamentally a summons to "scrupulous subjectivity," does this find expression in penitence or protest, in a theology/ideology of shame or one of resistance? Are we correct to pose the question in either/or terms? Perhaps we should think of lament and penitence as shifting accents within a common response to historical calamities.[51] Perhaps scholars select from these shifting accents, valuing one more than the other (lament over penitence or vice versa), in response to their own interpretive contexts. In any event, we need more attention to the attendant ideological, sociological, and theological roles of lament and penitence, within both ancient and modern cultures, if we are to have clarity about the "institutionalization" of prayer.

(3) Boda has sharpened our understanding of the lively intersection between prophetic and priestly traditions in the development of penitential prayer. Westermann's suggestion of a more or less straight line of influence from the Deuteronomistic theologians must now be judged, I believe, as insufficient. The intersection between prophetic and priestly understandings of the role of penitence vis-à-vis lament merits further investigation, especially in view of J. Milgrom's discernments concerning the "priestly doctrine of repentance."[52]

In Milgrom's view, the priests postulated, for the first time in history, that repentance is both desired and required by God for the mitigation of divine retribution. In support of this argument, he notes that four Priestly texts (Lev 5:5; 16:21; 26:40; Num 5:7) explicitly require confession, presumably before bringing sacrifice, as the only possible remedy for transforming advertent sins into inadvertent sins, thus making them eligible for expiation. Of these four texts, only Lev 26, from the Holiness Code, which Milgrom considers to be a product of the Hezekian period, dispenses with the requirement of sacrifice. Thus, Lev 26 "approximates, and perhaps influences, the prophetic doctrine of repentance,

---

50. Said, "Between Worlds," 567.

51. Cf. Bautch's instructive observation that "penitence is no way univocal" in the prayers of the Second Temple period. Its predominance in prayers like Ezra 9 and Neh 9 is rooted, he suggests, in the "theological pessimism" that begins in the Persian period, when Jews were confronted with the loss of Israel's important religious institutions, such as the monarchy and the Solomonic temple (*Developments in Genre*, 159–61).

52. For a concise summary of Milgrom's view, see *Leviticus 1–16* (AB 3; New York: Doubleday, 1991), 373–78.

which not only suspends the sacrificial requirement, but eliminates it entirely."[53] In sum, Milgrom argues that although the doctrine of repentance informs the teaching of all of the prophets, "it is not their innovation."[54]

Boda has followed up the arguments in his book for a strong Priestly/Ezekielian influence with an article that examines the connections between Lev 26 and the prophetic liturgy in Jer 14:1–15:4.[55] He concludes that Jeremiah was cognizant of Lev 26, which he accepts as a preexilic priestly agenda for reversing covenant curses with confession of sin. Jeremiah's rejection of the priestly agenda (Jer 15:1–4) raises for Boda a critical question: Who among Israel's tradents would have the ability to discern when a particular historical moment requires lament or penitence? Boda hypothesizes that it was the prophets, with their access to the council of God, who were uniquely positioned to make the call.[56]

This is a plausible hypothesis, but given the priestly roots of prophets like Jeremiah and Ezekiel, not to mention the importance of the "priestly-oriented society" at Qumran that Falk suggests continues to exercise its interpretive influence on prophetic emphases, is it not equally plausible that it is the priests who play the decisive role in deciding whether the experiences of history require lament or penitence? If this question has merit, then another follows in its wake. Is there any evidence from the priestly tradition that lament and protest could be a legitimate response to suffering? The conventional answer to the question has been no. But in view of the lively dialogue that seems to have occurred between priestly and prophetic circles concerning the meaning of penitence, is it not possible that the interaction also included discussion of the meaning and value of lament?

(4) This last question may be pursued a step further. Bautch has invited attention to the significance of the Book of Job for understanding the trajectory of penitential prayer. Noting points of contact between "penitential preaching" in Ezra and Nehemiah and prophetic warnings in Amos, Ezekiel, and Micah, he suggests Job 29, a postexilic lament with literary connections to the prophetic corpus, may provide a "missing link." He singles out three features that suggest Job is shaped by the prophetic warning in ways that broadly parallel the penitential prayers: (1) Job's orientation to the righteous and the wicked (e.g., Job 29:14–16, 17) sheds light on both the communal lament in Isa 63:7–64:11 and the confession of sin in Neh 9; (2) Job's understanding of the binding relationship between justice and faith (Job 29:24–25) is comparable to both Neh 9:33 and to the Qumran covenanters (4Q504); and (3) the structure of Job 29–31 has affinities with the

---

53. Jacob Milgrom, *Leviticus 23–27* (AB 3B; New York: Doubleday, 2001), 2330.

54. Milgrom, *Leviticus 1–16*, 375.

55. Mark J. Boda, "From Complaint to Contrition: Peering Through the Liturgical Window of Jer 14,1–15,4," *ZAW* 113 (2001): 186–97.

56. Ibid., 196.

communal lament psalm. It is this genre, Bautch argues, that was transformed in the postexilic period by the emerging dominance of the confession of sin.[57] In sum, postexilic prayers of penitence like Isa 63:7–64:11, Ezra 9:6–15, and Neh 9:6–37 "have received the same prophetic deposit as has Job, but they employ it for their own purposes."[58]

I second Bautch's invitation to include Job in the discussion of penitential prayer, and I suggest that it might be strengthened with an additional observation. Perhaps Job is also a missing link to what may have been an internal priestly debate concerning the appropriateness and/or requirement of repentance. To use Bautch's language, perhaps Job also received the same *priestly* deposit as Ezra and Nehemiah. Given the uncertainties in dating the book, it is unwise to suggest any straight-line connection between Job and the Priestly literature.[59] Nevertheless, a number of intriguing clues indicate that some sort of connection merits further investigation.[60] To cite but one oblique yet suggestive piece of the post-biblical interpretive tradition, the Talmud embellishes the biblical instructions concerning the Day of Atonement (Lev 16) by stipulating a seven-day period of preparation for the priest. Included among the required exercises during this period are readings from the biblical books of Job, Daniel, Ezra, and Nehemiah (*m. Yoma* 1:6). The Talmud offers no explanation for this selection of texts. We may speculate that Daniel, Ezra, and Nehemiah are included because they model the prayers of personal and corporate repentance that the priest will require from a sinful people. The reading from Job may be for a similar reason since Job is profiled in both the Prologue and Epilogue as one whose intercessory prayers were effective (cf. Job 1:5, 42:8). But we may be permitted to wonder if Job might have been considered important for other reasons as well. Perhaps the priestly tradition also knew and valued the legacy of Job's refusal to relinquish lament for rituals of penitence that may be too inflexible to countenance a legitimate protest of innocence.[61]

---

57. Bautch, *Developments in Genre*, 161–65.

58. Ibid.

59. The book of Job is notoriously difficult to date. Absent any explicit chronological markers within the book itself, scholars have proposed a wide spectrum of possibilities, ranging from the early seventh century to the fourth-third centuries, that is, deep into the Second Temple period.

60. Mary Douglas has noted, for example, almost in passing, that the treatment of the law of talion in Lev 24, and more broadly its general reflections on God's justice, makes an "opening … for the complex view of retribution celebrated in the Book of Job." In her judgment, Leviticus "reaches forward to the book of Job" (*Leviticus as Literature* [Oxford: Oxford University Press, 1999], 212, 250). See also Israel Knohl, who has called attention to a similar trajectory in Job and the "Priestly Torah" (*The Sanctuary of Silence: The Priestly Torah and the Holiness School* [Minneapolis: Fortress, 1995], 165–67).

61. For a preliminary exploration of these matters, see further Samuel E. Balentine, "Job as Priest to the Priests," *Ex Auditu* 18 (2003): 29–52.

Confession as Theological Expression:
Ideological Origins of Penitential Prayer

Mark J. Boda

Introduction

Over the past decade there has been a veritable explosion of published research on penitential prayers in early Second Temple Judaism. The focus of these works has been varied, ample witness to the creativity of the human pursuit of knowledge. However, to a lesser and greater degree each of these works has touched on traditio-historical aspects of this prayer tradition.

The decade began with the publication of four monographs providing overviews of the large corpus of prayers associated with the Judeo-Christian tradition. In his 1993 contribution Stefan Reif traced the development of Jewish liturgy from its biblical roots to the modern day. The book begins with a review of the early liturgical texts within the Hebrew Bible and beyond. In the process he highlights several penitential prayers, offering a cursory description of each with a focus on form as well as content. More focused attention was afforded prayers from the biblical period in Samuel Balentine's volume from the same year. Balentine limits his attention to prose and nonpsalmic prayers within the Hebrew Bible. His approach avoids fixation with the forms of biblical prayers and focuses rather on the "literary and theological function" of these prayers within their narrative contexts.[1] Balentine offers an extended analysis of the biblical penitential prayer tradition in a chapter related to the prayers which Weinfeld identified as Deuteronomic liturgical orations.[2] His analysis reveals the deep theological character and orientation of this prayer tradition. Two years later a third overview appeared in print, this time from Patrick Miller who traced the form and theology of prayers

---

1. Samuel E. Balentine, *Prayer in the Hebrew Bible: The Drama of Divine-Human Dialogue* (OBT; Minneapolis: Fortress, 1993), 25.

2. Balentine, *Prayer in the Hebrew Bible*, 89–117; cf. Moshe Weinfeld, *Deuteronomy and the Deuteronomic School* (Oxford: Clarendon, 1972), 32–45.

in the Old and New Testaments.³ He devoted one chapter to the analysis of penitential prayer in the Old Testament, delineating both the form and the theological content within this tradition.⁴ Finally in 1996, Michael Thompson published his review of prayer in the Old Testament. His chapter on prayers in Ezra, Nehemiah and Daniel deals with various types of prayer within that particular corpus, but does devote ten pages to the penitential prayers.⁵ Thompson wisely notes the intertextual reliance of these prayers on the Torah and discerns that they not only detail Israel's guilt, but also stress God's faithful character. Although limited in the space they could afford for the discussion of penitential prayer, these four initial works laid a deep foundation and set the broader liturgical context for the study of penitential prayers, especially as to their traditio-historical and theological dimensions. Little did they know that no less than seven works would appear in the wake of their overviews.

The first came from Volker Pröbstl, who devoted his 1997 monograph to Neh 9 and Pss 106 and 135, three prayers in the Hebrew Bible that contain elongated historical reviews.⁶ For each of these Pröbstl concluded that there was a special reliance on Deuteronomic texts (seen in the continuous employment of Dtr formulae) and that, in particular, Neh 9 and Ps 106 presuppose the Deuteronomic view of the history of Israel. However, he wisely notes that the prayers deviate from the Deuteronomic tradition stream consistently and adds that there are many connections to Priestly texts, even if again there is evidence of modification of the Priestly.

Rodney Werline's 1998 consideration of the traditio-historical background of penitential prayer echoes the longstanding assumption that these prayers trace their origins to the Deuteronomistic stream of tradition.⁷ He focuses considerable attention on texts such as Deut 4 and 30 which outline the appropriate response of a people exiled for their sin, that is, the response of repentance. However, these texts are not adequate to explain the supplicatory dimension of penitential prayer. For this Werline highlights the key role that a later phase of reflection, represented by 1 Kgs 8, played, with its reinterpretation of Deut 4 and 30 to show that "the people could enact Deuteronomy's demand for repentance through penitential prayer."⁸ A similar transformation of this Deuteronomic theology is discerned

---

3. Patrick D. Miller, *They Cried to the Lord: The Form and Theology of Biblical Prayer* (Minneapolis: Fortress, 1994).

4. Miller, *Biblical Prayer*, 244–61.

5. Michael E. W. Thompson, *I Have Heard Your Prayer: The Old Testament and Prayer* (Peterborough, U.K.: Epworth, 1996), 64–88, esp. 71–82.

6. Volker Pröbstl, *Nehemia 9, Psalm 106 und Psalms 136 und die Rezeption des Pentateuchs* (Göttingen: Cuvillier, 1997).

7. Rodney A. Werline, *Penitential Prayer in Second Temple Judaism: The Development of a Religious Institution* (SBLEJL 13; Atlanta: Scholars Press, 1998).

8. Ibid., 62.

by Werline in Jer 29:10–14, a passage which seeks to shape the response of the people at the end of the "exilic" seventy years. This response was to include calling (קרא), praying (פלל) so that God may hear (שמע).[9] Werline does not restrict his reflection to the Deuteronomistic tradition, but, clearly emphasizes this stream of influence for the creation of the "religious institution" of penitential prayer. He is aware of "the influence of Priestly traditions," displayed especially in the fact that the "authors refer to the prayers as 'confessions.'"

It is this Priestly stream that is highlighted in my 1999 volume on the penitential prayer in Neh 9.[10] In a chapter investigating the traditio-historical background of the earliest penitential prayers, I argue that although Deuteronomic idiom is obvious throughout these prayers, several features of these prayers "move beyond classic deuteronomism."[11] I highlighted what I called evidence of "Priestly transformations" within the Deuteronomic idiom of the individual prayers and traced several features common to the prayer tradition to Priestly sources.[12] In contrast to Werline, I placed far greater emphasis on the role of Lev 26 and Ezekiel on this prayer tradition and suggested that although 1 Kgs 8 is presently embedded in a "Deuteronomic" context, it is structured in Priestly formulations. I also introduced Joshua 7 as representing an important influence on this prayer form, a passage that is also presently found in a "Deuteronomic" context and yet evidences strong Priestly vocabulary and themes. This Priestly influence for the *Gattung* as a whole was confirmed in the traditio-historical evaluation of Neh 9. Further reflection has led to the publication of articles on the relationship between penitential prayer and such passages as Jer 14:1–15:4, Lamentations, and Zech 1–8, each with attention to form-critical and traditio-historical issues.[13] Jeremiah 14:1–15:4 contains two prophetic liturgies of request rooted in the final years of the kingdom of Judah. Their close affinity with the Priestly agenda for repentance, in particular that expressed in Lev 26, and the ultimate rejection of such a penitential rite in this Deuteronomic context shows

---

9. Werline (ibid., 29) makes the odd claim that Jer 29:10–14 shows "no detectable influence from 1 Kings 8." Although one cannot always determine direction of influence with precision, it is interesting that he then notes similarities between 1 Kgs 8:48–49 and Jer 29:12 (p. 30).

10. Mark J. Boda, *Praying the Tradition: The Origin and Use of Tradition in Nehemiah 9* (BZAW 277; Berlin: de Gruyter, 1999).

11. Ibid., 72.

12. Ibid., 72–73.

13. Mark J. Boda, "From Complaint to Contrition: Peering through the liturgical window of Jer 14,1–15,4," *ZAW* 113 (2001): 186–97; idem, "Zechariah: Master Mason or Penitential Prophet?" in *Yahwism after the Exile: Perspectives on Israelite Religion in the Persian Era* (ed. Bob Becking and Rainer Albertz; Studies in Theology and Religion; Assen: Van Gorcum, 2003), 49–69; idem, "The Priceless Gain of Penitence: From Communal Lament to Penitential Prayer in the 'Exilic' Liturgy of Israel," *HBT* 25 (2003): 51–75.

that the agenda of penitential prayer is closely allied with Priestly rather than Deuteronomic circles. In Jeremiah, however, the form still retains elements of lament, possibly an indication that the silencing of lament itself should be traced to Deuteronomic rather than Priestly sources. A close look at the central poem of the book of Lamentations (chapter 3) reveals, however, the impact of a shift from Zion theology to the Character Credo on the development of penitential prayer. Finally, an investigation of Zech 1:1–6 and 7:1–8:23 highlighted the close affinity between Zecharian circles and the penitential prayer tradition. These three articles strengthened the view that the transformation from lament to penitential prayer was a process that was taking place during the sixth century B.C.E.

Judith Newman's 1999 consideration of the technique of scripturalization expands the traditio-historical discussion beyond the purview of penitential prayer to include the breadth of Jewish prayer traditions.[14] However, her analysis of Neh 9 confirms the presence of both Deuteronomic and Priestly resources for scripturalization in Neh 9, although tipping the scales in favor of the Deuteronomic,[15] and adds to these resources a third, the latter prophets.[16] Newman highlights the use of materials from the Golden Calf incident in Exod 32–34 in Neh 9:17–18, especially the citation of Exod 34:6a. Trends that she observes in scripturalization in Neh 9 are traced also into other longer prayers found in the books of the prophets and psalms, including some that are related to the typology of penitential prayer: Jer 32:16–25; Isa 63:7–64:12; and Ps 106.

Emphasis on the Priestly dimension in penitential prayer is strengthened by Falk's oral paper at the Fifth International Symposium of the Orion Center for the Study of the Dead Sea Scrolls and Associated Literature (19–23 January 2000).[17] In this paper, the purpose of which was to argue that the motivation for communal prayer was not necessarily to replace sacrifice within the Jewish community, Falk affirms Werline's Deuteronomic sensibilities. However, he takes him to task for a lack of focus on the Priestly tradition. Drawing heavily upon Milgrom's work on the Priestly doctrine of repentance (see further below), Falk argues that Lev 26:39–42 mediates the Priestly doctrine of repentance for a people caught in the conditions of exile. Interestingly, Werline has the identical material in an excur-

---

14. Judith H. Newman, *Praying by the Book: The Scripturalization of Prayer in Second Temple Judaism* (SBLEJL 14; Atlanta: Scholars Press, 1999); cf. idem, "Nehemiah 9 and the Scripturalization of Prayer in the Second Temple Period," in *The Function of Scripture in Early Jewish and Christian Tradition* (ed. Craig A. Evans and James A. Sanders; JSNTSup; Sheffield: Sheffield Academic Press, 1998), 112–23.

15. Newman, *Praying by the Book,* 115: "Nehemiah 9 uses scriptural traditions from all parts of the Bible including the Priestly source, not just the Deuteronomistic material, although the latter strongly influenced the author."

16. Ibid., 55–108, esp. 103.

17. http://orion.mscc.huji.ac.il/symposiums/5th/main5.shtml. See Daniel Falk's contribution to the forthcoming second volume of the Penitential Prayer consultation.

sus in his first chapter, but does not capitalize on the implications of this evidence for the origins of penitential prayer.

Michael Duggan's 2001 monograph offers a synchronic literary analysis of Neh 7:72b–10:40. He offers a close reading of this section with attention to the penitential prayer in Neh 9, which he considers the "theological summit" and "hermeneutical key" to Ezra-Nehemiah.[18] His work offers summative reflections on tradition-historical background of the prayer which he considers a "mosaic of traditions" drawing from Deuteronomic, Priestly, and Prophetic traditions. He offers a review of key theological themes within the prayer in Neh 9 as well as in the penitential prayer tradition in general.[19]

Although focused on form-critical issues,[20] Richard Bautch (2003) does provide reflection on the tradition-critical background because, as he writes: "an awareness of sources and their use can be critical to understanding a prayer's formal arrangement and logic."[21] Focusing attention on the proto-penitential composition, Isa 63:7–64:11, and the penitential prayers, Ezra 9 and Neh 9, Bautch emphasizes the strong stamp of Deuteronomic thought. For Isa 63:7–64:11, Deuteronomic thought is not simply the dominant, but the only classic tradition stream that is evident in the prayer. Bautch associates this prayer with those exilic and postexilic priestly lay theologians posited by Albertz.[22] "Conventional adherence to Deuteronomic traditions" can also be discerned in Ezra 9:6–15, even though he does admit there is sensitivity also to "the Levitical code of purity."[23] Deuteronomic dominance, however, is further muted in Neh 9, which "consolidates the traditions of Dtr and P while employing each to differing degrees," a technique that he calls "an interpenetration of the two traditions [that] allows both to be represented significantly at the levels of language and ideas."[24] Bautch is careful, however, to note that the "prayer appears to be partial to Dtr's language and presentation" even if "in each case the prayer acknowledges P's view of the matter."[25] Referring to the stream of scholarship we have been reviewing, Bautch warns: "As scholars devote increasing attention to P's influence upon the

---

18. Michael W. Duggan, *The Covenant Renewal in Ezra-Nehemiah (Neh 7:72b–10:40): An Exegetical, Literary, and Theological Study* (SBLDS 164; Atlanta: Society of Biblical Literature, 2001), 230, 298. In his final conclusion (298) he argues that the three penitential prayers in Ezra-Nehemiah are united in rhetorical function to show how the devotion of the two key leaders, Ezra and Nehemiah, exemplified in their penitential prayers now "pervades the community."

19. Ibid., 228–33.

20. Richard J. Bautch, *Developments in Genre between Post-exilic Penitential Prayers and the Psalms of Communal Lament* (SBLAcBib; Atlanta: Society of Biblical Literature, 2003), 11.

21. Ibid., 11 n. 47.

22. Ibid., 61–62.

23. Ibid., 88; see 84–88.

24. Ibid., 132.

25. Ibid.

prayer, they need not overlook the contribution of Deuteronomy and the Deuteronomistic schools operative during and after the exile."[26]

These seven works have provided much needed research into the traditio-historical background of these liturgical texts which played a key role in shaping the community of Jews in the wake of the destruction and decimation of Judah.[27] They each highlight in one way or another the key role that the Deuteronomic and Priestly streams within Israelite tradition have played in the development of this prayer form.

The goal of the remainder of this paper at hand is to offer further reflections, clarifications and integrative conclusions on crucial theological streams discernible within the earliest penitential prayers (Ezra 9; Neh 1; 9, Dan 9; Ps 106).[28]

---

26. Ibid., 133.

27. This does not include many articles that have appeared during this period as well, including Manfred Oeming, "'See, We Are Serving Today' (Nehemiah 9:36): Nehemiah 9 as a Theological Interpretation of the Persian Period," in *Judah and Judeans in the Achaemenid Period* (ed. Oded Lipschits and Manfred Oeming; Winona Lake, Ind.: Eisenbrauns, 2006), 571–88; Hans van Deventer, "The End of the End, Or, What Is the Deuteronomist (Still) Doing in Daniel?" in *Past, Present, Future: The Deuteronomistic History and the Prophets* (ed. Johannes C. de Moor and Harry F. Van Rooy; OtSt 44; Leiden: Brill, 2000), 62–74; Paul L. Redditt, "Daniel 9: Its Structure and Meaning," *CBQ* 62 (2000): 236–49; Pieter M. Venter, "Bybelse Teologie en skuldbelydenis," *HvTSt* 55 (1999): 533–62; Harm W. M. van Grol, "'Indeed, Servants We Are': Ezra 9, Nehemiah 9 and 2 Chronicles 12 Compared," in *The Crisis of Israelite Religion: Transformation of Religious Tradition in Exilic and Post-exilic Times* (ed. Bob Becking and Marjo C. A. Korpel; Leiden: Brill, 1999), 209–27; Pieter M. Venter, "Intertekstualiteit, kontekstualiteit en Daniël 9," *IDS* 31 (1997): 327–46; Harm W. M. van Grol, "Schuld und Scham: Die Verwurzelung von Esra 9,6–7 in der Tradition," *EstBíb* 55 (1997): 29–52; Rolf Rendtorff, "Nehemiah 9: An Important Witness of Theological Reflection," in *Tehillah le-Moshe: Biblical and Judaic Studies in Honor of Moshe Greenberg* (ed. Mordechai Cogan, Barry L. Eichler, and Jeffrey H. Tigay; Winona Lake, Ind.: Eisenbrauns, 1997), 111–17; Rainer Kessler, "Das kollektive Schuldbekenntnis im Alten Testament," *EvT* 56 (1996): 29–43; Pieter M. Venter, "Die aard van die geloofsgemeenskap in Nehemiah 9 (Afrikaans)," *HvTSt* 51 (1995): 720–31.

28. See also a short summary of some of these themes in Boda, "Priceless Gain," 51–75. This study is not meant to be exhaustive. Compare the recent thesis of Frederico G. Villanueva Jr. ("Confession of Sins or Petition for Forgiveness: A Study of the Nature of the Prayers in Nehemiah 1, 9, Daniel 9, and Ezra 9" [masters thesis, Asia Graduate School of Theology, 2002]), which focuses on four key themes (covenant, theology (God), divine retribution, and restoration), and Balentine's four themes: divine-human relationship, God, humanity, and faith. As for the choice of these five compositions as the earliest penitential prayers, it is admitted that disagreement over the precise dating of these prayers will continue *ad infinitum* or, one may say, *ad nauseum*. See my views in Boda, *Praying the Tradition*, and for Dan 9 see, more recently, Redditt, "Daniel 9," 236–49, who places the prayer in the sixth century B.C.E. Even if these prayers are dated to a later period, they remain some of the earliest prayers. It is difficult to believe that there is a gap of a few centuries between the beginning of the transformation from the lament to penitential prayer (evident in materials often linked to the sixth century: Jer 14–15, Lam 3, Isa 63–64) to its maturity in the prayers cited above.

This follows the lead of Balentine, whose monograph on the broader phenomenon of prose prayer in the Hebrew Bible was "concerned to attend to the use of prayer as a means of conveying ideological and theological perspectives,"[29] and also Miller, who sought "to discern something of the theology of prayer, but even more determinedly of the character of the God to whom these prayers are lifted, the human ones who utter them in joy and sorrow, and what we can discern from them about the divine-human relation."[30] Although traditio-historical perspectives and techniques will not be abandoned in this paper, the hope is to shift to a description of the resulting theological orientation of the earliest prayers in this grand tradition.

Theology of Repentance

It is obvious to all that key to the form under consideration is the belief that prayer is an essential component of authentic penitence that will bring an end to the exile and that such prayer must contain a confession of sin. Such an orientation was linked by Werline to the agenda set out in the Deuteronomic prayer of Solomon in 1 Kgs 8 and the prophetic message of Jer 29:10–14, texts that, according to Werline, betray links to the Deuteronomic agenda for repentance set out in Deut 4 and 30.[31] These two texts transform the Deuteronomic agenda to include prayer as an essential component of this repentance, and for 1 Kgs 8 also a declaration of one's sinful acts.[32]

The Deuteronomic tradition's perspective on repentance is clearly evident within the theology of repentance in the early penitential prayers.[33] Within the

---

29. Balentine, *Prayer in the Hebrew Bible*, 29. See his results in his theological summary of chapter 10 (260–71). So similarly Oeming on Neh 9: "Its meaning is to be found not merely in poetic-aesthetic considerations, nor in historiographic intention, but rather in theology" (Oeming, "Nehemiah 9").

30. Miller, *Biblical Prayer*, 2.

31. Werline, *Penitential Prayer*, 11–64, esp. 25 n. 50; see now Mark J. Boda, "Renewal in Heart, Word, and Deed: Repentance in the Torah," in *Repentance in Christian Theology* (ed. Mark J. Boda and Gordon T. Smith, Collegeville, Minn.: Liturgical Press, 2006), 3–24.

32. Falk, in his superb oral paper, cites evidence for the combination of prayer and repentance in Hos 14:1–2 in Jer 36:7; Daniel K. Falk, "Motivation for Communal Prayer in the Dead Sea Scrolls and Early Judaism" (paper presented at the Fifth Orion International Symposium—Liturgical Perspectives: Prayer and Poetry in Light of the Dead Sea Scrolls, 19–23 January, 2000, Hebrew University of Jerusalem, 2000). However, it is important to note that these examples, along with Jer 29:10–14, do not mention confession of sin.

33. Cf., for example, Carl R. Anderson, "The Formation of the Levitical Prayer of Nehemiah 9" (Th.D. diss., Dallas Theological Seminary, 1987); cf. Moshe Greenberg, *Biblical Prose Prayer as a Window to the Popular Religion of Ancient Israel* (Los Angeles: University of California Press, 1983), 63 n. 1; Balentine, *Prayer in the Hebrew Bible*, 103–4; Miller, *Biblical Prayer*, 418 n. 32; Boda, *Praying the Tradition*. On the Deuteronomic-Prophetic stream, see Jacob Mil-

Deuteronomic tradition the prophet is the key promoter of repentance among the people, sent by God to call the people to the penitential (Ezra 9:11; Neh 9:26, 30; Dan 9:6, 10). The prophetic witness is not innovative, but rather merely calls the people back to Torah as covenant document. In the Deuteronomic tradition the prophets are intimately linked not only with the declaration and preservation of Torah, but also the creation of Torah, highlighted in Deuteronomy's presentation of Moses as prophet. The same breadth of function can be discerned in presentation of prophet and law in the penitential prayers. Most important to the Deuteronomic-prophetic theology of repentance is the use of the vocabulary of שׁוּב (šûb), a word that appears regularly in the early penitential prayers (Neh 1:9; 9:26, 29, 35; Dan 9:13). This kind of repentance means both turning from covenant violations (Neh 9:35; Dan 9:13) and turning to covenant relationship typified both by relationship with God (Neh 1:9; 9:26, 35) and obedience to Torah (Neh 1:9; 9:26; 29). The influence of Deuteronomic conceptions on penitential prayer is most vividly displayed in the prayer of Neh 1 in which the agenda of Deut 30 with its emphasis on שׁוּב (šûb) is clearly enunciated (see further below). That such repentance is expressed through confession of sin in prayer is often linked to the agenda laid out in 1 Kgs 8, a link that can be easily demonstrated through the appearance of vocabulary from this prayer in penitential prayers.[34] However, there is another stream of tradition that needs to be introduced at this point, one that both Daniel Falk and I have emphasized elsewhere as playing an influential role on the development not only this prayer form, but also on developments in Deuteronomic theology showcased in passages like 1 Kgs 8 and Josh 7.[35]

It is in Lev 26:39–40 that one finds emphasis not just on prayer in the wake of the exile but also on confessing sin, using the terminology for confession (הִתְוַדָּה, hitwaddâ) found in the various contexts of penitential prayer. To understand the theological roots of this agenda in Lev 26, however, one must focus even more intently on the Priestly tradition and in particular the Priestly doctrine of repentance that underlies this text in Lev 26.

Probably the most concentrated research on this aspect of Priestly tradition has been Milgrom's investigation of the אָשָׁם (ʾāšām) offering, often translated as

---

grom, *Cult and Conscience: The Asham and the Priestly Doctrine of Repentance* (SJLA 18; Leiden: Brill, 1976), 121–23.

34. See Boda, *Praying the Tradition*, 43–45, 189–97.

35. Falk, "Motivation for Communal Prayer"; cf. Daniel K. Falk, *Daily, Sabbath, and Festival Prayers in the Dead Sea Scrolls* (STDJ 27; Leiden: Brill, 1998); and Boda, *Praying the Tradition*, 43–73. Werline is aware of the Priestly theology but does not appear to capitalize on it in the end and even speaks of "the minimal influence that Levitical traditions had on [the penitential prayers]" (Werline, *Penitential Prayer*, 193). See also Bautch (*Developments in Genre*, 145–48) on this Priestly influence, even if his mixing of תּוֹדָה (tôdâ) and הִתְוַדָּה (hitwaddâ) is inappropriate, see Mark J. Boda, "Words and Meanings: ידה in Hebrew Research," *WTJ* 57 (1995): 277–97.

"guilt offering."³⁶ Milgrom contradicts the dominant lexicography on the root אשם, which defines the noun as "guilt" and the verb as "is guilty."³⁷ In contrast, he argues that this root in the cultic texts refers to the consequential אָשָׁם (ʾāšām).³⁸ Thus he concludes that this root can be used in four ways: as a noun for either "reparation" or "reparation offering" and as a verb for either "incur liability (to someone)" or "feel guilt (without a personal object)".³⁹ Rather than the usual "be guilty" (which connotes legal guilt), the last meaning refers to "the self-punishment of conscience, the torment of guilt."⁴⁰ The feeling of guilt is the punishment for the behavior.

After this careful definition, Milgrom then goes on to identify the circumstances that necessitate this kind of offering. He demonstrates this by highlighting the link between the sacrifice and the word מַעַל (maʿal), a term that describes a sin against God, in contrast to a sin against humanity (חטא, ḥṭʾ; see Num 5:6). Such sins against God can be divided into two basic categories: the *sancta* trespass, that is, inappropriate physical contact with that which was holy (Lev 5:14–19; 14:10–14, 21–25; 22:14–16; Num 6:12; Jer 2:3; Ezra 10:19); and the oath violation, that is, the violation of God's name that was sworn in the oath (Lev 5:20–26; Num 5:6–8). He concludes: "*maʿal*, then, means trespassing upon the divine realm either by poaching on his *sancta* or breaking his covenant oath; it is a lethal sin which can destroy both the offender and his community."⁴¹

What is important for the study of penitential prayer is Milgrom's work on the oath violation. Although clearly linked to Lev 5:20–26, Num 5:6–8 has a few

---

36. Milgrom, *Cult and Conscience*, 11; cf. Jacob Milgrom, "Priestly Doctrine of Repentance," *RB* 82 (1975): 186–205. Although I consulted Milgrom in my earlier work and was aware of the Priestly stream of repentance, I am indebted to Rod Werline (ironically) and Daniel Falk for the importance of this stream of research by Milgrom to the study of penitential prayer.

37. For a classic expression of this view, see Paul P. Saydon, "Sin-Offering and Trespass-Offering," *CBQ* 8 (1946): 393–98.

38. That is, the retribution associated with the behavior, not the behavior itself; thus, for example, *ḥṭʾ* can refer to both the sin and its punishment.

39. Milgrom, *Cult and Conscience*, 11.

40. Ibid.; see idem, "Further on the Expiatory Sacrifices," *JBL* 115 (1996): 511–14, and idem, *Leviticus 23–27: A New Translation with Introduction and Commentary* (AB 3; New York: Doubleday, 2001), 2446–52, where he responds to Adrian Schenker, "Interprétations récentes et dimensions spécifiques du sacrifice *ḥaṭṭaʾt*," *Bib* 75 (1994): 59–70. Milgrom does not distinguish between presumptuous and intentional sins, explaining that deliberate sin is considered presumptuous without penitential rites. Contradicting Milgrom, however, is Nobuyoshi Kiuchi, *The Purification Offering in the Priestly Literature: Its Meaning and Function* (JSOTSup 56; Sheffield: JSOT Press, 1987), 31–34, who distinguishes between objective and subjective aspects of אָשָׁם (ʾāšām), suggesting the translation "realize guilt" instead of "feel guilt." For Milgrom's response see his *Leviticus 1–16: A New Translation with Introduction and Commentary* (AB 3; New York: Doubleday, 1991), 338.

41. Milgrom, *Cult and Conscience*, 21.

innovations, the most important of which is the stipulation that confession must precede restitution.⁴² Noting that each of the cases in which confession occurs in Priestly sources "deals exclusively with deliberate sin (Lev 5:1–4; 16:21; 26:40; Num 5:6f)," Milgrom concludes: "For involuntary sin, *ʾšm* or remorse alone suffices; it renders confession superfluous. But for deliberate sin there is the added requirement that remorse be verbalized; the sin must be articulated and responsibility assumed."⁴³ Such confession "means to 'acknowledge' the sin by identifying it and accepting blame."⁴⁴ In this approach to repentance, "his remorse (*ʾšm*) and confession (*htwdh*), reduces his intentional sin to an inadvertence, thereby rendering it eligible for sacrificial expiation."⁴⁵ Balentine echoes Milgrom's conclusions when he asserts:

> Confession is the cotter pin that joins contrition to reparation and reparation to a public commitment to change. Without confession, sin seeks the camouflage of secrecy, the status remains quo, and brokenness continues to diminish the 'very good' world God has created.⁴⁶

In dealing with oath violation, Milgrom notes that the regular use of מַעַל (*maʿal*) in connection with idolatry is reasonable in light of the covenant oath: "Since the swearing of fidelity is the root purpose of the Lord's covenant it is hardly surprising that the maʿal of oath violation usually turns out to be idolatry."⁴⁷ This helps us to understand Lev 26:39–40, in which repentance is required in the wake of the exile, an event that was precipitated by the hostility of Israel against the Lord through idolatrous violation of their covenant oath (Lev 26:27–30). Thus the מַעַל (*maʿal*) that brought on the exile must be rectified through a confession that transforms the voluntary sin of the people into involuntary status and thus becomes rectifiable through reparation. While sacrifice is impossible in such a

---

42. Such an innovation can be seen elsewhere in the ancient Near East, e.g., Hittite; ibid., 106–7.

43. Ibid., 109–10. In this Milgrom challenges the traditional reading of Num 15:30b, that is, the absence of forgiveness for presumptuous violation of the law: "sacrificial atonement is barred to the *unrepentant* sinner, to the one who 'acts defiantly' … but not to the deliberate sinner who has mitigated his offense by his repentance." Contrast Baruch A. Levine, *Leviticus* (JPS Torah Commentary; Philadelphia: Jewish Publication Society, 1989), 28, who sees this confession as necessary because the acts under discussion were private in character and thus would never have come to light apart from confession. Also note Gordon J. Wenham, *The Book of Leviticus* (NICOT; Grand Rapids: Eerdmans, 1979), 100, for whom the sins in Lev 5:1–6 are sins that slipped one's memory: "In each case, when conscience smites the forgetful person, he must confess his sin and bring a purification offering" (p. 93).

44. Milgrom, *Cult and Conscience*, 110.

45. Milgrom, "Priestly Doctrine," 117.

46. Samuel E. Balentine, *Leviticus* (IBC; Louisville: Westminster John Knox, 2002), 57.

47. Milgrom, *Cult and Conscience*, 20.

context, with an inoperative temple,⁴⁸ it is possible that the sacrifice is equated here with their suffering in exile (26:41: "pay for their sin") or that there was an expectation that once they were returned to the land they would sacrifice.⁴⁹

Further insight into the Priestly doctrine of repentance can also be discerned by investigating one other use of the term הִתְוַדָּה (hitwaddâ) in the Priestly material: the Yom Kippur ritual in Lev 16. While some see the original design of this ceremony as a means to cleanse the defiled sanctuary which was later expanded to include the cleansing of the people,⁵⁰ there is no need to distinguish these two purposes, in light of the intimate connection between people and sanctuary.⁵¹ A key act in this complex ritual is described in Lev 16:21 following the sacrifice of the first goat, a sacrifice that was designed to make atonement *(kipper)* for the most holy place, the tent of meeting and the altar (16:20). After this Aaron was instructed to take a second goat, the scapegoat which would be released into the desert, and while laying hands on the goat's head, confess over it the sins of the people, thereby transferring the sins of the people onto the goat. Interestingly, on this day the people were to "deny themselves" (תְּעַנּוּ אֶת־נַפְשֹׁתֵיכֶם), an action linked elsewhere with sackcloth, fasting, and humbling oneself (Isa 58:3, 10; Ps 35:13).⁵² Milgrom argues that this ritual served the same purpose as the other instances of confession, dealing with intentional unrepented sins⁵³ which have

---

48. The main purpose of Falk's 2000 paper was to consider the question of the relationship between sacrifice and prayer.

49. For the former, see Milgrom, *Leviticus 23–27*, 2333, where he claims that "H wants to stress that Israel, deprived of its sacrificial cult, would express its atonement by contritely and patiently accepting its punishment of exile until the land made up its neglected Sabbath years"; for the latter, see Milgrom, *Leviticus 23–27*, 2330: "the assumption 'may well be' that once Israel is restored and cult reestablished that the appropriate sacrifices would be made." It is possible that this lays the ground for prayer replacing sacrifice, but this does not seem to have been understood by Ezra in his use of penitential prayer in Ezra 9–10 alongside the אָשָׁם (*'āšām*) offering (Ezra 10:19).

50. E.g., Levine, *Leviticus*, 99.

51. Balentine, *Leviticus*, 132, showcases the function of the sanctuary within the life of the people by isolating the two purposes for this purification: "to cleanse the sanctuary, thereby, restoring its capacity to sustain creation's sacred intersection between the presence of a holy God and the common life of the people...to purify themselves by removing sins that fray their commitment and subvert their covenantal partnership with God." For literary arguments, see Angel M. Rodriguez, "Leviticus 16: Its Literary Structure," *AUSS* 34 (1996): 269–86.

52. Cf. Levine, *Leviticus*, 109; Balentine, *Leviticus*, 134; Wenham, *Leviticus*, 236.

53. Notice the list of עָוֹן פֶּשַׁע חַטָּאת in Lev 16:21 and פֶּשַׁע חַטָּאת in 16:16. Balentine, *Leviticus*, 128, notes that reference to these three categories, especially says the reference to "uncleanness ... transgressions ... sins" shows, especially the second of these, פֶּשַׁע, shows that "what are being addressed are not only Israel's ritual impurities but also its ethical transgressions."

rendered the people and their sanctuary defiled (טָמְאָה).⁵⁴ The Yom Kippur legislation in Lev 16, thus, shows us the Priestly doctrine of repentance not only on a liturgical, but also on a communal plane, providing an important precedent for our consideration of penitential prayer.⁵⁵

The influence of this Priestly doctrine of repentance on penitential prayer can be discerned in the regular appearance of the verb הִתְוַדָּה (*hitwaddâ*) both in the narrative contexts in which they are embedded (Ezra 10:1; Neh 9:2, 3; Dan 9:4, 20), as well as in one of the prayers proper (Neh 1:6). This influence is confirmed in the regular appearance of the root מַעַל (*ma'al*) in these prayers (Neh 1:8; Dan 9:7), demonstrated most vividly in the use of penitential prayer in Ezra 9–10. Here one finds the violation of מַעַל (*ma'al*; 9:2, 4; 10:2, 6, 10) which is met with penitential prayer (9:3–15) focused on אָשָׁם ('*āšām*; 9:6, 7, 13, 15) and leading to an אָשָׁם ('*āšām*) offering (10:19). Furthermore, one can discern a close relationship between the final redaction of Dan 9 and the Priestly Yom Kippur ritual preserved in Lev 16.⁵⁶ Following the segue of Dan 9:22–23, which

---

54. Milgrom, *Leviticus 1–16*, 1034, 1042–44; idem, *Cult and Conscience*, 109 n. 406, and notice the link there to the penitential prayer tradition. In this I concur with Milgrom contra, for instance, Levine, *Leviticus*, 106, who links the confessional to a ritual designed to exorcise sin: "Ancient peoples believed that sinfulness, like impurity, was an external force that had clung to them; it was necessary, therefore, to 'drive out,' or detach, sins"; and Frank H. Gorman, *Divine Presence and Community: A Commentary on the Book of Leviticus* (ITC; Grand Rapids: Eerdmans, 1997), 97, in which the confession in Lev 16: "The high priest actualizes or concretizes the sins through confession and puts them on the goat, which carries them into the wilderness, away from the camp" (for this view see the chapter in this volume by Jay Hogewood). Levine does not take into account the various instances of confession in the Priestly material as Milgrom has. This view also stands in contrast to Wenham, for whom the need for such elaborate Day of Atonement ceremony was necessary because the sin was of a higher degree. The purification offering dealt with pollution caused by sin, a pollution that defiled the house of God. The seriousness of the pollution depended on the seriousness of sin and this seriousness gauged by status of the sinner (this clearly contrasts Milgrom who sees it as types of sins, as opposed to Wenham's types of sinners): a private citizen (only limited pollution, thus only smear horns of altar of burnt sacrifice), but if the whole nation or high priest, then blood was to be taken into tabernacle and sprinkled on the veil and altar of incense. Milgrom does, however, see that the need for the Day of Atonement is linked to national accumulation of guilt: "Finally, over the period of a year the sins of the nation could accumulate to such an extent that they polluted even the holy of holies, where God dwelt. If he was to continue to dwell among his people, this too had to be cleansed in the annual day of atonement ceremony" (Milgrom, *Cult and Conscience*, 95).

55. There is much debate over the precise date of the genesis of the Yom Kippur ceremonies. See Boda, *Praying the Tradition*, 49 n. 19; and further Rodriguez, "Leviticus 16," 269–86; Joseph Gutmann, "The Strange History of the Kapporet Ritual," *ZAW* 112 (2000): 624–26

56. Scholars often emphasize Deuteronomic evidence in this prayer, something that is not difficult to see; see van Deventer, "End of the End," 62–75. However, I have nuanced this in my *Praying*, 71–72; see also John J. Collins, *Daniel: A Commentary on the Book of Daniel*

transitions the reader from the penitential prayer of Dan 9:4–21 to the angelic interpretation, a statement summarizing the angelic message is provided in verse 24. Here one finds the appearance of the three terms for sin that lie at the center of the confession in the Day of Atonement ceremony עָוֹן פֶּשַׁע חַטָּאת (Lev 16:21) connected with the key verb כִּפֶּר. Interestingly, this Priestly lexical combination occurs within an interpretation that takes the Jeremianic seventy year tradition and elongates it using the principle of multiplication by seven, a technique that can be observed in Lev 26 (vv. 18, 21, 24, 28) in a Priestly passage that reaches its climax in the exile of the nation.[57] Here we see a narrative connection between penitential prayer and the Priestly tradition of penitence through confession exemplified in the Yom Kippur ritual but mediated through the exilic perspective of Lev 26. Evidence from both Ezra 9 and Dan 9 suggests that links to ancient Priestly conceptions and rituals of the penitential were not lost on those responsible for the preservation of the earliest penitential prayers within the biblical text.[58]

The backdrop of the Priestly doctrine of repentance, mediated as we can see through the Holiness Code's use of this doctrine in Lev 26, is essential to the theology of repentance found in penitential prayer. While 1 Kgs 8 is an important text, I have argued elsewhere that it most likely has been drawn from a Priestly source and thus shows the impact of the Priestly doctrine of repentance on Deuteronomic streams in Israel.[59]

(Hermeneia; Minneapolis: Fortress, 1993), 360, who sees here "an implicit rejection of the Deuteronomic theology of history." For diversity of tradition in this prayer, see also Venter, "Daniël 9," 327–46. However, I do agree with Gerald H. Wilson, "The Prayer of Daniel 9: Reflection on Jeremiah 29," *JSOT* 48 (1990): 91–99, that Dan 9 is, indeed, seeking to fulfill the conditions of Jer 29, only those responsible are not necessarily Deuteronomic tradents.

57. For this see John Goldingay, *Daniel* (Word Biblical Themes; Dallas: Word, 1989), 232; contra Redditt, "Daniel 9," 247–48, who sees the play on the rhythm of Jubilees, that is, here ten Jubilees. Due to the connection at the outset of Dan 9 with the Jeremianic seventy-year tradition, the focus is on the equation 70 x 7, not on 10 x Jubilee. For other priestly motifs in Dan 9, see Boda, *Praying the Tradition*, 71–72, esp. n. 123.

58. For evidence of preexilic influence of Lev 26 on penitential liturgy, see also Boda, "Complaint," 186–97. Note also the recent work of Jonathan Klawans, *Impurity and Sin in Ancient Judaism* (New York: Oxford University Press, 2000), who shows the impact of Priestly purity language on Ezra 9.

59. See Newman's (*Praying by the Book*, 39–52) review of research on the background of this prayer. Although one cannot deny Deuteronomic vocabulary (Gary N. Knoppers, "Prayer and Propaganda: Solomon's Dedication of the Temple and the Deuteronomist's Program," *CBQ* 57 [1995]: 229–254), it is interesting that the structuring devices for the prayer are Priestly and also, as Newman (50–51) notes so well, that the conclusion to the prayer (vv. 52–53) picks up on the priestly vocabulary of separation. One author not cited by Werline, J. Gordon McConville, "I Kings VIII 46–53 and the Deuteronomic Hope," *VT* 42 (1992): 67–79, draws a clear distinction between 1 Kgs 8 and Deut 30, the former of which "stands consciously over against … deliberately distances itself from" the latter (71). In his conclusion he warns: "a question is

Thus, the earliest penitential prayers are dependent upon two streams of penitential theology now discernible in the final form of the Old Testament.[60] On the one side lies the penitential theology of the Priestly tradition with its concern over the ultimate מַעַל (ma'al) that led to the exile and demanded a penitential confession to restore covenantal relationship. On the other side lies the penitential theology of the Deuteronomic tradition with its concern for a return to the observance of Torah as covenant document that fosters the eternal relationship between God and his people. This intersection of theological streams in penitential prayer is further displayed in a closely related theological theme to which we now turn.

Theology of Sin

The consideration of the theology of repentance above could not avoid consideration of the theology of sin and to this we now turn for a closer look. Within the penitential prayer tradition, repentance includes confession of sin, the admission that the community has failed, expressed through reviews of specific events within the history of Israel both past and present and in lists of words expressing the full lexical stock of Hebrew words for sin and guilt (מָרָה; מַעַל; רֶשַׁע; עָוֹן; חָטָא; אַשְׁמָה; מֶרֶד).[61] While many of these words do not suggest any particular tradition group and most of them are used (especially רֶשַׁע; עָוֹן; חָטָא) in stereotypical and generic form,[62] we have already noted the importance of מַעַל for tracing the origins of this prayer form, especially in light of the intimate link between אָשָׁם ('āšām), מַעַל (ma'al), and הִתְוַדָּה (hitwaddâ).

Drawn from the Priestly ethos, מַעַל (ma'al) is a violation against God, most likely referring (due to reliance on Lev 26) to the people's violation of their oath

---

placed on against the undistinguishing use of vocabulary as a diagnostic tool in the identification of Deuteronomic literature. Too often, similar vocabulary or phraseology is taken, without further ado, to imply similar origins and meaning. The case I have examined [1 Kgs 8] shows that the writer's use of vocabulary may be self-conscious and intend both to express a measure of identity with a tradition and criticize it" (78).

60. It is easy to tip the balance in favor of the Priestly over the Deuteronomic in order to challenge prevailing emphasis on the Deuteronomic in the prayer, but I am reminded of the need for balance by Bautch, *Developments in Genre*, 21, when he notes that the Deuteronomic sequence of retribution theology is "a point of reference for understanding the confession of sin in penitential prayer."

61. See Boda, *Praying the Tradition*, 203.

62. Such expressions do not mean that sin is viewed as a general condition, as Miller, *Biblical Prayer*, 246, has aptly put it: "Confession of sin in the Old Testament is characteristically for specific sinful acts—though they may be recurring or prolonged sinful acts—rather than for a general condition of sin." However, one should note the statement in the influential prayer in 1 Kgs 8:46: כִּי אֵין אָדָם אֲשֶׁר לֹא־יֶחֱטָא ("for there is no human who does not sin").

in covenant relationship through idolatry.⁶³ This may help us make sense of the fact that in penitential prayer the most common specific sin that is mentioned is that of idolatry (Ezra 9:11-14; Neh 9:18, 26; Ps 106:19-20, 28, 35-39). As we have already seen from the Priestly literature, מַעַל (ma'al) is identified as willful sin against God, that which necessitates oral confession of sin lest the person fall under the defiant category of Num 15:30-31 and risk capital punishment.⁶⁴ However, there is another aspect of מַעַל (ma'al) that is important to note, which has implications for the theology of sin in penitential prayer.

There are indications in the Hebrew legal literature and that of the ancient Near East in general that מַעַל (ma'al) had serious consequences beyond the individual transgressor. As Milgrom has argued, there are intragenerational implications for מַעַל (ma'al) as demonstrated most poignantly in the example of Achan (Josh 7; 22:20; 1 Chr 2:7).⁶⁵ Collective punishment, however, was only a divine right and could not be exercised by any human agents. This Priestly stream of collective punishment has had an impact on penitential prayer, communicated through the agenda of Lev 26:39-40. In v. 39 we are told that the remnant will live in the lands of their enemies and do so on account of their sins and the sins of their אָבוֹת. This is repeated in the following exhortation to confess not only "their sins" but also the sins of their אָבוֹת. Collective guilt here has expanded, however, from intragenerational to intergenerational. The roots of this theology are ancient in Israel, clearly enunciated in the Decalogue in which the sins of the fathers will be visited upon the children. It is important, however to make a distinction with Tigay, between "cross-generation retribution" (such as in Exod 34:7b) and compound retribution (such as in the Decalogue).⁶⁶ Cross-generational retribution involves the transfer of the ancestors' sins while compound retribution involves the addition of the ancestors' sins to the children's sins. Important for our present purposes is the fact that Tigay considers Lev 26:39-40 an example of compound retribution, a point which has been vigorously challenged by Milgrom who argues that:

---

63. So Milgrom, *Leviticus 23-27*, 2331: H is "notorious for converting the precise terminology of P into wide-ranging metaphors" and later connects this to the covenant relationship.

64. See above n. 43.

65. Milgrom, *Cult and Conscience*, 33-35.

66. Jeffrey H. Tigay, *Deuteronomy* (The JPS Torah Commentary; Philadelphia: Jewish Publication Society, 1996), 436-37; as Joel S. Kaminsky, *Corporate Responsibility in the Hebrew Bible* (JSOTSup 196; Sheffield: Sheffield Academic Press, 1995), 44, has so aptly described the latter: "Trans-generational retribution is a form of corporate retribution in which the guilt of a sinful generation and its consequent punishment are stored for a generation or more and then released against a later generation. It does not exclude the idea that the recipient may also be somewhat deserving of punishment."

there is nothing in these verses or in all of Leviticus that implies the cancellation of vertical retribution if the children are virtuous. The existence of the *kārēt* penalty, endorsed by H as well as P, implies the reverse: the line of the sinner will be cut off, even if his descendants remain steadfastly virtuous. Moreover, H's vertical retribution also functions horizontally. Note that in H, not only do the descendants suffer, but also the extended family (e.g., the family of the Molek worshiper, 20:5) and, at times, the entire nation (e.g., its exile, though not all have sinned, 18:25; 26:14–39).[67]

Thus for Milgrom the doctrine of collective responsibility is "a cardinal plank in the structure of Priestly theology."[68]

Leviticus 26, however, does not appear to bear the weight of Milgrom's conclusion. Leviticus 26 does not state that the remnant lives in exile only because of the sins of the fathers, but rather also because of "their sins" and, furthermore, links the safe return to the land with the confession not only of the sins of their fathers, but also of "their sins." Thus, it appears that Tigay is correct. The latest development in the Priestly traditions now showcased in Lev 26 had incorporated this compound aspect, something that has had a profound influence on penitential prayer.

Milgrom continues in his typology of the theology of intergenerational sin through D, Jeremiah and Ezekiel.[69] He argues that D expounds both intergenerational as well as individual retribution theologies. While in Deut 5:9–10 D retains the intergenerational retributive principle, in Deut 24:16 retribution is reserved for the culpable generation only (cf. Deut 7:9–10). One may see the same diversity within the Deuteronomic history as well, where one finds in 2 Kgs 14:5–6, a citation of Deut 24:16 to explain why the sons of the killers of Joash were not executed by Amaziah, and yet also throughout the history many narratives that depict punishment passed between generations, the most obvious of which is the climactic accusation of Manasseh as the sinful forefather whose sin caused the downfall of the southern kingdom (2 Kgs 21:10–15; 23:26–27; 24:2–4). Similarly, in Jeremiah one finds both streams of theology, both intergenerational retribution (Jer 15:4; 32:18–19, 30–31), as well as individual generational retribution (Jer 18:1–12; 31:29–31). Only in Ezekiel, according to Milgrom, does one find an

---

67. Milgrom, *Leviticus 23–27*, 2327.
68. Ibid., 2331.
69. Baruch Halpern, "Jerusalem and the Lineages in the Seventh Century BCE: Kinship and the Rise of Individual Moral Liability," in *Law and Ideology in Monarchic Israel* (ed. Baruch Halpern and Deborah W. Hobson; JSOTSup 124; Sheffield: JSOT Press, 1991), 11–107, identifies social forces initiated during the reigns of Hezekiah and Josiah as the source for the shift from the corporate to the individual. These two kings attempted to wrest control of the state from the clans by linking individuals directly to the monarchy.

absolute denial of "the existence of collective (both vertical and horizontal) retribution (chaps 18 and 33).":[70]

This classic expression, however, has been nuanced more carefully in Kaminsky's monograph on corporate responsibility in the Hebrew Bible.[71] Kaminsky shows that intra- and transgenerational retribution were key aspects of Deuteronomic theology and stood alongside another retributive theology that stressed "the individual and his or her direct relationship to God."[72] He notes that scholars have suggested (von Rad, Daube) and denied (Scharbert, Eichrodt) tension between these two theological streams, both based on evolutionary processes.[73] Kaminsky asserts, however:

> Although there is evidence of some movement toward an innovative new theology that individualizes retribution, to read this movement as a radical shift toward individualism that completely rejected older corporate notions is problematic. It both oversimplifies the relationship between corporate and individualistic ideas by portraying these two sets of ideas as poles in an evolutionary schema, and it often leads scholars to read every passage that highlights the individual as automatically rejecting corporate ideas.[74]

---

70. Milgrom, *Leviticus 23–27*, 2328. Contrast here Halpern, "Jerusalem and the Lineages," 14, who claims that P limits and maybe even eliminates vertical (Num 26:10–11; cf. Num 16:31–33; Deut 11:6) and horizontal (Lev 4:3, 13) corporate identity. Kaminsky, *Corporate Responsibility*, 120 and n. 10, challenges this in light of Lev 4; 20:5; and 26:39. Also contrast here Kaminsky's work on Ezek 18, who claims that Ezek 18 qualifies and complements but does not contradict the older corporate ideas (177–178). Moshe Greenberg, *Ezekiel 1–20* (AB 22; Garden City, N.Y.: Doubleday, 1983), 338–41, traces this development in later materials to concerns over the injustice of God related to the exile of the later generation.

71. Kaminsky, *Corporate Responsibility*; cf. Joel S. Kaminsky, "Joshua 7: A Reassessment of Israelite Conceptions of Corporate Punishment," in *The Pitcher Is Broken: Memorial Essays for Gösta W. Ahlström* (ed. Steven W. Holloway and Lowell K. Handy; Sheffield: Sheffield Academic Press, 1995), 315–46; J. S. Kaminsky, "The Sins of the Fathers: A Theological Investigation of the Biblical Tension between Corporate and Individualized Retribution," *Judaism* 46 (1997): 319–32.

72. Kaminsky, *Corporate Responsibility*, 116. Kaminsky shows (ibid., 53) how the ideology of trans-generation recompense can be discerned in the two key theological centers of Deuteronomism, the Davidic tradition (2 Sam 7; 2 Kgs 8:19) and Sinai tradition (1 Kgs 21:29; 2 Kgs 20:16–18). Kaminsky seems to be caricaturing Weinfeld when he claims (42–43) that Weinfeld denies that the Deuteronomist spoke of cumulative guilt; rather, Weinfeld argues in similar ways to Tigay's compound retribution, as Weinfeld writes: "the conception that God only requites the sins of the fathers on the children only if the latter propagate the evil ways of the fathers is, in effect, the underlying view of the concept of retribution in the Deuteronomic history" (Weinfeld, *Deuteronomy and the Deuteronomic School*, 319).

73. For the former (suggesting tension), this is explained as an evolution from corporate to individual, from worst to best and for the latter (denying tension) the individual was "a natural unfolding of ideas that were latent within the older corporate conceptions" (Kaminsky, *Corporate Responsibility*, 117).

74. Kaminsky, *Corporate Responsibility*, 119.

His argument is based on the fact that passages such as Deut 24; Jer 31; and Ezek 18, which are used to highlight individualism, are found in books that contain strong statements about corporate responsibility. Kaminsky has wisely concluded: "Ultimately, the two conceptions function in a complementary, rather than in a contradictory fashion."[75]

This important clarification of the classic view of the development of corporate ideology in the Hebrew Bible helps us avoid simplistic contrasts between theological streams in ancient Israel. At the same time, Kaminsky has convincingly argued that "the Deuteronomic historian's covenantal understanding of the concept of corporate guilt was strongly influenced by *earlier* conceptions of sin, bloodguilt, holiness and divine wrath."[76] Especially in his chapters on Josh 7 and 2 Sam 21, Kaminsky demonstrates that the Deuteronomic concepts of corporate responsibility go back to precursors related to *herem* and holiness that have been drawn into the Deuteronomic History and linked to covenant. Such concepts are clearly at home in the Priestly ethos, something I suggested in my earlier work on Josh 7.[77] In his view, the "idea of corporate punishment has now been given more sophisticated covenantal explanation, but it is still evident that this notion originated in the matrix of older religious notions of sin, bloodguilt, holiness and divine wrath."[78] At this point Kaminsky falls into the evolutionary trap for which he criticizes others. He also fails to deal with the literary context of Lev 26 with its emphasis on covenant (26:42, 44, 45), a passage that once again provides the link between Priestly theology and penitential prayer.

Penitential prayer, therefore, relies heavily upon the foundational notions of corporate guilt that link the present generation of the pray-ers with the past generation of guilt. This leads to the consistent articulation of the sinfulness of Israel as something related to both past and present generations (Ezra 9:6; Neh 1:6; 9:32–37; cf. 9:2; Dan 9:5–6, 8; Ps 106:6). The roots of the transgenerational aspect can be seen clearly in the ancient confession of God's character of discipline

---

75. Ibid., 178. Note the opposing view of Gordon Matties, *Ezekiel 18 and the Rhetoric of Moral Discourse* (SBLDS 126; Atlanta: Scholars Press, 1990), esp. 145–46. Halpern, "Jerusalem and the Lineages," 12–15, highlights the fact that corporate and individual punishment existed alongside one another in the legal traditions of Israel, while expressing the classic view for his interpretation of Jeremiah and Ezekiel.

76. Kaminsky, *Corporate Responsibility*, 55.

77. See Boda, *Praying the Tradition*, 57–61, where I argue for the priestly character of Josh 7. On Priestly influences in the book of Joshua, see also John E. Petersen, "Priestly Materials in Joshua 13–22: A Return to the Hexateuch?" *HAR* 4 (1980): 131–46. Note also Halpern, "Jerusalem and the Lineages," 12, who highlights the importance of the ideology of collective responsibility (both ancestral and contemporary) to biblical prophecy and historiography, claims that such ideology has diverse theological underpinning, only then to note that key to this is the belief that "Pollution—moral or cultic—stains the fabric of the environment" (12), a notion clearly at home in the priestly stream.

78. Kaminsky, *Corporate Responsibility*, 112.

now preserved in Exod 34, where ancestors' sins impact subsequent generations (cross-generational). However, the notion exemplified in penitential prayer is compound guilt, a concept which espouses that guilt is cumulative, but only has implications for future generations if they replicate illicit behavior. This compound aspect is expressed beautifully in Ezra's cry: "Our sins have risen higher than our heads, and our guilt has mounted to the heavens" followed immediately by the rationale: "From the days of our fathers to this day we have been in great guilt" (Ezra 9:6–7).

This approach of compound guilt is linked to the later Priestly theology of the holiness code, showcased in Lev 26:39–40, but also seen in the Decalogue ("of those who hate me"), and clearly in the Deuteronomic history (2 Kgs 21:10–16; 23:26–27; 24:3–4). Although these concepts are not rejected completely in Deuteronomy, the DtrH, Jeremiah, or Ezekiel, they are clearly challenged and complemented by statements of individualized approaches to such sin. penitential prayer is an expression of the repentance of the present generation, but does so in a way that shows closer links to the corporate notions, something not surprising in light of the fact that the theology of repentance above has shown clear links to Lev 26.

Theology of God

As a form of supplication to the Lord, penitential prayer is (as expected) theocentric in its focus. So pronounced is this aspect, according to Balentine, "that the pray-ers themselves recede into the background" so that their prayers "reflect not so much their own inner character as that of the God to whom they are addressed."[79] This characteristic is common in Hebrew prayer, as can be seen in the lament tradition of the Hebrew Psalter from which penitential prayer is drawn, a tradition for which allusions to God's character and action often form the motivation for the appeal.[80] Within the earliest prayers of this tradition (both proto-penitential prayers and penitential prayers proper) there is a focus on God using narrative forms of discourse. Interestingly, two of von Rad's later examples of his "das kleine geschichtliche Credo" are some of the earliest examples of penitential prayer (Ps 106; Neh 9).[81] As Oeming has recently stated about Neh 9:

---

79. Balentine, *Prayer in the Hebrew Bible*, 90–91.

80. See Hermann Gunkel, *The Psalms: A Form-Critical Introduction* (Facet Books Biblical Series 19; Philadelphia: Fortress, 1967), Claus Westermann, *The Psalms: Structure, Content & Message* (Minneapolis: Augsburg 1980), Walter Brueggemann, *The Message of the Psalms: A Theological Commentary* (Augsburg Old Testament Studies; Minneapolis: Augsburg, 1984), 55.

81. Gerhard von Rad, *Gesammelte Studien zum Alten Testament* (TBü 8; Munich: Kaiser, 1958), 9–86; idem, *The Problem of the Hexateuch and Other Essays* (London: Oliver & Boyd, 1966), 1–78.

The prayer of confession has the character of a creedal summary. In contrast to Gerhard von Rad, who understood this short formula to be the origin of the tradition, I would suggest that this text is the final stage of a summary: a concentrate. It clearly exhibits catechismal elements, i.e. it is a kind of 'Creed' of the Persian era, a confession of the faith held by the post-exilic congregation. The primary intention of the text is twofold: to define the nature of God and to define the true Israel.[82]

Nehemiah 9 along with its counterpart Ps 106 employs the theological story of Israel in two ways within penitential prayer. First of all, they provide a clear picture of the consistent sinfulness of the people and through this function as implicit confession of sin. Summary statements such as Neh 9 (וְאֶת־מְלָכֵינוּ שָׂרֵינוּ כֹּהֲנֵינוּ וַאֲבֹתֵינוּ לֹא עָשׂוּ תּוֹרָתֶךָ וְלֹא הִקְשִׁיבוּ אֶל־מִצְוֺתֶיךָ וּלְעֵדְוֺתֶיךָ אֲשֶׁר הַעִידֹתָ בָּהֶם) merely condense the preceding long story of covenant unfaithfulness within the historical review.

Secondly, and more important to our purposes here, these reviews of the story of Israel in Neh 9 and Ps 106 function as theology, subtly preparing the way for the cry for mercy in the latter part of the prayer. Thus, when Ps 106:8 notes that God saved them "for his name's sake to make his power known," and verse 45 depicts God's mercy in exile when it declares, "For their sake he remembered his covenant and out of his great love he relented," the supplicant is preparing the way for his cry in 106:47: "Save us, O Lord our God and gather us from the nations." At the same time, however, the description of God's disciplinary actions in verses 26, 29, 40–41, each time linked to Israel's disobedience, emphasizes an important theological reality: God has and will discipline a recalcitrant people. Additionally, this form of theology has a subtle effect on the prayers by revealing a general pattern of God's action which provides hope for salvation in the present.

As I have argued elsewhere, the composer(s) of the prayer in Neh 9 employs both the discipline and patience sequencing models in order to lay a foundation for the request proper in 9:32.[83] The patience model carries the story from Abraham to the conquest (when the Abrahamic promise is fulfilled) and provides an opportunity to point back to God's promise to Abraham as foundational for hope in the present. The discipline model carries the story from the Conquest until the present and provided an opportunity to point back to an aspect of the story in which God responds to the penitential.[84]

Although this narrative aspect is dominant in only two of the penitential prayers,[85] there are shorter narrative pieces in the other early penitential prayers:

---

82. Oeming, "Nehemiah 9."

83. For this see Boda, *Praying the Tradition*, 81–87.

84. Further examples could be drawn from key proto-penitential forms such as Isa 63:7–64:12; Jer 32:17–26.

85. Although cf. proto-penitential prayers Isa 63:7–64:12 and Jer 32.

Ezra 9:7, 8–9, 13; Neh 1:10; Dan 9:15. Thus, one key stream in these prayers is that of the narrative creed, focusing attention on the God of action who saves and disciplines the people.

Another stream of theology that provides a foundation for the passionate cry of penitential prayer focuses attention on the character of God. The ancient character creed of Israel can be isolated in what is identified as the proclamation of the name of the Lord (קָרָאתִי בְשֵׁם יְהוָה) which is linked to the revelation of the goodness of the Lord in Exod 33–34 (כָּל־טוּבִי; 33:19; 34:6).[86] This ancient creedal form is announced in Exod 34:6–7:[87]

נֹצֵר חֶסֶד לָאֲלָפִים נֹשֵׂא עָוֺן וָפֶשַׁע וְחַטָּאָה וְנַקֵּה לֹא יְנַקֶּה אֵל רַחוּם וְחַנּוּן אֶרֶךְ אַפַּיִם וְרַב־חֶסֶד וֶאֱמֶת פֹּקֵד עֲוֺן אָבוֹת עַל־בָּנִים וְעַל־בְּנֵי בָנִים עַל־שִׁלֵּשִׁים וְעַל־רִבֵּעִים:

Echoes of this ancient creedal form can be discerned in various parts of the Hebrew Bible, notably in Num 14:18; Pss 86:15; 103:8; 111:4; 145:8; Joel 2:13; Jonah 4:2; Nah 1:3; 2 Chr 30:9.[88] It is not insignificant for our purposes that the majority of contexts into which this formula is incorporated are related to the issues of repentance, renewal, forgiveness and punishment. This creedal statement highlights both the gracious and disciplinary character of the Lord with the two linked through the transitional phrase: נֹשֵׂא עָוֺן וָפֶשַׁע וְחַטָּאָה, a threefold declaration of sin parallel to the Yom Kippur ceremony discussed above.

Allusions to this character creed tradition can be discerned throughout the penitential prayer tradition, the early prayers of which employ the full breadth of Hebrew lexical stock for grace to allude to the mercy of God.[89] What should not be missed, however, is that in the penitential prayer tradition the focus is on the

---

86. George E. Wright, *God Who Acts* (SBT 1/8; London: SCM, 1952), who saw the enterprise of Old Testament theology as "a recital or proclamation of the redemptive acts of God, together with the inferences drawn therefrom" (11) and defined biblical theology as "the confessional recital of the redemptive acts of God" (13), was certainly aware of the character creed, even if he relegated it to a footnote, thereby ignoring its theological significance (see p. 85 n. 2).

87. For focused work on this creedal form, see Josef Scharbert, "Formgeschichte und Exegese von Ex 34,6f und seiner Parallelen," *Bib* 38 (1959): 130–50; Robert C. Dentan, "The Literary Affinities of Exodus XXXIV 6f," *VT* 13 (1963): 34–51; Michael A. Fishbane, *Biblical Interpretation in Ancient Israel* (Oxford: Clarendon, 1985), 335–50; Thomas B. Dozeman, "Inner-Biblical Interpretation of Yahweh's Gracious and Compassionate Character," *JBL* 108 (1989): 207–23.

88. See Katharine D. Sakenfeld, *Faithfulness in Action: Loyalty in Biblical Perspective* (OBT 16; Philadelphia: Fortress, 1985), 49.

89. Ezra 9:8–9, 13, 15; Neh 1:10; 9:17, 19, 27, 28, 31, 33, 35; Dan 9:9, 13, 15, 17–18; Ps 106:1, 4, 7, 45. Newman, *Praying by the Book*, 89–91, notes the impact of the character creed on Neh 9 and Miller, *Biblical Prayer*, 258. See also my work on this aspect in penitential prayer as well as the proto-penitential prayer in Lam 3: Boda, "Priceless Gain," 51–75.

first part of the creed, that is, the vocabulary that comes prior to the center phrase נֹשֵׂא עָוֹן וָפֶשַׁע וְחַטָּאָה, and is focused on the grace of God.[90] As Newman has so aptly expressed this in relation to Neh 9:

> This ancient formula, crystallized and bound up with other sacred scripture over time, came to be used as a focus and refrain in this prayer as a true representation of God's gracious and compassionate character. For the author of Nehemiah 9, there was divine self-revelation to this effect in the past as well as evidence from divine salvation during the course of Israelite history.[91]

This avoidance of the latter half of the credo, the section associated with cross-generational discipline, not only reveals that the emphasis in penitence was placed on grace, but also confirms our assertion above that the cross-generational conception of sin is avoided in favor of the compound conception.

One further development in this creedal tradition that represents a key shaping influence on the earliest penitential prayers is the Deuteronomic form: הָאֵל הַגָּדוֹל וְהַנּוֹרָא שֹׁמֵר הַבְּרִית וְחֶסֶד לְאֹהֲבָיו וּלְשֹׁמְרֵי מִצְוֹתָיו.[92] Weinfeld has argued that this expression, which is cited in full or in part in three of the early penitential prayers (Neh 1:5; 9:32; Dan 9:4), has come from the Deuteronomic liturgical tradition.[93] In each case this creed is given priority of place at the outset of the petition[94] and brings the focus of attention on the covenantal relationship between God and people, reminding both partners of the reciprocity of this relationship, so important at a juncture in Israel's redemptive history when the penitential is necessary. It also establishes an important theological foundation for the future, for the God who keeps covenant is the God who will keep covenant and bring restoration to his people.[95]

The fact that the "great and awesome God" establishes relationship with this people, as was done at Sinai, is a subtle reminder for the people not to take this relationship lightly, as has been highlighted in the various depictions of the story

---

90. See Newman, *Praying by the Book*, 36–39, who notes with J. Milgrom, *Numbers* (JPS Torah Commentary; Philadelphia: Jewish Publication Society, 1990), 392–98, on Num 14:13–19 that the truncated form is typical of Jewish penitential prayer.

91. Newman, *Praying by the Book*, 115.

92. Noted also by Balentine, *Prayer in the Hebrew Bible*, 104; Miller, *Biblical Prayer*, 256. Cf. Weinfeld, *Deuteronomy and the Deuteronomic School*, 330–31; Scharbert, "Ex 34,6f.," 130–50; Sakenfeld, *Faithfulness in Action*, 111–39. See further Weinfeld, who includes these in his list and discussion of Deuteronomic liturgies, noting Deut 7:21; 10:17; 28:58; Jer 32:18 for the first half (pp. 39–41) and Deut 7:9, 12; 1 Kgs 8:23 for the second half (pp. 38, 41, 76 n. 3, 77).

93. Weinfeld, *Deuteronomy and the Deuteronomic School*, 32–45, esp. 40, 41.

94. Neh 9:32 is clearly the place in the prayer where the supplicant(s) move from the historical rehearsal to the present request, seen most notably in the employment of the formulaic וְעַתָּה.

95. Balentine, *Prayer in the Hebrew Bible*, 108.

of rebellion. This allusion to the "awesomeness" of God suggests another aspect of God's character, that is, his disciplinary character. Although these prayers consistently emphasize the grace and mercy of their covenant God,[96] one cannot avoid references to his disciplinary side. This aspect can be discerned in the references to God's punishment and anger (Neh 9:27, 28, 30; Ezra 9:13, 14; Dan 9:11, 16).

Finally, straddling these two categories of mercy and discipline is the reference to God as one who is righteous (Ezra 9:15; Neh 9:8, 33; Dan 9:14) and who possesses righteousness (Dan 9:7, 16). These terms highlight God's faithfulness to his covenant promises, a characteristic that is regularly contrasted with the infidelity of the people who have broken the covenant through their sin and rebellion.[97]

The early penitential prayers, thus showcase key theological streams of the Israelite tradition. They draw on the core recital of divine salvation that lay at the foundation of their story and use this foundational narrative to highlight the opportunity for both human penitence and divine rescue in the present. They also draw on the core recitation of divine character which offered hope for and understanding of their present predicament.

Theology of People

Clearly the declaration of God's character is a dominant feature in the penitential prayers, a view articulated by Balentine in the conclusion to his chapter on these compositions: "It is not the pray-ers themselves who are the fixed point of attention, but God."[98] However, one cannot ignore the human side of the covenant relationship, for the very depiction of God through narrative and character has consistently included the human partner as a reference point for understanding the divine.[99] Several aspects of this theology have already been articulated, that is, they are a people defined by sin, guilt and shame, as well as by their connection with past generations. But there are several other key theological themes that articulate the view of the people of God in these prayers.

First of all, the people are defined by the concept of remnant. This is clearly articulated in the prayer of Ezra 9, which employs the precise vocabulary שְׁאָר,

---

96. For this emphasis in penitential prayer and Lam 3, see Boda, "Priceless Gain," 51–75.

97. In this I differ from several others who see theodicy at work here; cf. Bautch, *Developments in Genre*, 153–54; Miller, *Biblical Prayer*, 257–58. The way the term is used in Neh 9 to structure the entire passage (9:8, 33; וְאַתָּה צַדִּיק), strongly suggests that this term is used to speak of God as righteous, that is, faithful to his covenant promises, rather than the usual just, that is, just in his discipline of Israel. That such theodicy is at play in this prayer tradition, is not in question. What is in question is the link between this phrase and theodicy.

98. Balentine, *Prayer in the Hebrew Bible*, 116.

99. This flies in the face of common popular theology that knowing God for who he is in himself is of a higher theological order than knowing God for what he has done for us.

שְׁאֵרִית, and פְּלֵיטָה (Ezra 9:8, 13, 14, 15), but is also evident in the background in the other prayers (Neh 1:8–9; cf. 1:3; 9:30–31; Dan 9:7; Ps 106:47). This understanding of the people is not surprising in light of the agenda of Lev 26: 36, 39 (note the vocabulary of שאר, vv. 36, 39), which provided guidance for Israel after discipline. This view of the people is one that directly relates to the conception of God as both gracious and disciplinary. As a remnant, the people are "those left over" after God's discipline of the people. But as a remnant, they are also "those preserved" by God through this discipline. The disciplinary side to this theology is seen in the regular articulation of the pain and suffering that has been and is being experienced by the pray-ers, expressed through such terms as humiliation (בֹּשֶׁת פָּנִים; Ezra 9:7; Dan 9:7, 8), hardship (הַתְּלָאָה; Neh 9:32), great distress (צָרָה גְדוֹלָה; Neh 9:37), calamity (הָרָעָה; Dan 9:13, 15),[100] and lists of abuses at the hands of the nations (Ezra 9:7; Neh 9:27–30, 35–37; Ps 106:41–43). The gracious side to this theology, however, is seen in the articulation that God did not eradicate the people completely, but rather preserved a remnant although the people did not deserve such (Ezra 9:8, 15; Neh 9:31; Ps 106:45–46).

Second, the people are defined by the land. One consistent emphasis throughout these prayers is the return of the land to the control of the Jewish community. The warning against intermarriage in Ezra 9:12 is bolstered by the hope that the people may enjoy the produce of the land and leave this land as an inheritance (ירש hip'il), for future generations. The prayer in Neh 1:9 draws from the promise of Moses that God would return the people after exile to the city of Jerusalem (אֶל־הַמָּקוֹם אֲשֶׁר בָּחַרְתִּי לְשַׁכֵּן אֶת־שְׁמִי שָׁם). The prayer in Neh 9 emphasizes this link between people and land consistently (Neh 9:8, 15, 23, 24, 25), a theme that sets up the lament over the lack of control of the land and its produce in their own time.[101] In Dan 9:16–17 the concern is similar to Neh 1, that is, focused on the city of Jerusalem and the temple mount. This intimate link between people and land betrays a people wearied by the experience of rootlessness and powerlessness.

Third, the people are defined by covenant and law. This is demonstrated most clearly in the recitation of the Deuteronomic creedal statement in Neh 1:5 and Dan 9:4, which states that God's grace is extended to those "who love him and keep his commandments," and in Neh 1:11, where the people of God are called

---

100. Cf. Neh 1:3: great trouble and shame (בְּרָעָה גְדֹלָה וּבְחֶרְפָּה).
101. Contra Oeming, "Nehemiah 9," who seeks to cast this section in a positive light in order to integrate this prayer into the larger context of Nehemiah as a whole. The difficulty with such an approach is that it does not deal adequately with the tone of the prayer to this point. For instance, since one finds the morphologically and semantically similar lexemes in Neh 9:27 as one finds in 9:37, referring to oppression, it is hard to forge a distinction between the two senses. Even more difficult, is the fact that the Dtr cyclical sequence ends in 9:30 with the negative scenario of the people given into the hands of their enemies, a situation that is seen as כָּל־הַתְּלָאָה in 9:32, which continues עַד הַיּוֹם הַזֶּה.

"your servants who delight to fear your name." Such programmatic statements resonate with regular emphasis in these prayers on the covenant relationship established with Israel, a relationship of love and fear that is expressed by the people through obedience to the commandments (see further below: Theology of Scripture).

Fourth, the people are defined over against the nations. Common to the narratives surrounding the prayers in Ezra 9 and Neh 9 is the separation of the people from foreigners, in both cases employing the verb בדל *nip'al* (Ezra 9:1–2; cf. 9:11–12; Neh 9:2). Even though the prayer in Ezra 9 does see in the present Persian occupation an aspect of God's חֶסֶד, even here this is not seen as ideal as the people remain in עַבְדוּת (9:8), a term used in Neh 9:17 to refer to slavery in Egypt. Similarly in Neh 9:35–37, the pray-ers express their pain over the present hegemony of the nations over their land and produce, identifying themselves as slaves in their own land.[102] The prayer in Daniel expresses deep consternation over the present desolate predicament of the city of Jerusalem and its sanctuary, noting how both city and people have become a byword among the surrounding nations (9:16). The petition proper of Ps 106 is focussed upon the return of the people from the nations with whom they mingled (idolatry) and among they have been brought low (106:35, 43, 47). These prayers reveal the deep struggle of a people in the process of defining themselves in the wake of the loss of political independence in the new world order. Even when they see signs of God's grace and discipline in the actions of the nations, they remain transfixed upon the goal of a pure community free from outside intervention.

Finally, the people are defined by God. This is encapsulated in such statements as Dan 9:19 in which the appeal to God is grounded in the fact that this people are "called by your name," in the consistent reference to the Lord as "our God"[103] and in the declaration of the Lord as "God of Israel" (Ezra 9:15).

These aspects of the theology of the people reveal to us the power of penitential prayer to express and shape the view of a community struggling for identity in the era after the fall of Jerusalem. This identity would continue to be founded upon those key ancient themes of God, law, and land, but such ancient themes would exist alongside the new realities of a people who now exist as a remnant in the midst of powerful nations.

---

102. Contra Oeming, "Nehemiah 9."
103. Ezra 9:8, 10, 13; cf. 9:6; Neh 9:32; Dan 9:9, 10, 13, 15, 17; cf. 9:18, 19.

Theology of Scripture

One final aspect of penitential prayer is the theology of Scripture with a focus on Torah.[104] As already seen in our review of the Deuteronomic character creed, God's faithfulness is extended to those who express their love for him by keeping his commandments (לְאֹהֲבָיו וּלְשֹׁמְרֵי מִצְוֹתָיו). The law plays an important role within the penitential prayer tradition as the code that defines covenant fidelity. This explains why sin is so often defined as violation of the law, employing various words used to denote this entity (תּוֹרָה/וֹת; מִצְוֹת; חֻקִּים; מִשְׁפָּטִים) and why the suffering of the people is linked to the curse of the law (Ezra 9:13–14; Neh 1:8; Dan 9:11). Torah, however, is not relegated to an abstract, objective legal code but rather is viewed consistently as the personal covenant demands of the Lord through the employment of the second-person singular objective suffix (Ezra 9:14; Neh 9:34; Dan 9:5) and the equation of violation of the law with personal rejection and defiance of the Lord (Neh 1:7; Dan 9:8, 11, 14). In addition, for penitential supplicants Torah defines the role of the prophets, who were commissioned as God's servants with keeping the Torah alive among the people, an emphasis drawn from the Deuteronomic stream of Hebrew theology (Ezra 9:11; Neh 9:26, 29–30; Dan 9:6, 10).[105]

These many instances of Torah vocabulary in the penitential prayer tradition not only showcase the high regard these pray-ers had for the law but also suggest a deeper role for the law in the prayer tradition. As I have argued elsewhere, there are two main approaches to Torah within the early penitential prayers.[106] On the one side, there are those prayers that represent an "anthology of pentateuchal law" (Ezra 9; Neh 1; Dan 9) and those that represent an "anthology of pentateuchal narrative" (Neh 9; Ps 106). What should not be missed here is that a similar traditio-historical process is at work as Torah is used to bolster authority, but also is leveraged to bring the ancient text to bear on new realities.[107] Thus the prayer in

---

104. See further Maurice Gilbert, "La place de la loi dans la prière de Néhémie 9," in *De la Tôrah au Messie* (ed. Maurice Carrez, Joseph Doré, and Pierre Grelot; Paris: Desclée, 1981), 307–16.

105. For the Deuteronomic tone here, see Boda, *Praying the Tradition*, 45, especially the phrase בְּיַד עֲבָדֶיךָ הַנְּבִיאִים. Cf. Weinfeld, *Deuteronomy and the Deuteronomic School*, 351.

106. See Boda, *Praying the Tradition*, 30–32.

107. Werline has shown sensitivity to this trend in his work on the prayers showing how this increases as time progresses in the penitential prayer tradition; Werline, *Penitential Prayer*, 63–64, 107–8, 158–59. Harm W. M. van Grol, "Exegesis of the Exile-Exegesis of Scripture? Ezra 9:6–9," in *Intertextuality in Ugarit and Israel: Papers read at the Tenth Joint Meeting of the Society for Old Testament Study and Het Oudtestamentisch Werkgezelschap in Nederland en Belgie (Held at Oxford, 1997)* (ed. Johannes C. d. Moor; Leiden: Brill, 1998), 31–61, seems to justify the appearance of "exegesis" in Ezra 9 by noting its similarity to sermonic forms. Although Ezra 9 does portray such affinities, such "exegesis" is a broader phenomenon of penitential prayer.

Ezra 9:10–12 uses the citation formula לֵאמֹר to introduce an anthology of legal material drawn from several places in Torah. As Milgrom has demonstrated for this technique (which he calls "Halachic Midrash"): "D's limited prohibition on intermarriages (Deut 23:4; cf. Neh 13:1–3, 23–27) is extended to all exogamous union. Next, Ezra derives from D that Israel is a *sanctum* and from P [108]that trespass upon sancta merits divine punishment. ... Ezra fuses them into a legal midrash directed against Israel itself which has allowed the 'enemy' to infiltrate by means of intermarriage. Thus, Israel, the 'holy seed', has been adulterated."[109] This technique is accomplished by employing a series of textual bites from both Deuteronomic and Priestly material to create a collage.[110] Again in the penitential prayer of Nehemiah 1 one finds the citation formula לֵאמֹר introducing what appears to be a "paraphrase" (Blenkinsopp) or "free summarizing quotation" (Clines) which echoes several passages from various parts of the Torah (interestingly again D and P).[111] In similar fashion Dan 9:11–13 is clearly alluding to the Deuteronomic warning of the curses that will fall upon covenant breakers in Deut 29:20–29 but paraphrases this passage and infuses it with Priestly vocabulary drawn from Num 5:21, the Torah instruction on dealing with infidelity in marriage. The interesting feature of these examples, especially the former two, is that these are presented as citations from the law itself, revealing an understanding that interpretation of the law could be regarded on the same level as the law itself. This trend of interpretation of inscripturated tradition was highlighted by Werline, but only for the later prayers in the penitential tradition, in an era when the verb דָּרַשׁ had subtly equated "seeking" as an activity of repentance (Deut 4; 28–30) with "interpreting," a later gloss for the root דָּרַשׁ. It appears from the observations above that interpretation of Torah was an integral part of penitential prayer from the outset, not surprising in light of the fact that one can trace the

---

108. Notice also the work of van Grol, "Schuld und Scham," 29–52; idem, "Exegesis of the Exile," 31–61, who notes intertextual links to Ezekiel.

109. Milgrom, *Cult and Conscience,* 72–73; D's belief that Israel is sanctum or holy people is seen in Deut 7:6; 14:2, 21; 26:19; 28:9; cf. also Bautch, *Developments in Genre,* 86–87, even though he cautions: "any sense of the prayer as interpretive literature should not be overstated" (88).

110. Joseph Blenkinsopp's terminology in *Ezra-Nehemiah: A Commentary* (OTL; Philadelphia: Westminster, 1988), 184; both David J. A. Clines, *Ezra, Nehemiah, Esther* (NCB; Grand Rapids: Eerdmans, 1984), 124; and Hugh G. M. Williamson, *Ezra, Nehemiah* (WBC 16; Waco, Tex.: Word, 1985), 137, call this "a mosaic" of passages, with the former citing Deut 7:1, 3; 11:8; 18:9; 23:6; Lev 18:24–30; Ezek 16:47; 2 Kgs 21:16; and the latter, Deut 7:1–3; 11:8; 23:6; 2 Kgs 21;16; Isa 1:19; Lev 18:24–30. See a similar view of halakic interpretation (in this case, in Neh 10) in D. J. A. Clines, "Nehemiah 10 as an Example of Early Jewish Biblical Exegesis," *JSOT* 21 (1981): 111–17.

111. Blenkinsopp, *Ezra-Nehemiah,* 209, notes Deut 30:1–5; 4:25–31; Clines, *Ezra, Nehemiah, Esther,* 139, Deut 30:1–5; Lev 26:14–15, 33; cf. Williamson, *Ezra, Nehemiah,* 172, who cites Deut 4:27; 28:64; 30:1–4; 12:5, etc.

origins of this prayer form to the Torah's prescribed response of the community to the discipline of the exile.[112]

For the second stream within early penitential prayer (Ps 106; Neh 9) the Torah remains a treasure chest for interpretation, but the focus is now upon the narrative of Torah. While from our modern perspective legal and narrative genres are distinct, for some within ancient Israel clear lines cannot be drawn as can be seen in the opening paragraphs of the book of Deuteronomy where Moses begins his exposition of the law with a review of the narrative of Israel, transitioning to legal material only in chapter 4.[113] Newman's work on Neh 9 has revealed key techniques in the reuse of Torah in Nehemiah, ranging from quotation (Neh 9:17–18), to "spin" (9:7, 13), to "biblicizing" (9:7, 17, 23, 16, 17, 29). Newman concludes:

> In this prayer in the book of Nehemiah, even as scripture is being written for the first time, scripture preys upon scripture as grist for a new composition. There is no clean divide between a canon of fixed scripture and its interpretation; rather, the two are enmeshed in this prayer. The process of tradition has long since begun.[114]

Although Newman and I published simultaneously, my own work concurs with her conclusion.[115] I discovered that even as this prayer was drawing from various parts of the Torah's narrative through an intricate series of textual allusions, echoes and citations on the micro level, it was simultaneously producing an innovative schema on the macro level that does not match the tradition sequencing found within the Torah from which it drew these allusions, echoes, and citations. The purpose behind this innovate tradition sequence can be seen in its usefulness to engender hope for the supplicants in their present predicament. Such evidence suggests a flexible hermeneutic parallel to the one which was noted for those early penitential prayers that create legal anthologies. As for Ps 106, my initial observations that Ps 106 portrays similar tendencies to Neh 9[116] only strengthen the far

---

112. Contra Bautch, *Developments in Genre*, 19 n. 80, who attacks Werline for imposing aspects seen in intertestamental literature onto texts from a much earlier era. I would have liked Werline to highlight this feature for these texts from the earlier era with greater vigor.

113. See also the recent dissertation of Lee in which he shows the close relationship between law and narrative in the Torah: Bernon P. Y. Lee, "Reading Law and Narrative: The Method and Function of Abstraction" (Ph.D. diss., University of St. Michael's College, University of Toronto, 2003).

114. Newman, *Praying by the Book*, 108.

115. See also Pröbstl, *Nehemia 9, Psalm 106 und Psalms 136*.

116. Boda, *Praying the Tradition*, 66–68.

more detailed work by Volker Pröbstl on this psalm,[117] the implications of which are summarized in his final paragraph:

> Die Darstellung von Neh 9, Ps 106 und Ps 136 verleiht dem Pentateuch einen besonderen Rang: Aus dem Pentateuch entnehmen die Verfasser die entscheidenden Daten ihrer Geschichtsdarstellung. Der vorliegende Pentateuch ist in seiner Grobgliederung verbindlich. Andererseits können sie Einzelepisoden umordnen, wie es ihren Absichten entspricht. Die Verfasser kennen den Text des Pentateuch und nehmen teilweise Formulierungen auf. Doch auch hier haben die Verfasser eine gewisse Freiheit, zuspitzend oder interpretierend abzuweichen.[118]

Such a view is expressed succinctly in the title of his conclusion: "Treue und Freiheit," that is, "Loyalty and Freedom." Such handling of Torah in penitential prayer is not unique within this later period, as can be seen, for instance, in the emerging intertextuality of the Persian period prophets.[119] What is fascinating, however, is how prayer becomes a vehicle for interpretation and exposition and such a move is only possible because of a certain theology of Torah that underlies this prayer form.

Conclusion

During the sixth century B.C.E. the state of Judah experienced a blow to its political and religious institutions that would shake it to its sociological and, in turn, theological core. At the same time, however, members of this same community introduced a liturgical transformation that would provide the theological foundation to enable this people to survive the demise of state and temple. Drawing on important themes expressed in Deuteronomic, Priestly, and prophetic traditions,

---

117. Newman, *Praying by the Book*, 110–11, mentions Ps 106 among a list including Ps 105; 106; 135; and 136 but focuses her attention on Ps 105.

118. "The presentation of Neh 9, Ps 106 and 136 gives to the Pentateuch a particular dignity. The authors take their crucial data for their historical presentation from the Pentateuch. The available Pentateuch is binding in its basic arrangement. On the other hand, the individual episodes can be reorganized, as it suits their intentions. The authors know the text of the Pentateuch and take up partial wordings. Nevertheless, even here the authors have a certain freedom to sharpen or to branch off in their interpretation" (translation mine).

119. See various articles in Mark J. Boda and Michael H. Floyd, eds., *Bringing Out the Treasure: Inner Biblical Allusion and Zechariah 9–14* (JSOTSup 370; Sheffield: Sheffield Academic Press, 2003); and bibliography in Mark J. Boda, "Reading between the Lines: Zechariah 11:4–16 in Its Literary Contexts," in Boda and Floyd, *Bringing Out the Treasure*, 277–91. Newman (*Praying by the Book*, 110–12) has also done us a great service by noting similar tendencies within other prayers that I have identified as proto-penitential prayers, that is, Isa 63:7–64:12; Jer 32:17–25.

these liturgists subtly shaped the theological life of a community on the brink of extinction. Little did they know that this liturgical tradition and the theology it would emphasize would provide an avenue for both expressing and strengthening faith for many centuries to come.

Socio-Ideological *Setting* or *Settings* for Penitential Prayers?*

Dalit Rom-Shiloni

Introduction

As a literary genre that developed mainly through the Persian, Hellenistic, and Roman periods, penitential prayer bridges the late biblical era and Second Temple Judaic literature.[1] Hence, this genre supplies a literary basis for the study of both continuity and evolution in the ideological-theological realm of Judaism.[2]

Yet the biblical roots of this genre are still somewhat obscure, or, to specify the enigma accurately: the circle/circles of authors responsible for the penitential prayers are unclear. Persuaded by Mark Boda's extensive traditio-historical study of Neh 9:6–37, I want to repeat his observation that this group of prayers (which also includes Ezra 9:6–14; Neh 1:5–11; Dan 9:4b–19) is "a type of prayer which reveals close affinities with Priestly-Ezekielian emphases drawing on a base of Dtr orthodoxy."[3] Indeed, the wide array of studies done on the literary sources of penitential prayers has shown that the prayers reflect an overall knowledge of the

---

* This study was conducted with the support of the Dorot Foundation and Hebrew Union College-Jewish Institute of Religion, Jerusalem, where I was a postdoctoral fellow during 2002–2004. Thanks are due to Dr. Ruth Clements, who not only improved my English but contributed tremendously to refine my thoughts. I am greatly indebted to Prof. Mark Boda for inviting me to join this inspiring project and for his helpful comments on this paper.

1. Samuel E. Balentine, *Prayer in the Hebrew Bible: The Drama of Divine-Human Dialogue* (OBT; Minneapolis: Fortress, 1993), 103–17.

2. Judith H. Newman, *Praying by the Book: The Scripturalization of Prayer in Second Temple Judaism* (SBLEJL 14; Atlanta: Scholars Press, 1999); Rodney A. Werline, *Penitential Prayer in Second Temple Judaism: The Development of a Religious Institution* (SBLEJL 13; Atlanta: Scholars Press, 1998); Daniel K. Falk, "4Q393: A Communal Confession," *JJS* 45 (1994): 184–207.

3. Mark J. Boda, *Praying the Tradition: The Origin and Use of Tradition in Nehemiah 9* (BZAW 277; Berlin: de Gruyter, 1999), 197. For additional biblical texts categorized as penitential prayers, cf. Werline, *Penitential Prayer*, 11–45.

earlier sources evoked in them. Scholars have noted explicit and implicit allusions to and exegesis of Deuteronomic sources,[4] historical traditions from the whole Pentateuch and from the Deuteronomistic History,[5] and Priestly phraseology.[6] It has also been suggested that these prayers allude to prophecies of Ezekiel,[7] Isaiah, Jeremiah, Haggai, Zechariah (1–8), and other prophetic books.[8] This is thought-provoking in itself, since by studying such innerbiblical allusions and exegesis scholars suggest that a vast biblical literature was available to the authors of penitential prayers. Yet, this literary phenomenon raises several questions. May we treat this amalgam of literary sources as an intrinsic characteristic of this genre, and, if so, can we mark out sources that these prayers rejected or polemicized against? What is the relationship between the penitential prayers and the classical *Gattung* of lament? And, finally, to what extent may we define communal laments as proto-penitential prayers?[9]

In this paper I want to reconsider the relationship between penitential prayers and communal laments. I will argue that penitential prayers do not simply continue communal laments diachronically, with certain generic-formal

---

4. For example, Neh 1:8–10 brings together Deut 4:27; 9:29; 12:11; 30:2, 4. See Werline, *Penitential Prayer*, 11–30. As for Dan 9, see André Lacocque, "The Liturgical Prayer in Daniel 9," *HUCA* 47 (1976): 119–42; Boda, *Praying the Tradition*, 89–187.

5. Neh 9 starts with the creation and goes through the historical traditions of Abraham, the exodus, the wilderness traditions, and the settlement; it incorporates the DtrH pattern of sin and judgment. See Boda, *Praying the Tradition*, 72–73.

6. Ezra 9:10–12 refers back to Lev 18:24–30; Deut 7:1–3; 12:28; 23:4–7; and Isa 1:19. See Boda, *Praying the Tradition*, 47–54, and throughout the detailed discussion on 89–187; and Werline, *Penitential Prayer*, 18–20. Yet, exposing Priestly influences on the penitential prayers is problematic. Allusions to the Holiness code (H, Lev 26) are traceable, but the question of Levitical liturgy is under debate; see Gerhard von Rad, "The Levitical Sermon in I and II Chronicles," in his *The Problem of the Hexateuch and Other Essays* (trans. E. W. Trueman Dicken; New York: McGraw-Hill, 1966), 267–80; and Richard J. Bautch, *Developments in Genre between Post-exilic Penitential Prayers and the Psalms of Communal Lament* (SBLAcBib 7; Atlanta: Society of Biblical Literature, 2003), 78–81.

7. Boda couples together Ezekelian and Priestly influences (*Praying the Tradition*, 62–66). Bautch found prophetic tones of warning in Ezra 9:6–15 and Neh 9:6–37 and allusions to the prophetic literature in both content and context (*Developments in Genre*, 82–84, 121–23, 159–63).

8. For Neh 9, see Jacob M. Myers, *Ezra-Nehemiah* (AB 14; Garden City, N.Y.: Doubleday, 1965), 167–69; for allusions to Jeremiah in Dan 9, see Lacocque, "Liturgical Prayer in Daniel 9," 119–42; and for Ezra 9, see Harm W. M. van Grol, "Exegesis of the Exile—Exegesis of Scripture? Ezra 9:6–9," in *Intertextuality in Ugarit and Israel: Papers Read at the Tenth Joint Meeting of the Society for Old Testament Study and Het Oudtestamentisch Werkgezelschap in Nederland en Belgie (Held at Oxford, 1997)* (ed. Johannes C. de Moor; OtSt 40; Leiden: Brill, 1998), 31–61; Boda, *Praying the Tradition*, 190–95.

9. Boda mentions Pss 74; 79; 89; Isa 63:7–64:11; 59:9–15; Jer 32:17–25; and Lamentations as "proto-forms of the later prayers" (see *Praying the Tradition*, 27, and the literature there). This idea has been carried further by Bautch, *Developments in Genre*.

transformations. Rather, during the sixth century B.C.E. penitential prayers polemicize *against* communal laments, suggesting "orthodox" alternatives to them. I will restrict myself to comments based on my previous research concerning concepts of God in the prophetic literature and poetry roughly dated to the Neo-Babylonian period, the first half of the sixth century B.C.E.[10]

PENITENTIAL PRAYERS AND COMMUNAL LAMENTS

PENITENTIAL PRAYERS IN THEIR LITERARY LOCATION

As noted above, the penitential prayers know and utilize pentateuchal and prophetic texts. However, a comparison of penitential prayers with communal laments, which presumably reflect the destruction of Jerusalem and the exile,[11] yields an impressive list of significant differences between these two bodies of literature in terms of both structure and content.[12]

GENRE, LITERARY STRUCTURE

In his studies on communal lament Claus Westermann suggested that these poems have a five-element structure: address (including introductory petition), lament (/complaint), turning to God (confession of trust), petition, and vow of praise.[13] Penitential prayers, however, silence the complaint,[14] usually refrain

---

10. Dalit Rom-Shiloni, "God in Times of Destruction and Exiles: Theology and Ideology in the Prophetical Literature and in the Poetry of the First Half of the Sixth Century B.C.E." (Ph. D. diss., Hebrew University of Jerusalem, 2001). This work will soon appear in Hebrew (The Hebrew University Magnes Press) and in English (SBL Academia Biblica).

11. In the present study, examples are adduced only from Pss 44; 74; 79; 80; 89; and 137, which are widely accepted as referring to the destruction of temple and city and the exile. For these and other lists, see Walter C. Bouzard, *We Have Heard with Our Ears, O God: Sources of the Communal Laments in the Psalms* (SBLDS 159; Atlanta: Scholars Press, 1997), 101–23; Bautch referred to Pss 44; 74; 78; 49; 80 (*Developments in Genre*, 24). The Psalms I considered in my dissertation were Pss 9–10; 42–43; 44; 74; 77; 79; 80; 89; 90; 94; 102; 103; 106; 123; 137 (Rom-Shiloni, "God in Times of Destruction and Exiles," 28–40).

12. Boda, *Praying the Tradition*, 25–26, 41; Bautch, *Developments in Genre*, 20–21.

13. Claus Westermann, *Praise and Lament in the Psalms* (trans. Keith R. Crim and Richard N. Soulen; Atlanta: John Knox, 1981), 52–64; idem, *Lamentations: Issues and Interpretation* (trans. Charles Muenchow; Minneapolis: Fortress, 1994), 95–98. Westermann based his work on Sigmund Mowinckel, *The Psalms in Israel's Worship* (trans. D. R. Ap-Thomas; 2 vols.; Oxford: Blackwell, 1962), 1:195–204. See also Craig C. Broyles, *The Conflict of Faith and Experience in the Psalms: A Form-Critical and Theological Study* (JSOTSup 52; Sheffield: Sheffield Academic Press, 1989), 220–21.

14. Boda considers "absence of complaint" to be the "most fundamental change" from lament to penitential prayer ("From Complaint to Contrition: Peering through the Liturgical

from explicit petitions for salvation,[15] and constantly emphasize confession of sins.

CONFESSION OF SINS

As presented by W. Sibley Towner, Samuel Balentine, and Richard Bautch, confessions dominate the penitential prayers in Dan 9; Ezra 9; and Neh 1; 9.[16] The function of these confessions is to praise God and to demonstrate the unbalanced relationship between God and his people.[17] God is celebrated for his salvific deeds, for his mercy and justice, whereas the people are despised for their ungrateful sinful behavior.[18]

In a few communal laments, confession does serve as justification for God's actions against his people (as in Lam 1:18; 4:6; Ps 79:8–9; and covertly in Ps 89:31–34).[19] However, such confessions are a debated element in the communal laments of Psalms and Lamentations. In fact, lack of a confession is one of the

---

Window of Jer 14,1–15,4," *ZAW* 112 [2001]: 186–97; phrased as "absence of lament" in *Praying the Tradition*, 55–61). See also, earlier, Peter R. Ackroyd, *Exile and Restoration: A Study of Hebrew Thought of the Sixth Century B.C.* (OTL; Philadelphia: Westminster, 1968), 77.

15. Bouzard sees these "importunities" as "the most consistent aspect of the communal lament; it is never missing." (*Sources of the Communal Laments*, 140). In contrast, penitential prayers have only covert hints of petitions for salvation, gathered from restricted descriptions of the present distress (Neh 9:36–37; but compare to Dan 9:6–11); and they rather explicitly focus on petitions for forgiveness (Dan 9:3–9; Ezr 9:6–15; Neh 1:6–11); this, of course, is the exact meaning of 'penitence' (see Balentine, *Prayer in the Hebrew Bible*, 89). Hence, I cannot accept Bautch's conclusion that the petition for salvation remains central in the penitential prayers (*Developments in Genre*, 136–37).

16. W. Sibley Towner, "Retributional Theology in the Apocalyptic Setting," *USQR* 26 (1971): 203–14; Balentine, *Prayer in the Hebrew Bible*, 103–17; Bautch, *Developments in Genre*, 21; and, regarding Neh 9, pp. 116–17.

17. Boda considered the confession of sins a Priestly influence on this genre, stemming from Lev 26 (*Praying the Tradition*, 47–54).

18. E.g. Neh 9:6, 7–8, 9–11, 12–21, 22–25, 26–31. Observing this dichotomy between God and the people, Towner understood penitential prayers to be "celebrating the manifest greatness of … God", and thus part of the doxology *Gattung* ("Retributions Theology," 203–14); See also Waldemar Chrostowski, "An Examination of Conscience by God's People as Exemplified in Neh 9,6–37," *BZ* 34 (1990): 253–61 (esp. 253–54).

19. This function of the confession of sins within prayers of the individual or of the community is a more generally shared element in biblical prayers (e.g., Exod 9:27; as also 10:16–17; 32:17–24; similarly Isa 38:17; Pss 32:5; 51; and likewise in the communal laments, Pss 90:8; 103:10–14; 106:6); See Moshe Greenberg, *Lectures on Prayer* [Hebrew] (Jerusalem: Academon, 1983), 15–17. A diversity of attitudes to confession characterizes Lamentations. Confessions appear in six verses in chapter 1 (vv. 8, 9, 14, 18, 20, 22), in four places in chapter 4 (vv. 6, 13, 22 [twice]), but only indirectly in chapter 2 (v. 14), in two verses in chapter 3 (vv. 39, 42), and once in chapter 5 (v. 16).

central characteristics of the communal laments (e.g., Pss 74; 77; 123; 137)[20] and pious protest may be heard in the psalmists' announcements of the people's complete loyalty to God (44:18–23; 80:19). Moreover, in further contrast to penitential prayers, the restricted confessions that do appear in a few communal laments do not exclude complaints and petitions for salvation.[21]

Hence, although prayers in general, and laments or penitential prayers in particular, have at their disposal a shared stock of "building blocks,"[22] the relative weight given to each of the three elements—complaint and petition, on the one hand, and confession of sins, on the other—is not merely a formal change of balance within the genre.[23] Rather, the transformative tactic of silencing the complaint and accentuating the confessional element designates an intentional theological innovation in the penitential prayers, which should be evaluated in its theological context.

Concepts of God in Their Theological Context

The theological discussion in the Neo-Babylonian period (the sixth century, prior to the Restoration) resembles the anxious search for a pious solution to the trilemma of theodicy as defined by Ronald M. Green:

> The "problem of theodicy" arises when the experienced reality of suffering is juxtaposed with two sets of beliefs traditionally associated with ethical monotheism. One is the belief that God is absolutely good and compassionate. The other is the belief that he controls all events in history, that he is both all-powerful (omnipotent) and all-knowing (omniscient). When combined ... these various ideas seem contradictory. They appear to form a logical "trilemma," in the sense that, while any two of these sets of ideas can be accepted, the addition of the third renders the whole logically inconsistent.... Theodicy may be thought of as the effort to resist the conclusion that such a logical trilemma exists. It aims to show that traditional claims about God's power and goodness are compatible with the fact of suffering.[24]

---

20. For parallels to this lack of penitential materials in the Mesopotamian *balag* and *ershemma* laments, see Bouzard, *Sources of the Communal Laments*, 53–99, 199–200.

21. Additional differences were suggested by Mark J. Boda, "The Priceless Gain of Penitence: From Communal Lament to Penitential Prayer in the 'Exilic' Liturgy of Israel," *HBT* 25 (2003): 51–75.

22. Moshe Greenberg argued that shared elements in prayers result "logically from the circumstances of the prayer" (*Biblical Prose Prayer As a Window to the Popular Religion of Ancient Israel* [Berkley: University of California Press, 1983], 11).

23. Compare to Westermann's description of the transformation of the lament in *Praise and Lament*, 171, 206; Boda suggested a similar tendency in Josh 7 (*Praying the Tradition*, 57–61); see also Bautch, *Developments in Genre*, 156–69.

24. Ronald M. Green, "Theodicy," *The Encyclopedia of Religion* (New York: Macmillan, 1987), 14:430–41.

This problem of theodicy in the face of the national crisis aroused a wide-ranging theological disputation among the Judahite people in Jerusalem and subsequently in Babylon, over God's three major qualities: omnipotence, omnipresence, and omniscience. (1) As omnipotent, God is considered the Lord of history, and his role in the destruction and exile of his people is central. (2) As omnipresent, God's presence and involvement in his people's destiny is in focus, and the possibility of a continuing God-people relationship after the destruction is contemplated. (3) As omniscient, God's attributes of justice, compassion, and the ability to forgive are major, and they raise bothersome questions regarding divine justice.

These theological topics are articulated along a vast spectrum of perceptions that were voiced by different speakers, and are recorded in the books of Jeremiah, Ezekiel, Lamentations, and selected Psalms. Explicit debates that present binary theological oppositions, lead me to observe the ideological-theological contention as dichotomized between speakers (or literary circles) in general categories of "ideological core" versus "ideological periphery," "mainstream" versus "dissident," "orthodox" versus "nonorthodox" perceptions.[25]

"Orthodoxy," according to Sheila McDonough, denotes its literal meaning as "correct or sound belief according to an authoritative norm."[26] On this "orthodox," or just "core" side of the division, stand historiographers (DtrH), priests (mainly of the Holiness school), and prophets. On the other side are sources that can be defined only negatively as not belonging to any of the former groups. Non-prophetic voices are found in relatively large numbers in Jeremiah and Ezekiel, in citations brought within these prophetic books.[27] As opponents of the prophets, the speakers are specified at times by their names (mostly the kings and their officials, Jer 21:2; 37:3) or grouped anonymously and generally as the *vox populi*, "all the people" (as in Jer 26:7).[28] This general division, however, does not intend to smooth over internal contentions within "orthodox circles." For instance, Jeremiah and Ezekiel faced other "orthodox" opponents, designated in the literature according to their social circles (e.g., "the priests and prophets," Jer 26:7; as also the peace prophets, Jer 23; 28; 29; Ezek 13). "Nonorthodox" writers stand behind

---

25. All these terms are of course sociologically inadequate, used here only to suggest theological oppositions. Yet none of the pairings seem satisfactorily to define the socio-theological dialectics under discussion here. Compare to Walter Brueggemann's "trial metaphor" with "core testimonial" and "countertestimonial" texts (*Theology of the Old Testament: Testimony, Dispute, Advocacy* [Minneapolis: Fortress, 1997], 117–26, 400–401).

26. Sheila McDonough, "Orthodoxy and Heterodoxy," *ER* 11:124.

27. Almost 140 quotations are found in Jeremiah, with more than 40 in Ezekiel (1–39), though not all of them are authentic. See Rom-Shiloni, "God in Times of Destruction and Exiles," 41–68 and appendix 1.

28. For the *vox populi* in opposition to the "writing" prophets, see James L. Crenshaw, *Prophetic Conflict: Its Effect upon Israelite Religion* (BZAW 124; Berlin: de Gruyter, 1971), 23–38.

most of the communal laments in Psalms and Lamentations. Their identity is unknown, but we can certainly detect a multifaceted independent expression of pious poetry. Furthermore, similarities have been noticed between arguments suggested in the quotations and themes presented in laments.[29] Hence, this opposition between "orthodox" (prophetic/historiographic/priestly) perspectives, on the one hand, and "nonorthodox" voices, on the other, demonstrates the complicated religious climate of that period.

In order to establish my argument regarding the theological relationship between penitential prayers and communal laments, let me suggest a theological inventory, which can help in situating penitential prayers in their theological context. This inventory is based on examination of the differences within the Judean religious worldview in the Neo-Babylonian period. I will restrict myself to one topic, the God-people relationship, the most persistent issue in both penitential prayers and communal laments.[30]

The God-People Relationship in Sources from the Neo-Babylonian Period

Sources from the Neo-Babylonian period exploit the general biblical patterns of covenant relationship between God and his people using two alternative sets of metaphors: metaphors taken from the sphere of political suzerainty treaties;[31] and metaphors from the family realm, marriage and adoption.[32] Both metaphors share the following constitutive elements: (1) the covenant as divine initiative; (2) commitments to the covenant, which may or may not mention (a) the people's obligations or (b) the divine commitment; (3) violation of the covenant, alternatively attributed to (a) the people or (b) God; (4) judgment, which explains the present distress; (5) prospects for renewal of the covenant relationship after the destruction and the exiles, again with the dual possibilities of (a) the people's continuing obligation; or (b) God's eternal commitment/recommitment, to his people.

---

29. Rom-Shiloni, "God in Times of Destruction and Exiles," 59–60, 90–155, 178–80, 284–318.

30. Balentine, *Prayer in the Hebrew Bible*, 216–64.

31. Moshe Weinfeld, "בְּרִית," *TDOT* 2:253–79. The political metaphor functions in DtrH (e.g., 2 Kgs 17:7–23; as in Jer 11:1–15; Ezek 20:1–38); in H (Lev 25, 26); as well as in nonprophetic voices (Jer 2:6, 8; Ezek 20:32); in Pss 44, 74, 80, 89, 106, and implicitly also Pss 77, 79.

32. The metaphor of marriage occurs in Jer 3:1–5; and in Ezek 16, 23; metaphor of adoption in Jer 31:9, 18; Ezek 16:1–43. See Moshe Weinfeld, *Deuteronomy and the Deuteronomic School* (2d ed.; Winona Lake, Ind.: Eisenbrauns, 1992), 80–81, 327; Shalom M. Paul, "Adoption Formulae: A Study of Cuneiform and Biblical Legal Clauses," *MAARAV* 2/2 (1979–1980): 173–85. Marriage and adoption are brought together in Ezek 16:1–14 and Jer 3:4. See Rom-Shiloni, "God in Times of Destruction and Exiles," 249–51.

While the two sets of metaphors function in all the above-mentioned literary contexts, the "orthodox" texts differ from the "nonorthodox" ones in terms of three elements: the commitments to the covenant taken on by the human and divine, their recognition of responsibility for violating it, and their commitments to its renewal.

Commitments to the Covenant

According to the political model, God, the suzerain, is the one who "makes a covenant" (e.g., Deut 5:2, 3; Jer 34:13; Ezek 34:25; and Ps 89:4), or "upholds a covenant" (e.g., Lev 26:9; Ezek 16:62) with his people.[33] Following this initiative, the suzerain has the privilege of obligating the people to fulfill his demands. Hence, God is the one who sets the terms, and the people are committed to being loyal by keeping "the words of the covenant" (Jer 11:2, 3, 6, 8; 34:18), and God's commandments (e.g., Deut 6:2, 17; 2 Kgs 17:19; Ezek 20:21).

In the "orthodox" sources, a long list of demands is put upon, or accepted by, the people (Jer 7:23; 11:4), whereas divine obligations are scarcely found at all.[34] Exceptional in this respect is the covenant formula, "That I may be your God and you may be My people" (e.g., Jer 7:23; as also Lev 26:12; Deut 26:17; 29:12), which syntactically suggests mutual obligations.[35] The contexts in which this formula appears indicate implicitly God's obligations (1) to be present within his people (Lev 26:11–13); (2) to give military aid and salvation from enemies (Lev 26:13; Deut 26:17–19); and (3) to fulfill the promise concerning the land (Deut 29:12).

This balance changes completely when we come to communal laments. As a rule (with the single exception of Ps 106:34–39), the laments on the one hand, do *not* mention any commitment imposed on the people, and, on the other, *do* emphasize the divine obligations for military aid and salvation from enemies. These obligations are mentioned in three contexts: in recitals of God's past deeds for the benefit of his people (Pss 44:2–9; 74:12–17; 80:9–12; 89:6–19, 20–38), in complaints about the present distress (44:10–17), and in petitions for future salvation (44:24–27; 80:15–20; 137:7–9).

---

33. On כרת and הקים ברית, see Jacob Milgrom, *Leviticus 23–27* (AB 3B; New York: Doubleday, 2000), 2343–44.

34. This phenomenon is well-attested in Neo-Assyrian suzerainty treaties, and it does not contradict the Suzerain's basic obligations of military aid, political backing and peace. See Simo Parpola and Kazuko Watanabe, *Neo-Assyrian Treaties and Loyalty Oaths* (SAA 2; Helsinki: Helsinki University Press, 1989), xiv–xv.

35. The covenant formula occurs seven times in Jeremiah (Jer 7:23; 11:4; 24:7; 30:22; 31:1, 33; 32:38) and five times in Ezekiel (Ezek 11:20; 14:11; 36:28; 37:23, 27), more than in any other biblical composition.

Violations of the Covenant

The DtrH and the prophets are united in their interpretation of the Babylonian victory and dominion over God's people. The present distress is a divine judgment in retaliation for Judah's one-sided violation of God's covenant (e.g., 2 Kgs 21; 23:26–27; 24:1–4, 20; Jer 11:1–14; Ezek 20:5–38). Judah brought upon itself the stipulations of the covenant, the long warning lists of curses of Lev 26 and Deut 28 against transgressions of the covenant obligation.[36]

However, communal laments generally do not mention any violation of the covenant on the part of the people and do not suggest present or past lapses in loyalty to God (so Pss 74; 77; 80; 89; 137). Rather, the psalmists ask the reason for the people's suffering (as in 74:1) or announce loudly the loyalty and innocence of the people who declare their commitment to the covenant (44:18–23; 80:19). Confession of "former iniquities" coupled with present sins does indeed appear in Ps 79:8–9, but this does not overshadow the declaration of faithfulness: "We, your people, the flock you shepherd" (v. 13).

Unlike "orthodox" sources, some communal laments do not describe Jerusalem's destruction or the people's defeat as a divine judgment in retaliation for the people's sins (e.g., Pss 74; 79). The destruction is mainly seen from one of two perspectives, either as a cruel act of war initiated by the human enemies, which God had no part in bringing against his people and city (Pss 74:1–15; 79:1–4; as also Jer 21:2), or as a direct act of God, who summons the enemy against his people, giving his people into their hands (44:10–17; 80:13; 89:41–43). In face of the people's faithfulness, both alternatives are theologically inexplicable, thus they elicit the psalmists' protests.

Moreover, laments charge *God* with violating his eternal covenant and oath (Ps 89:39–40). They explicitly call God to recommit himself to the covenant (Ps 74:20; as also Jer 14:21); they protest against God's withdrawal from his major obligation as Warrior who saves his people in times of distress (Pss 44:10–17, 24–25; 77:8–10; 79:15,20; 80:2–3; 89:39–46);[37] and they furthermore question God's continuing anger during the exile (Pss 74:1; 79:5; 80:5).

Renewal of the Covenant Relationship

In accordance with their perspectives on the commitments to the covenant and its violation, communal laments urge God to return and to bring his people back to him (Ps 80:3, 8, 20), to wake up (44:24), to turn his face to his people (80:3, 8,

---

36. Delbert R. Hillers, *Treaty Curses and the Old Testament Prophets* (2d ed.; BibOr 16; Rome: Pontifical Biblical Institute, 1964).

37. Psalm 44 adds an implicit protest against the divine justice (particularly vv. 18–23); see Dalit Rom-Shiloni, "Psalm 44: The Powers of Protest," forthcoming.

20), to see and hear (80:15), to remember (89:48–52), and to save his people as their sole Warrior (e.g., 79:20–23; as also Jer 14:7–9). There is no mention of any break in the people's loyalty to God while in distress. Rather, communal laments reflect the opposite. Using language of abandonment, the verbs זנח, נטש, עזב, and מאס, the psalmists express the feeling that God has deserted his people and withdrawn from the covenant (Ps 44:10, 24; as also 74:1; 77:8; 89:39; and Jer 33:24);[38] furthermore, he has abandoned the land ("The Lord does not see us; the Lord has abandoned the country," Ezek 8:12; 9:9). Whether deliberately absent or voluntarily uninvolved in the events because he hides his face (Ps 44:25), God does not see, hear, or speak; he does not employ his qualities of knowledge and remembrance to renew his past commitments to his people (תשכח "ignoring our affliction and distress," Ps 44:25). The complaints and the petitions addressed to God in the laments designate *him* as the partner who should be called to renew the covenant relationship with his loyal, patient, though suffering, people (Lam 5:19–22).

This is, of course, in contrast to the historiographic, priestly, and prophetic viewpoints. Focusing on the *people's* violation of the covenant, DtrH, Jeremiah, and Ezekiel use the verbs עזב, נטש, זנח, and מאס almost exclusively with the people as agents, and God or his commandments as objects, as for instance: "For all their wickedness: they have forsaken me" (Jer 1:16).[39] Furthermore, Jeremiah and Ezekiel refute the people's expressed feeling of desertion (Ezek 8–11, and Jer 33:24–27; 31:37).[40] In these sources the people are directed to return and seek God from their places of exile (Deut 4:29–31; 30:1–10; Lev 26:39–42). The prophets call for penitence and repentance (Jer 3:12–13, 14–18, 19–25; Ezek 18:21–32), and Ezekiel even projects a one-sided divine salvation of the exiles, in which God will conduct an internal transformation of their hearts to assure the

---

38. עזב, נטש, זנח with the objects of people and land, are among the verbs that describe God's absence and uninvolvement. מאס refers to God's abhorrence of a previously chosen king (Ps 89:39), priest (Hos 4:6), cult (Amos 5:21), the city (2 Kgs 23:27), and likewise the people (Lev 26:44; 2 Kgs 17:20; Jer 33:24; Isa 54:6, etc.).

39. Jeremiah uses נטש and עזב with God as agent in divine threats against the people only in Jer 12:7 (נטש) and 7:29; 23:33 (עזב). Regularly, however, does עזב occur in Jeremiah with the people as agents and God as object (Jer 1:16; 5:7–8, 19; 16:11; 19:4; 22:9; and metaphorically, 2:17, 19); so also implicitly within the refutations of the quotations in Ezek 8–11 (8:12; 9:9). In Dtr sources: Deut 28:20; 31:16; Josh 24:16; Judg 10:10, 13; 1 Sam 12:10; 1 Kgs 11:33; 2 Kgs 22:17; and see queries 2 Chr 15:2; 24:20. More than the other three verbs, מאס is connected with covenant phraseology and usually occurs with the objects תורה, חקות, משפטים, and דבר to denote the misconduct of the people toward God (Jer 4:30; 6:19; 8:9; 9:12; Ezek 5:6; 20:13, 16, 24; as also Lev 26:15; 2 Kgs 17:15); cf. נטש Jer 15:6.

40. Cf. Deut 31:20 to 31:6, 8. We also find the negation of abandonment verbs in the laments: לא זנח, Lam 3:3; לא נטש, Ps 94:14; לא עזב, Pss 9:11; 94:14. Yet only in Deutero-Isaiah's prophecies, alongside the announcements לא עזב (Isa 41:17; 42:16), do we see prophetic approval of this feeling of abandonment among the exiles in Babylon (Isa 49:14; 54:6–8).

exiles' obedience (Ezek 11:19–20; 36:26–27).[41] This "orthodox" approach to the renewal of the covenant thus reflects and understanding that the *people* violated the covenant through their continual sins (Lev 26:15), whereas God's judgment was *not* a final break in the God-people relationship (Lev 26:44–45).[42]

The evidence points to several conclusions. First, fundamental differences of perspective characterize the major conflict between the "orthodox" historiographic and prophetic sources, on the one hand, and the "nonorthodox" sources in the quotations and the communal laments, on the other. The "orthodox" sources argue that the *people* transgressed the covenant, whereas the "nonorthodox" ones claim that *God* has abandoned God's eternal commitment to Israel. Second, as heterogeneous and independent literary compositions, laments demonstrate several alternative concepts when they describe God's role in the destruction and his relationship with his people. Yet, the common denominator in these various conceptions of the God-people relationship is the people's full devotion to God and to his covenant in the face of their frustrating encounter with an abandoning, hiding, sleeping, uninvolved God. Third, this confidence in the people's devotion leads to the particular elements that characterize the communal laments: the praise for past deeds, the complaints, the petitions, and the lack (or rare occurrence) of confessions of sin.

The God-People Relationship in the Penitential Prayers

To express their overall perspective on the God-people relationship, penitential prayers utilize the political metaphor. Nehemiah 9 mentions a covenant with Abraham (Neh 9:7–8);[43] God is referred to as "our God" (Dan 9:9, 10, 14, 15, 17; Neh 9:32; Ezra 9:13); ה' אלהי ישראל (Ezra 9:15); the people are his servants (Neh 1:6, 10) or "your people" (Dan 9:16; Neh 1:10), and so forth. Repeatedly God is given the epithet שמר הברית והחסד ("who stays faithful to his covenant," Neh 1:5; 9:32; Dan 9:4).

If we apply to the penitential prayers the theological inventory developed above concerning the God-people relationship, none of the concepts that exemplify the perspectives of communal laments match the perspective within the extant penitential prayers.

---

41. Moshe Greenberg, *Ezekiel 21–37* (AB 22A; New York: Doubleday, 1997), 735–38.

42. Milgrom suggested that "I will remember in their favor the covenant with the ancients" (Lev 26:45) denotes God's maintenance of both the Sinaitic and the patriarchal covenants (*Leviticus 23–27*, 2337–42).

43. Fredrick C. Holmgren, "Faithful Abraham and the *ămānâ* Covenant, Nehemiah 9,6–10,1," *ZAW* 104 (1992): 249–54.

Commitments to the Covenant

Penitential prayers suggest that the people were committed to God through the laws and commandments given to Moses or to his servants, the prophets (Ezra 9:11–12; Neh 1:8–9; 9:13–14; Dan 9:10–11). Most of the references use only general language: "laws, commandments, and teaching" (Neh 9:14); "commandments and rules" (Dan 9:5), and the like; yet two of the penitential prayers allude to specific laws in Deuteronomy and in Leviticus (Ezra 9:10–12 to Lev 18:24–30; Deut 7:1–3; 23:4–7; and Neh 1:8–10 to Deut 4:27–29; 9:29; 30:2–5).

In contrast to communal laments, but in additional agreement with the historiographic and prophetic sources, penitential prayers do not explicitly mention God's obligations toward his people. An exception is the historical recital in Neh 9, which refers first to the divine promise of the land to Abraham and the fulfillment of this promise (Neh 9:7–8); second, to the fulfillment of the promises of progeny and the giving of the land to the second generation after the exodus (9:9–23) and third, to military assistance in confronting the Canaanite peoples (9:24–25).

Violation of the Covenant

In the penitential prayer traditions, responsibility for violating the covenant is put entirely upon the people's shoulders. For instance, Dan 9 contrasts God as one "who stays faithful to his commandments" (v. 4) with six expressions of the people's transgressions: "We have sinned; we have gone astray; we have acted wickedly; we have been rebellious and have deviated from your commandments and your rules and have not obeyed your servants the prophets" (vv. 5–6). In penitential prayers, the speaker(s) confess sins at length, sins committed by both the forefathers and the present generation (Dan 9:16, and vv. 6, 8; Ezra 9:7). The sins are catalogued in keeping with historiographic and prophetic models;[44] they are phrased in conventional Dtr and Priestly language;[45] or they use *hapax* phrases that allude to Dtr/Priestly concepts.[46]

---

44. For Neh 9, see Boda, *Praying the Tradition*, 81–87.

45. To mention some examples: ולא שמענו בקול ה' אלהינו ללכת בתורתיו (Dan 9:10); ולא שמרנו את (Dan 9:6); ולא שמענו אל עבדיך הנביאים (Dan 9:5); וסור ממצותך וממשפטיך (Dan 9:8); חטאנו לך (Neh 1:7); המצות ואת החקים ואת המשפטים אשר צוית (Dan 9:15); חטאנו רשענו (Dan 9:9); מרדנו בו (Dan 9:16); בחטאינו ובעונות אבתינו ולא חלינו את פני ה' (Dan 9:13); אלהינו לשוב מעוננו ולהשכיל באמתך (Dan 9:7); במעלם אשר מעלו בך. This general phraseology persists also when the specific violation of rules is mentioned (Ezra 9; Neh 1).

46. ויעשו נאצות גדולת ("thus committing great impieties," Neh 9:18, 26), e.g., is a *hapax* connected in this prayer to the sin of the golden calf (v. 18) and to the idolatry after the settlement in the land (v. 26). But since עשה נאצות stands for violation of the covenant in general, Neh 9:25–26 seems to allude to Deut 31:20 more strongly than to the wilderness tradition, as suggested by Boda, *Praying the Tradition*, 152–53.

According to the penitential prayers, in afflicting his people, God responded to the people's disobedience in a manner fully consistent with criteria of justice (Dan 9:12–14) and of steadfast love (חסד, Ezra 9:9). God's past mercy is repeatedly mentioned (Neh 9:19, 27, 31), and he is called by the epithets "a forgiving God, gracious and compassionate, long-suffering and abounding in faithfulness" (Neh 9:17; and see Dan 9:9). God's celebrated quality is righteousness (צדיק אתה "You are benevolent," Ezra 9:15; Neh 9:8, 33), the one who has justice at his disposal "With you, O Lord, is the right" (Dan 9:7).[47]

Judgment is thus completely justified, producing no complaint or protest. On the contrary, according to Ezra 9 God has brought the mildest judgment possible given the severity of the sins: "Though you, our God, have been forbearing, [punishing us] less than our iniquity [deserves]" (Ezra 9:13).[48]

The description of the past and present crises states that God gave the people into the hands of their enemies (Neh 9:27–29): "You abandoned them to the power of their enemies, who subjugated them" (Neh 9:28); "You delivered them into the power of the peoples of the lands" (Neh 9:30); "we … have been handed over to foreign kings" (Ezra 9:7b). All resemble the intermediate position (most often appearing in DtrH), that God himself had summoned the enemies to fight his people. Exceptions appear only in Dan 9, where exile is introduced once as the place to which God has banished his people (Dan 9:7) and where God is the sole agent of the distress (Dan 9:12–14).

Renewal of the Covenant Relationship

The confessional element in penitential prayers paves the way for the people's expected repentance, in agreement with the concept of exile in Deut 4:29–31; 30:1–10; Lev 26:39–42 (and 1 Kgs 8:46–50). Penitential prayers emphasize the people's violation of the covenant and at the same time accentuate God's constancy as שמר הברית והחסד ("who stays faithful to his covenant," Neh 1:5; 9:32; Dan 9:4). Hence, in contrast to communal laments, penitential prayers do not await divine renewal of the covenant. With no intervening break, God has always been obligated to his people through the covenant. Thus, there is no need to call him to renew it, as there is no place for pleas and petitions of salvation.[49]

---

47. See also ככל צדקתך ("as befits your abundant benevolence," Dan 9:16); as also Lam 1:18 and, in a personal context, Jer 12:1. See Rolf Rendtorff, "Nehemiah 9: An Important Witness of Theological Reflection," in *Tehillah le-Moshe: Biblical and Judaic Studies in Honor of Moshe Greenberg* (ed. Mordechai Cogan, Barry L. Eichler, and Jeffrey H. Tigay; Winona Lake, Ind.: Eisenbrauns, 1997), 111–17.

48. A similar argument occurs in Ps 103:10–11.

49. However, contextually Neh 9:1–10:1 presents the prayer as part of a renewal ceremony; see Boda, *Praying the Tradition*, 32–38.

Furthermore, repeatedly in Neh 9 God is said not to have left or abandoned his people, even at the worst point of their disobedience (Neh 9:17, 19, 31). Ezra 9:9 emphasizes God's commitment to his people as specifically apparent in their present tremendous distress "though even in our bondage God has not forsaken us, but has disposed the king of Persia favorably toward us." On the contrary, God is praised for giving his people a remnant (Ezra 9:8–10; 13–14).

This short comparison establishes the theological context of penitential prayers, and suggests close conceptual similarities between penitential prayers and the "orthodox" sources: DtrH, the Holiness code within the Priestly sources, and the prophetic literature.

The Polemical Position of Penitential Prayers

The differences between penitential prayers and communal laments are usually explained diachronically. Being preexilic or exilic, communal laments precede penitential prayers, which are considered to be a later transformation of exilic and mainly postexilic lament literature.[50] Yet this diachronic sequence is highly speculative. First, dating the communal laments is a riddle, and at least some of them are definitely exilic (Pss 44; 74; 79; 137; etc.).[51] Second, this theological diversity with regard to concepts of the God-people relationship was apparent in Judean religious thought as early as the first half of the sixth century. Hence, it seems more reasonable to perceive the ideological relationship between communal laments and penitential prayers as roughly synchronic.[52]

Moreover, judging both from literary references and from ideological-theological perspectives, penitential prayers cannot be taken simply as a linear evolution of communal laments, transforming lament to penitence. Rather, penitential prayers should be evaluated as contemporaneous polemical response to communal laments. In contrast to the "nonorthodox" milieu of poetic communal laments, penitential prose prayers originated in Deuteronomistic, priestly, and

---

50. See Westermann's reconstruction of "a history of the lament" from preexilic literature to the Apocrypha and Pseudepigrapha (*Praise and Lament*, 171–72, 195–213).

51. For a recent discussion, see Adele Berlin, "Psalms and the Literature of Exile: Psalms 137, 44, 69, and 78," in *The Book of Psalms: Composition and Reception* (ed. Peter W. Flint and Patrick D. Miller; VTSup 99; Leiden: Brill, 2005), 65–86.

52. Dan 9:4–19 and Neh 9:6–37 have been dated to the exilic or early Persian periods (before 500 B.C.E.). See Lacocque, "Liturgical Prayer in Daniel 9," 119–42 (especially 125–27). Hugh G. M. Williamson considered Neh 9 a composition of the Judean community that remained in the land after 587 ("Laments at the Destroyed Temple," *BRev* 6/4 (1990): 12–17, 44), whereas Chrostowski suggested that the author of Neh 9:6–37 was one of Ezekiel's disciples ("An Examination of Conscience," 253–61). Based on literary and thematic connections to Haggai and Zech 1–8, Boda thought of the early Persian period (520–500 B.C.E.) (*Praying the Tradition*, 190–95).

prophetic circles of authors during the Neo-Babylonian and early Persian periods. These prayers indeed display a complicated relationship to communal laments, a relationship of explicit and implicit rejection, on the one hand, and of implicit acceptance, on the other.

Explicit Rejection

As suggested above, penitential prayers rejected "nonorthodox" concepts of the God-people relationship (as found in communal laments) in the aftermath of the destruction. In contrast to the laments, penitential prayers retained the "orthodox" balance: God had obligated the people to the covenant through demands of loyalty and specific commandments; the people had violated the covenant by deserting God and his commands, but, nevertheless, God had not abandoned his people. The special emphasis given to the abandonment language expresses a vast contrast with laments.

Implicit Rejection

Using their awareness of the form and content of communal laments, the authors of the penitential prayers changed the typical structures and themes of the laments in a way that produced counter-answers. The three major characteristics of penitential prayers—silence of the complaint, muting of petitions (except for Dan 9), and accentuation of the confession—are all formal features that respond to the communal laments' special concepts of God. The changes in penitential prayers are aimed at minimizing the elements of protest and complaint, in order to maximize the confession and, even more so, the praise given to God.[53] Moreover, while communal laments express protest and doubt with regard to God's involvement in his people's distress, his ability and wish to save his people, and so forth, penitential prayers pronounce the opposite: God had acted fiercely against a sinful people (yet he never deserted them), and as always, he is completely involved in their life at the present time.

Implicit Acceptance

The dialogue that Neh 9 conducts with communal laments in general, and above all with Ps 106, has been presented time and again.[54] However, given the wide and diverse theological expressions of sources from the sixth century, Neh 9 joins the theological discussion in a very sophisticated way.

---

53. Compare to Bautch, *Developments in Genre*, 116–19.
54. Boda, *Praying the Tradition*, 24–25, 66–68; Bautch prefers Ps 78 (*Developments in Genre*, 114–19).

First, Neh 9 indeed presents explicit confessions of sin on behalf of past generations (vv. 16–18, 26, 28–31) and once even joins the present generation to its forefathers (vv. 33–34). Yet throughout the prayer the author distinguishes between the ancestors and the present generation of repatriates. Third-person plural dominates the historical recital, whereas first-person plural appears only in verses 33–34 and in the closing verses that describe the present distress (vv. 36–37).[55] This morphological variation illustrates, even if only implicitly, the author's anxious desire to define accurately the differences between his generation and previous ones, arguing that the present generation is not following the forefathers' misconduct.[56]

Second, the historical recital in Neh 9 emphasizes God's past presence and involvement on behalf of his people in times of distress (vv. 9–11, 12–21, 30a), as well as his patience and mercy in the face of the continuing disobedience of the people in past generations (vv. 17, 19, 27, 31). These are presented down to the eventual stage of destruction (vv. 30–31). However, the final verses of this penitential prayer (vv. 32–37), which focus on the present generation of repatriates in Yehud, demonstrate a deafening silence about these divine qualities: there is no mention of mercy, of patience, of involvement on behalf of this loyal community under subjugation in its own promised land, no positive statement that God has not abandoned the people this time.

This distinction between past and present could certainly supply a typical lament with complaints and petitions for salvation. Yet these two components are deeply buried under the "orthodox" disguise of this penitential prayer.

It seems, then, that the authors of penitential prayers distanced themselves intentionally from communal laments and preferred the "orthodox" concepts.[57] In their prayers they supplied total justification of God and full acceptance of his judgment, which gave alternative opportunities for expressions of protest and doubt.[58] This choice of alternative concepts caused immediate significant

---

55. This differentiation is clearly discernible even without Chrostowski's interpretation of ואנחנו הרשענו (ו)את מלכינו "Also we condemn both our kings." He thus argues that vv. 32–37 present a request for salvation and a complaint ("An Examination of Conscience," 255–58). Yet I would accentuate the implied tone of these verses.

56. Contra Holmgren, "Faithful Abraham," 252. Yet, I agree with Holmgren that, given the self-identification of the repatriates with Abraham, Neh 9 is an expression of the community's "hope for the future" (253).

57. For instance, Neh 9 reverses the communal lament's perspective regarding divine justice, presenting the binary opposition between God as צדיק and the people as רשע (v. 33); see Bautch, *Developments in Genre*, 117–19, 153–56.

58. The themes and rhetorical traits of protest, were discussed in my "Psalm 44: The Powers of Protest," a presentation at the Psalms Section at the SBL Annual Meeting in Philadelphia, November 2005, and will appear in writing.

formal deviations that distinguished penitential prayers from the genre of communal lament.[59]

CONCLUSIONS

In answer to the question posed by the title of this article—socio-ideological *setting* or *settings* for penitential prayers?—I place the "orthodox" circles as the socio-ideological setting of penitential prayers.[60] The communal laments, stemming from "nonorthodox" circles, would have been considered contemporary antagonistic expressions, which penitential prayers attempted to reject through major thematic and consequently formal changes.[61] From this perspective, communal laments can hardly bear the burden of being "proto-penitential prayers." The present discussion suggests an alternative description of the penitential prayers' literary reliance on prior or contemporary sources. On the one hand, "orthodox" sources (DtrH, Priestly, and prophetic traditions) serve as the penitential prayers' literary and theological background. They supply the rhetoric of the prose style, the phraseology, and the themes. On the other hand, shared elements of structure and style from biblical prayers provide the repertoire of forms for the penitential prayers. From this diverse biblical prayer tradition the penitential prayers draw and encounter the essential thematic characteristics of the communal laments: the themes of lament, protest and doubt, and mostly the lack or minimized place of the confession of sins.

Therefore, we can confidently assume that not only were the authors of penitential prayers highly knowledgeable of the genre of communal laments,[62] but they also intentionally constructed an "orthodox" counterpart to these laments that "cleaned up" inappropriate concepts, yet left enough traces to allow us to discern a complicated dialogue between prayer and lament.

As repeatedly happened in late biblical history, the "orthodox" line of thought prevailed. The diachronic sequence in the "history of the lament" suggested by Westermann is thus the product of an extraliterary (social) process that gained dominance and excluded lament in favor of repentance. While "nonorthodox"

---

59. Bautch, in contrast, measures the transformation in formal criteria and further regards Isa 63:7–64:11 and Neh 9:6–37 as "innovative" in their use of the communal laments (*Developments in Genre*, 156–57).

60. See Werline: "penitential prayer is not isolated to fringe groups, but stands at the center of Israel's religious system" (*Penitential Prayer*, 64).

61. In this I suggest a somewhat different perspective on the relationship between the two genres; cf. Boda, "From Complaint to Contrition," 186–87.

62. Robert E. Culley pointed out the biblical poets' ability to cite "stock phrases and stereotyped expressions" as part of their creative work in composing poetry (*Oral Formulaic Language in the Biblical Psalms* [Near and Middle East Series 4; Toronto: University of Toronto Press, 1967], 5–9).

voices, including the communal laments, apparently vanished in the course of the postexilic period, penitential prayers, their "orthodox" counterpart, flourished.

The Speech Act of Confession: Priestly Performative Utterance in Leviticus 16 and Ezra 9–10

Jay C. Hogewood

Introduction

The priestly legislation uses the verb התודה to prescribe the ritual act of confession. Evidence of this particular manifestation of confession appears in Lev 5:5; 16:21; 26:40; and Num 5:7. This verbal performance serves as the central component in the activity of confessing sins, not only in restoring relationships within the community of Israel (Lev 5:5; Num 5:7), but also in the purification of sins as the worshiping community approaches YHWH. Confessing transgressions represents the significant moment of handling and cleansing the entire community in the annual Day of Atonement (יום הכפרים) ritual as seen in Lev 16:20–22. Accordingly, Levitical legislation exemplifies the prescription for ritual utterance. Confession represents the performance of an utterance in rituals for casting out (התודה) sin, transgression, and iniquity.

By employing the action of penitential prayer in Second Temple rituals, the worshiping community uses confession to separate itself from sin and impurity. The following examples of confessionary procedure serve to highlight the significance of a word's force: Dan 9:4, 20; Ezra 10:1; Neh 1:6; 9:2, 3; and 2 Chr 30:22.[1] התודה again functions as the word that engages a particular rite to rid the community of transgression. Even more, confession or the act of confessing is the introductory tag placed on these penitential liturgies by the narrator (Ezra 10:1; Neh 9:2, 3) or the biblical character (Neh 1:6; Dan 9:4, 20). Unlike the priestly ritual in which confession is an imbedded (legislated) or implicit activity that

---

1. 2 Chr 30:22 is problematic: Does Hezekiah call for confession of praise or confession of sin? Whichever way we understand the confessionary episode, the force of the utterance applies. In terms of confession as praise, see Jacob Milgrom, *Leviticus 1–16* (AB 3; New York: Doubleday, 1991), 301–3; for confession of sin, see Mark J. Boda, "Words and Meanings: ידי in Hebrew Research," *WTJ* (1995): 285–88.

commits the community to rid sin from its midst, the penitential liturgies of Ezra, Nehemiah, and Daniel are explicit prayers that shape the behavior of the community in an effort to separate from unfaithful practices.

In both Levitical legislation and Second Temple penitential prayer, saying confession separates sin from the community. For that reason, התודה serves as a performative utterance: the act of speaking performs a particular rite in priestly guidelines for ridding the community of sin. Throughout this essay on confessionary procedure, I benefit from John L. Austin's work with performative utterances in *How to Do Things with Words*.[2] Austin's empirical philosophy of language use, while not initially connected to the exegesis of scripture, plays a formative role in this present interpretive enterprise. Austin provides an easily adaptable taxonomy that relates to the force of utterances that perform a certain act by speaking a word or phrase in a particular convention or rite. Continued work with such a methodology, I will demonstrate, appears fruitful for biblical exegesis, and more should be done to broaden speech-act theory's application, particularly to Hebrew scripture. Although *Semeia* 41 explored the usefulness of speech-act theory and Austin's methodology, only one article in the volume focuses on the text of the Hebrew Bible.[3] In relation to the rites of sin's riddance associated with Lev 16 and Ezra 9–10, the performance of confession initiates the liturgy in penitential prayer, which rids the Second Temple community of its transgressions. The performative utterance of confession achieves meaning in the ways that communities practice the articulation of sin before YHWH in relationship to other rituals or liturgies.[4]

---

2. Saying confession is a speech act. By saying confession, an action is performed: saying something is doing something. The work of John L. Austin serves as the methodological and hermeneutical filter through which I interpret the activity of priestly confessionary ritual and penitential prayer liturgies. See John L. Austin, *How to Do Things with Words* (ed. J. O. Urmson and Marina Sbisa; 2d ed.; Cambridge: Harvard University Press, 1975), 1–11; idem, *Philosophical Papers* (Oxford: Clarendon, 1961), 220–39; Donald D. Evans, *The Logic of Self-Involvement: A Philosophical Study of Everyday Language with Special Reference to the Christian Use of Language about God as Creator* (London: SCM, 1963), 11–78; and John R. Searle, *Speech Acts: An Essay in the Philosophy of Language* (London: Cambridge University Press, 1969), 16–61.

3. Susan S. Lanser, "(Feminist) Criticism in the Garden: Inferring Genesis 2–3," *Semeia* 41 (1988): 67–84. In that issue of *Semeia*, Martin Buss ("Potential and Actual Interactions between Speech Act Theory and Biblical Studies," *Semeia* 41 [1988]: 125) surmises: "The potential contribution of speech act theory can be viewed either in terms of a theoretical reconceptualization of the process of exegesis or in terms of a refinement of exegetical procedures in their application to specific passages." According to these terms, I seek to realize the second potential contribution: dealing with specific texts, while being informed by theory.

4. I adapt the work of Rodney A. Werline, "Defining Penitential Prayer" (see pp. xiii–xvii in this volume). Concerning words and their meanings, Werline notes: "A word achieves its meaning by the way that a community uses the word by placing it in relationship to other words or ideas" (xiii). Werline comes remarkably close to speech-act theory in his comments, for Austin

Since confession is a significant element of rituals for sin's riddance and penitential liturgy, do the use and the force of התודה provide a point of connection between priestly patterns of atonement and Second Temple penitential practice? To what extent do penitential prayer liturgies owe their existence to priestly ritual utterance? Confession of sin, as seen in Lev 5; 16; 26; and Num 5, is efficacious without the surrounding situation (gestures and/or prayer) of penitence, yet the liturgies of penitential prayer would not be complete without confession, as evidenced in Dan 9; Ezra 9–10; and Neh 1 and 9.[5] Samuel Balentine highlights the significance of confession: "Confession is the cotter pin that joins contrition to reparation and reparation to a public commitment to change."[6] Extending Balentine's imagery, I propose that confession is the foundation upon which penitential prayer builds the community's performance of repentance; confession is the point of connection between Levitical legislation of ritual and the ongoing vestiges of priestly utterance that shapes the worshiping community in Second Temple rites of repentance. The genre known as penitential prayer is built upon the existing strata of priestly ritual utterance. In other words, the speech act of confession serves as the cornerstone of Second Temple penitential prayer.

By this proposal, I suggest that one ongoing issue concerning rites of repentance is the impact of priestly confessionary rituals upon penitential prayer. Other scholars have established significant connections between the use of התודה and penitential liturgies. Additionally, scholars within this consultation have contributed in creative and profound ways to the understanding of the theological and ideological origins, development, and impact of penitential prayer.[7] However, viewing confession through the lens of speech-act theory and performative utterance reveals the ritual-critical dimensions and hermeneutical

---

concludes that the forcefulness/effectiveness of a speech act involves its use in conventional situations. See Austin, *How to Do Things with Words*, 13–19.

5. See Eileen M. Schuller's contribution to the next volume in this Penitential Prayer series ("Penitential Prayer in Second Temple Judaism: A Research Survey"), in which she insightfully catalogues the defining elements of penitential prayer and serves as a helpful resource to view diverse scholars' interpretations of penitential prayer texts.

6. Samuel E. Balentine, *Leviticus* (IBC; Louisville: Westminster John Knox, 2002), 57. See also Balentine's contribution to the present volume ("I Was Ready to Be Sought Out by Those Who Did Not Ask"), in which he notes: "A new generation of scholarship on penitential prayer has now moved texts and traditions that had been of rather marginal interest front and center, and as a result the landscape of our understanding about the 'conventions' of prayer has changed in significant ways" (above p. 1). For this, I am a glad beneficiary.

7. See the contributions in the present volume of Mark J. Boda ("Confession as Theological Expression: Ideological Origins of Penitential Prayer") and Dalit Rom-Shiloni ("Socio-Ideological Setting or Settings for Penitential Prayers") as well as those of Russell Arnold ("Repentance and the Qumran Covenant Ceremony") and Daniel K. Falk ("Biblical Inspiration for Penitential Prayer in the Dead Sea Scrolls") in the next volume.

implications of the relationship between priestly rituals of confession and Second Temple penitential prayer.

In order to explicate the connection of confessionary ritual to penitential liturgy, I shall investigate two representative texts from both of these genres, first, Lev 16, which is paradigmatic of the priestly legislated speech act, and secondly, Ezra 9–10, which exemplifies a penitential liturgy in the Second Temple era. These two texts exhibit the nature of confessionary procedure and the ways in which penitential prayer benefits from and builds upon priestly formulations of performative utterance. In order to show these features of confession and penitential prayer, I will first identify the conventions around which confession works, and explain how the act of confessing sin draws boundaries between the sacred and the sinful. Using ritual-critical sensitivities, I will establish the importance of confession as a building block to penitential prayer. Second, I will map the force and meaning of confession in the rite of riddance of sin in Lev 16:20–22. Drawing on the Priestly prescription for confession, I will chart the meaning and force of confession in the liturgy of penitence in Ezra 9–10. Third, I will examine the ritual-constructing force and several sociological features of confession. Acknowledging sin commits the community to rid itself of sin, iniquity and transgression, while it also shapes the behavior of the community.

The Force of Confession:
Performative Utterances within Penitential Rites

How do Austin's methodology and the theory of performative utterance benefit the exegesis of Hebrew scripture? More specifically, does speech-act theory offer the interpreter any advantage by understanding confession as performance? Confessionary speech acts occur in the complex conventions of ritual purgation (Lev 16:20–22) and the community's approach to God through prayer (Ezra 9). By identifying the context in which the performative is uttered, the interpreter of the biblical text sees more clearly the significance of language used in the human-to-God communication. As a result, no longer does the function of certain words in the Hebrew Bible rely on some mysterious power assumed to be inherent in words.[8] Instead, speech-act theory focuses precisely on the ritual context of prayer in Priestly legislation and in Second Temple liturgies. That is, speech-act theory demonstrates that confession is efficacious because it

---

8. See Anthony Thiselton, "The Supposed Power of Words in Biblical Writings," *JTS* 25 (1974): 283–99. Thiselton debunks the earlier work of Gerhard von Rad, *Old Testament Theology* (trans. D. M. G. Stalker; New York: Harper & Row, 1965), 2:80–98. Thiselton applies the work of Austin to refute the notion that the Hebrew scripture witnesses a primitive understanding of incantation and word-magic. Thiselton writes, "The relation between words and this is certainly not 'by nature,' but rests on use, social tradition, and rules of convention" (287).

functions in a particular setting, not because the use of התודה is an inherently magical term. Words of confession (imbedded in penitential prayer or implicit in priestly ritual) carry force only when functioning in rites that are conducive to their meaningfulness. The force and meaning of confessionary utterance display an interdependent relationship, for force establishes meaning as meaning locates force.

Speech-act theory assists biblical criticism by emphasizing the *locutionary*, *illocutionary*, and *perlocutionary* forces in performative utterance.[9] These three forces engaged in the speaking of certain utterances are characterized as follows. (1) The locutionary act is the act *of* saying something. Thus, the locution of confession: Moses says to the high priest, "Confess their sin." In the process of saying so, Moses means by "confess" to confess and referring to "their sin" the sin of the Israelite community. (2) The illocutionary act is *the performance of an act in* saying something. The illocution of confession: Ezra confessed the sin of the congregation. (3) The perlocutionary act is *the performance that results from* saying something. The perlocution of confession: Ezra or the high priest led the congregation of Israel in their liturgical act of confession whereby atonement is performed.

The significance of illocutionary and perlocutionary forces is relevant to the speech act of confession. When seen in the textual evidence of the priestly legislation and in the liturgical features of the Second Temple community's penitential prayer, the force of confession adheres to its function in shaping the congregation of Israel to voice its sin and behave in ways conducive to covenant life with Yhwh. While Austin does not explicitly address the notion of confession as performative, nevertheless the sense of confession's force is clearly connected to the idea that in saying "I confess" or "we confess" or "they confess," I or we or they are doing confession.[10] As is indicative of the perlocutionary force of the performative, when the confessor as a representative for the Israelite community says

---

9. Austin, *How to Do Things with Words*, 94–147. Austin's lectures 8–11 (the William James Lectures delivered at Harvard University, 1955) comprise the specific delineation of terminology for the nature of performative force. My brief overview involves only my examples from confessionary utterance. That is, the concepts are Austin's, but the examples center upon the force of confession in the biblical text.

10. Austin does not ultimately offer the use of "I confess" as an example of a performative. Other examples such as "I apologize" and "I commiserate" and "I declare my intention" do arise in his twelfth and final lecture. Part of this enterprise shows that the use of confession is indeed a performative. That the term does not come to Austin's mind does disappoint my sensibilities; however, it does not undermine the effort. Rather, Austin's list of examples by his own admission (*How to Do Things with Words*, 150) is not exhaustive and serves to fuel the imagination that is willing to apply his empirical theory to the force of utterances. For a vivid example of illocutionary language particular to human communication with God, see Evans, *Logic of Self-Involvement*, 11–78.

"We shall confess our sin," the community is doing the confession of sin. Even more, the community joins the speech act of confession with gestures of expiation (sacrifice, separating clean and unclean elements, and blood manipulation in Lev 16:20–34) and penitence (crying, hand gestures, and separating from foreign influences in Lev 26:40; Dan 9:4, 20; Ezra 10:1–11; Neh 1:6; 9:2, 3).

Accordingly, Lev 16:20–22 and Ezra 9:6–10:1 provide clear examples of forceful and effective speech events as illocutionary utterances. In the priestly ritual of Lev 16, purgation is enacted as the community commits to confessing sin. By way of confession, the sin is transferred upon the head of the live goat, then removed to the wilderness. In the penitential prayer of Ezra, the community separates from sins of exogamy as their behavior is shaped by the confession of Ezra, then by the community as a whole (Ezra 10:11). Two classes of illocutionary force apply to the confession of sin in Lev 16:20–22 and Ezra 9:6–10:1.[11] To confess sin (according to these examples) carries the force to change behavior and to commit oneself to another way of acting, thinking, speaking, and/or being. Therefore, saying confession is doing confession: as a commissive force in Lev 16:20–22 and as behabitive force in Ezra 9–10.

"Building Blocks": Priestly Utterance, Penitential Action[12]

The passages of Lev 16:20–22 and Ezra 9–10 are verbal rites.[13] The Priestly instruction that constructs the ritual of atonement and the penitential liturgy that comprises Ezra's prayer indicate the sound of repentance.

Leviticus 16

In Lev 16 the verbal elements of the day of purgation arise when the priest gives voice to the sin committed by the community. The confessionary procedure of

---

11. Austin actually distinguishes five classes of illocutionary force: verdictive, exercitive, commissive, behabitive, and expositive (*How to Do Things with Words*, 150–64).

12. For use of "building blocks," see Rom-Shiloni in the present volume (p. 55). The sharing of "building blocks" between penitential liturgies and prayers in general is a matter of interest, particularly as it relates to the conventions within which prayer is scripted (voiced). See Moshe Greenberg, *Biblical Prose Prayer as a Window to the Popular Religion of Ancient Israel* (Los Angeles: University of California Press, 1983), 11. Greenberg identifies a "natural pattern" in biblical prayers: address, petition, and motivation. See also Patrick D. Miller, *They Cried to the Lord: The Form and Theology of Biblical Prayer* (Minneapolis: Fortress, 1994), 55–133; Samuel E. Balentine, *Prayer in the Hebrew Bible* (OBT; Philadelphia: Fortress, 1993), 118–98.

13. See Israel Knohl, "Between Voice and Silence: The Relationship between Prayer and the Temple Cult," *JBL* 115 (1996): 17–30; cf. idem, *The Sanctuary of Silence: The Priestly Torah and the Holiness School* (Minneapolis: Fortress, 1995). Leviticus 16 is the exception to the rule of silence in the sanctuary, as well as the sacrificial system. The idea of a "verbal cult" stems from the priest's communication with Yhwh on the day of purgation. Ezra 9, which produces the wording of the prayer, is straightforward in its explicit communication with Yhwh.

Lev 16:20–22 is not explicitly recorded in the biblical text; we do not know how the priest confesses or the way in which he voices the sin, transgression and iniquity of Israel. We only know that Yhwh through Moses instructs Aaron to do so. So the text is left to speak to the interpreter (16:21b):

והתודה עליו את־כל־עונת בני ישראל ואת־כל־פשעיהם לכל־חטאתם

Why leave the confession unstated in the legislation? Why did the Priestly tradents not share the language that the high priest used to articulate the sinfulness of the congregation?

The gap in the text apparently proved bothersome to the ancient rabbis. The Mishnah speaks where the biblical legislation keeps silent. In *m. Yoma* 6:2, the rabbis fill in the gaps in the biblical text by offering details (wording) for confession:

> He [Aaron] then came to the scapegoat, and he laid his two hands upon it and made confession; and thus he said, "I pray, O Eternal! Thy people, the house of Israel, have done wrong, they have transgressed, they sinned before Thee. I pray, by Thy Name! Pardon, I pray, the iniquities, the transgressions, and the sins which Thy people, the house of Israel, have wrongly committed, and which they have transgressed, and which they have sinned before Thee, as it is written in the Law of Moses, Thy servant, for on this day shall atonement be made for you to cleanse you from all your sins, before the Eternal shall you be clean."[14]

The priestly task, as indicated by the legislation for the rite of riddance in Lev 16:20–22, is clearly unconcerned with the wording of the confession. Rather, the implication of the text and its use of performative speech through confessionary utterance resound through the function of confession. Instead of a preoccupation with wording the procedure, the cultic formula emphasizes the force that confessing sin has to separate the community from sin via the goat bound for עזאל. This instruction for confession functions in two ways: first, the prescription for Aaron to give voice to the community's sin moves the community from contrite intentions to penitential actions (16:22–34); and, second, the cultic legislation rids communal sin by turning the silence of guilt into the prescription for the sound of sin's riddance via the priest's articulation (16:20–21).

The wording of the confession is not given because it is unnecessary. Sin is to be made known by a representative sinner (priest or intermediary). The detail of the confession is left to the confessor. Since the wording is not made explicit by Yhwh (or the priestly editors), a social analogy of confession is in full force. A precise utterance is unnecessary for the community to give voice to sin and

---

14. Extracted from Philip Blackman, trans., *Mishnayoth* (6 vols.; Gateshead, N.Y.: Judaica, 2000), 300.

experience expiation. How can this be? Or, as Greenberg asks, "What justified such confidence [that the worshiper could rightly utter confession of sin]?" Did the Levitical legislator suppose that a commoner could voice confession in an efficacious way? Simply put, yes. As Greenberg states: "The practice of modeling confessionary prayer [is] after the pattern of interhuman confessionary speech—a simple natural pattern, corresponding to the dynamics of the transaction and therefore known to everyone."[15]

The high priest, as a representative of the congregation in confessing the collective sin burden, breaks the silence alone in the holy shrine. Greenberg's social analogy, as well as Austin's theory of performative utterance, shows that the instruction to the cultic personnel prescribes how to confess without creating (or writing) a liturgy. Instead, "anyone capable of conventional interhuman discourse was capable of praying; equally, that the prayer of anyone was deemed acceptable by God."[16]

As Aaron confesses the transgression, iniquity, and sin of the community on the head of the goat bound for the wilderness, he serves as an envoy for the congregation. Yet even while his role is representative of the larger community before Yhwh, the holy congregation is not without responsibility. The worshipers must also give voice to their transgression. The conclusion of the ritual's instruction includes the motions of contrition to match the utterance by the priest. This rite is comprised of gestures of self-denial (תענו את־נפשׁתיכם), strict observance of Sabbath (שׁבת שׁבתון), and cessation of labor (וכל־מלאכה לא תעשׂו).

The basis for confession as it occurs in Priestly legislation comes from patterns of interhuman dialogue: the need for pardon, the desire to repair a relationship damaged by wrongdoing, and the subsequent recognition of guilt that is given voice by the one seeking to make amends. In voicing the wrong, the confessor connects again to the one wronged by establishing a shared evaluation of the blameworthiness of the one confessing. The communication that comes though confessionary utterance, while free from fixed form in the priestly instruction, is adjudicated by the high priest and is governed by conventions that guide the ritual of the day of purgation.

---

15. Greenberg, *Biblical Prose Prayer*, 30. The understanding of "social analogy" parallels the performative theory of conventions: certain elements provide the framework within which confession (in this case) and atonement are effective. Austin's example of the wedding ceremony is popular. The "I do" of each spouse is only forceful or binding as it is spoken in the context of a ritual (in a church, a synagogue, a mosque, or county courthouse). Likewise, for the gestures and utterances associated with the Day of Atonement, the rite of the live goat bound for Azazel is only efficacious when speech and actions are performed in the convention of atonement.

16. Ibid., 38. Yet, concerning the exceptional nature of worship in the holy sphere and sacrificial expiation, Greenberg modifies his analogy: "Both are prescriptions of the schooled; they belong to a class of experts. The piety of the populace was mediated and probably refined through them" (ibid., 6–7).

Such guidelines or conventions aid the confessor in two distinct ways. First, conventions for confession enable every person to customize the pattern of utterance into the specific situation of transgression. Each person who confesses sin is thereby encouraged to "play his or her momentary role by filling the empty lines of the pattern with substance tailored to the situation."[17] Second, the guidelines for confession provide the confessor with the notion that there is a means of communicating with Yhwh that lies between a set ritual prayer and free innovations of the one praying. Ultimately, the prescription for the priestly confession offers a mechanism that transforms the gravest of sin into expiable transgressions.[18]

The speech act of confession transfers the sin and uncleanness of the community upon the head of the live goat. The intention of sorrow and guilt is turned into action through the utterance of confession. Saying confession acts as a way of handling sin as the interior disposition of contrition accompanied by the speech act of confession moves Yhwh to render harmless the sin of the community that contaminates the *sancta*. Additionally, by confessing sin the high priest commits the congregation to join ritual confession with acts of contrition. Therefore, sin is cast away by a voice that separates the element of sin from the holy community and the holy place of worship.

Ezra 9–10

The performative utterance found in Ezra 9–10 originates with Ezra as priest and scribe of the postexilic congregation. The confessionary utterance of Ezra 9:6–15, the result of members of the community violating marriage stipulations, is a canonical depiction of communication between human and God. We know precisely (per the biblical record) how the priest-scribe Ezra confesses and the ways in which he articulates the sin of the community, which the community overhears. He does not term his prayer a confession. Rather, that designation, the category by which we understand Ezra's penitential language, comes from the narrator (Ezra 10:1):

וכהתפלל עזרא וכהתודתו בכה ומתנפל לפני בית האלהים

Ezra 9–10 stands as a textual unity in which both the text of prayer and the subsequent response by the congregation formulate the people's desire to return to the covenantal relationship with Yhwh. Thus, this act of desired restoration culminates in a liturgical moment in which Ezra's gestures and utterances create a penitential mood that is suitable for approaching God. Through such actions,

---

17. Ibid., 44–45.
18. Milgrom, *Cult and Conscience*, 110. See also Boda, "Confession as Theological Expression," 30.

Ezra dramatizes the return to God. In such a context, prayer itself becomes a performance in the process of return. The text depicts a performative drama: gestures of contrition and Ezra's verbal encounter with Yhwh.

Ezra's confession focuses upon the acts of separation (בדל) from sin and of driving out (להוציא) the "unfaithful" from the congregation. Ezra does not utilize the terminology of re/turning (שוב) from sin. Repentance, expressed through the idea of turning from (שוב) sin, however, is a prominent feature of Neh 1:9; 9:26, 29, 35; and Dan 9:13. Ezra, instead, shares the priestly terminology within his penitential prayer. The issue of confession through the use of התודה remains unchanged: the confession of sin, whether imbedded in the narrative and named the act of "confessing" by the narrator or in the language of prayer itself, demonstrates the force of a performative utterance. Saying confession performs an action that commits the congregation to acknowledge sin (Lev 16:20–22) and modifies the behavior of the congregation to repent of sin (Ezra 9–10). Levitical legislation influences later penitential prayer. Boda recognizes such and insightfully concludes: "It is in Lev 26:39–40 that one finds emphasis not just on prayer in the wake of the exile but also on confessing sin, using the terminology for confession (התודה) found in various contexts of penitential prayer."[19]

Another feature of Levitical legislation also informs the interpretation of confession and its force in rites of penitence. The appropriation of אשם "guilt" or "remorse" that appears in Lev 5:5 and in Ezra 9: 6, 7, 13; and 10:10 represents a trespass that has to do with incurring guilt or realizing an emotion that is connected to shame. The term associates with the meaning of confession as a worshiper communicates "feeling guilty" or "realizing guilt."[20] Milgrom notes that term closely relates to "remorse," while Kiuchi indicates that the meaning has more to do with "consciousness of sin."[21] In either translation, the use of the term in Lev 5:5 is a prescription for verbal encounter, for it deals with a deliberate attempt by the sinner to withhold evidence. The wrongdoer is fraudulent, and only by coming to realize his or her error does the wrongdoer experience remorse for the sin of omission. To reverse the potential damage of the consciousness of sin, the person confesses that he or she sinned. In turn, the sin is made expiable

---

19. Boda ("Confession as Theological Expression," 28). See also Rodney A. Werline, *Penitential Prayer in Second Temple Judaism: The Development of a Religious Institution* (SBLEJL 13; Atlanta: Scholars), 47–48.

20. Lester L. Grabbe, *Leviticus* (OTG; Sheffield: Sheffield Academic Press, 1993), 35. Cf. Milgrom, *Leviticus 1-16*, 373–78; and Nobuyoshi Kiuchi, *The Purification Offering in the Priestly Literature: Its Meaning and Function* (JSOTSup 56; Sheffield: Sheffield Academic Press, 1987), 32–36. Milgrom and Kiuchi disagree as to the precise definition of אשם, but their arguments are formulated in the larger situation of sins related to ritual expiation. As such, whether one chooses to translate the term with "feeling guilt" (Milgrom) or "realizing guilt" (Kiuchi), the matter of handling sin and its devastating effects remains for confession's efficacious force.

21. Milgrom, *Leviticus 1-16*, 301; Kiuchi, *Purification Offering*, 32–34.

through sacrifice. This is, according to Milgrom, the most important capacity that confession carries. The spoken acknowledgement of sin "is the legal device fashioned by the Priestly legislation to convert deliberate sins into inadvertences, thereby qualifying them for sacrificial expiation."[22] Perhaps no greater connection exists between the particular nature of sin in terms of אשם and the ritual utterance of confession. The "realization of guilt" or "remorse" or "feeling guilt" comes to public attention through its utterance—the speech act of confession.

Ezra 9:6–15, the actual prayer of confession and repentance, signifies the confessionary utterances of the mediating voice of Ezra. This communication begins with Ezra getting up (קמתי), tearing his clothing (בקרעי), bowing down (אכרעה), and spreading out his hands (אפרשׂה). From gesture to articulation, Ezra shifts from his own performance to the collective effect of Israel's transgression before God. He speaks to the Lord: "I said to my God, 'I am ashamed and I am humiliated'" (v. 6). Ezra then shifts to the first common plural possessive of "our iniquities" (עונתינו) and "our guilt" (ואשמתנו) later in verse 6. The move from the singular to the plural indicates that the prayer is communal confession: an individual's cry of communal transgression.[23] As the text shows, Ezra's performance attracts the attention of a large crowd (10:1–13). The act of confessing is a public affair; the utterance occurs in a larger event of penitence.

As mentioned above, the Israelites' intermarriage with the people of the land (העם הארץ) jeopardizes the holiness of the Second Temple community and its relationship with Yhwh (Ezra 9:2). This practice of exogamy is abhorrent to Yhwh, at least as Ezra construes the instruction of God. "It is of no small significance that Ezra's crisis pertains to the very nature of the community."[24] The penitential prayer in Ezra, unlike the prescriptive tone of Priestly legislation, works by shaping the community's response away from its sinfulness. The speech act of confession in Ezra functions to modify the Israelite behavior of intermarriage.

The liturgical convention in which Ezra's confession is performed is comprised of four themes.[25] First, Ezra expresses the shamefulness of the sin. Second,

---

22. Milgrom, *Leviticus 1–16*, 301–2. For the connection of guilt to idolatry, see also Jonathan Klawans, *Impurity and Sin in Ancient Judaism* (Oxford: Oxford University Press, 2000), 33–35.

23. See Joseph Blenkinsopp, *Ezra-Nehemiah: A Commentary* (OTL; Philadelphia: Westminster, 1996), 181. The nature of such confessional utterance, as seen in the Second Temple uses of התודה, means that while prayers are personal, they are also communal. Private prayer does not occur in the use of confessionary performance. Ezra's example, like those of Aaron in Lev 16:21 and Daniel in Dan 9:4–20, shows clearly this representative expression of corporate guilt. For more on the communal aspect of the confession, see Tamara Cohn Eskenazi, *In an Age of Prose: A Literary Approach to Ezra-Nehemiah* (Atlanta: Scholars Press, 1988), 68–69.

24. Eskenazi, *In an Age of Prose*, 68.

25. See Lester L. Grabbe, *Ezra-Nehemiah* (Old Testament Readings; London: Routledge, 1998), 33–34.

the congregation understands that its shame results from its guilt before Yhwh. Third, the community's burden of sin is not limited to the current generation; the sins of previous generations are compounded upon the present generation.[26] Fourth, exile is the punishment for unfaithfulness.

Where Lev 16:20–22 prescribes a ritual solution (via confessionary utterance and gesture) to separate sin from the holy sphere and people on the day of purgation, Ezra 9–10 describes the penitential liturgy (via worded prayer and gesture, plus the recognition that the utterance is the act of confessing) in order to shape the community's ongoing behavior before God after exile. One might also examine the uses of confession in the penitential prayers of Dan 9 and Neh 1 and 9 for additional evidence that the act of confessing is the common element in a larger convention of repentance. In these other prayers, the chief aim of the confession is to remove the threat of exile for the "unfaithful" Israelite community. The counteractive force for unfaithfulness comes through confessionary utterance: an appeal to God that results in the community's will to modify its actions in ways consistent with covenantal faithfulness, not otherwise.

Constructing the Ritual

The primary relationship between the rite of sin's riddance and the liturgies of penitential prayer is based upon the meaning and force of confession. As an illocutionary force, the speech act of confession performs: in Lev 16 it prescribes (commits participation in) the ritual of atonement via the transference of sin upon the live goat bound for עזאזל, while in Ezra 9 it shapes the behavior of the Israelite community through the liturgy of repentance that separates sin from the postexilic congregation. Both situations, while different in form and historical setting, are rituals of separation from sin that involve verbal engagement with Yhwh.

The force and function of performative language provide the key to establishing ritual and liturgy. All ritual acts, including the Priestly legislation that informs and shapes later penitential prayer, are bound by specific conventions in the community's life before Yhwh. The ritual of confession forms around "specific processes of a society that are embedded in, integrally related to, supported

---

26. For more on the differences between collective and compound retribution, see Boda, "Confession as Theological Expression," 34–39. Additionally, concerning the terminology of unfaithfulness (מעל) and exile, much has been made of the connection between Priestly and Deuteronomistic strands assimilated in Lev 26:40 (again, the use of התודה is noteworthy). While this paper does not pursue this conversation, this scripture only adds to the priestly foundation upon which later penitential prayers develop. For associations of Lev 26:40 with the Second Temple genre of penitential prayer, see Balentine, "I Was Ready to Be Sought Out," 11–16; and Mark J. Boda, *Praying the Tradition: The Origin and Use of Tradition in Nehemiah 9* (BZAW 277; Berlin: de Gruyter, 1999), 48–51.

by, and which give support to specific socio-cultural contexts of which they are a part."[27] The language of confession occurs in particular sets of performances that are enacted for a specific purpose, at a particular time, in a certain place, within a specific situation.

By expressing or giving voice to sin, the phenomenology of confession highlights the human capacity to practice a performance that is situational, strategic, partly a result of misrecognition, and committed to reimaging the order of the world.[28] First, the force of confessionary procedure is practiced in specific contexts. According to Lev 16, once each year on the day of purgation, the high priest handles the transgression, iniquity, and sin of the community. In Ezra, the priestly scribe (and the congregation) must handle the sin before it irreparably damages the community's standing before God. The immediate contexts of the function and force of confession develop from practices associated with the sacrificial system and penitential prayer. The formulation of voice to sin, if pulled from its immediate convention of rites of repentance, is an act that would lose is directedness and logic of promise.

Second, the procedure of confession is practiced with a certain strategy. To some extent confession is an effort by the confessor(s) to shape the nature of atonement and/or forgiveness. The biblical evidence suggests that one element of giving voice to sin involves the community's recognition of its need for cleansing its defilement. The strategy for the ritual of confession comes from the representative's understanding of when, how, and what to confess.

Third, the experience of confession finds fulfillment when the confessor misrecognizes that God already knows the sin that the confessor has committed. In light of this misrecognition of what God knows and how God responds to the conventions of confession, the practice of giving voice to sin is mysterious and cannot be practiced as a mindless performance. The confessor must be mindful

---

27. Frank H. Gorman, *The Ideology of Ritual: Space, Time and Status in the Priestly Theology* (JSOTSup 91; Sheffield: Sheffield Academic Press, 1990), 14. For more on ritual theory and its relation to elements of confessionary procedure, see Mary Douglas, *Purity and Danger: An Analysis of the Concepts of Pollution and Taboo* (London: Routledge, 1966), 59–66; idem, *Leviticus as Literature* (Oxford: Oxford University Press, 1999), 247–51; Catherine Bell, *Ritual Theory, Ritual Practice* (Oxford: Oxford University Press, 1992), 30–117; idem, "Performance," in *Critical Terms for Religious Studies* (ed. Mark C. Taylor; Chicago: University of Chicago Press, 1998), 205–21; and idem, *Ritual: Perspectives and Dimensions* (Oxford: Oxford University Press, 1997), 68–76. The body of Douglas's and Bell's work is substantial, and my treatment of it pertains only to the insights offered to the phenomenology of confession. Bell explicitly connects the linguistic analysis of Austin and Searle to the meaningfulness of social dramas in *Ritual Theory*, 38–113. She also forms a linchpin in this approach to biblical rituals. As I conceive the connection of Austin's speech-act theory to biblical texts, Bell indicates how speech acts relate to performance theory. For a related connection of performance theory to Lev 16, see the imaginative work of Gorman, *Ideology of Ritual*, 61–102.

28. Bell, *Ritual Theory*, 81–88.

that variables exist in the convention of sacrifice and penitential prayer. Therein, the practice of confession forces the community to step boldly from intention—the silent contrition over sin—to action, which means to acknowledge audibly the transgression before Yhwh.

Fourth, the procedures of confession comprise the worshiping congregation's will to act. The priestly legislation and the Second Temple penitential prayers guide the performance of confession, which is motivated by the desire to reorder the relations between the Israelite community and Yhwh. Sin confuses the lines of distinction between holy and profane, as well as it contaminates the clean and causes uncleanness. Confession reconfigures the lines of holiness and profanity, cleanness and contamination.

Conclusion

The force of confession, originating from the priestly ritual of purgation, informs, develops, and shapes later penitential prayer. Penitential prayer draws upon the force of confession to extend prescriptive (unfixed, unworded legislation) rites of sin's riddance into descriptive (fixed, worded liturgy) articulations to shape the community after exile.

Within Levitical legislation, confession is commissive. Five elements of commissive utterance occur. First, the legislation commits the high priest to give voice to sin. Second, confession commits the transfer of sin upon the live goat. Third, confession commits the ritual personnel to engage in sin's transfer to the land of separation (גזרה). Fourth, confession commits the community an annual right of self affliction. Fifth, confession commits the later readers of the text to give voice to sin through the ongoing dynamic of self-involving hermeneutics.

Within penitential prayer, confession is behabitive. Four aspects of this force develop in Ezra's confessionary procedure. First, confession transforms Israelite marriage practice by reinterpreting the nature of sin. Second, confession urges the community to conform to covenantal guidelines. Third, confession shapes the attitudes and action of the community by defining insider/outsider roles for the returning Israelite congregation. Fourth, Ezra's confession shapes subsequent readers' understanding of confession and worship according to definitions of sin and covenantal relationship with God.

Lament Regained
in Trito-Isaiah's Penitential Prayer

Richard J. Bautch

Introduction

In ancient Israel, lament was a type of prayer comprising formal elements that often included bitter complaint against God for the misfortune and distress at hand. Lament occurred in the psalms and other, largely preexilic, types of prayer. In the second half of the past century, there arose among scholars the conviction that such lament ceased in Israel as a result of the Babylonian exile and theological developments in the wake of this catastrophe.[1] Scholars today routinely speak of the "loss of lament."

During and after the exile, lament certainly underwent transformation that involved a degree of decline or diminution. Postexilic literary developments involving lament, however, are complex and heterogeneous such that they cannot be subsumed under a single concept such as loss. There are alternative ways to document lament in the postexilic period, as this study sets out to do. The following analysis of Isa 63:7–64:11 takes as its thesis that lament exerted a certain influence upon those responsible for this poignant prayer of penitence and that the authors of this text adopted and adapted the classic lament for their composition. In *their* work, lament has not been lost.

The goal of this study is to begin a reconsideration of the notion of lament lost by examining a later prayer in which lament has, I will argue, been retained, and in this sense regained. If this be the case, then lament can be retained in contemporary scholarship as well. At the very least, our study will engage anew

---

1. The scholars in question, principally Claus Westermann and Walter Brueggemann, are discussed below in the section "Lament Lost?" Theologically, a doctrine of divine retribution that is elaborated in the Deuteronomistic History (Dtr) becomes pronounced in the prayers of lament that are composed after the exile. Many of these prayers evince an acceptance of divine judgment as justifiable in light of the people's transgressions (Ezra 9:13, 15; Neh 9:33; Dan 9:7, 16).

certain ideas about lament and its historical development that have become engrained in biblical scholarship. Thus, a brief history of scholarship as well as a discussion of lament constitute our preliminary considerations.

Lament Implies Complaint

In this study, references to "lament" often denote "complaint," an element of prayer that is voiced individually and communally within the Psalter and elsewhere in the biblical literature. The complaint is a response to acute pain resulting most often from political events that usually are not without a religious dimension.[2] In the political or geo-political fray, the destruction or desecration of religious structures and institutions has led the people to hold God personally responsible for their misery and in this sense to complain against God.

In these complaints, the people typically interpret their misfortune as evidence of God's wrath against them. The wrath is expressed as God offending, insulting or rejecting them. In the extreme case of Ps 44, to be examined in detail below, God is charged with leading Israel to slaughter like sheep that are sold at a discount (44:12–13). No less grievously, other authors accuse God of forgetting Israel (44:24–25) and remaining indifferent to its plight (Pss 10:1; 89:47). Certain complaints imply that God has ceded control of the world to dark forces that vex the people (Ps 58:2–5; Hab 1:13–17). These intimations, all theological, compound the people's pain and contradict what their religion had led them to believe. In the words of Hermann Gunkel:

> Dem Inhalt nach sind diese Klagelieder der Verzweifelungs und Hilfeschrei eines gequälten und in seinem heiligsten Empfinden beleidigten Volkes, eine Klage, so herzzerreissend und zugleich so andauernd, wie sie vielleicht niemals wieder in der Welt erflungen ist.[3]

Lament Lost?

Gunkel's concluding observation implies a terminus to the biblical complaint, and indeed scholars tend to date the loss of lament to the exilic and particularly the postexilic periods. The seminal work in this regard is that of Claus Wes-

---

2. Political misfortune gives rise to lament in Pss 44:10–17, 20, 23–25; 60:3–5, 12; 74:4–11; 79:1–4; 80:5–7, 13; 89:39–46; Isa 26:14, 17–18; Jer 10:25; 31:18; Hab 1:13–16; and Lam 1:9; 3:42–51; 5:2–18. In select instances the complaint addresses problems of nature such as drought (Jer 14:2–6) and a plague of locusts (Joel 1:18–20).

3. Hermann Gunkel, *Einleitung in die Psalmen: Die Gattungen der religiösen Lyrik Israels* (ed. J. Begrich; Göttingen: Vandenhoeck & Ruprecht, 1933), 124–25.

termann, who posited the historical development of lament in three phases.[4] Initially the lament enters the literature of ancient Israel as a brief interrogative ("Why?") uttered to God in the course of unfortunate events (Exod 5:22; Josh 7:7; Judg 6:13). The first phase points toward the second. In the second phase the interrogatives become more numerous and varied ("Why?" "How long?") as they are clustered together with accusations against God (Pss 44:9; 60:10; 89:38; Lam 3:42–45). In this phase, Westermann notes, those voicing complaint often insist that they are innocent of any wrongdoing, and confession of sin is rare.[5] The compositions of the second phase, which include most of the Psalter's individual and communal laments, are generally thought to be preexilic, although this dating is open to critique.[6] In the third stage, understood to be exilic and postexilic, an Israel stripped of its sovereignty changes the way that it prays. It no longer challenges God with lament and complaint but rather confesses its sin and guilt publicly in a manner that supplies the rationale for God's retributive justice meted out in terms of the people's misfortune. In Westermann's view, the Deuteronomistic theology that underwrote such a view of justice was the catalyst for this third phase.[7] For Westermann these developments have decisive consequences theologically. As penitential prayer supplants the lament psalm with its trenchant complaint against God, so Israel's theology is reduced to two categories, sin and punishment, and its God to one attribute, righteousness.[8]

Following Westermann, Walter Brueggemann has further explored the theological consequences of lament lost as well as its societal implications. He asks:

> What difference does it make to have faith that permits and requires this form of prayer [i.e., lament]? My answer is that it shifts the calculus and *redresses the distribution of power* between two parties, so that the petitionary party is taken

---

4. The description to follow is set forth in Westermann's "Struktur und Geschichte der Klage im Alten Testament," *ZAW* 66 (1954): 44–80; and his *Praise and Lament in the Psalms* (trans. Keith R. Crim and Richard N. Soulen; Atlanta: John Knox, 1981), 165–213.

5. *Praise and Lament*, 206.

6. Elsewhere in this volume Dalit Rom-Shiloni holds that the date of the communal laments is a "riddle," as she claims that certain of these psalms are exilic. See her "Socio-Ideological *Setting* or *Settings* for Penitential Prayers?" 64.

7. *Praise and Lament*, 171–72. Rom-Shiloni suggests that Deuteronomistic historiographers joined by certain priests and prophets actively opposed the theology of the complaint and succeeded in silencing it: "silencing the complaint and accentuating the confessional element designates an intentional theological innovation in the penitential prayers, which should be evaluated in its theological context" ("Socio-Ideological *Setting* or *Settings*," 55).

8. *Praise and Lament*, 203. In addition to the Deuteronomistic theology current in the postexilic period, Westermann associates the loss of lament with the dictates of Christian piety and the tendency of many modern biblical interpreters to belittle the lament. Both of these later causes he cites in *Die Klagelieder: Forschungsgeschichte und Auslegung* (Neukirchen-Vluyn: Neukirchener, 1990), 78–81.

seriously and the God who is addressed is newly engaged in the crisis in a way that puts God at risk.[9]

Lament puts God at risk in the sense that God takes seriously the petitioner's pained speech and becomes available to act upon it. In turn, lament that is taken seriously is valued and legitimated. With lament's loss, however, the complaint is devalued and the one who would issue it becomes docile and submissive, according to Brueggemann.[10] Theology becomes reductive, in the manner that Westermann had suggested, and there is reinforced "a theological monopoly" that squelches theodicy.[11] The resulting social patterns "reinforce and consolidate the political-economic monopoly of the status quo."[12] The loss of lament that constricts theology and society, in Brueggemann's opinion, is more pernicious than many people realize.[13]

It would be anachronistic to search the postexilic literature for evidence of lament's loss in terms of a constricted theology or a reductive monopoly of the same. Yet if lament were irrevocably lost in the postexilic period, its absence should be noticeable, and there should be no counter data. That is, a theological passivity should typify the prayer of this period, and the prayer itself should be bereft of complaint. To help determine whether this is so, we now examine one such prayer, Isa 63:7–64:11.[14]

Overview of Trito-Isaiah's Penitential Prayer

There are six parts to the prayer in Trito-Isaiah: (1) a historical section (63:7–14); (2) a lament (63:15–63:19a) followed by (3) an appeal (63:19b–64:4a); (4) a confession of sin (64:4b–6); (5) a final appeal that both asserts confidence (64:7–8) and issues a second lament (64:9–10); and (6) a conclusion (64:11). In terms of content and sequence, the prayer's form-critical repertoire compares well with those established by Gunkel[15] and Mowinckel[16] for the psalms of communal

---

9. Walter Brueggemann, "The Costly Loss of Lament," in *The Psalms and the Life of Faith* (ed. Patrick D. Miller; Minneapolis: Fortress, 1995), 98–111, here 101, emphasis original; repr. from *JSOT* 36 (1986): 57–71.
10. Ibid., 102.
11. Ibid. "Theodicy" is the effort to reconcile God's goodness, God's omnipotence and the reality of human suffering, in light of the fact that asserting any two of these points logically precludes the third.
12. Ibid.
13. Ibid., 111.
14. The text of the prayer is taken from MT with translations by the author.
15. Gunkel, *Einleitung in die Psalmen*, 125.
16. Sigmund Mowinckel, *The Psalms in Israel's Worship* (2 vols.; New York: Abingdon, 1992 [1962]), 1:195–219.

lament, and a detailed study of the prayer and its context confirms this comparison.[17] An awareness of form is helpful background for considering the prayer's overriding theological concerns.

The impetus of the prayer is strain placed upon the people's relationship with God when instability and vulnerability come to characterize the covenant. The covenantal nature of the human-divine relationship is established in 63:7–14,[18] and the strain upon the relationship is evident in the lament of 63:15–19a. The people thus petition God to visit them anew as God once did at Sinai (63:19b–64:4a), and the request is literally framed by the preceding lament and a subsequent confession of sins (64:4b–6). The sequence of lament-request-confession forms the center of the prayer. At this center is a request by a people who lament that God has become distant as they suffer the consequences of their sin. Set in a central position, the lament is reminiscent of those found in the psalms of communal lament; in both cases the lament plays the role of anticipating the petition. Later in the prayer, a second lament (64:9–10) is issued in anticipation of the prayer's conclusion (64:11). The authors' self-conscious use of lament warrants further study.

Lament in the Prayer of Trito-Isaiah

Isaiah 63:15–19a

This lament clearly revolves around God, albeit indirectly. God's strength and compassion (63:15) are conspicuous by their absence, while God is removed and no longer acting as the people's guide (63:17) and sovereign (63:19a). Abandoned and dispossessed of their sanctuary (63:18), the people join in lament. They consider their wrongdoing (63:17a) and ask God to relate to them as redeemer (גאלנו) and, especially, father (אבינו). These divine appellations, on the one hand, imply the familial piety that was current after the exile.[19] On the other hand, the

---

17. See Richard Bautch, *Developments in Genre Between Post-exilic Penitential Prayers and the Psalms of Communal Lament* (SBLAcBib 7; Atlanta: Society of Biblical Literature), 40, 47–48.

18. The covenantal nuances of Isa 63:7–10 are established in 64:7, where MT's חסדי יהוה may be translated as "the LORD's covenant deeds." Although not all translators choose to emphasize the covenantal nature of the divine human relationship, it is very much implicit when this term is used in the context of communal lament, as noted by Mowinckel, *Psalms in Israel's Worship*, 1:205; for further indications of covenant making in this passage, see Elizabeth Achtemeier, *The Community and Message of Isaiah 56–66* (Minneapolis: Fortress, 1982), 113; and most recently Joseph Blenkinsopp, *Isaiah 56–66: A New Translation with Introduction and Commentary* (AB 19B; New York: Doubleday, 2003), 259–60.

19. From the time of the exile onward, there is a trend toward personal piety; the relationship with God finds its analogy in familial ties, not history, as God is invoked as parent—father

people's self-identification points to an earlier period. In 63:17 they are "servants" (עבדיך, 63:17b) understood as those who serve the Lord by diurnal devotions. Moshe Weinfeld notes that in the Deuteronomic literature, this sense of the root עבד is always accompanied by other devotional expressions, such as "fearing the LORD."[20] Thus, in Isa 63:17b, the reference to servants is preceded directly by a reference to "fear of you" (i.e. the LORD). Of itself, "fearing the LORD" has a generic, Deuteronomic resonance, as does its parallel in the beginning of 63:17, "(erring from) your ways" תתענו יהוה מדרכיך (Deut 9:12, 16; 11:28; 31:29).[21]

Here the verb, תתענו, requires examination, but before doing so we must recognize its stridency and potential for polemic.[22] תתענו is an imperfect form of תעה in *hipʻil* and is translated "you cause us to err." It is an accusation against God, who, according to the complaint, has caused Israel to commit sins that remain unspecified but that may be the object of the confession in 64:4b–6. In the context of a national catastrophe, that is, the desecration of the temple (63:18), the assertion that God has caused the people's wrongdoing as God has hardened their hearts amounts to a protest of innocence. Theologically, the expression "you cause us to err" reflects a move toward theodicy as it juxtaposes God who is good, divine causation, and the experience of alienation from God. Literarily, the accusation against God echoes the lament psalms and more generally the classical literature of ancient Israel.

Analysis reveals that the pivotal verb in Isa 63:17, "you cause us to err," תעה in *hipʻil*, is typical of classical sources, namely, the prophets of the eighth century (Isa 3:12; 9:15; Hos 4:12; Amos 2:4; Mic 3:5). As such, it evokes not an exilic or postexilic context but rather an earlier one. Similarly, God's zeal (קנאה, 63:15) is a theologoumenon of the preexilic ("YHWH-alone") prophets, whose use of the term connoted divine love, jealousy, power, and determination to reward and punish (see Deut 4:26; 5:9; 6:15).[23] Precise dating of the term קנאה is difficult because this byword for zeal passed on to the Deuteronomistic school and anchored its theological system during and after the exile (Deut 32:16, 21b; Exod 34:14). There *is*, nevertheless, a basis for relating 63:15 and surely 63:17 to the time of the pre-

---

(Deut 32:6b; Jer 3:4, 19) and mother (Isa 46:3; 49:15; 66:13). The trend is discussed in Rainer Albertz's *A History of the Israelite Religion* (2 vols.; Louisville: Westminster John Knox, 1994 [1992]), 403.

20. Moshe Weinfeld, *Deuteronomy and the Deuteronomic School* (Oxford: Clarendon, 1972), 332.

21. "Fear of the LORD" is well attested in Deuteronomy: 4:10; 5:26; 6:2, 13, 24; 8:6; 10:12, 20; 13:5; 14:23; 17:19; 28:58; 31:12, 13.

22. My gratitude to Mark Boda for offering this observation in the course of our discussions.

23. Morton Smith, *Palestinian Parties and Politics That Shaped the Old Testament* (London: SCM, 1987 [1981]), 39.

exilic prophets. One may conclude that this lament's predominant echoes are to those sources that represent an *early* articulation of Deuteronomic theology.[24]

ISAIAH 64:9–10

These verses constitute a distinct lament over Jerusalem. The holy city, Zion/Jerusalem, is said to be in desuetude (64:9), and the temple has been burned after its precious vessels were plundered (64:10). These events correspond well to an exilic point of reference.[25] It is furthermore important that the temple is characterized not as a sacrificial cult but as the locus of general worship used by the ancestors (אשר הללוך אבתינו). The perspective may be characterized as Deuteronomic, based on the work of Weinfeld, who notes that with the shift from pre-Deuteronomic to Deuteronomic literature expressions of cultic worship were transformed into devotional worship not dependent on a cult.[26]

In the final analysis, the prayer showcases two laments, Isa 63:15–19a and Isa 64:9–10, whose origins reach back generations. They are vestiges of the complaints issued by the preexilic and exilic forebears. Nonetheless, the two laments remain influential and effectively voice the pain of postexilic Jews. By these laments, the people engage questions of theodicy. If the religious tradition in question, postexilic Judaism, had lost lament, it had also regained it through the redaction of earlier expressions that challenged God.

Moreover, these are not isolated incidences of such redaction. The technique of adopting and adapting earlier complaints and working them into postexilic compositions is visible elsewhere, but in each case the theological calculus is different. In the prayer of Neh 9, for example, portions of the historical recital parallel the complaint element that is found in the psalms. That is, the psalmic complaint is echoed in the people's crying out from their oppression (Neh 9:9, 27–28). In these passages, the crying out elicits God's mercy and so establishes a basis for

---

24. Yairah Amit provides a discussion of Deuteronomic discourse in the early part of the seventh century. Her point of reference is the book of Judges, whose Deuteronomic phrasing is not, in her opinion, secondary. Amit holds that Deuteronomic phrasing originated in Judges and subsequently influenced the Deuteronomic movement. See *The Book of Judges: The Art of Editing* (Leiden: Brill, 1999), 364–75.

25. With H. G. M. Williamson I date the second lament (Isa 64:9–10) and the verses surrounding it to late in the exilic period, but other portions of the prayer require earlier and later dating based on their preexilic or postexilic content. See Williamson's "Isaiah 63:7–64:11: Exilic Lament or Post-exilic Protest?" *ZAW* 102 (1990): 48–58, esp. 57–58; and Bautch, *Developments in Genre*, 60–61.

26. Weinfeld, *Deuteronomy and the Deuteronomic School*, 332. See too Albertz, *History of the Israelite Religion*, 476.

hope in the future.²⁷ Contemporary texts from the community at Elephantine offer another example. Bezalel Porten suggests that reading the psalms of communal lament brought these fifth-century Jews to focus on literary expressions such as "save," "help," "answer," and "deliver."²⁸ These distinctive imperatives, Porten notes, were incorporated into personal names that are attested at Elephantine; he speculates that this lexical linkage *is* intentional and reflects a people in distress finding their protection in the Lord.²⁹

Confession of Sin in the Prayer of Trito-Isaiah

There is another aspect of the penitential prayer in Trito-Isaiah that illumines the phenomena of lament lost and lament regained in the postexilic era. Studies of prayers such as this remark upon the predominance of the confession of sin, and often scholars relate this fact to the wane of lament in the same prayers.³⁰ On occasion, the relationship between confession and lament is glimpsed in its complexity:

> The type of the psalm of lamentation, with its apparent complaints at the silence and inactivity of the deity, is turned into its obverse—though this is in reality part of that psalm form—in which the acceptance of the rightness of divine judgment is in itself an anticipation of what may follow.³¹

Peter Ackroyd suggests that a vindication of God, such as that associated with the confession of sin, is gained by reversing the theological polarities of the classical lament. In other words, the lament remains an influence upon the prayers, but in the manner of a negative image. The prayers reflect lament indirectly, and they do so through elements such as the confession of sin. Is Ackroyd correct, and if so may it be said that lament is regained in the penitential prayers via the confession of sin? To see this matter clearly, one must compare confessional expression in the penitential prayer of Trito-Isaiah with the language of complaint in the

---

27. This source-critical study of the prayer in Nehemiah 9 is corroborated by Michael Duggan, who also holds that the theological import of Neh 9:9, 27–28 is one of hope. See *The Covenant Renewal in Ezra-Nehemiah (Neh 7:72b–10:40): An Exegetical, Literary and Theological Study* (SBLDS 164; Atlanta: Society of Biblical Literature, 2001), 231.

28. Bezalel Porten, *Archives from Elephantine: The Life of an Ancient Jewish Military Colony* (Berkeley and Los Angeles: University of California Press, 1968), 146–47.

29. Ibid.

30. Westermann states: "The lament is replaced by the confession of sins, thus transforming the psalms of communal lament in which the lament recedes to the background and in its place another motif comes to dominate the psalm" (*Praise and Lament*, 206).

31. Peter Ackroyd, *Exile and Restoration: A Study of Hebrew Thought of the Sixth Century B.C.* (Philadelphia: Westminster, 1968), 77.

psalms of communal lament. Three passages in Isa 63:7–64:11 provide the occasion for such comparison.

Isaiah 63:7–10

Confessional expression first occurs in Isa 63:7–14, a section about God's saving deeds in the history of Israel. The first half of the unit (vv. 7–10) considers the covenantal rapport that has existed between God and God's people.[32] While God is gracious, merciful, and eminently faithful to the covenant, the people are false to the covenant (שקר) and rebellious (מרה) to the point of grieving (עצב) God and turning God against them. At first, God in 63:8 claims the people as God's own and declares them incapable of deceit (לא ישקרו).[33] Here dramatic irony prevails as שקר represents an impossibility to the speaker, but it has a foreboding and quite different meaning to those who understand the situation better. The latter view surfaces in 63:10, which confirms that the people are imbued with שקר. They rebel and grieve God's holy spirit. Thus God turns and fights against them. The operative terms, rebel and grieve (עצב and מרה), although not inherently penitential, may be construed as confessional because they involve a frank admission of guilt on behalf of the people.

Moreover, in the postexilic period when the prayer of Trito-Isaiah assumed its final form, the term מרה occurs regularly in texts that accuse Israel of rebellion in the face of God's public, historical deeds, especially those in the wilderness.[34] That is to say, the prayer reflects the meaning of מרה associated with the postexilic literature as well as Pss 78 and 106.[35] In these two psalms מרה appears predominantly (seven times) and denotes

---

32. The covenantal nuances of Isa 63:7–10 are discussed in n. 18.

33. In light of 1 Sam 15:29 and Ps 89:34, it is as if divine steadfastness is being projected onto humanity.

34. See Rolf Knierim, "מרה," *TLOT* 2:688. Historically, the meaning of מרה as "obstinate" is rooted in Deuteronomic law (Deut 21:18–21); in the Dtr, מרה accrues "nomistic nuance" and conforms to one of two stock usages, neither of which is attested in the prayer from Trito-Isaiah. The "nomistic nuance" is treated in Ludger Schwienhorst, "מרה," *TDOT* 9:7, 9.

35. Although Pss 78 and 106 both provide historical recitals, they are not easily classified by genre. Psalm 78, for example, may be understood as a wisdom psalm on the basis of 78:1–4. Furthermore, Ps 78 is akin to the psalms of communal lament in that it relates the people's distress when they are separated from God. Like the psalms of communal lament, Ps 78 is generally dated to the preexilic period, and there is ample evidence for doing so. The psalm nowhere refers to the temple's destruction, and it has "origins in a common cultic tradition which may belong to a much earlier period than the psalm's literary record." That is, in Artur Weiser's view the psalm is early even though "the ideology of the psalm" is most compatible with later texts such as Deut 32 and, I would add, the postexilic prayers of penitence. See his *The Psalms: A Commentary* (trans. Herbert Hartwell; OTL; Philadelphia: Westminster, 1962), 540.

the rebellious conduct of the patriarchal generation (Ps 78:8) during the wilderness period (78:17, 40; 106:7, 33) and the occupation (78:56; 106:43). Also, in this time מרה appears with many synonyms; besides those of Deuteronomistic origin we find expressions from the language of wisdom and the general terminology of sin [including] עצב (Ps 78:40).³⁶

Like Ps 78, Isa 63:10 employs מרה in a manner particular to those generations after the exile who shift their Dtr focus from law to historical conceits such as the wilderness. In fact, Isaiah's terms of indictment, עצב and מרה, correspond remarkably to those of Ps 78:40: "How often they rebelled against him in the wilderness and grieved him in the desert." Nowhere else does the Bible join these two terms of wrongdoing, although a close approximation is found elsewhere in Ps 78: "Yet they still sinned more against him, rebelling against the Most High (למרות עליון) in the desert" (v. 17). Psalm 78:17, 40 both recognize a specific type of misdeed that is later elaborated by the author of Isa 63:10.

The term שקר (Isa 63:8) enjoys a similar affinity with the psalms of communal lament. Its basic meaning, "to behave contrary to a contract, faithlessly, perfidiously,"³⁷ is consonant with the Old Aramaic Sefire inscriptions.³⁸ Genesis 21:23 and other verses confirm שקר as a biblical term no less rooted in treaty law. Psalm 44:18 reads: "We have not forgotten you nor been unfaithful to your covenant (ולא־שקרנו בבריתך)." Given the covenantal context of 63:7–10, שקר (63:8) finds its parallel in Ps 44's expression of being untrue to the covenant, from the psalms of communal lament. Yet there is one significant difference. In Ps 44:18 the people assert that despite great calamity they have not forgotten God or been false to the covenant. The psalm affirms their innocence and laments their plight. The prayer in Trito-Isaiah, however, depicts a rebel people false to the covenant.

Within the first half of the prayer's historical section (63:7–10), confessional language has the stamp of the psalms and specifically of the psalms of communal lament.³⁹ By adopting three deliberate expressions of penitence, שקר, מרה, and עצב, the composer is able to underscore both the people as sinners and God

---

36. Schwienhorst, "מרה," 9:9.
37. Martin A. Klopfenstein, "שקר," TLOT 3:1399.
38. Joseph Fitzmyer, *The Aramaic Inscriptions of Sefire* (Rome: Pontifical Biblical Institute, 1995 [1967]), 107.
39. Richard Clifford similarly concludes that Isa 63:7–14 is an extension of the lament that is found in earlier biblical material, although the psalms are not among the antecedents he cites. He lists rather pentateuchal passages involving Moses because he focuses on the narrative dimension of Isaiah's text, not confession of sin. Clifford's work complements our study inasmuch as both present aspects of the background of lament from which Isa 63:7–14 emerges. See his "Narrative and Lament in Isaiah 63:7–64:11," in *To Touch the Text: Biblical and Related Studies in Honor of Joseph A. Fitzmyer* (ed. Maurya P. J. Horgan and Paul J. Kobelski; New York: Crossroad, 1989), 93–102.

as alienated from the covenant by their sins.⁴⁰ The prayer's foci are essentially two. The first is the traditional subject of lament, God's distance from the people in travail. The second is the cause of this distance, understood by the prayer's authors as human faithlessness to the covenant.

ISAIAH 64:4B-6

The verses 64:4b–6 are the prayer's most self-conscious attempt at confession. Similar to 63:8, 10, the section correlates references to sin and iniquity with the people's alienation from God. The terms for sin and iniquity are חטא (64:4b) and עון (64:5b, 6b); God is described as one who is angry and not apt to save (64:4b), whose name and strength are no longer invoked (64:6), and who has become at best a hidden presence (64:6b). Human sin and God's lamentable remoteness are at the center of a complex, troubled relationship.⁴¹

Thus, 64:4b keynotes this short confession: "Behold, you grew angry; we have sinned." The statement, on the one hand, is conventional because in psalms of lament חטא routinely connotes the causal connection between one's ill-chosen action and its consequence.⁴² The syntax, however, is counterintuitive as one expects human sin to spur divine anger, and not vice versa. In light of the conditional construction in Gen 43:9,⁴³ Isaiah's verse has been read as legal discourse whereby God's anger stands as the verdict against a sinful people. Only upon conviction is Israel subjected to the full depths of its own sin, in this view first proposed by Franz Delitzsch.⁴⁴ His interpretation is grammatically defen-

---

40. The terms also echo the book of Isaiah itself, as in 30:9: "For they are a rebellious people, lying sons, who will not hear the instruction of the LORD."

41. The difficulties are reflected in the pericope itself. Isa 63:7–64:11 is a prayer with challenging syntax (64:4bα) and signs of textual corruption (64:4bβ, 64:6bβ). Exegeting the confessional expressions is further complicated by the fact that wrongdoing and its consequences are expressed literally (64:4b), cultically (64:5a), and figuratively (64:5b).

42. K. Koch, "חטא," *TDOT* 4:313–14.

43. Judah says to his father Jacob, "I myself will be surety for him; you can hold me accountable for him. If I do not bring him back to you and set him before you, then let me bear the blame forever" (Gen 43:9). Psalm 36:3 holds that the evildoer's self-flattery mitigates against his iniquity being found out and hated, thus providing another instance of this view that public knowledge heightens a misdeed's reprehensibility.

44. Delitzsch holds that the *waw* forms the imperfect consecutive: "So haben wir denn gesündigt (Folgerung der Sünde aus der Strafe), richtiger aber wie Gen. 43,9: so stehen wir denn als Sünder, als Schuldige da—die Strafe hat Isr. vor der Welt und vor sich selber als das hingestellt was es ist" (*Commentar über das Buch Jesaia* [Leipzig: Dörffling & Franke, 1889], 609). An alternative exegesis considers the second clause to be epexegetical: "You were angry, we having sinned," as John Oswalt, *The Book of Isaiah: Chapters 40–66* (NICOT; Grand Rapids: Eerdmans, 1998), 619. Yet a third interpretation takes the first clause to be concessive: you grew

sible⁴⁵ and makes much sense in light of the composer's larger agenda to craft a confession based on God's apparent flight from sinful humanity. It is from this point of view that the verse's final three words, about salvation, can be understood. While some editors would emend the text, it reads rhetorically: "(We are) forever (implicated) in them (our sins), and we shall be saved?" Despite the verse's difficulties, its first-person confession of sin is quite direct and almost formulaic. Among the psalms of lament, such forthright use of חטא is found in Ps 79:9b and in Ps 78:32, also a keynote to a section of confessional material.⁴⁶

The next verse, 64:5, sketches the breadth and depth of the people's defilement in terms that are cultic (64:5a) and figurative (64:5b). Common to both expressions is the self-referential "all of us." The cultic expression, involving the designation "unclean" (טמא), reflects how uncleanness has become a metaphor for immorality after the exile. Jacob Neusner interprets 64:5a as a commonplace critique of someone who "while ritually pure, does impure deeds."⁴⁷ The critique, he notes, is not unique to prophetic literature, and another striking example is found in Hag 2:13–14.

The figurative language in 64:5b reads: "And we have fallen like a leaf, all of us" (ונבל כעלה כלנו), a use of the root בלה⁴⁸ that is not unknown to the prophets.⁴⁹ When the stich concludes, "Like the wind, our iniquities carry us away," the likeliest source is Ps 1:3–4, where a distinction between lawful and wicked mentions the leaf *not* withering and the wind driving away the chaff. Unlike the psalm, Isa 64:5b applies both expressions pejoratively and implies that iniquity determines the direction of people's lives. Wrongdoing's effects or consequences appear to be emphasized when this usage of "iniquities" (עון) is

---

angry, "and yet we sinned"; so R. Norman Whybray, *Isaiah 40–66* (NCB; Grand Rapids: Eerdmans, 1981), 264.

45. "The imperfect expresses the practical consequences" (Edward Young, *The Book of Isaiah* [3 vols.; Grand Rapids: Eerdmans, 1965–72], 3:495).

46. By indentation, MT indicates Ps 78:32–39 as a distinct unit. Richard Clifford designates vv. 33–40 as meditation or reflection on the miracles and punishments of vv. 12–32. See his "In Zion and David a New Beginning: An Interpretation of Psalm 78," in *Traditions in Transformation: Turning Points in Biblical Faith* (ed. Baruch Halpern and Jon D. Levenson; Winona Lake, Ind.: Eisenbrauns, 1981), 121–41, here 133.

47. Neusner further notes that equating impurity with evil doing is typical of the book of Isaiah as a whole, as witnessed by Isa 6:5. See Jacob Neusner, *The Idea of Purity in Ancient Judaism* (Leiden: Brill, 1973), 13.

48. If the verb is a *hip'il* imperfect, first common plural, MT's form and pointing would indicate the root to be בלל, which *BDB* crosslists. The expected form of the verb is found in 1QIsaᵃ, which thus witnesses to the root בלה. See Millar Burrows, *The Dead Sea Scrolls of St. Mark's Monastery* (New Haven: ASOR, 1950), vol. 1, plate LI.

49. Isa 1:30; 34:4; Jer 8:13; Ezek 47:12.

compared to others.⁵⁰ God's help is nowhere to be had. The expression "driving wind" occurs in Ps 78:39, where God stays the divine wrath because mortals are merely a wind that passes and comes not again. Where the psalm notes human foibles, Isa 64:5b laments "our iniquities"; Trito-Isaiah has brought wrongdoing more to the fore.

The concluding verse to this section compounds the people's failure with God's abandoning them. In Isa 64:6a lament and confession blend together flawlessly: "There is no one calling upon your name, no one rousing himself to take hold of you." The first idea is a psalmic conceit found in the communal laments (Pss 75:1; 79:6; 80:18).⁵¹ In the psalms, calling upon God's name is tantamount to revelation in all its mystery and wonder. As calling upon God's name implies that God is immanent, its negation underscores God's absence. The second expression of Isa 64:6a, מתעורר, about rousing oneself, is both psalmic and Isaian. Typically, it is God who is called to rise up and help the people.⁵² That God is not doing so is lamentable; that no mortal rises up to take hold of God is in fact an indictment, possibly against a human leader.⁵³ In its extent, Isa 64:6a captures a loss of grace and human nerve in the milieu of divine abandonment.

Fittingly, the confession's crescendo, Isa 64:6b, continues: "For you have hidden your face from us, and made us to melt because of our sins." The bearing and/or hiding of God's face is well attested in the prophetic literature⁵⁴ and especially the psalms.⁵⁵ Among the communal laments, Ps 80 concludes with this image and equates it with salvation: "Restore us, O LORD, God of hosts. Let your face shine, that we may be saved" (80:19). Psalm 44's final section also speaks of God's hidden face, and does so amid repeated calls for God to rise up. Psalm 44:24 reads: "Why do you hide your face, why do you forget our oppression and affliction?" While the verse visits the divine and human realms, it nowhere links God's absence to human sin. However, Isaiah does.

Isaiah 64:6bβ concludes: "You have made us melt by means of our iniquities." Our translation, with the second clause expressing agency, is most probable, over and against a different rendering of ביד based on an appeal to Ugaritic.⁵⁶ Another term at issue is MT's וַתְּמוּגֵגוּ, which we read as the contracted *polel* of מוג, the

---

50. *BDB*, 5771; cf. *KBL*, 689. According to these lexica, Isa 64:5 is unique with עון referring to the consequence of or punishment for iniquity. More frequently attested synonyms for the term include offense/transgression and the *guilt* of iniquity.

51. In the Psalter, the expression also occurs in Pss 99:6; 105:1; 116:4; 13, 17.

52. Pss 44:23, 78:65; Isa 42:13–16, 51:9–11.

53. Weiser, *The Psalms*, 73–74.

54. Isa 8:17, 54:8; Jer 33:5; Ezek 39:23, 24, 29; Mic 3:4.

55. Pss 13:2; 22:25; 27:9; 69:8; 88:15; 102:3; 143:7.

56. As Mitchell Dahood has noted ("Hebrew-Ugaritic Lexicography I," *Bib* 44 [1963]: 301–2), the Ugaritic lexeme ביד can mean "because," as in Jer 41:9, Job 8:4.

root for "melt."⁵⁷ "Melt" connotes moral dissipation elsewhere in the Hebrew Bible (Exod 15:15; Jer 49:23). Certain ancient translators, however, have rendered ותמוגגו differently. 1QIsaᵃ reads a different root, מגר: "You have cast us into our iniquities."⁵⁸ Another ancient variant, "you have delivered us up," is obtained by emending MT and doubling the *nun* to reflect the root מגן. While "delivered us up" is found in the Old Greek translation,⁵⁹ "melt" remains superior on two counts. It has the advantage of *lectio difficilior* and makes the best sense contextually. That is, God's absence in 64:6bα is paralleled by the people's diminution, their moral melting away. Human iniquity is the root of this decline and as such provides the signature upon the confession Isa 64:4b–6.

ISAIAH 64:8

In Isa 64:8, the individual's vow of confidence, the theme of confession is sounded in now familiar words: "Be not excessively angry, LORD, and do not remember iniquity forever. Behold, consider, we all are your people." God is not to remember iniquity forever, and while the negative particle normally precedes the verb directly, here the temporal adverb intervenes to emphasize "forever."⁶⁰ If punishment must be prolonged, let it not be forever. Unlike 64:4b–6, this capsule confession involves no figures of speech or cultic jargon; it is a sanguine appeal that God consider God's people and requite iniquity with mercy, not anger.

The verse has been compared to the psalms of communal lament, especially Ps 79,⁶¹ which reads:

> Do not remember against us the iniquities of our ancestors;
>> let your compassion come speedily to meet us, for we are brought very low.
> Help us, O God of our salvation, for the glory of your name,
>> deliver us, and forgive our sins, for your name's sake. (Ps 79:8–9)

The psalm and the prayer from Isaiah both embellish lament with elements of confession, and this is their greatest similarity. Nonetheless, they have quite different perspectives on wrongdoing and God's redress of the same. The psalm

---

57. *GKC* §72cc.

58. ותמגדנו ביד עוונננו. While the root in question appears to be מגר, the text from Qumran reflects some confusion of the letters *dālet* and *rêš*. See Burrows, *Dead Sea Scrolls*, vol. 1, plate LI.

59. LXX = παρέδωκας ἡμᾶς (מגן), "you have delivered us up because of our sins."

60. Paul Joüon and T. Muraoka, *A Grammar of Biblical Hebrew* (Rome: Pontifical Biblical Institute, 1991 [1923]), 604.

61. Arthur S. Herbert, *The Book of Isaiah Chapters 40–66* (CBC; Cambridge: Cambridge University Press, 1975), 180.

recognizes iniquity but displaces it upon an earlier generation. It speaks of "our sin" but in a context of consolation, that is, beholding God's face. The psalm invokes divine compassion and supposes that it may come speedily. The prayer, on the other hand, speaks only of God's anger ceasing and presumes no compassion. Moreover, the prayer forebodes an extensive penitence; the request that God not remember forever implies a dispensation that is not anon. In sum, the psalm recognizes sin but is quick to attenuate it while focusing on God's rescue of a people in duress. Isaiah 64:8 is less confident and situates the psalms' traditional language of lament in a different context. As the prayer takes seriously the penitential phrases that had been grafted onto the likes of Ps 79, Isa 64:8 turns on the sober hope that God requite iniquity with mercy, not anger.

Shared Theological Aspects

In Isa 63:7–64:11, the confessions of sin echo the psalms of communal lament, especially Pss 44; 79; and 80. There are found in the confessions of Isa 63:7–10; 64:4b–6; and 64:8 at least seven lexical correspondences to the psalms of communal lament.[62] While it is not always possible to determine whether the correspondences are due to direct borrowing or the common usage of stock phrases in circulation, the continuity between the lament psalms and Isaiah's prayer remains noteworthy. Most important, however, are the theological points of contact within these correspondences.

God's absence from history is of preeminent concern in the psalms of communal lament. As the psalms hold God accountable for the misfortune that befalls an abandoned people, they explore the culpability of God. Yet as the exile gave fresh impetus to retribution theology generally, so the prayer Isa 63:7–64:11 reconsiders culpability *in terms of the human condition*. Culpability becomes an illuminating dimension of *human* history; any statement in the psalms may be reconstrued and recast in light of what human sin has wrought. Thus in Isa 63:7–64:11 confession of sin is seminal data whose importance is on a level with God's seeming to take leave of human history. In the postexilic period, confession expresses a deeply held belief: God's distance from the people in travail is an effect of human faithlessness to God's ways.

Yet are the postexilic prayers of Trito-Isaiah and others so very different from the psalms of lament? It is striking to note how the prayer and the psalms, despite reaching opposite theological conclusions on issues such as culpability, both explore a God no longer present to the human realm, and they do so in

---

62. The correspondences are based not on words alone but on the patterned associations of words. By contrast, a parallel text of penitence in Trito-Isaiah, Isa 59:1–15, does not compare as positively with the psalms of communal lament and draws its confessional language primarily from the individual laments' descriptions of oppressors (59:5–8, 13–15a).

similar terminology. God's presence and, especially, absence are stated in terms of the covenant (Isa 63:7, 10; Pss 44:18; 89:34), the divine name (Isa 64:6a; Ps 79:6, 9) and the divine countenance (Isa 64:6b; Pss 44:24; 80:19). Concomitant with this divine dispatch is human deceit (Isa 63:8; Ps 44:18), sin (Isa 64:4b; Pss 78:32; 79:9) and iniquity (Isa 64:5b, 6b, 8; Ps 79:8). The similar terminology bespeaks consonant theologies.

The theology of Trito-Isaiah's prayer owes a debt to the psalms of lament and especially to the complaints contained therein. By reversing the theological polarities of the complaint, the prayer pronounces confessions of sin that justify God and so serve as sure defense against charges that God mistreats the people. Historically speaking, lament is the penultimate point in the theological progression that concludes in the confession of sin, and it is in this sense that lament is a proximate influence upon the penitential prayer. The prayers reflect lament, though perhaps dimly, through the confession of sin. Drawn from the lament is the confession's language as well as its interest in concepts such as culpability. Lament is thus "regained" in the penitential prayers via the confession of sin.

Conclusion: Lament Regained

Without disputing that lament, understood as complaint against God, was subject to a quantitative decrease in the postexilic period, this paper has demonstrated that it would be erroneous to hold that lament was univocally "lost" at that juncture in history. In postexilic writings such as Isa 63:7–64:11, one may document lament functioning as an influence that is vestigial and proximate. It is a vestigial influence in Isa 63:15–19a and Isa 64:9–10, two laments whose origins significantly predate the final form of the prayer in Trito-Isaiah. As echoes of the complaints issued by the preexilic and exilic forebears, the two laments effectively voice the pain and theological bewilderment of postexilic Jews. The religious tradition in question, postexilic Judaism, had "lost" lament only to regain it through the redaction of much earlier endeavors in theodicy. Lament is a proximate influence inasmuch as the theology of Isa 63:7–64:11 stands upon that of the psalms of lament as it is keyed by the complaints therein. The prayer, however, reverses the theological polarities of the complaint. As a result, the prayer's confessions of sin exonerate the God whom the laments would indict. Lament is indeed the penultimate point in the theological progression toward the confession of sin, and in this sense lament is a proximate influence upon the penitential prayer.

Through an analysis of Isa 63:7–64:11, we have documented the important influence of lament upon postexilic literature. Lament is regained, but to what end? Lament in Isa 63:7–64:11 is perhaps a device that enriches the text both literarily and theologically by creating a tension between the past and the present, between the preexilic and the postexilic. Rodney Werline observes such tension throughout the prayer as he notes that "the coupling of lament with confession of sin ... generates a tension."[63] The tension results from the people asking why God has not delivered them, or lamenting, precisely as they confess their sins. Werline concludes:

> While a modern reader might think that the authors are inconsistent, obviously ancient writers had no problem expressing both complaint and confession within the same text. The phenomenon may be analogous to the shifting between praise and complaint in several of the canonical psalms.[64]

Alternatively, the prayer in Trito-Isaiah is evocative of the lament psalms construed as retorts to biblical texts that propound Dtr theology. In the analysis of Carleen Mandolfo, the two types of literature form "a dialogic relationship of the testimony/counter testimony variety."[65] She has observed that laments in the Psalter provide "just the leverage needed to keep Deuteronomistic theology viable as the basis of a worldview or theology."[66] Similarly, the prayer of Isa 63:7–64:11 incorporates time-honored lament that serves as countertestimony, and in this sense is theologically proximate, to the multiple confessions of sin that evince the prayer's Dtr theology. The Dtr theology and the elements of lament thus form a relationship that is in process and under negotiation, much like the theology of this period in general.

To conclude, as the authors of Isa 63:7–64:11 adopted and adapted the lament for their composition, the lament came to serve as a vestigial and proximate influence upon this poignant prayer of penitence. Although in their day lament was waning, these biblical authors reclaimed this classical literary form and allowed it to help shape their prayer and so their lives.

---

63. Rodney A. Werline, *Penitential Prayer in Second Temple Judaism: The Development of a Religious Institution* (SBLEJL 13; Atlanta: Scholars Press, 1998), 42.

64. Ibid., 44.

65. Carleen Mandolfo relies on the work of Bakhtin as well as Brueggemann in her analysis of the lament psalms as a theological counter to Deuteronomistic theology. See her *God in the Dock: Dialogic Tension in the Psalms of Communal Lament* (JSOTSup 357; London: Sheffield Academic Press, 2002), 142–43.

66. Ibid.

The Affirmation of Divine Righteousness in Early Penitential Prayers: A Sign of Judaism's Entry into the Axial Age

William Morrow

Introduction

Petitionary prayers made on behalf of Second Temple Jewish communities often use penitential motifs. This situation stands in contrast to that of collective pre-exilic and exilic biblical prayers, which prefer the rhetoric of complaint, including protests against divine actions. It is the thesis of this chapter that the preference for penitence as opposed to protest can be connected to Judaism's emergence into what philosopher Karl Jaspers called the "Axial Age." Among other biblical writings, the poems of the Second Isaiah and the book of Job attest to the emergence of a theology that dissipated the energies of communal lament in the exilic period and afterwards. An emphasis on divine transcendence severed the polarity between praise and protest that was characteristic of lament. The permanence of this theological development ensured the domination of the penitential posture in prayer.

Penitential prayer is more easily identified by stereotypical contents than structure. Traits of penitential prayer include an emphasis on divine sovereignty, mercy and justice, the influence of Deuteronomic theology and rhetoric, and expressions of confession of sin and contrition.[1] Biblical prayers of penitence include Dan 9:4–19; Ezra 9:6–15; Neh 1:5–11; 9:5–37.[2] Extrabiblical examples include Bar 1:15–3:8;[3] 1 Esd 8:74–90;[4] the Prayer of Azariah,[5] and *Pss. Sol.* 2;

---

1. Samuel E. Balentine, *Prayer in the Hebrew Bible: The Drama of Divine-Human Dialogue* (OBT; Minneapolis: Fortress, 1993), 103–4; Rodney A. Werline, *Penitential Prayer in Second Temple Judaism: The Development of a Religious Institution* (SBLEJL 13; Atlanta: Scholars Press, 1998), 1–2.

2. Balentine, *Prayer in the Hebrew Bible*, 103; Werline, *Penitential Prayer*, 45–64.

3. Claus Westermann, *Praise and Lament in the Psalms* (trans. Keith R. Crim and Richard N. Soulen; Atlanta: John Knox, 1981), 206.

4. Ibid.; 1 Esd. 8:74–90 is a paraphrase of Ezra 9:6–15.

5. Carey A. Moore, "Daniel, Additions to," *ABD* 2:19.

8; 9.[6] Fragments of the same genre are also attested in the Dead Scrolls: 4Q393 (4QCommunal Confession) and 4Q481c (4QPrayer for Mercy).[7]

In the Bible, collective penitential prayers are rarer than community laments and are absent from the Psalter.[8] A large number of the corporate psalms for help contain complaint against God. Psalms of community lament containing motifs of complaint against God protest national defeat (Isa 63:7–64:11; Pss 44; 74; 79; 80; 89; Lam 5) and the conditions of the postexilic period (Pss 9–10; 60 [=108]; 77; 83; 85; 94). Expressions of repentance or confessions of sin are not common in these poems (but cf. Isa 64:4–5; Ps 79:8–9).

This situation changes in the prayers preserved in extrabiblical Second Temple sources. One indication of this fact emerges from a consideration of the prayers that show a similar form to the psalms of communal lament. None of the extrabiblical examples contain direct complaint against God (cf. Add Esth 13:9–17;[9] 14:3–19;[10] Jdt 9:2–14;[11] 3 Macc 2:2–20;[12] 6:2–15;[13] and Pr Azar 3–22[14]).

---

6. Westermann (*Praise and Lament*, 206) identifies *Pss. Sol.* 9 as a genuine prayer of repentance. Werline (*Penitential Prayer*, 185–88) perceives *Pss. Sol.* 1; 2; 8 as written under the influence of penitential theology. Here I include *Pss. Sol.* 2 and 8 as examples of the penitential psalm genre because both explicitly justify God while confessing the sins of Jerusalem.

7. Esther G. Chazon, "Hymns and Prayers in the Dead Sea Scrolls," in *The Dead Sea Scrolls after Fifty Years: A Comprehensive Assessment* (ed. P. W. Flint and J. C. VanderKam; 2 vols; Leiden: Brill, 1999), 1:259. Penitence and confession of sin loomed large in the consciousness of the sectarians of Qumran. 4Q504–506 (4QWords of the Luminaries) is a collection of daily prayers that includes among their elements confessions of Israel's sins; see Werline, *Penitential Prayer*, 147–59. I have not included a discussion of the penitential liturgy in 1QS 1.16–2.18, since this is not a prayer text per se. For a discussion of penitential theology in the *Rule of the Community*, see Werline, *Penitential Prayer*, 135–38.

8. Psalm 106, in which confession of sin is prominent, is not considered part of this genre by Westermann (*Praise and Lament*, 206); cf. also the list of Werline, *Penitential Prayer*, 1; and the remarks of Richard J. Bautch, *Developments in Genre between Post-exilic Penitential Prayers and the Psalms of Communal Lament* (SBLAcBib 7; Atlanta: Society of Biblical Literature, 2003), 160. For a contrary view, see Mark J. Boda, *Praying the Tradition: The Origin and Use of Tradition in Nehemiah 9* (BZAW 277; Berlin: de Gruyter, 1999), 66–68.

9. The form of Add Esth 13:9–17 contains: address (v. 9a), confession of trust/praise (vv. 9b–11), declaration of innocence (vv. 12–14), petitions (vv. 15–17), including enemy-complaint motif (v. 15b).

10. Identified in Westermann, *Praise and Lament*, 202. The form of Add Esth 14:3–19 contains: address (v. 3a); personal petition, including I-complaint and trust motifs (vv. 3b–4); confession of trust/retrospect (v. 5); confession of sin, including justification of divine righteousness (vv. 6–7); enemy-complaint (vv. 8–10); petitions (vv. 11–14); declaration of innocence (vv. 15–18); collective petitions (v. 19a); personal petition (v. 19b).

11. Identified in Westerman, *Praise and Lament*, 204. The form of Jdt 9:2–14 contains: address (v. 2); retrospect (vv. 2b–4a); petition (v. 4b); confession of trust (vv. 5–6); enemy-complaint (v. 7); petitions (vv. 8–10); confession of trust (v. 11); personal petitions (vv. 12–13); petition for the nation (v. 14).

These prayers show connections to penitential prayers by virtue of their justifications of divine righteousness while describing the causes of the plight of the nation and confessions of sin. The influence of penitential theology was not complete, however. In an earlier paper I showed that the books of the Maccabees and various late apocalypses attest to a practice of informal protest prayer that continued to assert itself in expressions of popular piety.[15] It was in the interest of community leaders to suppress such sentiments,[16] but this tradition would continue to find expression in especially dark junctures in Jewish history. Examples include complaints that were uttered during the massacres of the Crusades, at the beginning of the Hasidic movement after the Chmielnitski pogroms, and in post-Holocaust literature.[17]

One may ask why the penitential tradition became dominant despite the fact that the tradition of lament rhetoric was not entirely forgotten. It is typical to explain the transformations of the lament tradition that characterize early postexilic penitential prayers by an appeal to a combination of historical and psychological conditions that impinged on the religion of Israel at that time.[18] But

---

12. Identified in Westermann, *Praise and Lament*, 203–4. The form of 3 Macc 2:2–20 contains: address (v. 2a), petition, including we-complaint motif (v. 2b); confession of trust/retrospect (vv. 3–12); petition, including confession of sin and we-complaint motif (v.13); enemy-complaint, including confession of trust motif (vv. 14–16); and petitions (vv. 17–20).

13. Identified in Westermann, *Praise and Lament*, 203–4. The form of 3 Macc 6:2–15 contains: address (v. 2); petition (v. 3), including we-complaint motif; confession of trust (vv. 4–8); petition (v. 9), including confession of trust and we-complaint motifs; and petitions (vv. 10–15), including enemy-complaint motif (v. 12) and trust motifs (vv. 12–13).

14. Identified in Westermann, *Praise and Lament*, 202. The form of Pr Azar 3–22 contains: address (v. 3); confession of sin (vv. 4–9), including justification of God's righteous actions; we-complaint (v. 10); petitions (vv. 11–13), including motif of historical retrospective; we-complaint (vv. 14–15); petitions (vv. 16–19) including confession of trust motif (v. 18).

15. William S. Morrow, "The Limits of Lament: The Fate of Late Second Temple Community Complaint Prayer in the Light of Rev 6:9–11" (paper presented at the annual meeting of the Canadian Society of Biblical Studies, Halifax NS, 31 May 2003). See, e.g., 1 Macc 2:7–13; 3:50–53; *2 Bar.* 3:1–9; *1 En.* 84:2–6; 2 Esd 3:28–36; 5:28; 6:55–59. The presence of questions about divine providence in apocalyptic literature points to a popular prayerful voice that continued to question divine justice, even if the apocalyptic writers themselves attempted to defuse such criticism.

16. See, e.g., discussions of rabbinic control of the "law court pattern of prayer" in Joseph Heinemann, *Prayer in the Talmud: Forms and Patterns* (SJ 9; Berlin: de Gruyter, 1977), 205–6; David Kraemer, *Responses to Suffering in Classical Rabbinic Literature* (New York: Oxford University Press, 1995), 216–19; Anson Laytner, *Arguing with God: A Jewish Tradition* (Northvale, N.J.: Aronson, 1990), 100–101.

17. Surveyed, e.g., in Laytner, *Arguing with God*; and David G. Roskes, *The Literature of Destruction: Jewish Responses to Catastrophe* (Philadelphia: Jewish Publication Society, 1989).

18. See, e.g., Rainer Albertz, *A History of Israelite Religion in the Old Testament Period* (OTL; 2 vols.; Louisville: Westminster John Knox, 1994), 2:508–11; Bautch, *Developments in Genre*, 172; and Boda, *Praying the Tradition*, 189–95.

the historical conditions that generated prayers such as those in Ezra 9; Neh 9; and Dan 9, and even the form of penitential prayer, did not continue unaltered.[19] Nevertheless, complaint against God did not reassert itself as a typical expression of community distress even in those cases where Second Temple writers continued to use the form of biblical laments. I suggest another factor must be taken into consideration to explain why the theological milieu that favored the emergence of penitential prayer continued to have influence: Israel's entry into the Axial Age.

The argument below highlights the use of the motif of divine righteousness in penitential prayers in contrast to psalms of community lament. This motif is related to a shift in the concept of divine transcendence characteristic of the development of monotheism among the writing prophets. An analogy to the theological dynamics of the book of Job illustrates the process whereby Axial Age thinking suppressed the rhetoric of complaint prayer. Other marks of the engagement of penitential theology with the emergence of the Axial Age will then be noted. Conclusions will be drawn about the implications of this study for a history of penitential prayer in Second Temple Judaism.

Reversal of the Rhetoric of the God-Israel Relationship in Penitential Prayer

The reason for the dominance of the complaint against God in community lament psalms lies in the God-Israel relationship these poems assume. Whether Israel had sinned or not does not appear to have been a principle concern to the writers of these prayers. Rather, these psalms spring out of a primary conviction that Yhwh has an obligation to act in order to protect the God-Israel relationship.[20]

The primacy of the God-Israel relationship in community complaint psalms is revealed in two features. First, God is considered the major perpetrator of Israel's misfortunes. It is Yhwh who has caused the people to lose, sold them to their military opponents, exiled them, and delivered them to unspeakable suffering.[21] It is Yhwh who is also chiefly responsible for their continuing desperate straits by virtue of his inactivity. The second indicator can be found in the petitions of these poems. All but absent are imprecations or cursing prayers against the enemy.[22] The enemies do not act on their own initiative; Yhwh's own decisions are always prior to whatever Israel's opponents are able to do. Consequently, throughout the

---

19. See Bautch, *Developments in Genre*, 159–72.

20. Murray J. Haar, "The God-Israel Relationship in the Community Lament Psalms" (Ph. D. diss., Union Theological Seminary, 1985), 129.

21. Rainer Albertz, *Persönliche Frömmigkeit und Offizielle Religion: Religionsinterner Pluralismus in Israel und Babylon* (Calwer Theologische Monographien Reihe A, Bibelwissenschaft 9; Stuttgart: Calwer, 1978; repr., Atlanta: Society of Biblical Literature, 2005), 38.

22. Ibid., 43.

poems of community complaint, it is Yhwh's actions that are the decisive factor, both in creating the community's distress and also relieving it.

But what motivates the conviction that Yhwh has an obligation to act in the community's favor? An easy answer would be to appeal to a covenantal theology. But the psalms of community complaint do not often invoke covenant terminology (see 44:18; 74:20; 89:4). Much more important is that Yhwh is thought to have authored Israel's history (44:2–9; 60:8–10; 74:2; 77:15–21; 80:9–12; 83:10–13; 89:20–38) and created all of its fundamental institutions, including covenant, kingship, and temple. It is a contradiction in terms that Israel should disappear or that its institutions should be destroyed. By the very virtue of creating them, of calling Israel into being, Yhwh has a responsibility to ensure their continuity.

The presuppositions of the God-Israel relationship are undone in early penitential prayers. In particular, the righteous party in the God-Israel relationship is redefined. According to Richard Bautch, this is apparent in three different ways: the use of the historical résumé; the function of the confession of sin; and the reference value of the binary pair "righteous and wicked." A good illustration is found in Neh 9:5–37. Whereas historical résumé is used in communal laments to remind Yhwh of the God-Israel relationship, its function in the penitential prayers is to motivate the people to confess their infidelity and to recognize their dependency on divine grace. By the same token, the confession of sin becomes a motivating element for petitions for help and deliverance. This is not its function in community laments, where confessions of sin are uncommon. A related reversal is manifested in the use of the binary pair "the righteous" and "the wicked." The tone of the communal laments implies that the people are righteous, while it is Yhwh who is culpably indifferent to the people's plight. Neh 9:33 is a key text in demonstrating how that logic is reversed in penitential prayer. The people penitently assert their wickedness while imputing all justice to God.[23]

Praise of divine justice and the transformative effects of such praise in Second Temple prayers that use the lament form have also been noted by Claus Westermann. In effect, the complaint against God is silenced by the constantly repeated statement that everything that has happened to the community was justified. What had once been the occasion for lament, became an opportunity for praising the righteous God. Therefore, the polarity between lament and praise, so characteristic of biblical psalms, was abolished.[24]

---

23. Bautch, *Developments in Genre*, 109–21.
24. Westermann, *Praise and Lament*, 202–3. Examples cited include Add Esth 14:6–7; Pr Azar 9; and *Pss. Sol.* 2:15–18; 8:7.

The Prophetic Background to Penitential Prayer and the Axial Age

According to the philosopher Karl Jaspers, the Axial Age encompassed 800–200 B.C.E., with a center at approximately 500.[25] Jaspers used the epithet "Axial" because this epoch heralded fundamental and revolutionary changes in human social, religious, and intellectual history. Many civilizations were affected (independently, but in analogous ways), including those of ancient Israel, Greece, Iran, China, and India.

The application of the Axial Age concept to the history of biblical religion has been promoted by the Israeli sociologist S. N. Eisenstadt. Axial Age civilizations perceived a large degree of tension between the transcendental and mundane orders of reality. This tension emerged and was expressed in ways that distinguish these societies from their predecessors. Human societies typically perceive the divine or spiritual realm as somewhat different, usually higher and more powerful, than everyday reality. In pre-Axial civilizations, this higher world was symbolically structured according to principles very similar to the mundane or lower one. In other words, the two worlds were thought to operate by similar principles and accessed by similar means. By contrast, in the Axial Age there developed the perception of a sharp disjunction between the everyday and transcendent worlds. The divine reality was no longer simply human reality writ large. Such a distinction created numerous problems in the construction of social institutions with respect to the cosmic order.[26]

Axial Age social, political, religious, and intellectual processes were closely connected with the emergence of new social elites. Examples include the Jewish prophets, Greek philosophers, the Chinese scholar-class, and Buddhist monks. They created new institutions and practices to manage the perceived tension between the transcendental and mundane orders. These new types of thinkers differed from the elites that had been ritual, magical, and sacred specialists prior to their society's Axial Age revolution.[27] Radical changes in the nature of knowledge partly account for the rise and influence of these new religious specialists. The Axial Age did not simply involve transformations in social structures; it portended significant changes in the conceptual worlds of human beings. In fact, these new elites produced the first true ideologies in that they offered comprehensive views of the world and how people should live in it.[28]

---

25. Karl Jaspers, *Vom Ursprung und Ziel der Geschichte* (Zürich: Artemis, 1949), 19.

26. S. N. Eisenstadt, "The Axial Age Breakthroughs—Their Characteristics and Origins," in *The Origins and Diversity of Axial Age Civilizations* (ed. S. N. Eisenstadt; SUNY Series in Near Eastern Studies; Albany: State University of New York Press, 1986), 1–3.

27. Ibid., 4–6.

28. Peter Machinist, "On Self-Consciousness in Mesopotamia," in Eisenstadt, *Origins and Diversity*, 183.

The emergence of ancient Israel into the Axial Age can be associated with the development of its monotheistic faith into a universal religious claim.[29] This claim was the product of a history of intellectual speculation that had been taking place among Israel's prophetic elite.[30] One has only to compare the more anthropomorphic picture of Yhwh in Isa 6:1–3 (mid eighth century) with that of Ezek 1:22–28 (early sixth century) to realize that a belief in a more transcendent deity, less amenable to the human imagination had been developing for some time. It was the prophets who were responsible for transforming the God of a small independent state into a universal deity. They did so under the pressure of, and partly in reaction to, imperial imagery and claims made by Israel's and Judah's overlords and conquerors: the empires of Assyria, Babylon, and Persia.[31] In this triangular process, the common object of desire of both Israelite and Ancient Near Eastern intellectuals was a deity competent to control history. The politics of empire was an impetus for the emergence of the Axial Age and the need for vision of a sufficiently transcendent order to comprehend this new international reality.[32]

There is a prophetic connection, therefore, both with Israel's entry into the Axial Age and with the articulation of a penitential theology that refuses the logic of lament. This later point has been made by researchers in the early history of penitential prayer. For example, Mark Boda finds such prophetic engagement with a rejection of the theology of complaint prayer in Jer 14–15 and Lam 3;[33] Rodney Werline and Richard Bautch find similar views connected with postexilic prophecy in Isa 63–64; Ezra 9; and Neh 9.[34]

The result of prophetic speculation was a deity more transcendent and more powerful than that envisaged in the older complaint psalm tradition: an imperial deity, king not only of Israel but unmatched emperor of the universe. A key figure here is Second Isaiah. Though there are antecedents, the late exilic prophet called Second Isaiah (Isa 40–55) can be considered the endpoint of the evolution of an

---

29. S. N. Eisenstadt, "The Axial Age Breakthrough in Ancient Israel," in Eisenstadt, *Origins and Diversity*, 128–29.

30. Karen Armstrong (*A History of God: The 4,000-Year Quest of Judaism, Christianity and Islam* [New York: Ballantine, 1993], 41–45) connects the emergence of the Axial Age in ancient Israel with the eighth-century prophets. I would argue, however, that they set in motion a process of intellectual and theological innovation that did not reach its fruition until the articulation of the monotheistic vision of Second Isaiah and the reorganization of Israel's religious institutions in the early postexilic period.

31. Moshe Weinfeld, "The Protest against Imperialism in Ancient Israelite Prophecy," in Eisenstadt, *Origins and Diversity*, 178–81.

32. Marcel Gauchet, *The Disenchantment of the World: A Political History of Religion* (New French Thought; Princeton: Princeton University Press, 1997), 41.

33. Mark J. Boda, "From Complaint to Contrition, Peering through the Liturgical Window of Jer 14,1–15,4," *ZAW* 113 (2001): 186–97; idem, "The Priceless Gain of Penitence: From Communal Lament to Penitential Prayer in the 'Exilic' Liturgy of Israel," *HBT* 25 (2003): 51–75.

34. Werline, *Penitential Prayer*, 45; Bautch, *Developments in Genre*, 161–65.

unambiguous and universal monotheism in Israel.³⁵ For Second Isaiah, Yhwh was not only sovereign over Israel; Yhwh was the only God that existed, and his sway was universal (e.g., Isa 45:15–25). Moreover, Yhwh was immeasurable and incomparable (e.g., Isa 40:12–18).³⁶ Consequently, there emerged a sharp distinction between transcendent reality and the human world. In the process of setting forth a convincing vision of Yhwh's control of both creation and universal history, Second Isaiah articulated a theology of hope for the exile that ruled out the possibility of complaint in favor of the anticipation of divine deliverance.³⁷

Job, the Axial Age, and Penitential Theology

The book of Job has been suggested as a missing link in the developments that lead from communal lament to penitential prayer.³⁸ A fuller treatment of Job and its engagement with Axial Age theology can be found elsewhere.³⁹ Here I can only digest a longer argument. The book of Job shows the influence of a theology that emphasized divine transcendence and righteousness to the exclusion of the rhetoric of lament.

Fundamental to my approach is the acceptance of a scholarly consensus that the book of Job is a postexilic composition (i.e., likely composed sometime in the fifth or fourth century B.C.E.).⁴⁰ It is also important to take seriously scholarly perception that the book of Job registers a spiritual crisis related to that historical context.⁴¹ Most obviously, the destruction of the First Temple by the Babylonians plunged the religion of Israel into much theological turmoil. Restoration of the Second Temple (dedicated in 515 B.C.E.) brought with it numerous problems about the reorganization of religious life.⁴² Chronologically, therefore, the

---

35. Benjamin Uffenheimer, "Myth and Reality in Ancient Israel," in Eisenstadt, *Origins and Diversity*, 168; John J. Scullion, "God in the OT," *ABD* 2:1042–43.

36. Scullion, "God in the OT," 2:1043.

37. William S. Morrow, "Comfort for Jerusalem: The Second Isaiah as Counselor to Refugees," *BTB* 34 (2004): 80–86; and idem, "Post-Traumatic Stress Disorder and Vicarious Atonement in the Second Isaiah," in *Psychology and the Bible: A New Way to Read the Scriptures* (ed. J. H. Ellens and W. Rollins; 4 vols; Westport, Conn.: Greenwood-Praeger, 2004), 1:163–87.

38. See Bautch, *Developments in Genre*, 163–65.

39. William S. Morrow, *Protest against God: The Eclipse of a Biblical Tradition* (Sheffield: Sheffield Phoenix, 2006), 129–46.

40. James L. Crenshaw, "Job, Book of," *ABD* 3:863–64.

41. James L. Crenshaw, *Old Testament Wisdom: An Introduction* (rev. ed.; Louisville: Westminster John Knox, 1998), 103–4; Leo G. Perdue, *Wisdom and Creation: The Theology of Wisdom Literature* (Nashville: Abingdon, 1994), 124. René Girard (*Job, the Victim of his People* [London: Athlone, 1987], 83) refers to the religious dilemma addressed by the book of Job as a "sacrificial crisis."

42. Albertz, *History of Israelite Religion*, 2:458–64.

postexilic era can be located within the emergence of the Axial Age in human intellectual history and associated with the composition of Job.

The book of Job is also engaged with the theology of lament. But there are no grounds for interpreting Job as a symbol of national distress or complaint. In the first place, Job's language fits in most clearly with the language of individual complaint, in particular with psalms emphasizing the innocence of the petitioner (cf. Job 6:28–30; 16:16–17; 23:10–12; 27:2–6 with Pss 17:3–5; 26:2–7).[43] Particularly significant is the use of an oath formula in Job 29–31, in effect, calling on God to curse the poet if his righteousness is not established (cf. Job 31:5–22; Ps 7:4–6). As Erhard Gerstenberger notes, such a procedure would have been considered highly risky unless the guiltlessness of the afflicted party was beyond doubt.[44] A second feature is the description of Job's God as personal creator in Job 10:8–12 (cf. Ps 22:10–11). Appeals to God as personal creator and protector mark the genre of individual complaint as distinct from community prayers.[45] Finally, along with these indicators one must also note the lack of any unambiguous reference to national catastrophe. This absence sets the book of Job apart from other biblical literature that explicitly wrestles with the destruction and exile of Jerusalem and Judah (e.g., Ezekiel, Lamentations, and Isa 40–55).

So how can Job's engagement with the theology of individual lament help to discern a movement toward the theology of corporate penitence? I would argue by analogy. Job registers theological currents related to the conditions of the Axial Age, which inhibit the posture of the petitioner as one with the right to indict God. In making this argument below, it is not my intention to propose *the* way to read this difficult and multivalent book. Nevertheless, I think that awareness of the dynamics of the Axial Age is an important heuristic tool in interpreting Job.

Two modes of rhetoric predominate in the dialogues between Job and his interlocutors (Job 3–27; 29–31): individual lament and the wisdom tradition of disputation speech. Throughout the dialogue both Job and his friends assume that God is primarily responsible for Job's predicament. At stake, is whether Job's suffering is justified or an exercise of divine power that can be challenged. In his speeches, Job continually protests the assumption that his suffering is warranted. The position of Job's erstwhile friends is that God acts justly, treating persons as they deserve.[46] The theological perspective of Job's friends was common in educated circles of the ancient Near East. It is associated with the ideology of wisdom. Wisdom thinking often endorses a doctrine of divine retribution in which there

---

43. John E. Hartley, "From Lament to Oath. A Study of Progression in the Speeches of Job," in *The Book of Job* (ed. Wim A. M. Beuken; Leuven: Leuven University Press, 1994), 90–91.
44. Erhard S. Gerstenberger, *Psalms: Part 1 with an Introduction to Cultic Poetry* (FOTL 14; Grand Rapids: Eerdmans, 1988), 65.
45. Albertz, *Persönliche Frömmigkeit*, 37–38.
46. Carol A. Newsom, "Job," in *The Women's Bible Commentary* (ed. Carol A. Newsom and Sharon H. Ringe; Louisville: Westminster John Knox, 1992), 132.

is a predictable cause and effect relationship between order and chaos, justice and suffering.

By the end of the dialogues, both parties remain entrenched in their theological positions. Job's resolute posture of protest continues undiminished. Eliphaz, Bildad, and Zophar are just as adamant in demanding that Job accept his suffering as punishment for sin. This situation stands in contrast to the social effects of complaint rhetoric in the Psalms. There, the language of complaint and affirmation of innocence were tactics used by ostracized people to win support from a hostile or indifferent community. In other words, protest against undeserved suffering functioned to rehabilitate individuals into their local support group.[47] What has happened to make Job's theologically motivated protest so ineffective? And why does the accompanying assertion of innocence not move Job's former support group to accept him? In the preexilic period, wisdom discourse existed as well as complaint rhetoric in ancient Israel. It is the assertion of wisdom theology to the exclusion of complaint rhetoric by Job's comforters that marks a theological turning point in the history of biblical thought. The intransigent refusal of Job's comforters to entertain the force of his complaint against God and his declarations of innocence points to their engagement with Axial Age influences.

Space prevents a full discussion of the various solutions to the Joban dilemma. I think that the original form of the book of Job substantially encompassed Job 1–27; 29–31; 38–42. In my opinion, the writer of Job 1–27; 29–31; 38–42 did not intend to resolve questions regarding the propriety of protest as a response to suffering in Israel's Axial Age. This version of the book works primarily as a vehicle to confront its readers with the paradox that faces all those who refer their existence to a single and righteous deity: the experience of unjust suffering in a world made by a God supposed to love justice. Traditional complaint rhetoric and wisdom discourse are juxtaposed in a way that defies resolution. Readers are left to infer their own solutions to the dilemma. Carol Newsom has observed that the book of Job not only ruptures the ideological closure of retribution thinking but that its structure actually resists all closure and all resolution of contradiction.[48] I follow that observation here. The Yhwh speeches do not necessarily support the traditional worldviews undergirding either complaint prayer or retribution theology.[49] But they refrain from articulating a vision to take the place of either theological construct.

---

47. Lea Jakobson, "The Individual's Suffering in Psalms and in Mesopotamian Narratives" [Hebrew], *Beth Mikra* 168 (2001): 33, 39–55; Erhard Gerstenberger, *Der bittende Mensch: Bittritual und Klagelied des Einzelnen im Alten Testament* (WMANT 51; Neukirchen-Vluyn: Neukirchener, 1981), 144–46.

48. Carol A. Newsom, "Cultural Politics and the Reading of Job," *BibInt* 1 (1993): 136.

49. William S. Morrow, "Consolation, Rejection, and Repentance in Job 42:6," *JBL* 105 (1986): 223–25.

The ambiguity and lack of clarity of Job 38–42 may well have been the reason why later hands added the Elihu speeches and the poem to divine wisdom in Job 28.[50] Job 28 places an emphasis on the distance between the divine and human realities that is characteristic of Axial Age theology. Nothing in creation knows the way to wisdom, not even the preternatural realms of death and the grave (28:20–22). As for human beings, not only have they not found wisdom, but it is so much beyond their attainment that they are not even able to assess it properly (28:16–19). Such distancing dissolves any analogy between human and divine wisdom. From the point of view of Job 28, it is category confusion to talk of human and divine wisdom as if they were the same thing. A subtle detail in vocabulary helps to convey this impression. It is wisdom with a definite article (i.e., "Wisdom") that God possesses in 28:12, 20. It is a less definite wisdom with no article ("wisdom") that is accessible to humanity (28:28). The content of these two sorts of wisdom is different. In the case of human beings, wisdom is the fear of Yhwh; it is not ultimate knowledge about the nature of creation.[51]

The psalms of individual complaint are filled with pleas to God to see, take notice, pay attention, and hear. But though human beings may search and see the hidden gems of the earth (Job 28:10), Wisdom is beyond their powers of perception (28:13). A sharp distinction is raised between divine and human perspectives. By contrast, argumentative prayer rests on a confidence that God will act as soon as he sees things the way the psalmists do. Ordinary language is sorely stretched in the distance between God and humanity depicted in Job 28.

The Elihu speeches in Job 32–37 appear to compete with the Yhwh speeches of Job 38–41 as an answer to Job's dilemma.[52] Elihu's reasoning essentially represents the positions of the first three friends of Job: God is always righteous and human suffering is connected to wrongdoing. Throughout there are signs of an Axial Age theology that rejects the human analogies on which protest prayer is based.

Elihu begins with a remarkable claim in Job 32:6–9: wisdom is not simply a benefit of age but is a possession of any human being in whom God's spirit dwells. The emergence of new elites who were not defined by the same categories used by their predecessors is characteristic of the Axial Age. In this case, Elihu rejects a traditional equation between age and wisdom and makes a claim for a kind of autonomy from ordinary processes of social validation. The wise person is the

---

50. For the secondary character of Job 28 and 32–37, see Yair Hoffman, *A Blemished Perfection: The Book of Job in Context* (JSOTSup 213; Sheffield: Sheffield Academic Press, 1996), 281–84, 289–93; and Leo. G. Perdue, *Wisdom in Revolt: Metaphorical Theology in the Book of Job* (JSOTSup 112; Sheffield: JSOT Press, 1991), 80–83.

51. Hoffman, *Blemished Perfection*, 278–81.

52. Christopher R. Seitz, "Job: Full Structure, Movement and Interpretation," *Int* 43 (1989): 12–13.

God-inspired person who speaks the truth, a claim that will later be made in Wis 4:7–9.[53]

Contrary to Job's claim that God does not speak, Elihu sets out two ways in which God makes his ways known: through dreams of warning and physical affliction that brings one close to death (33:12–22). The worldview of the psalms of individual complaint would have little problem with these claims. What distinguishes Elihu's analysis from the worldview of individual complaint is that both dreams and sickness are always regarded as means for explaining suffering as a punitive experience.

In addition, Elihu introduces the idea of a mediating angel (following the translation tradition represented by the NRSV) between God and suffering humans as a means of deliverance (33:23–26). Angelic figures as emissaries of God appear elsewhere in scripture (e.g., Num 22:31; Judg 2:1; 13:6; and 2 Sam 24:16). What distinguishes the imagery of Job 33:23–26 is the role of the angelic figure as one who both announces to the petitioner the reason for his illness and acts as intercessor for the suffering person before God.[54] Nowhere in the psalms of individual complaint is it implied that the psalmist does not have direct access to Yhwh. The role of angels in bringing the prayers of the pious before God is characteristic of the highly developed angelology of postexilic Judaism.[55] This is a function of the transcendence of the divine reality that is characteristic of the Axial Age. Unlike the world of the psalms of individual complaint, a mediator is needed in Elihu's religious imagination because the gap between the divine and human realities has grown significantly.

Behind the imagery of Elihu's angelic intermediary, scholars have detected the shadow of a ritual expert who oversaw an individual complaint liturgy. Such a person would have been either a prophetic or priestly figure. His responsibilities included informing the petitioner about the cause of his illness as well as leading in intercessory prayer to God for its deliverance. Alongside ritual actions, the prayer mandated by Elihu in Job 33 required both praise of God and confession of sin. In other words, a form of prayer related to the complaint psalm liturgy was still permitted, but it was purchased at the price of expunging any claim to innocence by the petitioner.[56]

Elihu then turns to Job's charges of divine injustice. God is supremely righteous and chastises those who have become estranged from him and oppressed others (34:21–30). God's transcendence is such that God is neither touched by human sin or human acts of goodness; wickedness and righteousness mainly have to do with our treatment of fellow persons (35:1–8). However, many of

---

53. Perdue, *Wisdom in Revolt*, 248–49.
54. James F. Ross, "Job 33:14–30: The Phenomenology of Lament," *JBL* 94 (1975): 43.
55. Carol A. Newsom, "Angels, Old Testament," *ABD* 1:252.
56. Gerstenberger, *Der bittende Mensch*, 138–39.

the oppressed are not liberated because they themselves rail against God and do not turn to him (35:9–15). In fact, God is great and righteous, rewarding people according to their works. Misfortune is but an instrument in the hands of God to save the guilty (36:5–16). Elihu ends his speech with lengthy praise to this exalted and ever righteous deity. The conclusion is that God is not within our reach. By reason of his power and righteousness, God is to be feared and reverenced. The divine being has no accounts to render to human beings (37:19–24).[57] Obviously, protests or doubts in connection with divine faithfulness or justice cannot be entertained in such a worldview.

Scripture and Holiness in Penitential Theology

The Axial Age theology articulated in the Elihu speeches undermine Job's right to complain against God. Similarly, in biblical and postbiblical penitential prayers, divine sovereignty and righteousness are beyond question: Yhwh is "the great and awesome God" (Dan 9:4; Neh 1:5; 9:32), who is in the right to afflict his people (Dan 9:7, 14; Ezra 9:15; Neh 9:33).[58] The same theology can be discerned in Bar 1:15; Pr Azar 4–9; and *Pss. Sol.* 2:15–16; 9:2.

The perception of divine righteousness is reinforced in the biblical penitential prayers by two shifts in perspective between the protests of national defeat and biblical penitential prayers that are diagnostic of Axial Age thinking. These occur in the historical retrospectives and confessions of sin. They are connected through their emphasis on scripture. The transformation of ancient Judaism into a scriptural religion reflects the dynamics of the Axial Age.[59]

Historical retrospectives occur in a number of community laments (e.g., Isa 63:7–14; Pss 44:2–4; 60:8–10; 74:2; 80:9–12; 83:10–13; 89:20–38). They also occur in Dan 9:7–15; Ezra 9:7–13; and Neh 1:7–9; 9:6–31. A comparison of the two groups shows that retrospects in the psalms emphasize the experience of exodus, conquest of the land of promise, and the gift of the Davidic dynasty. There is no mention of the bestowal of divine commandments on the nation as part of the descriptions of salvation history. The closest to this theme is the retrospect in Ps 89:20–38, which mentions the precepts and laws given to the Davidic dynasty (v. 31). In contrast, the historical retrospects of biblical penitential prayers all mention the gift of commandments and divine instruction to the nation in its early history (Dan 9:10; Ezra 9:10–11; Neh 1:7; 9:14).

---

57. Édouard Dhorme, *A Commentary on the Book of Job* (London: Nelson, 1967), lvii.

58. Balentine, *Prayer in the Hebrew Bible*, 104; Patrick D. Miller, *They Cried to the Lord: The Form and Theology of Biblical Prayer* (Minneapolis: Fortress, 1994), 257–58.

59. Michael E. Stone, "Eschatology, Remythologization, and Cosmic Aporia," in Eisenstadt, *Origins and Diversity*, 244.

The emphasis on disobedience to divine commandments also stands in contrast to confessions of sin that belong to the late preexilic or exilic period. Witnesses to community confessions from these eras can be obtained from material in the Deuteronomistic History and prophetic citations: Judg 10:10, 15;[60] Isa 59:9–15a;[61] Jer 3:22b–25;[62] 14:7–9, 19–22.[63] Such texts confess idolatry and rebellion against Yhwh, but they fail to make mention of a specific body of commandments. The confessions of sin in the postexilic penitential prayers, however, are closely connected with their historical retrospectives: the nation possessed a body of scriptural instruction from which it deviated.[64] This perspective sets the confessions of sin in Dan 9; Ezra 9; Neh 1; 9 apart from earlier expressions of communal contrition. Evidently, some kind of theological development has taken place by time the postexilic prayers of communal repentance were composed.

The scriptural context of the confessions of sin in penitential prayers and their associated historical retrospectives shows a new form of self-awareness in the community. The theology of penitential prayers suggest that a self-evident sense of belonging to the community has been lost; in its place one finds indications of a sense of belonging that is conscious and reflected.[65] Such deliberate and self-critical processes are marks of Axial Age civilizations.[66]

---

60. This text is recognized as an interpretative passage bearing the perspective of the Deuteronomistic History, see Norman K. Gottwald, *The Hebrew Bible: A Socio-Literary Introduction* (Philadelphia: Fortress, 1985), 242.

61. The dimensions of this text are disputed. Anton Schoors (*I Am God Your Savior: A Form-Critical Study of the Main Genres in Is. Xl–LV* [VTSup 24; Leiden: Brill, 1973], 37) identifies vv. 15b–20 as an oracular response to a community lament in vv. 9–15a. Claus Westermann (*Isaiah 40–66* [OTL; Philadelphia: Westminster, 1969], 345–50) regards several portions of Isa 59 as belonging to a lament that underwent expansion. In his view, the original text included vv. 1, 9–11, and 15b–20, which portrays the longed-for divine epiphany. But there is no petition to link vv. 15b–20 to the preceding complaint; therefore, vv. 15b–20 are best considered as the prophet's answer to the people's complaint.

62. The text cites a communal lament that is followed by an oracular response in Jer 4; see Schoors, *I Am God Your Savior*, 37.

63. Some commentators also read Jer 14:2–6 as a citation of complaint prayer, but according to William L. Holladay (*Jeremiah* [Hermeneia; 2 vols.; Philadelphia: Fortress, 1986, 1989], 1:424) vv. 2–6 and vv. 7–9 are best read as two different poems. Jer 14:2–6 can be read as a description of the disastrous drought that occasions the lament rather than as complaint proper; see Robert P. Carroll, *Jeremiah* (OTL; London: SCM, 1986), 309. Therefore, identification of lament will be limited to vv. 7–9 and 19–22; cf. Moshe Greenberg, *Biblical Prose Prayer as a Window to the Popular Religion of Ancient Israel* (Taubman Lectures in Jewish Studies, Sixth Series; Berkeley and Los Angeles: University of California, 1983), 60.

64. Werline, *Penitential Prayer*, 64.

65. Balentine, *Prayer in the Hebrew Bible*, 116–17.

66. Yehuda Elkana, "The Emergence of Second-Order Thinking in Classical Greece," in *The Origins and Diversity of Axial Age Civilizations* (ed. S. N. Eisenstadt; SUNY Series in Near Eastern Studies; Albany: State University of New York, 1986), 63–64.

The connection between penitential theology and scripture also has connections with holiness thinking. Although Israel Knohl's dating of the Priestly movement is controversial, his characterization of P's reforms of Israel's cultic space remains valid, "[T]he cultic relation between humans and the dimension of God represented by the name Yahweh is detached from all aspects of mutual dependence. Instead, two principles are at the heart of the ideal cultic system: holiness and commandment."[67] Publication of the Torah in a written form was part of an agenda to combine holiness and morality in a way that would encompass the people as a whole. This program of extending the limits of the sacred to include national morality can be viewed as an Axial Age transformation.[68]

The principles of holiness and commandment are both assumed in postexilic penitential prayer. Emphasis on commandment in the penitential prayers is obvious from their historical retrospectives and confessions of sin. Connections with holiness thinking have been disputed.[69] However, references to holy categories are attested in penitential prayers, as in "holy mountain" (Dan 9:16), "holy place" (Ezra 9:8), "holy Sabbath" (Neh 9:14), "Israel your holy one" (Pr Azar 12), and multiple occurrences in 4Q504.[70] Terminology related to holiness thinking includes allusions to uncleanness and pollution (1 Esd 8:87; *Pss. Sol.* 2:3, 13; 8:11–12, 22) as well as to cleansing and purification (*Ps. Sol.* 9:6; 4Q393 frg. 3:5).

The equation of national morality with holiness reinforced perceptions that Israel's (mis)fortunes were tied to its covenant (in)fidelity. The study of Neh 9:5–37 by Mark Boda has underscored the engagement of Priestly as well as Deuteronomistic theology in the generation of the prayers of community repentance.[71] Holiness thinking is also visible in the penitential prayer of Ezra 9, which emphasizes the uncleanness and impurity of the people in its allusion to the Deuteronomic instructions. In fact, the vocabulary of "abomination" is not used by Deuteronomy in connection with mixed marriages. Its appearance in Ezra 9:11 establishes an exegetical bridge between the marriage instructions in Deut 7:1–3; 23:3–7; and Lev 18, an instruction on impurity and defilement. According

---

67. Israel Knohl, *The Sanctuary of Silence: The Priestly Torah and the Holiness School* (Minneapolis: Fortress, 1995), 149. Knohl dates writings in the P-style to both the preexilic period and postexilic era (201). Here I assume the dominance of P in the postexilic era, following the consensus of critical scholarship.

68. Israel Knohl, "Axial Transformations within Ancient Israelite Priesthood," in *Axial Civilizations and World History* (ed. Johann P. Árnason, S. N. Eisenstadt, and Björn Wittrock; Jerusalem Studies in Religion and Culture 4; Leiden: Brill, 2005), 213–15, 221.

69. Werline (*Penitential Prayer*, 193–94) de-emphasizes the influence of Priestly thought on the formation of penitential prayer. For the opposite point of view, see Boda, *Praying the Tradition*, 196–97.

70. Conceded by Werline (*Penitential Prayer*, 193), who acknowledges Levitical vocabulary in Ezra 9 and allusions to the Day of Atonement in 4Q504.

71. Boda, *Praying the Tradition*, 186–87.

to Lev 18:26–30, the peoples cut off from the land were abominators. This link authorizes the exclusion of those who persist in the practice of mixed marriages lamented by Ezra 9.[72]

Holiness thinking, therefore, reinforces the kind of theological reasoning that analyzes the distress of the people as due to their willful negligence of scriptural commands. The actions of God in bringing disaster upon his people are not arbitrary according to this construction, but a result of "evil deeds and … great guilt" (Ezra 9:13). That Israel continues to survive at all is an expression of divine benevolence (v. 15). A theology that emphasizes divine transcendence and holiness while affirming the presence of a body of divine instructions accessible and known to the community undermines the perception that experiences of divine absence or affliction are exercises in arbitrary power. The only conclusion that the community can draw from such a theology is that it has itself to blame for its misfortunes on its failures to obey the divine commandments; its deity remains in the right even when the nation fails to prosper. In such circumstances, protest gives way to penitence.

Summary and Conclusions

The problem that I raised at the beginning of this article concerned the continued dominance of the penitential posture in Second Temple prayer. While historical or psychological conditions may have favored early articulations of penitential prayer, neither the historical circumstances nor the mood of the various communities that belonged to Second Temple Judaisms remained constant. What is the "missing link" that connects the emergence of the penitential prayer with the suppression of lament in the community supplications of Second Temple Judaism?

To date, accounts of the emergence of penitential prayer in postexilic Judaism have focused on innerbiblical developments. Influences on the development of penitential prayer that have been previously identified include Deuteronomistic and Priestly theologies and rhetorical traditions found in the prophetic texts. My contribution is not intended to contradict this work but to suggest how it may be supplemented. Underlying these particular theological developments, I suggest, a more global theological shift was also at work, one for which the success of penitential theology in Second Temple Judaism is symptomatic. Israel's entry into the Axial Age was predicated on the perception of a deity much more transcendent to the vicissitudes of human history than earlier theologies envisaged. This development had a profound effect on the religious imagination of ancient Judaism.

Axial Age categories are the missing link attested by the book of Job in terms of the emergence of penitential prayer and the suppression of the theology of lament. The same factors were also at work in the prophetic influences and

---

72. Bautch, *Developments in Genre*, 88–89.

scriptural consciousness implicit in the generation of biblical penitential prayers. By the same token, a significant reason for the continuing success of the penitential posture in Second Temple communal prayers was due to the persistence of Axial Age theological categories. Axial Age theology inhibited the practice of complaint, promoted the emergence of penitential prayer, and ensured its continuing dominance throughout the Second Temple era and beyond.

WHEN NONE REPENTS, EARTH LAMENTS: THE CHORUS OF LAMENT IN JEREMIAH AND JOEL

Katherine M. Hayes

INTRODUCTION

In his *Old Testament Theology* Gerhard von Rad observes the "radical differences in literary form between the prophetic witness of the book of Jeremiah and that of earlier prophets."[1] He speaks of the breaking up of the classic forms of accusation and announcement of judgment and the insinuation of new forms of first-person speech for both God and prophet as well as the indirect presentation of Israel's deviance through divine lament. He notes the pervasive tone of lament and, in sum, the lyric, epic, and dramatic qualities of this prophetic book.[2] Studies of Jer 11–20 in particular have stressed the "dialogic" and dramatic character of this section of the book by relating the prophetic confessions to the divine speeches with which they are interspersed.[3] A. R. Diamond, for example, conceives of Jer 11–20 as a "prophetic drama" that "relies primarily upon dialogue in order to create a sense of narrative development" and that "portrays Jeremiah's prophetic mission as a dialogue in which prophet, Yahweh, and nation are participants."[4] Other studies find dramatic interaction in Jeremiah more broadly. Mark Biddle, for example, identifies dramatic personae and interactions throughout Jer 7–20

---

1. Gerhard von Rad, *Old Testament Theology* (trans. D. M. G. Stalker; 2 vols.; New York: Harper & Row, 1965), 2:193.
2. Ibid., 193–95. Most of the passages von Rad cites in his illustration of these tendencies are found within Jer 1–20.
3. See, e.g., Kathleen M. O'Connor, *The Confessions of Jeremiah: Their Interpretation and Role in Chapters 1–25* (SBLDS 94; Atlanta: Scholars Press, 1984); A. R. Diamond, *The Confessions of Jeremiah in Context: Scenes of Prophetic Drama* (JSOTSup 45; Sheffield: Sheffield Academic Press, 1987); Mark S. Smith, *The Laments of Jeremiah and Their Contexts* (SBLMS 42; Atlanta: Scholars Press, 1990), esp. 50–53, 61–64.
4. *Confessions of Jeremiah*, 181–82.

in his book *Polyphony and Symphony in Prophetic Literature: Rereading Jeremiah 7–20.*[5]

This essay focuses on the juxtaposition of prophetic and divine lament in Jer 12:1–13 within the wider context of interaction between different voices in Jer 1–12.[6] In this wider context the break up of prophetic speech into diverse voices creates a type of prophetic drama in which different responses to an imminent reversal of circumstances are enacted. The dynamic between voices pulls on the attention of the witnessing audience and elicits their response,[7] and this dynamic can be viewed in light of Aristotle's remarks in his *Poetics* on the mechanisms of Greek tragedy. Singling out the role of both the reversal of expectations (*peripeteia*) and the movement from ignorance to recognition (*anagnōrisis*) in complex tragic plots, Aristotle defines tragedy as the imitation (*mimēsis*) of an action of serious magnitude so as to move its audience through pity and fear to a catharsis, or purification, of such emotions.[8] Since many discussions of *catharsis* allow for its cognitive as well as emotional dimensions,[9] this concept may help elucidate the relation between lament and penitential prayer as responses to catastrophic events.[10] A relationship between lament and penitence is evident in the call to lament and repent in Joel 1–2.

---

5. Mark Biddle, *Polyphony and Symphony in Prophetic Literature: Rereading Jeremiah 7–20* (SOTI 2; Macon, Ga.: Mercer University Press, 1996). On the dramatic character of Jer 14:1–15:9, see Willem A. M. Beuken and Harm W. M. van Grol, "Jeremiah 14,1–15,9: A Situation of Distress and Its Hermeneutics, Unity and Diversity of Form–Dramatic Development," in *Le livre de Jérémie: Le Prophète et son milieu, les oracles et leur transmission* (ed. Pierre Bogaert; BETL 54; Leuven: Peeters, 1981), 297–342. On the use of dialogue in Jeremiah, see John T. Willis, "Dialogue between Prophet and Audience as a Rhetorical Device in the Book of Jeremiah," *JSOT* 33 (1985): 63–82; cf. Thomas W. Overholt, "Jeremiah 2 and the Problem of 'Audience Reaction,'" *CBQ* 41 (1979): 262–73; and Walter A. Brueggemann, "Jeremiah's Use of Rhetorical Questions," *JBL* 92 (1973): 358–76.

6. I focus on Jer 1–12 here rather than, e.g., on the larger unit Jer 1–20, due to the space constraints of this essay.

7. By "witnessing audience" I mean the audience of the book.

8. Aristotle, *Poetics*, 1449b (ch. 6) and 1452a (ch. 9).

9. See, e.g., Charles Segal, "Catharsis, Audience, and Closure in Greek Tragedy," in *Tragedy and the Tragic: Greek Theatre and Beyond* (ed. M. S. Silk; Oxford: Clarendon, 1996), 149–72; P. E. Easterling, "Weeping, Witnessing, and the Tragic Audience: Response to Segal," in Silk, *Tragedy and the Tragic*, 173–81; Elizabeth S. Belfiore, *Tragic Pleasures: Aristotle on Plot and Emotion* (Princeton: Princeton University Press, 1992), 255–360; Andrew Brown, *A New Companion to Greek Tragedy* (Totowa, N.J.: Barnes & Noble, 1983), 54–56.

10. In reading Jeremiah with Aristotle's *Poetics* in mind, I do not intend to match point by point biblical prophetic texts with Aristotle's prescriptions for tragic drama. As many classical scholars observe, Aristotle's comments do not even apply to the whole range of Greek tragedy, but rather represent his concept of the ideal tragic plot (see, e.g., Gerald F. Else, *Introduction to Aristotle: Poetics* [trans. Gerald F. Else; Ann Arbor: University of Michigan Press, 1970], 7–8; Brian Vickers, *Towards Greek Tragedy* [London: Longman, 1973], 62–63; Brown, *New Com-*

In what follows I will delineate major voices in the first twelve chapters of Jeremiah and draw attention to the dynamic of lament in these chapters.[11] I will then examine the dramatic configuration of the interrelated poems Jer 12:1–6 and 12:7–13, in which prophetic and divine distress are contrasted with the indifference of the people. Common to both poems is a reference to the mourning earth, which, I will suggest, assumes a parallel role to that of the tragic chorus, guiding the response of the text's audience. This motif of the mourning earth recurs in the call to lament in Joel 1, which envisions a universal response of lament and which precedes the summons to lament and repent in Joel 2, thereby anticipating a twofold movement from insensibility to lament to penitence. I will conclude by considering the implications of the focus on lament in these texts for the question of the development of penitential prayer in the postexilic period.

Major Voices in Jeremiah 1–12

Although the interweaving of divine, prophetic, and communal speech in Jeremiah is widely noted, the difficulty of identifying the speakers of particular speeches is also acknowledged,[12] and this is evident in the conflicting analyses

---

panion, 44–45). I simply find that Aristotle's discussion of elements of the representation of tragic events in Greek drama can help elucidate the literary elements of other tragic genres and contexts. M. H. Abrams (*A Glossary of Literary Terms* [6th ed.; Fort Worth, Tex.: Harcourt Brace College, 1993], 212) warns that attempts to extend Aristotle's analyses to later tragic forms have tended to blur his categories and ignore significant diversities in literary expression. Yet Abrams concedes, "when flexibly managed, however, Aristotle's descriptions apply in some part to many tragic plots, and his analytic concepts serve as a suggestive starting point for identifying the differentiae of various non-Aristotelian modes of tragic construction." See also Vickers, *Towards Greek Tragedy*, 3–5, 63–64 and M. S. Silk, "Tragic Language: The Greek Tragedians and Shakespeare," in Silk *Tragedy and the Tragic*, 458–96.

11. In this endeavor I will read the text for the most part synchronically as a deliberate, albeit redactional, composition intended to move a hearing or reading audience distinct from the prophetic audience portrayed in the text itself. I presume a postexilic redaction that integrates preexilic material but in a way that does not reflect chronological sequencing and that speaks most directly to a postexilic audience. For recent articulations of this approach to reading Jeremiah, see, e.g., Biddle, *Polyphony and Symphony*, 76, 82, 125–27; and Christopher R. Seitz, "The Place of the Reader in Jeremiah," in *Reading the Book of Jeremiah: A Search for Coherence* (ed. Martin Kessler; Winona Lake, Ind.: Eisenbrauns, 2004), 67–75. J. Gordon McConville (*Judgment and Promise: An Interpretation of the Book of Jeremiah* [Winona Lake, Ind.: Eisenbrauns, 1993], 23–26, 178–81), who places the composition and original audience of the book of Jeremiah in the exilic period and within the lifetime of the prophet, also emphasizes the redactional unity of the book in the sense that all of its parts reflect knowledge of the exile experienced in 587 B.C.E.

12. Willis, "Dialogue between Prophet and Audience," 68; Biddle, *Polyphony and Symphony*, 22, 80–81; O'Connor, *Confessions of Jeremiah*, 140 n. 77; Beuken and van Grol, "Jeremiah 14,1–15,9," 313; Terence Fretheim, "The Earth Story in Jeremiah 12," in *The Earth Bible 1: Read-*

in commentaries.¹³ The divine and prophetic voices, for example, seem often to merge, and the distinction between the prophet delivering the first-person speech of Yhwh and obeying the divine mandate to prophesy by speaking himself in the first person appears fluid.¹⁴ Sometimes, too, the people's voice and that of the prophet seem to blend, especially in passages where the first-person plural is used.¹⁵ Overall Jer 1–12 conveys a convergence of voices raised in lament, alarm, and regret in a way that is not always easy or possible to sort out. The identity of voices in particular speeches is thus open to reinterpretation and, as Naama Zahavi-Ely has recently suggested, often deliberately ambiguous, so as to blend human (communal and prophetic) and divine responses to the tragic collapse of Israel as a nation.¹⁶

One of the first indications of the breakdown of straightforward prophetic speech into different dramatic personae in Jeremiah is the posing of rhetorical questions by Yhwh to Israel in Jer 2:4–37.¹⁷ Such questions evoke a conversation partner and beg a response, if only rhetorically. This impression is heightened as Yhwh articulates the response the people and their leaders have *failed* to make, for example, in 2:6: "They did not say, 'Where is the Lord,/who brought us up from the land of Egypt?'"¹⁸

As the divine questioning continues, Yhwh cites and argues with the actual responses of the people: "How can you say, 'I am not defiled,/I have not gone after the Ba'als'?" (2:23).¹⁹ The presentation of the content of prophetic preaching in the book of Jeremiah thus opens with a divine speech that, though it is a mono-

---

ings from the Perspective of Earth (ed. Norman C. Habel; Sheffield: Sheffield Academic Press, 2000), 98; William L. Holladay, *Jeremiah 1* (Hermeneia; Philadelphia: Fortress, 1986), 289.

13. See, e.g., differences in identification of the speaker in Jer 4:19–22. Biddle (*Polyphony and Symphony*, 20–21) identifies the speaker as Lady Zion; J. J. M. Roberts ("The Motif of the Weeping God in Jeremiah and Its Background in the Lament Tradition of the Ancient Near East," in idem, *The Bible and the Ancient Near East: Collected Essays* [Winona Lake, Ind.: Eisenbrauns, 2002], 139–40) as Yhwh; and Holladay (*Jeremiah 1*, 160–63) as Jeremiah. See also the discussion in Biddle (*Polyphony and Symphony*, 28–32) of differing analyses of the speakers in Jer 8:18–9:2 and 9:9.

14. See, e.g., Jer 4:16–17; 9:16–18. So von Rad, *Old Testament Theology* 2:193. See also the comments by Terence Fretheim, cited by Roberts, "Motif of the Weeping God," 135 n. 4; and Timothy Polk, *The Prophetic Persona: Jeremiah and the Language of the Self* (JSOTSup 32; Sheffield: JSOT Press, 1984), 96–97.

15. See, e.g., Jer 4:5, 8; 6:24–26.

16. Naama Zahavi-Ely, "Multiple Speaking Voices in the Book of Jeremiah: A Survey of a Poetic Convention and Its Effects" (paper delivered at the of the Society of Biblical Literature Annual Meeting, Philadelphia, November 2005).

17. See 2:4, 11, 14, 17, 18, 21, 23, 28, 29, 31–32. On the use of rhetorical questions in Jeremiah as a literary technique, see Brueggemann, "Rhetorical Questions," 358–74.

18. See also 2:8.

19. See also 2:25, 27, 35.

logue, gives the impression of being a spirited exchange in which Israel is evoked as a collective character.[20]

In several places in Jer 1–12 Yhwh appears to be self-questioning: "Shall I not punish them for these things, says Yhwh,/and shall I not avenge myself against a nation like this?" (Jer 5:9, 29; 9:8).[21] The effect here is twofold. First, imparting the inner deliberations of Yhwh makes the deity a character in the round, with whom sympathetic identification is possible. Second, the questions imply a listening audience distinct from the people about whom Yhwh is deliberating and invite a response from that audience.[22] The divine voice becomes even more personal if it is recognized in various expressions of lament in Jer 1–12.[23] These, too, can be heard as directed toward a witnessing audience, rather than to the people over whom God is lamenting.[24]

The people's voice, with which the book's audience most readily identifies, is heard frequently through allusions to it in divine/prophetic speeches. In 4:8 the divine command puts words in the people's mouth as they are directed to put on sackcloth, lament and wail: "The fierce anger of the Lord/has not turned away from us."[25]

Elsewhere the voice of the people seems to interrupt divine or prophetic speech, often without introduction, strengthening the impression of a prophetic drama. The cry of alarm in 4:13, which follows an announcement of judgment on the people in the form of a windstorm in 4:11–12, can be heard as the voice of the people or, more precisely, as that voice projected into the near future, when catastrophe is upon them:

Look, he comes up like clouds,
    his chariots like the storm,
His horses are swifter than eagles,
    woe to us, for we are ruined![26]

---

20. The speech is addressed in 2:4 to the "house of Jacob" and "all the families of the house of Israel"; the naming of priests, shepherds, and prophets in 2:8 and of kings, princes, priests, and prophets in 2:26 spell out the leadership of this collectivity.

21. For another example, see Jer 8:4–5.

22. Easterling ("Weeping," 177–78) notes that in Greek tragedy similar questions posed by a character are directed not simply to other characters but to the audience in the theater, guiding their response to the drama.

23. See Roberts, "Motif of the Weeping God," 132–42; Mark S. Smith, "Jeremiah IX, 9—A Divine Lament," *VT* 37 (1987): 97–99; Biddle, *Polyphony and Symphony*, 28–34; see 34–40 for Biddle's identification of divine lament in Jer 13:15–17; 14:17–18; and 15:5–9.

24. For a discussion of the primary audience of the discourses in Jeremiah as the "book's readership" see Biddle, *Polyphony and Symphony*, 47–49, 113–28, esp. 121–22.

25. Cf. Jer 4:8; 8:19b; 9:20.

26. See also Jer 6:24; 8:14–15, 20a; 9:18.

The personification of daughter Zion in these chapters adds another element to the collective characterization of the people, as in 4:31: "Woe is me! I am fainting before killers!"[27]

The prophetic voice is clearly evident in the first-person laments, or confessions, in 11:18–20 and 12:1–4. But this voice also breaks out in the first person in 6:10, in a speech that begins with self-questioning: "To whom shall I speak and give witness/that they may hear?" Again, the question reaches out from the speaker to the hearing audience. Elsewhere, divine speech singles out the prophet as a distinct persona, as in 5:14:

> Thus says the LORD,
>   the God of hosts,
> "Because they have spoken this word
>   I am now making my words in your mouth like a fire."[28]

Further, the ambiguity of voices in various laments over the fate of Jerusalem allows the book's audience to hear and respond to the prophetic as well as the divine and communal voice in personal expressions of grief.[29]

This cursory depiction of some of the voices given expression in Jer 1–12 is meant to convey a sense of the dramatic enactment of the prophetic message that precedes the exchange between the prophet and Yhwh in Jer 12:1–13.[30] That these different voices are intended to be heard as interacting, and not simply juxtaposed, is evident in the instances where verbal exchanges are apparent. In the sequence in Jer 6:22–30, for example, Yhwh announces the coming of the enemy from the north (6:22–23), the people (or the prophet and the people) respond in fear and anguish (6:24–25), the prophet directs the people to lament (6:26), Yhwh affirms the prophetic mission (6:27), and Yhwh (or Yhwh and the prophet) announces its outcome (6:28–30). Although allowance needs to be made for interpretive differences in the delineation of voices, the interweaving of two or three dramatic voices is apparent here and in other passages as well.[31]

---

27. Cf. 10:19–20, as well (perhaps) as 4:19–21 (on this identification, see Biddle, *Polyphony and Symphony*, 20–21). Zahavi-Ely ("Multiple Speaking Voices") suggests that the exclamation in 4:31 can also be heard as coming from the prophet or even from Yhwh.

28. See also Jer 6:27, 7:16; 11:14.

29. See, e.g., 8:18–9:1; 9:17–20.

30. Note also the unidentified cries of alarm in Jer 4:15–16; 10:22 and the voice of the enemy in 6:4a, 5.

31. See, e.g., Jer 4:9–10, 19–22; 5:1–5; 6:4–5, 10–12; 8:14–17; 10:17–25.

The Dynamic of Lament

Biddle draws attention to the polyphonic quality of Jer 7–20, in which diverse speakers embody different, even conflicting, perspectives, representing the relationship between God and God's people as defying "resolution and systemization."[32] Yet certain thematic threads draw these voices together at different points, creating dramatic patterns. A predominant thread in Jer 1–12 is that of lament. The people are summoned to lament (4:8; 6:26; 7:29; 9:17, 19) and, either as a collective or as personified Zion, raise their voices in lament (4:13; 4:19–21, 31; 6:4b, 24–25; 8:14–15, 19–20; 9:18, 20; 10:19–20). In places, prophetic and divine laments seem to merge or converge (8:18–9:2; 9:9–10; 12:1–13). Lament takes different forms among these different voices, however.

Linked to the people's expressions of woe and lament is their failure to value and turn to the God they have forsaken (2:13, 19, 27, 32; 3:21; 5:7–8, 23–24; 6:10, 16–17; 8:5–6). This failure brings them into the crossfire of God's judgment in a sense unwittingly, since they do not recognize their wrongdoing (2:23, 34–35; 4:22; 6:15; 8:8, 11–12) or its dangerous ramifications. Even when struck by the Lord, they are unfazed and refuse to return:

> You have struck them, but they show no distress (ולא־חלו)
>   you have destroyed them but they refuse to take instruction
> They have made their faces harder than rock,
>   they have refused to return (לשוב). (5:3)[33]

Rather, in 5:12 they remain confident:

> They have lied about the Lord
>   and said, "Not he—
> Evil will not come upon us
>   neither sword nor famine we will see."

They are thus destined to walk blindly toward full catastrophe in the form of conquest by a nation from far away, whose language they do not know (5:15–17).

The lamentation foretold for the people and for Zion, then, represents the cry of those mourning a bitter reversal that they did not look for, in which they may recognize God's anger (4:8) but which they do not fully understand.[34] The people's apparent admission of fault in Jer 8:14–15 and 10:23–25 does not sig-

---

32. Biddle, *Polyphony and Symphony*, 40, 49, 85–86.
33. See also 3:3.
34. So Biddle (*Polyphony and Symphony*, 41–42) on the voices of the people and the city in the nonoracular lament materials in Jer 7–20.

nificantly alter their expectations. They confess in 8:14 that God has "stilled us" because "we have sinned" (חטאנו), but 8:15 shows confusion: "hoping for peace, but there is no good,/for a time of healing, yet terror is there."[35] Personified Zion even presumes to critique divine discipline in 10:24:"Discipline me, Lord, only in just measure,/not in your anger, lest you reduce me to nothing."[36]

The divine/prophetic laments, in contrast, reflect a deep anguish fully cognizant of what has led to the current predicament of the people and of the gravity of their reversal.[37] This is apparent in the linked laments in Jer 12:1–13.

JEREMIAH 12:1–13

The breakdown of voices in Jer 12:1–13 assumed here identifies 12:7–13 as a divine lament answering the prophetic lament in 12:1–6. Jeremiah 12:7–13 could, perhaps, also be heard as the prophet's response to his own lament, or as carrying that undertone.[38] In what follows I trace one dramatic scenario, acknowledging the undertones that accompany it and that create other interactions, making the whole complex and rich.

The prophetic and divine speeches placed side by side in these verses are often referred to as laments, or as lament-like.[39] Whatever their precise genre, the two speeches are interrelated, illustrating the general mode of dramatic interac-

---

35. Cf. 2:26–27, which expose the superficiality of the people's appeal to YHWH in time of trouble. William McKane (*Jeremiah* [vol. 1; Edinburgh: T&T Clark, 1986], 189–92) and Jack R. Lundbom (*Jeremiah 1–20* [AB 21A; New York: Doubleday, 1999], 524–27) take Jeremiah, in his role as "representative of the people," as the speaker of 8:14–15. Holladay (*Jeremiah 1*, 289) attributes 8:14 to the voice of the people in Jeremiah's imagination and 8:15 to Jeremiah.

36. For a similarly skeptical view of this prayer, see Holladay, *Jeremiah 1*, 339, 343–44. The penitential response of the people in 3:22b–24 to YHWH's plea to return (שובו) in 3:22a appears as the projection of an ideal future confession. It does not recur in the subsequent portrayals of judgment on an unexpectant people in Jer 4:5–6:30. So also Biddle, *Polyphony and Symphony*, 42; cf. Willis, "Dialogue between Prophet and Audience," 66–67. McConville (*Judgment and Promise*, 35, 39) points out that YHWH's offer to "heal" the turning away (משובתיכם) of the people in Jer 3:22a suggests that they are incapable of repentance.

37. See Biddle (*Polyphony and Symphony*, 42–44) on the divine response.

38. So Naama Zahavi-Ely, "Multiple Speaking Voices." I hear the divine voice as dominant because the first-person possessive forms ("my house," "my possession," "my own beloved," "my vineyard," "my field") evoke YHWH's claim over the people and land of Israel.

39. On Jer 12:1–6 as a lament or lament-related, see, Diamond, *Confessions of Jeremiah*, 37–39; Smith, *Laments of Jeremiah*, 6–11; Holladay, *Jeremiah 1*, 368–69. Walter Baumgartner (*Jeremiah's Poems of Lament* [Sheffield: Almond, 1987], 62–71) considers it, along with several other poems, lament-like more in content than in form. He notes that the use of מדוע ("why") is reminiscent of psalm laments, although למה is exclusively used for "why" in the psalms. The phrase עד מתי, "how long" (12:4), is also found in psalms of lament and related psalms (see, e.g., Pss 6:4; 74:10; 80:5; 82:2; 90:13; 94:3). On the lament-like tone of Jer 12:7–13, which also includes elements of judgment and lacks the phraseology characteristic of psalm laments, see

tion in Jer 1–12[40] and a typical convergence of prophetic and divine voices. The poems share language, images, motifs, and a focus on definitive judgment against the people of Israel/Judah.

The sequence of the poems creates a dialogue. The prophetic lament in 12:1–4 raises questions that the divine response in 12:5–6 answers only obscurely. A more explicit answer is provided by the divine speech in 12:7–13. In the resultant dialogue—divine lament answering prophetic lament—the finality of judgment against a people who neither lament nor repent (12:4, 11) is clarified. An additional persona, which appears in 12:4 and 12:11, is that of the mourning earth.

Jeremiah's complaint in 12:1–4 begins in 12:1a with legal idioms: the prophet has a dispute with YHWH (אריב) and wishes to take up a case (משפטים אדבר). The scene is thus set for a dramatic interchange, and a pair of questions follows that open the dialogue and beg a response: "Why does the way of the wicked prosper? Why are all who deal treacherously at ease?" (12:1b). Jeremiah's concern here is the delay of divine justice and the apparent divine tolerance of the wicked.[41] God has not only planted these people in the land but has allowed them to take root and bear fruit, in essence multiplying wickedness (12:2a). God is far from their affections and sensibilities (מכליותיהם), however often they use God language (12:2b; cf. 5:2). Jeremiah, in contrast, is known by the Lord, and his will or mind (לב) has been tested: it is with YHWH (12:3a). The distinction between the prophet and the wicked inhabitants of the land, then, consists in knowing, or recognition: in being known by the Lord and in knowing the Lord, that is, having one's heart and mind with God.[42]

From this position Jeremiah demands that YHWH uproot the wicked, for, he implies in 12:4, they have plunged the land into mourning:

How long will the earth mourn (תאבל)
    and the grass of every field wither? (ייבש)
From the wickedness (מרעת) of those who live in it,
    animals and birds are swept away,
For they say: "He cannot see our end." (12:4)

The personification of earth as mourning is a common prophetic motif, appearing in a comparable passage in Hos 4:3 as well as in Amos 1:2; Isa 24:4; 33:9; and Joel 1:10 and three times elsewhere in Jeremiah: 4:28, 12:11; 23:10. The

---

Baumgartner, *Jeremiah's Poems of Lament*, 86; Holladay, *Jeremiah 1*, 385–86; Smith, *Laments of Jeremiah*, 47–48; Lundbom, *Jeremiah 1–20*, 51

40. See Smith, *Laments of Jeremiah*, 49–50.
41. So Diamond, *Confessions of Jeremiah*, 48. Cf. Ps 94:1–11.
42. Note the paralleling of כליות and לב in Jer 11:20; 17:10; 20:12; Pss 7:10; 26:2. These two aspects of the inner self are clearly related in these texts.

metaphor involved in this personification is doubly effective in these passages because of the dual associations of the verb אבל. The primary meaning of אבל is "to mourn," and it is used with human subjects in various depictions of grief and anguish. Where the earth, or an aspect of the earth, is the subject of אבל, the context is physical devastation. In three of these instances, אבל is used in parallelism with, or close proximity to, the root יבש, "to wither" or "dry up," as here.[43] Whether or not a second root אבל with the meaning "to dry up" exists as a cognate of Akkadian *abālu*,[44] the Old Testament usage of אבל suggests that the primary meaning "mourn" accommodates the nuance of "drying up." One might see the desiccation of the land and decimation of its creatures in Jer 12:4, then, as physical signs of the earth's mourning and loss.

This reading is enhanced in the light of biblical mourning rituals, which include fasting, stripping or tearing of clothing, the cutting of hair, sprinkling the body with dust, and bowing down toward the ground. All these activities bear resemblance to the withering, stripping, and diminishment of the earth and its plant and animal life in times of drought.[45] Further dimensions of meaning are introduced when the range of contexts in which biblical mourning rituals are described is considered. According to Saul Olyan's comprehensive survey, these include, in addition to mourning for the dead, mourning over calamity and both penitential and nonpenitential petitionary mourning.[46] Since earth's mourning is mute, it may potentially express various types of grief and distress.

---

43. See also Amos 1:2; Jer 23:10. The form הוביש in Joel 1:10, which occurs with the subject "new wine," is ambiguous. This form can be read as both the *hip'il* of יבש, "to dry up," and the *hip'il* of בוש, "to be ashamed," as in Joel 1:11, where the farmers are called to show shame (הובישו). The occurrence of the *qal* form יבש in Joel 1:12 (and 1:20) suggests deliberate word play with homonyms, as does the use of הוביש/הביש with the subject "the vine" in 1:12a and "joy" in 1:12c.

44. So *HAL* 6b–7a.

45. For a fuller discussion of the verb אבל and its uses with nonhuman subjects, see Katherine M. Hayes, *"The Earth Mourns": Prophetic Metaphor and Oral Aesthetic* (SBLAcBib 8; Atlanta: Scholars Press, 2002), 12–18.

46. *Biblical Mourning: Ritual and Social Dimensions* (Oxford: Oxford University Press, 2004), 19–27. Olyan includes mourning connected with skin disease as a separate category. Biblical depictions of mourning in these different contexts share common vocabulary (the roots אבל and ספד) as well as references to rituals such as fasting, tearing of garments, wearing sackcloth, cutting off hair, sitting on the ground, and sprinkling the body with dust. Mark J. Boda, ("The Priceless Gain of Penitence: From Communal Lament to Penitential Prayer in the 'Exilic' Liturgy of Israel," *HBT* 25 [2003]: 60) notes the association of biblical penitential prayers with mourning rites in Ezra 9; Neh 1:9; Dan 9.

In Jer 12:4 the earth mourns and suffers harm from, or because of, the wickedness of its inhabitants (מרעת ישבי־בה) and laments its own diminishment.[47] Such an interpretation of the mourning of the earth is presented in Jer 23:10:

> For the earth is full of adulterers,
>   because of the curse (כי־מפני אלה) the earth mourns
>   the pastures of the wilderness are dried up (יבשו).

In this passage the earth is cursed with drought and becomes a vehicle of punishment for those who live in it.

At the same time, in 12:4 the mourning of the earth is contrasted with the unperturbed confidence of those who say of YHWH: "He cannot see our end." Earth does not simply suffer from, but recognizes the wickedness of, its inhabitants and, implicitly, its woeful outcome.[48] The prophet petitions the Lord for a "day of slaughter" in 12:3, and earth's mourning can be seen as a response to the inevitability of greater mourning to come, in which none can claim immunity.[49] The people, ironically, display their own blindness by failing to see both the reality of divine justice (cf. Ps 94:8–11) and the warning of a bleak future in earth's distress. It is this impenetrable self-assurance that prompts the prophet's anguished question, "How long?"—a question that demands a divine response and at the same time commands the attention of the witnessing audience.[50]

The question is answered indirectly by YHWH in 12:5–6, in which "Long enough!" seems to be the divine reply. The divine soliloquy in 12:7–13, however, offers a second response that echoes the prophet's distress with God's own.[51] Parallels in vocabulary and semantic field as well as word play link this divine *cri de couer* with the preceding prophetic outburst: לב ("heart"); אבל ("mourn"); צאן/רעים ("sheep"/"shepherds"); תבואת, חטים, פרי/זרע, שרש, נטע ("plant," "take root," "fruit"/"sow," "wheat," "harvest"); and יבש/בוש ("dry up"/"be ashamed").[52]

YHWH's lament begins by announcing the decision to abandon the people (12:7). A command follows in 12:9—"Go, gather all the wild animals/bring them to devour!"—that unequivocally answers the prophet's plea "How long?" in 12:1.

---

47. See the comparable use of מחרון, "because of the anger," in Jer 12:13. On the identification of the wicked in 12:1–4 as the entire nation, see Diamond, *Confessions of Jeremiah*, 46–47.

48. See also in Hos 4:1–3 the dual sense of the earth's mourning as a consequence of and response to the aberrations of its inhabitants.

49. So Diamond, *Confessions of Jeremiah*, 47–50.

50. The recurrence of this question in Jer 4:14, 21 provides a backdrop for its occurrence here.

51. So Smith, *Laments of Jeremiah*, 47.

52. The links between יבש and בוש are not only phonological in this context; see the discussion of the interplay between the two roots in Joel 1 in n. 43, above. On the linguistic parallels between Jer 12:1–6 and 12:7–13, see further, Smith, *Laments of Jeremiah*, 47–48.

Yet the personal anguish of the divine voice is transparent in the way YHWH refers to the people in 12:7–8. They are "my house" (ביתי), "my possession" (נחלתי), and "my own beloved" (ידדות נפשי), even though they have turned divine love into hate. YHWH vocalizes the shock and intensity of the process of separation from the people in a question: "Is my possession a hyena's den to me?/Are birds of prey circling over her?" (Jer 12:9b).[53] Again, the question is posed to the witnessing audience, drawing them into the prophetic drama.

The divine decision in 12:7 is expressed in perfect (*qatal*) forms: עזבתי, "I have abandoned," and נטשתי, "I have forsaken." Yet the imperative "Go, gather, all the wild animals" in 12:9 implies that the decision is just now being implemented. The reversion to perfect forms in the description of devastation in Jer 12:10–13, then, creates ambiguity.[54] Are these "prophetic perfects," sharpening the vision of what is to come?[55] Or, as in 12:4, is the devastation of the land, here brought about by invading armies, an ongoing reality?[56] The unaffected attitude of the people in 12:11b, which states that "no man lays it to heart," at least allows the possibility that the divinely determined annihilation is not yet complete.[57] So, too, in 12:13, the form ובושו, which can be read as a converted perfect (*weqatal*), "they will be ashamed," and the reference to the harvest, a symbol of completion, suggest a current state of woe that will culminate in the near future. Earth's mourning, then, may represent both sorrow over the immediate damage inflicted on the land and cognizance of the fullness of loss to come.

In any case, in 12:11 the mourning of the earth reflects divine distress but is again set in opposition to human lack of recognition:

> It has been made a desolation;
>   it mourns to me, desolate.
> All the earth is made desolate
>   yet no man lays it to heart.

The structure of this verse, in which the first colon of 12:11a, שמה לשממה, "it has been made a desolation," is echoed in the first colon of 12:11b, נשמה כל־הארץ,

---

53. This line is notoriously difficult to translate, but it is generally read as a question. For a discussion of the translation here, see Hayes, "The Earth Mourns," 105; and John A. Emerton, "Notes on Jeremiah 12,9 and on Some Suggestions of J. D. Michaelis about the Hebrew Words *naḥā*, *'aʿbrā*, and *jadāʿ*," ZAW 81 (1969): 182–91.

54. For a discussion of tense in Jer 12:7–13, see McKane *Jeremiah*, 277–78.

55. Such is the leaning of McKane, *Jeremiah*, 278; Holladay, *Jeremiah 1*, 386. The commentary of Ronald E. Clements (*Jeremiah* [IBC; Atalanta: John Knox, 1988], 83–84) reflects this interpretation.

56. So P. Albert Condamin, *Le livre de Jérémie* (Paris: Gabalda, 1936), 111; Peter C. Craigie, Page H. Kelley, and Joel F. Drinkard Jr., *Jeremiah 1–25* (WBC 26; Dallas: Word, 1991), 184.

57. So, presumably, in Jer 5:3–6.

"the whole land is made desolate," deepens the contrast between the second cola of each line. Thus אבלה עלי שממה, "it mourns to me, desolate," is parallel antithetically to כי אין איש שם על־לב, "yet no man lays it to heart."

The phrase אבלה עלי, "it mourns to (or upon) me," implies a turning toward God and, perhaps, an implicit, if inarticulate, petition. This posture of the earth contrasts with the failure of the people to acknowledge the devastation that is happening around them and what it portends. Earth's mourning over her diminishment, however, is in sympathy with the divine lament over the reversal of love to hate. The emotional timbre of both responses solicits a sympathetic reaction from the audience.[58]

The configurations of *dramatis personae* in Jer 12:1–6 and 12:7–13 are similar. In the first poem the voice of the mourning earth echoes the lament of the prophet; in the second it is directed toward Yhwh and parallels the divine lament. The two laments themselves correspond, the prophetic anger of 12:1–4 being matched by the divine passion of 12:7–13. The people stand outside this circle of voices that call out to, respond, and echo one another. The interaction among the other voices does not affect them: they are both oblivious and hostile.

Yet an inherent relationship between the people and the earth is suggested by the language of 12:7–13, beginning in 12:7 with Yhwh's renunciation of ביתי, "my house," נחלתי, "my possession," and ידדות נפשי, "my own beloved." The primary reference of these expressions seems to be to the people. Yet נחלה is used widely of both the land given to Israel by Yhwh and of the people themselves as belonging to Yhwh.[59] The "house" of Yhwh evokes both the temple and the house of Israel/Judah.[60] Yet in Hos 9:15b, in a similar context of judgment, ביתי seems to refer to the land.[61] In this matrix of associations, the designation ידדות נפשי which Yhwh has "given into the hands of her enemies," takes on a dual reference as well.

The association of land and people recurs in Jer 12:10, which speaks of shepherds destroying כרמי, "my vineyard," and חלקתי, "my field" or "my portion." In a concrete sense this verse depicts damage done to the cultivated land. Yet כרם is clearly evocative of the people of Israel[62] and lends this association to its parallel, חלקה. The first-person suffixes on the nouns in this verse echo the earlier expressions ביתי, נחלתי, and ידדות נפשי with their multiple associations.

Both land and people are evoked again in the personification of the earth or land (ארץ) in 12:11. A collective persona, the ארץ both encompasses and repre-

---

58. In the *Poetics*, 1456a (ch. 18), Aristotle speaks of the sympathy or human feeling (*to philanthōpon*) aroused by tragedy; he links it with pity and fear in 1452b (ch. 9).
59. See BDB, 635.
60. Cf. the reference to the "house of Judah" in Jer 12:14 and BDB, 108–10.
61. Note the use of the verb שנא, "to hate," in both Hos 9:15b and Jer 12:8b.
62. As, e.g., in Jer 5:10 and 6:9.

sents the people who inhabit it.⁶³ The phonological and syntactical parallels in phraseology between the earth's and the people's responses in Jer 12:11 accentuate the relationship, as well as the stark contrast, between these two personae: אבלה עלי שממה says Yhwh of the earth, כי אין איש שם על-לב.

The semantic disjunction between these two similarly phrased responses signals disjunction between two collective entities that are essentially enfolded one within the other. The mourning of the earth calls for an echo from the people but finds none. At the same time, earth's mourning appeals to its collective counterpart in the witnessing audience to lament.

Mourning Earth and Tragic Chorus

In this sense the role of the mourning earth in the two laments resembles the role of the Greek tragic chorus, that collective persona present throughout a drama and offering various forms of witness, including silent witness, to the interchanges of the actors.⁶⁴ In Greek tragedy the chorus introduces a communal dimension to what might be seen as a personal or familial drama; in the paired laments of Jer 12:1–13 the people are already present as a collective character.⁶⁵ But the earth in these laments represents an alternative collective presence, one able to grieve over the wickedness that inhabits it and the suffering inflicted on it. According to John Gould the witness of the tragic chorus is usually "normative," drawing on "the inherited stories and the inherited, gnomic wisdom of social memory and of oral tradition."⁶⁶ The response of the earth in Jer 12:1–13 implicitly manifests a communal ethos that recognizes wickedness and its effects, both short term and long term. Gould's observation that the tragic chorus often represents marginal segments of the community—old men, women, captives, foreigners—who articulate an experience other than that of the hero or heroes offers an additional perspective on the role of the earth in Jer 12:1–13.⁶⁷

---

63. On the dual aspects of ארץ as both the physical land and a political entity, see BDB, 76.

64. So John Gould, "Tragedy and Collective Experience," in Silk, *Tragedy and the Tragic*, 233. See also Pat E. Easterling ("Form and Performance," in *The Cambridge Companion to Greek Tragedy* [ed. Pat E. Easterling; Cambridge: Cambridge University Press, 1997], 163): "One of the major functions of the chorus is to act as a group of 'built in witnesses,' giving collective and usually normative responses to the events of the play." Note that as in the biblical laments under discussion here, the actors on stage in a given scene in Greek tragic drama never number more than three and are often limited to two.

65. Cf. Norman K. Gottwald ("Tragedy and Comedy in the Latter Prophets," *Semeia* 32 [1984]: 88), who assigns the people the role of "tragic hero" in the prophetic writings.

66. Gould, "Tragedy and Collective Experience," 233. Frederick W. Dobbs-Allsopp, ("Tragedy, Tradition, and Theology in the Book of Lamentations," *JSOT* 74 [1996]: 49–50) ascribes a "choric role" to the "ethical vision" underlying Lamentations.

67. Gould, "Tragedy and Collective Experience," 219–25, here 224. Note that the broad analogy made here between the role of the mourning earth and that of the tragic chorus does

A key function of the tragic chorus is to intensify the dynamic between the dramatic action and its audience. As the collective element on stage, the chorus dramatizes a response to the action, as the audience itself reacts.[68] The chorus, further, guides the audience's responses, as P. E. Easterling has observed: "they offer possible models for the onlookers' emotional responses: pity for Cassandra, for example, or grief for the murdered king in *Agamemnon*."[69] Their job, in essence, is to "help the audience *become involved in the process of responding*, which may entail wrestling with conflicting or contrasting emotions."[70]

Certainly a key response to tragic action is lament, an aspect stressed by Charles Segal: "Drama effects a concrete, public sharing of grief through the collective response of the chorus and more broadly through the community of spectators in the theatre."[71] For Segal the shared release of emotions (pity and fear) aroused by the reenactment of tragic events is a major aspect of the ritual closure achieved through tragedy. In a number of tragedies, the weeping on stage of the chorus, or of an actor, cues the audience to respond similarly.[72] Such expressions of grief enlarge the sensibility and compassion of the onlookers, and this is part of the purification of emotions associated with Aristotle's concept of catharsis.

In a response to Segal, Easterling offers a more comprehensive view of catharsis and of the chorus that goes beyond lamentation. In the enactment of a story, the community is called not just to grieve but to "watch," that is, to "take cognizance of what the characters do and suffer."[73] The chorus guides the audience in understanding what they are seeing, whether the appropriate emotional response is sorrow, outrage, or even celebration. The public sharing of grief brought about through the mimesis of tragedy may entail, in addition to emo-

---

not preclude consideration of other, more particularized roles for the earth in Jer 12:1–13 and in other biblical prophetic contexts. The invocation of heaven and earth as witnesses to oaths, including covenants, comes to mind. Within the lawsuit (ריב) framework of Jer 12:1–4, the earth's mourning can be seen as testimony to a ruptured agreement. I am indebted for this interpretative possibility to Steven Weitzman.

68. Simon Goodhill, "The Audience of Athenian Tragedy," in Easterling, *Cambridge Companion to Greek Tragedy*, 67.
69. Easterling, "Form and Performance," 163.
70. Ibid.
71. Segal, "Catharsis, Audience, and Closure," 149.
72. Ibid., 153–57.
73. Easterling, "Weeping," 177. In another essay Easterling ("Form and Performance," 164) stresses the intellectual and even philosophical guidance, as well as the emotional guidance, given the audience by the chorus. Note that Segal ("Catharsis, Audience, and Closure," 155) does concede that the "intellectual pleasures of recognition and learning are fundamental to *mimesis* (artistic representation) as chapter 4 of the *Poetics* points out (especially 1448b12–19)."

tional expressions of sorrow, "the recognition that we are all vulnerable—and potentially guilty, too."[74]

Another aspect of the Greek tragic chorus seems pertinent to the role of the mourning earth in the laments under discussion here. The chorus is eloquent even when it is silent. Its continuous presence on stage raises the expectation of an outcome to the dramatic action it is witnessing, exerting pressure on the exchanges between actors that is sensed by the audience.[75]

The dramatization effected within and between the prophetic and divine laments in Jer 12:1–13 include the same collective witness: the personified earth. In 12:4, the earth responds to the wickedness and indifference it witnesses (that of the people) as well as to the onset and prospect of major loss, as in 12:11. Earth's mourning is silent but visualized by the text's audience, prompting them to ponder the outcome of what they are hearing about and modeling for them an alternative response to that of the people. The personalization of both prophet and deity in expressions of distress and anger creates a climate of lament that pulls on the sympathy of the audience as well as alerting them to the tragic dimensions of the situation. The persona of the earth, linked with the people through word play, appeals directly to the audience to merge their cognizant lament with the withering and diminishment displayed before them.

Joel 1–2

The call to communal lament in Joel 1 introduces a similar set of personae but a different configuration of voices.[76] Here an earth chorus is joined by the people and the prophet to raise a single multivocal lament to God in the context of a plague of locusts. In the present form of the book of Joel this composition is linked to the announcement of the day of Yhwh, the call to lament and repent, and the subsequent divine response in Joel 2.[77]

---

74. Easterling, "Weeping," 178–79.

75. Gould, "Tragedy and the Collective Experience," 232–33.

76. On the genre of Joel 1:5–14 as a call to lament, preceded by a call to attention and introduction to the disaster in 1:2–4 and followed by illustrations of lamentation in 1:15–20, see Hans W. Wolff, *Joel and Amos* (Hermeneia; Philadelphia: Fortress, 1977), 20–22.

77. So Wolff, *Joel and Amos*, 6–7; Barton, *Joel and Obadiah*, 14; Ferdinand E. Deist, "Parallels and Reinterpretation in the Book of Joel: A Theology of the Yom Yahweh?" in *Text and Context: Old Testament and Semitic Studies for F. C. Fensham* (ed. Walter T. Claassen; JSOTSup 48; Sheffield: Sheffield Academic Press, 1988), 63–70; Olyan, *Biblical Mourning*, 65–68. Jörg Jeremias ("Joel/Joelbuch," *TRE* 17:92–93) identifies all of Joel 1:2–2:17 as one call to lament. Although there are no clear textual references to assist the dating of Joel 1–2 (or the final redaction of the book of Joel as a whole), most commentators would place these chapters in a postexilic context. See the discussion in John Barton, *Joel and Obadiah* (OTL; Louisville: Westminster John Knox, 2001), 14–18; and in Hayes, "The Earth Mourns," 185–89.

There is little dramatic enactment of voices in Joel 1–2, yet the specification of individual members within the community as they are roused to lament and congregate evokes an array of voices.[78] Further, Joel 1:2–3, which introduces the prophetic response to the locust plague, seems to appeal to an audience outside the text as well as to those in the text who are under attack. Joel 1:2 begins with the standard prophetic call to attention: "Hear this, O elders, give ear all inhabitants of the land," but it is followed by a rhetorical question that demands not simply attention but retrospective contemplation: "Has such a thing happened in your days, or in the days of your fathers?" In 1:3 the prophet's audience is mandated to tell their children and children's children about what has happened. The absence of details particular to the locust plague in these two verses and the open-ended temporal references to past, present, and future allow an audience distinct from the community summoned to lament in 1:5–20 to hear themselves addressed. The broad designation of the prophet's audience in 1:3 as "elders" and "inhabitants of the land" contrasts with the characterization of the community in 1:5, where the call to lament proper begins, as "drunkards" and "drinkers of sweet wine." This initial distinction in the opening verses remains in the mind of the reader, despite the later reference to the elders and inhabitants of the land in the body of the call to lament (1:14).

The summons to lament begins, following a description of the destruction caused by the locusts in 1:4, with an appeal to a stupefied community:

> Awake you drunkards and weep
> and wail, all you drinkers of wine. (1:5)

The gravity of this appeal is stressed in 1:8: "Lament like a virgin dressed in sackcloth/for the husband of her youth." Members of the community are then directed to mourn—farmers and vinedressers (1:11), priests and ministers (1:13), elders (1:14)—as well as all the inhabitants of the land (1:14).

Interwoven with the commands to lament, be ashamed, wail, put on sackcloth, and fast in these verses are depictions of elements of the community and of the land as already in a state of mourning. Through common vocabulary, wordplay, and simple juxtaposition the responses of people and earth to the damage done by the locusts are drawn together into a scene of common lament. The priests mourn (אבלו) in 1:9, and the ground mourns (אבלה) in 1:10; the new wine dries up (הוביש) in 1:10, and the farmers are commanded to show shame (הבישו) in 1:11. In 1:12 the vine dries up (הובישה), all the trees of the field dry up (יבשו), and joy dries up or is shamed away (הביש) from the people. In 1:17 the

---

78. See also the movement from communal petition to divine response in 2:18–27. The switch from imperatives to first-person expressions of lament in 1:15–20 and the rhetorical question in 1:16, further, represent shifts in the tone and placement of the prophetic voice.

grain dries up (הביש). The priests are enjoined in 1:14 to call (קראו) an assembly, directing the elders and all of the inhabitants of the land to cry out (וזעקו) to God; in 1:19 the prophetic speaker calls out to God (אקרא); and in 1:20 the wild animals long (תערוג) for God. In 1:18 the animals sigh (נאנחה) and the herds of cattle are confused (נבכו).[79]

The content of this communal lament is unspecified, but it is clearly centered around the temple, the "house of the LORD your God" (1:14). The seriousness of the plague is manifest in the cutting off of cereal and drink offerings for the temple (1:9, 13) as well as of all gladness and exultation (1:15). The elders and all the inhabitants of the land are to be gathered into the temple to raise their cry to the Lord (1:14), suggesting, at the least, recognition of divine agency in the disaster they confront and, perhaps some form of petition.

A second call to lament is issued in Joel 2:12–17, this time directly from YHWH:

> Yet even now, says the LORD,
> Return (שבו) to me with all your heart
>   with fasting, weeping, and mourning;
> And rend your hearts and not your garments
>   and return (ושובו) to the LORD your God. (2:12–13a)

Much of the language in 2:12–17 either echoes or replicates the call to lament in Joel 1:5–20: the summons to weep and mourn (2:12; cf. 1:5, 8, 9); the reference to grain and drink offerings (2:14; cf. 1:9, 13); the appeals to sanctify a fast, call an assembly, and gather the people (2:15; cf. 1:14), and the specific entreaty to priests as ministers of the Lord (2:15; cf. 1:13). This language occurs in 2:12–17 in a penitential framework, however.

The context of the appeal to lament and repent in 2:12–17 is different as well. This summons is a response not to the locust plague per se but to the full catastrophe it signals: the day of the Lord: "Let all the inhabitants of the land tremble,/for the day of the LORD is coming, it is near" (2:1). This day of judgment is envisioned in 2:1–11 as the invasion of a "great and vast people" who destroy everything in their path (2:2–3). They are described, however, as the locusts of Joel 1:4–7 writ large, leaping over mountains and devouring stubble (2:5).[80] The declaration in 1:15 that the "day of the LORD is near" further suggests that the locusts are to be seen as forerunners of the more terrible, definitive catastrophe evoked in 2:1–11.[81]

---

79. On this blending of voices, see also Theodore Hiebert, "Joel," *ABD* 3:877.

80. To reinforce the link, in 1:6 the locusts are compared to an invading nation.

81. On the locust plague as prefiguring the day of the Lord, see Samuel R. Driver, *The Books of Joel and Amos* (Cambridge: Cambridge University Press, 1897), 25–34, 35; Wolff, *Joel*

In the sequence of Joel 1 and 2, the summons to lament in the house of God in Joel 1 serves as a prelude to the call to whole-hearted repentance in Joel 2. This fuller response is invoked following prophetic elucidation of the significance of the locust plague as a portent of total reversal. Recognition of the tragic enormity waiting upon the present experience of loss brings to expression a more profound human response. In Joel 2:12–17, the community is called to respond to calamity in a way that acknowledges and articulates their grief over what has already been suffered and set in motion and their potential role in halting it.[82] It is this deeper, cognizant response that the Lord answers in 2:18–27 with promises of restoration, reversing the onset of reversal.[83] The converted imperfect (*wayyiqtol*) forms ויקנא and ויחמל in 2:18a ("and the Lord became jealous for his land and took pity on his people") suggest in fact that the Lord's relenting is dependent on the expressions of penitential lament that precede it.[84]

In Joel 1–2 earth and the human community join with the prophet in a multivocal chorus that models for the witnessing audience a response to crisis. This response entails raising a communal lament over distress already inflicted and then, having recognized its full import, reorienting themselves toward God. The clamor of lament evoked in these chapters, again, draws the reading audience to experience loss and alarm with the personae of the text and to move with them toward fuller awareness and a deeper turning toward God.

---

and Amos, 20, 33–35, 41–43, 48–49; Deist, "Parallels and Reinterpretation," 69–70; Jeremias, "Joel/Joelbuch," 91–97. As a number of commentators point out, the prevalence of perfect (*qatal*) forms and imperatives in the description of the locust plague in Joel 1:5–20 strongly evokes a present reality, in contrast to the future reference created by the many imperfect (*yiqtol*) forms used to portray the day of Yhwh in 2:1–11. The argument of Barton (*Joel and Obadiah* 13–14, 45–48, 70) that the verb forms in 1:5–20 can be read as prophetic perfects and his conclusion that 1:2–20 and 2:1–17 represent two renditions of the same invasion of locusts does not fully address the differences between the two passages or the literary sequencing they have been given.

82. Cf. the blending of lament and penitence in Lamentations, as noted by Boda, "The Priceless Gain," 66–68. Boda also finds this mixture in penitential prayer, "which encourages passionate expression of the pain while maintaining self-awareness of the sin of humanity" (72).

83. Gottwald ("Tragedy and Comedy," 84–87) observes that all the prophetic books, in their present form, describe restoration following upon judgment and thus exhibit a comic rather than a tragic trajectory. Yet, he cautions, the tragic/comic balance of these writings needs to be appraised in each case. Cf. the equilibrium achieved at the end of the third drama (*The Eumenides*) in the *Oresteia*, the Aeschylean tragic trilogy that begins with *Agamemnon*.

84. On the role of repentance in averting the judgment inherent in the day of Yhwh, see Driver, *Joel and Amos*, 30. Note that Joel 2:14 offers no guarantees, however: "Who knows if he may turn and relent and leave a blessing behind him?"

Implications for the Development of Penitential Prayer

The prophetic drama enacted in Jer 12:1–13 draws its audience to recognize the reality of irrecoverable loss—of *peripeteia*—in the drama they are witnessing as well as the human failure that lies behind this reversal. The prospect of devastation raised up before them is tragic because of its magnitude—the closing down of a nation—and because it is at least potentially, or theoretically, avoidable.[85] The mourning earth—a collective voice not unlike that of the tragic chorus—displays a response to the onset of reversal that is sensitive to the ruinous effects of human wrongdoing and arrogance. This response accords with the distress of both prophet and deity, but clashes with the indifference of the people, who do not see the hand of God in what is happening around them. If earth's lament is ignored by the people, however, it can still arouse a response, emotional and cognitive, from the dramatic audience.

There is less dramatic enactment in Joel 1–2, in which the prophetic speaker, voicing the word of Yhwh, presses the community to lament. Yet the prospect of active, universal mourning raised by the figure of the mourning earth in Jer 12:1–13 is realized here. Elements of the earth—its soil, fields, vines, yields, and animals—appear as members of a larger chorus of voices, as all the members of the human community are directed to assemble in the temple and raise their cry to the Lord.

The expression of grief is fundamental to these texts. In Jer 12:1–13 it allows a catharsis in which the painful dimensions of tragedy—in heaven and on earth—are acknowledged and mourned by the witnessing audience. In Joel 1–2 lamentation moves both the people in the text and its audience toward repentance and a new starting point. The emphasis on lament in both compositions and the sequence of lament leading to repentance in Joel 1–2 suggest a dynamic with implications for the emergence of penitential prayer, with its emphasis on the confession of sin and of the righteous character of God, in the Second Temple period.[86]

Foretellings and voicings of lament predominate over the few articulations of penitence in Jer 1–12. As argued above, these last are presented as reflecting fear, confusion, and mistaken expectations rather than the community's recognition

---

85. That is, if the people would respond in sympathy with the other characters: God, prophet, earth. The people may be incapable of such a response at this point (see Biddle, *Polyphony and Symphony*, 47–54, 72), but the expressions of divine/prophetic disappointment and distress in Jer 1–12 suggest that this failure is not a given. Aristotle speaks in the *Poetics* (1452b–1453a [ch. 13]) of the construction of the tragic plot, which should, in order to arouse pity and fear in the audience, concern a protagonist who is neither wholly wicked nor wholly virtuous, but one who falls between these two extremes.

86. Mark J. Boda ("Confession as Theological Expression," in the present volume) speaks of penitential prayer as including both the acknowledgement of sin and articulations of faith concerning the character of God.

of failure to know YHWH for who he is.[87] The people are shown to be incapable of full confession of their sinfulness and cannot see the dimensions of their own blindness.[88] The communal acknowledgment of wrongdoing in Jer 3:22b-25, with its identification of YHWH as the source of salvation for Israel, its declaration of shame and dishonor, its claim of responsibility for having sinned (חטא) both in present and past generations, and having failed to listen to the voice of God, is exceptional. It seems to serve as an illustration for what is lacking in the precrisis prophetic audience and a model for the postcrisis readership of the book.[89]

The failure of the paired communal laments in Jer 14 to elicit a divine reprieve can be seen in this light. Penitential elements (14:7b, 20) and even an affirmation of YHWH's power in contrast to the idols of the nations (14:22) are mixed with expressions of complaint and challenge (14:8–9a, 19) in these petitions for deliverance.[90] As prayers of penitence they are incomplete, revealing the same sense of confusion found in earlier appeals of the people to YHWH.[91] The first complaint in 14:8, for example ("Why should you be like a sojourner in the land,/and like a traveler turning aside in the night [וכארח נטה ללון]?"), echoes the divine/prophetic lament in 9:1 ("O that I had in the desert a traveler's lodging [מלון ארחים],/that I might leave my people and go away from them"). The phraseological link between these two questions emphasizes the people's ignorance of the divine perspective. This ignorance is apparent in the complaint raised in 14:19 (which echoes that in 8:15, discussed above):

> Why have you struck us down,
> > So that there is no healing for us?
> We look for peace, but find no good,
> > For a time of healing, but there is terror instead.

The insertion of a dialogue in 14:13–16 between YHWH and the prophet concerning the false prophets who promise peace (14:13) primes the reader to interpret this complaint as arising out of a delusion (cf. 14:18).

The two laments of Jer 14 include flashes of confession, that is, of the recognition of sin and of the true character of YHWH as the hope and savior of Israel (14:8), who resides in the midst of the people (14:9) and is the only cosmic power

---

87. See, e.g., Jer 5:4–5; 8:7; 9:2, 5.

88. See, e.g., Jer 2:34–35; 6:15; 8:12.

89. So Biddle, *Polyphony and Symphony*, 4; Zahavi-Ely, "Multiple Speaking Voices"; Seitz, "Place of the Reader," 71.

90. Mark J. Boda ("From Complaint to Contrition: Peering Through the Liturgical Window of Jer 14,1–15, 4," *ZAW* 113 [2001]: 197) points to the mixture of complaint and penitence in Jer 14:19–21 as one explanation for why this petition is rejected.

91. Biddle, *Polyphony and Symphony*, 26–28, 41–43.

(14:22). Yet these confessions are counterbalanced by the people's faulty perceptions of their situation and their God.[92]

The response of Yhwh to these laments in 14:10–12 and 15:1–4 further suggests that there is a point where words are not enough. In responses to the prophet Yhwh faults the people for their actions, which speak against their words. They have "loved to wander" and "have not held back their feet" from doing so (14:10).[93] Similarly, in 15:1–4 the divine insistence on the fourfold destruction of the people is explained on the basis of what King Manasseh did in Jerusalem (15:4). In the end Yhwh's responses to the people's appeal revert back to the mode of divine/prophetic lament familiar from earlier chapters:

> You shall say to them this word:
> Let my eyes run down with tears night and day,
>   and let them not cease,
> For with a great blow the virgin daughter—my people—is struck down,
>   a very damaging blow. (14:17; cf. 8:23; 9:17)

The divine soliloquy in Jer 15:5–9 sounds a similar tone of distress over irreversible judgment.[94]

The recurrent summons to and expressions of lament in Jer 1–12 draw the reading audience toward sympathetic grieving. Attention must be paid, to borrow the words of a modern tragedian, to the damage that ensues from a tragic course of action. That damage must be experienced, recognized, and mourned over before there can be any talk of resolution or reconfiguration.

Biblical texts that convey the necessity of a gap between the crisis of exile and the full restoration of relationship with Yhwh may help to explain the primacy of lament in Jeremiah as well as in Joel 1–2. The prophet's letter to the exiles in Jer 29 makes clear that this community will have to endure a lengthy passage of time before they can hope to enter into an intimate relationship of prayer and response with God:

> Only when Babylon's seventy years are completed will I visit you.... And you will call on me and come and pray to me, and I will hear you. And you will search for me, and you will find me, when you seek me with all your heart. And I will be found by you, says the Lord. (29:12–14; cf. 25:11)

---

92. According to Boda ("From Complaint to Contrition," 197), Jer 14:19–21 represents a "transitional form on the way to penitential prayer." For a negative evaluation of the communal prayers in Jer 14, see Beuken and van Grol, "Jeremiah 14,1–15,9," 326–27, 330–31, 336–38; Willis, "Dialogue between Prophet and Audience," 74–75.

93. Beuken and van Grol ("Jeremiah 14, 1–15, 9," 330) point out the irony of Yhwh's response to a people who complain that God himself has become to them like a passing traveler.

94. See ibid., 314–23.

Deuteronomy 30:1–6 places *after* the experience of blessing and curse (30:1a) a "returning to heart" (השב אל־לבב) and a return (שוב) to Yhwh in the place of exile (30:1b-2).[95] The penitential prayer in 1 Kgs 8 implies a similar sequence, in similar language, in verse 47: "and they will return to their hearts (והשיבו אל־לבם) in the land where they have been taken captive, and they will return (ושובו) and entreat you in the land of their captivity, saying, 'we have sinned and done wrong, we have acted wickedly'" (cf. 1 Kgs 8:35).[96]

The penitential prayer in Dan 9:1–19 alludes to the seventy years of Jeremiah (9:2) and seeks divine disclosure of the meaning of this prophecy, within a narrative framework set in the Persian period (9:1, 3).[97] In response to Daniel's entreaty, Gabriel appears to explain that Jeremiah's seventy years are in fact seventy weeks of years. This is the length of time set "to finish the transgression, to put an end to sin, and to atone for wrongdoing, to bring in everlasting righteousness, to seal both vision and prophet, to anoint a most holy [place or one]" (9:24).

These texts posit an interval before the completion of the process of reintegration with Yhwh. In Ezek 36:16–32, this process includes a discernment of sin that is not possible before God scatters and then gathers the people, purifying them and implanting in them a new heart and spirit. Only at this point, the prophet proclaims, "You shall remember your evil ways and your treacherous acts that were not good, and you shall loathe yourselves for your wrongdoings and your abominable deeds" (36:31).

Baruch 1:15–3:8, a penitential prayer that draws extensively on earlier texts, makes an explicit connection between grieving and confession of the true character of God:

> For the dead who are in Hades, whose spirit has not been taken from their bodies, will not ascribe glory or justice to the Lord, but the person who is deeply

---

95. On the dating, provenance, and translation of this passage, see Mark Zvi Brettler, "Predestination in Deuteronomy 30:1–10, in *Those Elusive Deuteronomists: The Phenomenon of Pan-Deuteronomism* (ed. Linda S. Schearing and Steven L. McKenzie; JSOTSup 268; Sheffield: Sheffield Academic Press, 1999) 171–88. Brettler argues that Deut 30:1–6 is a very late addition to Deuteronomy, influenced by Jeremiah, especially Jer 31:31–34. He reads 30:1a as a protasis that is followed by a long apodosis beginning in 30:1b and extending through 30:6. David Lambert ("Reconsidering the 'Penitence' in 'Penitential Prayer,'" [paper delivered at the Society of Biblical Literature Annual Meeting, Philadelphia, November 2005]) alerted me to this article.

96. Other texts simply mention a set period during which Israel must suffer punishment. Isaiah 40:2 speaks of a term of servitude that has been fulfilled (מלאה צבאה), during which Israel's punishment has been "accepted" (נרצה). Lamentations 4:22 refers to "the completion (תם) of your punishment, O daughter of Zion," and promises, "he will no longer take you into exile."

97. So Rodney A. Werline, "Prayer, Politics, and Social Vision in Daniel 9," in the next volume in this Penitential Prayer series.

grieved, who walks bowed and feeble, with failing eyes and famished soul, will declare your glory and righteousness, O Lord.

Taken together, and in light of the movement from lament to penitence in Joel 1–2, these passages suggest that grieving and lamenting are a necessary part of the process of realignment with God and a prequel to repentance. Possible parallels to the anthropology and theology of biblical mourning rituals come to mind here.[98] Seventy years of exile may be seen as corresponding in some way to the seven days traditionally set aside for grieving over the dead. During these seven days mourners are ritually separated from daily life and from the cult.[99] They are ritually impure through corpse contamination and must both wait out the seven-day period of impurity (Num 19) and undergo an extensive ritual of purification. Their appearances are altered through the rending of clothing, pouring of dust or ashes on the head, shaving the head or allowing hair to hang loose, abstaining from anointing, and ritual behaviors such as fasting, weeping, and lamenting also set them apart. Some of these rituals signal the debasement or diminishment of the mourner, as indicated in Jer 9:18, with its expressions of shame. According to Olyan, ritual debasement may convey a form of identification with the dead.[100]

A primary purpose of this period of separation and identification with the dead, Olyan argues, is to reconfigure the social relationships that have been disrupted by death. In the case of mourning over a death, separation from normal activities allows mourners time to re-envision life without the deceased and to assume new social roles in his or her absence.[101] In the case of mourning over a catastrophe, the rituals create a context in which those affected "can enact and communicate their sorrow, shame, and personal or corporate diminishment as well as create, affirm, or modify social relationships"[102] and, perhaps, relationships with the divine. The tragedy of the exile as portrayed in the book of Jeremiah partakes of both calamity and death—it is a catastrophic blow that represents the end of life in the land (Jer 4:23–26).

The emphasis in Jer 1–12 on lament is appropriate to its preexilic setting, in which the people are portrayed as indifferent and unknowing. The occasional summons to or expressions of repentance in these chapters, whether incomplete or voiced as an unrealized ideal, speak to the post-crisis audience of the book, pointing ahead to a future movement within the community from lament to con-

---

98. As noted above, this connection is made by Olyan (*Biblical Mourning*, 19–27), who relates "non-death related mourning rituals," such as those enacted in mourning over a catastrophe, to those of mourners over the dead.
99. Ibid., 32–39, 59–60.
100. Ibid., 39–42.
101. Ibid., 42–45.
102. Ibid., 98.

fession/recognition of God and of their own blindness.[103] This dual movement is displayed in Joel 1–2, which is given, if not a specified postexilic setting, then one that is not defined by the explicit threat of exile.[104] In these two chapters the community's openness first to lament over a natural disaster, then to recognize in it a warning of eschatological reversal and to move toward a deep-seated reorientation toward Yhwh averts a total tragedy. In this broader sense, it can be affirmed that the origins of penitential prayer lie in communal lament.

Segal sees in the rites of lamentation enacted in tragic drama and in the collective sharing of grief effected in the audience a means of ritual purification from strong and violent emotions and the restoration of order and communal solidarity.[105] Olyan evaluates the role of mourning over calamity in biblical texts similarly. Both assessments point to the role of conscious mourning and lament in bringing participants to a new understanding of themselves. Consideration of the ways in which Jer 12:1–13 and Joel 1–2 appeal to and model responses for a reading audience suggests an intended transformation in that audience, especially, perhaps, in the sense of bringing them to the recognition that they, too, are "vulnerable and potentially guilty."[106] The experience of lament into which the audience of the biblical texts discussed here is invited serves both to clarify the tragedy that is played out before them and to forestall the tragedy that has not yet been enacted among them.

---

103. Cf. Seitz ("Place of the Reader," 71) on the composition of Jeremiah: "The book has been shaped to allow the reader to participate in the refusal of an earlier generation to heed God's calls to repentance and to experience the judgment they eventually experienced, though now with a clear confession of wrongdoing."

104. Note the figurative language of the vision of the Day of Yhwh in Joel 2:1–11, in which the invading forces are depicted as *like* horses, *like* chariots, *like* a people arrayed in battle (2:4–5).

105. Segal, "Catharsis, Audience, and Closure," 163–66. See also the remark with which he opens his essay (149): "It is a deeply held assumption among the Greeks of the archaic and classical periods that the sharing of tears and suffering creates a common bond of humanity between mortals."

106. Easterling, "Weeping," 179.

"...WHY DO YOU LET US STRAY FROM YOUR PATHS..." (ISA 63:17): THE CONCEPT OF GUILT IN THE COMMUNAL LAMENT ISA 63:7–64:11*

Judith Gärtner

INTRODUCTION

The communal lament in Isa 63:7–64:11 at the end of the book of Isaiah is generally seen as postexilic and is described as a communal lament with a hymnic beginning, an extended historical recital, and a confession of sins.[1] A different picture emerges, however, if one leaves the form-critical consensus and considers the redactional significance of the psalm upon the entire book. Three approaches to this problem are discernible in German scholarship. While Wolfgang Lau, Irmtraud Fischer, and Klaus Koenen regard the lament in Isa 63:7–64:11 as a

---

* The following chapter summarizes part of my dissertation (Ph.D., Philipps-Universität Marburg), now published as *Jesaja 66 und Sacharja 14 als Summe der Prophetie: Eine traditions- und redaktionsgeschichtliche Untersuchung zum Abschluss des Jesaja- und des Zwölfprophetenbuches* (WMANT 114; Neukirchen-Vluyn: Neukirchener, 2006).

1. See the detailed description of Irmtraud Fischer, *Wo ist Jahwe? Das Volksklagelied Jes 63,7–64,11 als Ausdruck des Ringens um eine gebrochene Beziehung* (SBB 19; Stuttgart: Verlag Katholisches Bibelwerk, 1989), 256. Similarly also Anneli Aejmelaeus, "Der Prophet als Klageliedsänger: Zur Funktion des Psalms Jes 63,7–64,11 in Tritojesaja," ZAW 107 (1995): 38–39; Michael Emmendörfer, *Der ferne Gott: Eine Untersuchung der alttestamentlichen Volksklagelieder vor dem Hintergrund der mesopotamischen Literatur* (FAT 21; Tübingen: Mohr Siebeck, 1998), 266–67; Johannes Goldenstein, *Das Gebet der Gottesknechte: Jesaja 63,7–64,11 im Jesajabuch* (WMANT 92; Neukirchen-Vluyn:Neukirchner, 2001), 27–28; Claus Westermann, *Das Buch Jesaja: Kapitel 40–66* (5th ed.; ATD 19; Göttingen: Vandenhoeck & Ruprecht, 1986), 306–7. Westermann shows the importance of the historical recital in Isa 63:7–64:11 as part of the communal lament. See further Willem A. M. Beuken, *Jesaja deel III B: De Prediking van het Oude Testament* (Nijkerk: Uitgeverij G. F. Callenbach, 1989), 10; Klaus Koenen, *Ethik und Eschatologie im Tritojesajabuch: Eine literarkritische und redaktionsgeschichtliche Studie* (WMANT 62; Neukirchen-Vluyn: Neukrichner, 1990), 157–68.

unit independent of tradition and only loosely connected with its context,[2] Odil Hannes Steck and Johannes Goldenstein take the almost opposite stance and describe Isa 63:7–64:11 as a compositional unit that was specifically formulated for the book of Isaiah and that must be understood in the context of Isaiah.[3] The third position, represented by Michael Emmendörfer and Anneli Aejmelaus, synthesizes these two positions. According to this view, the significance of the prayer is not sufficiently grasped as a unit taken from the tradition and placed in the context of Isaiah. Moreover, it is inadequate to explain the prayer only in terms of its redactional function as a continuation of the end of the book of Isaiah. Instead, Emmendörfer and Aejmelaus attempt to describe the formation of the prayer by regarding its psalmic and prophetic tradition as a composition formulated for the Trito-Isaianic context (Isa 56–66).[4] The following considerations attempt to contribute to this discussion about the significance of the lament in the context of the book of Isaiah. Attention will be given to the perceptions of sin and guilt, which are central to the prayer, in order to show how the principal features of Isaianic theology are concentrated and developed in the prayer and to demonstrate their importance for the redactional shape of the book.

The Concept of Guilt in Isaiah 63:7–64:11

The communal lament begins in hymnic style in verse 7 by urging the people to commemorate Yhwh's glorious deeds. This appeal is followed by two historical reflections in verses 8–10 and vv. 11–14.

Verse 8 begins with a statement of Yhwh's commitment to Israel. Israel (המה) is Yhwh's people (עמי), and his children do not lie. These two statements of relation are repeated in the subsequent prayer in both the lament and petition parts: Israel is God's people (63:11, 14, 18; 64:8) and his children (63:16; 64:7). God's act of redemption is contrasted in verse 10 by the rebellious acts of the people (והמה *waw adversativum*). The use of מרה and עצב *pi'el* suggests the complaining of the wilderness generation.[5] Already in the beginning, when the relation between God and people is initiated, the people respond to God's salvific

---

2. Wolfgang Lau, *Schriftgelehrte Prophetie in Jes 56–66: Eine Untersuchung zu den literarischen Bezügen in den letzten elf Kapiteln des Jesajabuches* (BZAW 225; Berlin: de Gruyter, 1994), 286–87; Fischer, *Wo ist Jahwe*, 278–80; Koenen, *Ethik*, 157–59.

3. Cf. Odil Hannes Steck, *Studien zu Tritojesaja* (BZAW 203; Berlin: de Gruyter, 1991), 233–42; Goldenstein, *Das Gebet der Gottesknechte*, 249–50.

4. Cf. Emmendörfer, *Der ferne Gott*, 277–89; and further Aejmelaeus, "Der Prophet als Klageliedsänger," 36–37, 46–49, who attributes the psalm as well as Isa 56–59 and 63–66 to Trito-Isaiah and dates it to the middle of the sixth century.

5. Cf. Emmendörfer, *Der ferne Gott*, 273. In the background of מרה is the complaining of the people as described in Exod 15:23 and Num 20:1. עצב *pi'el* is only further attested in Ps 56:6. The *hip'il* in Ps 87:40 attacks the behavior of the wilderness generation.

action not with trust but with complaining and rebellion. Yhwh responds by becoming their enemy and fighting against them. Yhwh's redemption and the destiny of the wilderness generation are of prime importance to the people offering this prayer.[6] Already in these verses Yhwh's glorious deeds and the rebellion of the people are juxtaposed.[7]

The second part of the lament (63:11–14) also contains historical reflection, but this time from the perspective of the people.[8] This section is likewise introduced by זכר. The main issue of this historical recital is the deliverance at the Red Sea, and this is emphasized in 63:12, 14b as a deed of Yhwh to glorify his name.[9]

The first petition and complaint section follows in verses 15–17. It begins with an imperative singular in verse 15 marking a main break in the text.[10] Verse 15b closes by replicating the איה- questions of verse 11 with a lament for the eagerness, strength, and mercy of Yhwh. These are held back from the praying person (אפק), and he or she laments being separated from Yhwh's devotion.

15a	Look down from heaven and see from your holy, glorious, and exalted dwelling!
15b	Where is your zeal, your power, the yearning of your heart and your compassion which have been withheld from me.
16aα	For you are our Father;
16aβ	Although Abraham does not know us, Israel not acknowledge us;
16b	yet you, Yhwh, are our Father, our redeemer from of old is your name.
17a	Yhwh, why do you let us stray from your paths, why harden our hearts, so that we do not revere you?
17b	Return for the sake of your servants, the tribes of your heritage

Verses 15–17 show a concentric structure of petition and complaint that climaxes with the theological explanation in verse 16. The following structure

---

6. The "days of old" refer to a central dimension of the text, which is woven into all passages of the prayer; cf. e.g., עולם in Isa 63:9, 11, 16; 64:4.

7. Cf. Emmendörfer, *Der ferne Gott*, 274.

8. זכר can refer to עמו (see Emmendörfer, *Der ferne Gott*, 263; Fischer, *Wo ist Jahwe*, 11; and Joseph Blenkinsopp, *Isaiah 56–66: A New Translation with Introduction and Commentary* [AB 19B; New York: Doubleday, 2003], 254) or to Yhwh (see Koenen, *Ethik und Eschatologie*, 252).

9. See Emmendörfer, *Der ferne Gott*, 275–76; and Goldenstein, *Das Gebet der Gottesknechte*, 82–85. Both develop the tradition of the exodus in Isa 63:8–11.

10. The structure of the psalm is discussed by Emmendörfer, *Der ferne Gott*, 269.

results: petition (v. 15a); complaint (v. 15b); explanation (v. 16); complaint (v. 17a); petition (v. 17b).

The explanation itself in verse 16 also shows a concentric structure. The key theological sentence אתה יהוה אבינו forms a bracket around the verse with כי introducing the two key clauses of the verse. Even though Abraham is ignorant of them and Israel does not acknowledge them, the supplicants declare Yhwh as their divine parent. On the one hand, this means that Yhwh, and not Israel's ancestors, is responsible for the salvation of the people and his own return to them.[11] The last part of the explanation in verse 16bβ emphasizes this by an additional reference to verses 8 and 11 through the use of עולם and to verse 14 through the reference to Yhwh's name. From the beginning Yhwh has been the redeemer of God's people, which is mentioned already in the historical reflections.

On the other hand, the explanatory כי sentence in verse 16a underscores the conclusion that the people can no longer be recognized as the assumed heirs of the Abrahamic tradition as a result of their entanglement in guilt from the very beginning.

It has become clear to this point that the people's entanglement in guilt is rooted early on in the relationship between Yhwh and Israel and that only Yhwh can save the people (vv. 15–16). Therefore Yhwh must repent, that is, turn himself to his people again. Consequently, the lament continues by asking: "Why do you let us stray from your paths, harden our heart so that we do not revere you?" (v. 17a). Verse 17b concludes with a petition: "Return for the sake of your servants." Yet the entanglement in guilt, which is also described in the following verses (64:4b–6b; English 64:5b–7b), becomes so abstract and pervasive that the text does not identify specific sins committed by the people. This is not done in order to claim innocence but with the knowledge that the possibility for conversion lies in Yhwh's hands alone.

In verses 18–19a the consequences of Yhwh's lack of devotion are described by the experience of foreign domination, and this reality prompts the urgent plea for theophany (63:19b–64:2). The transition to Isa 64:3–4a is fluent.[12] Verse 3 depicts the intervention of Yhwh from eternity (63:19, מעולם) as an unsurpassable event, and verse 4a describes the effects on the righteous.

The confession follows in Isa 64:4b–6b (5b–7b English).

---

11. The allusion to the Abrahamic tradition is discussed by Fischer, *Wo ist Jahwe*, 118; and Emmendörfer, *Der ferne Gott*, 279.

12. The attested text of Isa 64:1a, 2b is controversial; for a detailed discussion, see Goldenstein, *Das Gebet der Gottesknechte*, 108–12.

4b	But when you grew angry, we sinned—on those [ways] eternally and we can still be saved.[13]
5aα	We have become like a thing unclean,
5aβ	all our righteous acts like a filthy rag,
5bα	we all shrivel up like a leaf,
5bβ	our iniquities bears us off like the wind
6aα	There is no one who invokes your name,
6aβ	who bestirs himself to hold on to you,
6b	for you have hidden your face from us and handed us over to our iniquities.

This section is formally framed by הן (but you were angry) in verse 4b and by כי (for you have hidden your face from us) in 6b. The framing elements are respectively bipartite. As in the appeal for Yhwh's return in 63:17, so also this confession focuses on Yhwh's absence, which has caused the people of God to remain imprisoned or entangled in guilt. As far as this is concerned, the sequence of tenses in verses 4b–6b is particularly striking. The perfect-tense verb form of קצף is followed by an imperfect consecutive of חטא and should be translated as "When you grew angry, we sinned," which seems to be a consequence of the divine wrath. Many regard this order as scandalous because it appears to be a reversal of the typical Old Testament correlation between the people's sin and God's wrath.[14] If one considers, however, the context of 63:15, it becomes clear that this does not deal with the sequence of sin and wrath in the conventional sense. The use of the perfect tense here does not suggest the beginning of the divine wrath but emphasizes the consequences of God's wrath for the present. This correlates with the sinful state of the people in the wilderness period.[15] An analogous structure can be found in verse 6b, in which the perfect-tense verb form סתר is again followed by an imperfect consecutive of מוג[16] or מגג and, thus, should be translated as: "For you have hidden your face from us and handed

---

13. The translation of this difficult verse follows the interpretation of Beuken, *Jesaja*, 38, "but in your ways we can be eternally be saved."

14. See the detailed argumentation of Walter Groß, "Jes 64,4: 'Siehe, du hast gezürnt, und dann haben wir gesündigt': Zu 2000 Jahren problematischer Redaktion zweier brisanter Sätze," in *Schriftauslegung in der Schrift* (ed. Reinhard G. Kratz, Konrad Schmid, and Thomas Krüger; BZAW 300; Berlin: de Gruyter, 2000), 163–73, who traces the trajectories from the early textual witnesses to today and detects that they all contain an alleviation similar to the order transmitted in MT.

15. See the historical reflections in vv. 8–10, 11–14.

16. See Fischer, *Wo ist Jahwe*, 4, 25–26; and Blenkinsopp, *Isaiah 56–66*, 256.

over to our iniquities." Once again the perfect is used to show the results of God's absence: Yhwh has hidden his face. This absence means that the people of God remain entangled in guilt.

With ועתה in 64:7–11 the second part of petition and lament begins. The petition of verse 8 repeats the structure of the earlier confession. Only when Yhwh is not wrathful any longer (קצף, v. 4b), does not remember the iniquities forever (עון, vv. 5–6a), and turns back to his people (נבט, v. 6b) will they share in his salvific presence again. Verses 9–10 return to the pictures of Yhwh's dwelling (v. 15), but now the cities of God's holiness are described as desolate. The same is true for Zion and Jerusalem, as well as for the temple. The temple in heaven and on Mount Zion are described in both verses as a dwelling place or a house of holiness (קדוש) and glory (תפארה). While the dwelling in heaven is marked by the second-person singular suffix as Yhwh's house of holiness and glory, the earthly temple is the house of holiness and glory of the praying people (first-person plural suffix), which is consecrated to Yhwh. The heavenly and the earthly temple are, thereby, clearly differentiated. Yet the earthly temple—because of its similar designation—as an image of the heavenly dwelling, serves as the place of communication with Yhwh, but only if Yhwh once again makes the earthly temple his dwelling.

The prayer ends with the question in verse 11 that accuses Yhwh: "In view of all this, will you stand aloof, O Yhwh? Will you be silent and afflict us beyond measure?"[17] The word אפק establishes again the connection between the petitions and the laments in verses 15–17. The closing question of the community's lament emphasizes again that the possibility of salvation is in Yhwh alone.

As this journey through the text has shown, the pressing demand for Yhwh's return to his people forms the center of the prayer (63:15–17; 64:8). In this context not only is the connection between the people's guilt and Yhwh's wrath in terms of a cause and effect relationship central to the prayer, but the people's entanglement in guilt and the consequent divine wrath fundamentally determine the relationship between Yhwh and the supplicants from its beginning. This irresolvable state cannot be rectified by those who pray, but only by the return of Yhwh, that is, the abating of his wrath that is justified from the very beginning of Israel's history. The matter of the people's guilt is key for understanding the prayer. But how far is it a specific characteristic of Isaianic theology, concentrated as it is at the end of the book and summed up in the form of a communal lament? What redactional function does the lament have at the end of the book? To pursue these questions, it is first of all necessary to integrate the psalm in the context of the book of Isaiah.[18]

---

17. The translation follows Blenkinsopp, *Isaiah 56–66*, 254.
18. The following considerations continue the works of Lau, *Schriftgelehrte Prophetie*, 286–315; Steck, *Studien zu Tritojesaja*, 237–42; and Goldenstein, *Das Gebet der Gottesknechte*,

Isaiah 63:7–64:11 in the Context of the Book of Isaiah

The accusation against Yhwh after his silence (64:11) initially connects the prayer to the larger literary context, a feature repeated in the section immediately following (the divine speech of judgment in Isa 65:1–7). At the same time, the first section of petition and lament (63:15–17), as well as the confession of sins (64:4b-6), struggle with the silence of Yhwh and his turning away from the praying people. Thus, verse 17 reads: "Yhwh, why do you let us stray from your paths, why harden our hearts, so that we do not revere you? Return for the sake of your servants, the tribes of your heritage." To express this state of distance from God, the praying people use two strands of tradition that they connect in verse 17. First, the idea that Yhwh hardens the heart of the supplicant calls to mind the vision of the central temple in Isa 6:1-11, which ends with the "*Verstockungsauftrag*" to the prophet. Thereby the contrite identify with the tradition of Yhwh's complete judgment against the people. At the same time, in Isa 63:17 those praying regard themselves as servants of Yhwh despite their experience of God's distance. This is a strand of theology that runs through Deutero-Isaiah. The petition of a hard-hearted people and their confident hope in Yhwh's return make sense only in light of the people's status as servants. This dialectic, the people's hardness of heart *and* their status as Yhwh's servants that culminates in the petition for an end to Yhwh's silence in verse 11, should be examined by means of traditiohistorical analysis and redactional criticism.

The Answer to Yhwh's Silence in Isaiah 65:1–7 and 65:8–12

The request for the end of Yhwh's silence is taken up again in the divine speech in Isa 65:1–7 and considered in a new light.[19] Verses 1–2 describe how Yhwh allowed himself to be found, how he had turned toward his people. The people, however, did not call on his name (קרא בשם). Thus the description of the people's sin here is formulated in a similar way to their renunciation of God in Isa 63:19; 64:6. Because of the people's incorrect behavior discussed in 65:3–5,[20] Yhwh

---

33–201, who also assesses the function of the prayer by analyzing its redactional connections. See especially the compilation of references in Goldenstein, *Das Gebet der Gottesknechte*, 148–51.

19. The subject of Yhwh's silence points to Isa 62:1 and 42:14. Isaiah 42:14 also contains the connection of חשה and אפק, creating a special proximity to the communal lament. Yhwh was silent for an eternity, but now he cannot hold back. Now he will act as hoped for in Isa 64:11.

20. These cultic iniquities are described in particular poignancy and are found in Isa 66:1–4 as well as 66:17. It has therefore been repeatedly debated if they refer to certain syncretistic practices or to a prophetic perspective with an incorrect understanding of guilt or to a combination of both. Since the practices cannot be reconstructed, one can only refer to its

cannot be silent (חשׁה v. 6). In contrast to the hoped-for breach of silence (חשׁה) in 64:11, Yhwh's address to his people does not initiate his return to redeem his people but rather to judge his people for their crime. "I will not keep silence, but will recompense … the iniquities of your parents." This first section of chapter 65 thus responds to the central theological claims of the prayer and so continues the literary unit. According to Isa 65:1-7, Yhwh was not silent and will not be silent; on the contrary, his speech means judgment. Further, it was not Yhwh but the people themselves who were silent because they did not respond to his turning to them. The reason for Yhwh's vengeance lies in the misdeeds of the people described in 65:3-5. So the condition of wrath is no longer central, but the misdeeds of the people are the reason for the judgment that has taken place.[21]

The next section describes just how legitimate the appeal for Yhwh's return for his servants' sake in 63:17 is in the light of the speech of judgment in Isa 65:1-7. With למען עבדי (for my servants' sake) Isa 65:8 describes *who* Yhwh's servants are. "I will bring forth descendants from Jacob and from Judah inheritors of my mountains, and my chosen ones shall inherit it and my servants shall dwell there" (v. 9). Yhwh's servants are the chosen ones, the inheritors of the holy mountains. For them Yhwh will return. That is the bold assertion of Isa 65:8-10: *the chosen ones* will take part in the coming time of redemption. The others, namely, those who have left Yhwh and forgotten his holy mountain (65:11), will be judged. Yhwh does respond to the original lament in Isa 63:7-64:11 calling for his return for the sake of his servants; however, the "servants" are redefined and no longer refer to the people as a whole. Isaiah 65:8-12 functions as a second answer to the communal lament and divides the people of God into two groups.[22]

These two answers thereby correct the central theological statements of the prayer. Presuming the entirety of God's people, the communal lament attributes the possibility for salvation solely in Yhwh himself because of the people's entanglement in guilt. Isaiah 65:1-12, however, differentiates two distinct groups within the community of God's people. This entails a differentiation of Yhwh's deeds. Thus, the petition for Yhwh to return for the sake of his servants has different consequences: salvation for the righteous, the actual servants; and judgment for those who forsake Yhwh. With this crucial distinction identified, the connection between guilt and wrath can also be rightly understood: Yhwh's servants in Isa 65:8-10 are exempt from his righteous wrath, and the guilt is attributed solely to the sinners within the community.

---

intention, which is a complete defamation of the sinners; see Koenen, *Ethik und Eschatologie*, 191-92; and Lau, *Schriftgelehrte Prophetie*, 175-77.

21. The references to Isa 65:1-7 are discussed, e.g., by Koenen, *Ethik und Eschatologie*, 162-64; Ulrich Berges, *Das Buch Jesaja. Komposition und Endgestalt* (HBS 16; Freiburg: Herder, 1998), 497-500; and Steck, *Studien zu Tritojesaja*, 218-25.

22. See Blenkinsopp, *Isaiah 56-66*, 274-76.

The following text describes the divine interaction with the righteous and the sinners and places it in a universal perspective. Both go beyond the prayers. The salvific action of God is invoked in the prayer but not carried out. The universal perspective, however, which integrates the whole cosmos and the nations in the eschatological vision, is unfamiliar to the supplicant whose focus is the relation between God and his people. With the idea of a newly created heaven and earth, Isa 65:13–25 expresses a universal rearrangement with corresponding consequences for the righteous: long life, safe living, eating what one sows, absence of suffering, and so forth (65:19–25). The vision is created using material from the Deutero-Isaianic tradition. Verse 17 says: "See, I am about to create new heavens and a new earth…"[23]

Not to remember (לא זכר) the former (הראשונות), because Yhwh renews (חדש), goes back to a central *topos* of Deutero-Isaianic theology most clearly seen in Isa 43:18–19.[24] In contrast to Isa 65:17, Yhwh declares a new exodus in Isa 43:18–19.[25] Isaiah 65:16b, however, no longer deals with the subject of homecoming. Instead, going back to Deutero-Isaianic statements about creation (see 45:18–19; 42:5–9), Yhwh proves to be the one who not only created heaven and earth but will create anew. At the same time, it is striking that statements about creation with ברא "heaven and earth" or "light and darkness" are not connected with the subject of "the new." Rather, they serve to establish the exclusivity of Yhwh as creator of the world and Lord over heaven and earth.[26] Isaiah 65:16b–25 connects the idea of renewal with the idea of Yhwh as creator by attributing renewal not to the exodus but to the creation of a new heaven and new earth. Isaiah 65:16b–25 thereby goes beyond its Deutero-Isaianic background. Yhwh is pictured as the creator of a cosmological renewal that goes beyond the existing cosmos and increases his exclusivity to the unsurpassable. The theme of Isa 65 is not creation and exodus but a new creation of heaven and earth as a reorganization of the cosmos.[27]

---

23. The translation follows Blenkinsopp, *Isaiah 56–66*, 283.
24. ראשונה (feminine plural) is found in Deutero-Isaiah: 41:22; 42:9; 43:9; 48:3; 46:9; 65:16–17.
25. See Joseph Blenkinsopp, *Isaiah 40–55. A New Translation with Introduction and Commentary* (AB 19A; New York: Doubleday, 2000), 227–28; and Klaus Kiesow, *Exodustexte im Jesajabuch: Literarkritische und motivgeschichtliche Analysen* (OBO 24; Göttingen: Vandenhoeck & Ruprecht, 1979), 76.
26. See, e.g., Isa 40:28; 42:5–9; 45:7–8, 12, 18; and further Jürgen van Oorschott, *Von Babel zum Zion: Eine literarkritische und redaktionsgeschichtliche Untersuchung* (BZAW 206; Berlin: de Gruyter, 1993), 69–74.
27. See Odil Hannes Steck, "Der neue Himmel und die neue Erde: Beobachtungen zur Rezeption von Gen 1–3 in Jes 65,16b–25," in *Studies in the Book of Isaiah: Festschrift Willem A. M. Beuken* (ed. Jacques van Ruiten and M. Vervenne; BETL 132; Leuven: University Press, 1997), 349–65.

Isaiah 66:1–24 appropriates this universal aspect of the new creation and connects it with a global temple theology so that the kingship of Yhwh becomes central: "Heaven is my throne, the earth is my footstool" (66:1), and "Did not my hand make all of these" (66:2).²⁸ In Isa 66 the concept of temple as the dwelling place of the deity is transferred to the whole cosmos.²⁹ The idea of Zion as Yhwh's holy mountain in combination with the throne-room vision (Isa 6) is the historical background for the impending judgment of the sinners as well as the salvific reconstitution of Zion. Just as the renewal of heaven and earth increase the vertical and horizontal dimensions, so also does the universalized temple theology in Isa 66: Yhwh is not in the temple, he is not even in heaven, but he sits enthroned on the heavens, so that the whole cosmos becomes the temple.³⁰ This increase in the vertical entails expansion in the horizontal as the inclusion of the nations in the eschatological salvation and judgment indicates. Again, in the book of Isaiah different ideas of the nations are interwoven. In Isa 66:18-23 Yhwh gathers all the nations so they see the divine *kabod*. This proves to be a *kabod* of judgment from which survivors from among the nations emerge.³¹ They are sent to the ends of the world to proclaim Yhwh's *kabod*.³² The response of the nations in verses 20–22 is an eschatological pilgrimage of the nations. This pilgrimage involves the nations bringing the Diaspora on horses, chariots, litters, mules, and dromedaries to Yhwh's holy mountain in Jerusalem in the same way that the Israelites bring *mincha* to Yhwh's house in pure vessels. Here three key concepts converge: (1) the idea of the nations being gathered for judgment; (2) the idea of the survivors from among the nations going on a pilgrimage to Zion; and (3) the idea of the

---

28. The translation follows Blenkinsopp, *Isaiah 56–66*, 290.

29. Cf. Matthias Albani, "'Wo sollte ein Haus sein, das ihr mir bauen könntet?' (Jes 66,1): Schöpfung als Tempel JHWHs?" in *Gemeinde ohne Tempel: Zur Substituierung und Transformation des Jerusalemer Tempels und seines Kults im Alten Testament, antiken Judentum und frühen Christentum* (ed. Beate Ego et al.; WUNT 118; Tübingen: Mohr Siebeck, 1999), 37–56.

30. The tradition-historical background is developed by Friedhelm Hartenstein, *Die Unzugänglichkeit Gottes im Heiligtum: Jesaja 6 und der Wohnort JHWHs in der Jerusalemer Kulttraditon* (WMANT 75; Neukirchen-Vluyn: Neukirchner, 1997), 57–68. Concepts of Yhwh enthroned in the temple are taken up, like the ones underlying Isa 6:1–13. These in turn have religion-historical parallels to El being enthroned on the floods. With the destruction of the temple and the experience of the exile, Yhwh's throne and his dwelling is transferred to heaven.

31. Since this expression of the survivors (פליט) only appears again in Isa 45:20 in connection with the nations, one can assume that this text underlies 66:18–21. It only becomes clear by the concept of the survivors that the nations are gathered for their judgment and the *kabod* Yhwh turns out in a threatening way for them. See Hans-Jürgen Hermisson, *Jesaja 45,8–49,13* (vol. 2 of *Deuterojesaja*; BKAT 11.2; Neukirchen-Vluyn: Neukirchner, 2003), 68. Cf. further Steck, *Studien zu Tritojesaja*, 259–60; and Blenkinsopp, *Isaiah 56–66*, 314–15.

32. These locations are also mentioned in Ezekiel's poem about Tyre (Ezek 27:10–25) and some of them in Ezek 38:1 and Isa 11:11; see Blenkinsopp, *Isaiah 56–66*, 314.

Diaspora Jews being repatriated. The pilgrimage of the nations together with the return of the Diaspora are already connected in Isa 60:4, 9; however, here the place of the journey is different.[33] The daughters are not carried on the side (60:4), but instead the Diaspora travels on horses and chariots. Unlike 60:4–9, the pilgrimage in Isa 66 does not deal with the rich tribute brought by the nations and kings to proclaim the universal kingship of Yhwh and to inaugurate his reign in Jerusalem.[34] Instead, the nations bring the Diaspora like the Israelites' *mincha* and thus gain a cultic function. The following verse expands on this cultic element when it states that Yhwh will take Levitical priests from these nations.[35] The nations who escaped from the judgment in 66:18–19 gain the privilege of cultic participation with God's people. They not only make a pilgrimage to Jerusalem to get *torah*, as in Isa 2:2–4. In Isa 66:18–21 the remnant of the nations who survive Yhwh's judgment are the righteous who come to worship Yhwh and participate in the eschatological Yhwh-cult. The community of God's people is now composed of all flesh (כל־בשׂר), including all the righteous from among God's people and the nations that endured Yhwh's judgment (Isa 66:23). They come from new moon to new moon, from Sabbath to Sabbath, to praise Yhwh.[36] Corresponding to the creator of the new heaven and the new earth, the Lord whose throne is heaven, is a universalized people, including all flesh, that is, the righteous of all flesh (Isa 65–66). The idea of כל־בשׂר again calls to mind the prologue of Deutero-Isaiah. Isaiah 40:5 promises that all flesh will see Yhwh's *kabod*. The fullest revelation of Yhwh's *kabod* is developed in the last chapter of the book, as shown above: the concept of creation and temple as the foundation of salvation for all flesh that escape judgment. At the end of time, Yhwh's *kabod* proves to be for salvation and judgment.

In light of these observations, Isa 65–66 is an obvious continuation of the communal lament. Central theological statements of the communal lament are modified by the idea of Yhwh's silence. Yhwh, according to Isa 65:1–7, has not been silent and will not be silent, and his speech announces judgment. Further, it is not Yhwh who has been silent but the people, because they did not respond to his affection. The reason for Yhwh's judgment is the guilt of the people, as verses 3–5 illustrate, and this is at the very center of the lament (not the state of entanglement in guilt). Moreover, it is necessary to recognize that this text implies a differentiation within the entity of God's people. Therefore, the petition in 63:17

---

33. Cf. Steck, *Studien zu Tritojesaja*, 97–100.
34. See Blenkinsopp, *Isaiah 56–66*, 212.
35. To whom וגם refers is very controversial. The context suggests the nations. See Koenen, *Ethik und Eschatologie*, 211; Blenkinsopp, *Isaiah 56–66*, 315; and Westermann, *Das Buch Jesaja*, 338.
36. See further Walter Groß, "Wer soll YHWH verehren? Der Streit um die Aufgabe und die Identität Israels in der Spannung zwischen Abgrenzung und Öffnung," in *Kirche in der Zeit* (ed. Hermann J. Vogt and C. Steiling; Munich: Wewel, 1990), 11–33.

for the return of Yhwh for the sake of his servants makes sense because the word "servants" signifies the righteous (65:8–12); for the sake of the (righteous) servants Yhwh returns, but the sinners experience judgment. On this modified basis the eschatological action of Yhwh unfolds in terms of new creation and universalized temple theology. Though Yhwh is called creator and father in Isa 64:7, the new creation in 65:16b–25 announces a universal reorganization of the cosmos with respective consequences. The same is true for Isa 66. The concept of a temple theology that describes the cosmos as temple (66:1–2; 66:18–24) and Yhwh's *kabod* as glory reveal connections to the concept of Yhwh's dwelling in heaven (63:15), but like the new creation aims at an eschatological reorganization of the cosmos.

The Communal Lament in Isaiah 63:7–64:11 as a Conclusion of the Book of Isaiah

The reinterpretation of the silence and division within God's people clearly identifies Isa 65–66 as a continuation of the communal lament. This raises the question: Could an earlier version of the book of Isaiah have ended with the communal lament? Here two strands of tradition are to be considered in the context of the book of Isaiah that are central to the prayer: the praying people's hardness of heart; and the identification of the praying people as servants.

The Hardness of Heart

The first part of the appeal in Isa 63:17 takes up the idea of the hardness of heart from Isa 6:1–11, which unfolds the reality of Yhwh's judgment in his holy place using the Jerusalem cult tradition as background. According to Friedhelm Hartenstein, the shaking of the doorposts, the smoke that filled the temple (Isa 6:4), and, in connection with this, the destruction of the whole country (6:11) describe the inability to approach Yhwh in his holy place. Yhwh's throne and the length of his train no longer yield salvation to the people.[37] The idea that the divine presence means judgment and not salvation for the praying people is also used in the prayer. The supplicants discern between the earthly destroyed temple in Isa 64:10, which is identified as the temple of the praying people by the first-person plural suffix, and Yhwh's dwelling in heaven (Isa 63:15). At the same time the earthly and the heavenly temple are described by the same attributes (קדוש, תפארה). On the one hand, the people are denied access to Yhwh's heavenly dwelling because of their entanglement in guilt. On the other hand, they hope that Yhwh will again turn the earthly temple, an image of his heavenly dwelling, into his dwelling place so they can experience Yhwh's salvific presence through

---

37. See Hartenstein, *Die Unzugänglichkeit Gottes im Heiligtum*, 109–83.

the temple again. While in Isa 6 the certainty of Yhwh's salvific presence in the temple is revoked, this is already the reality of the praying people (Isa 63:15–17). They suffer because Yhwh has evaded them.

Isa 6:10[38]	Isa 6:10
<u>Dull</u> this people's <u>mind</u>	השמן לב־העם הזה
stop their ears,	ואזניו הכבד
and seal their eyes,	ועיניו השע
lest they see with their eyes,	פן־יראה בעיניו
hear with their ears	ובאזניו ישמע
and understand with their <u>hearts</u>,	ולבבו יבין
and turn to be healed.	ושב ורפא לו

This presence of judgment means for Israel that their hearts (לב) become fat (שמן), their ears (אזניים) become heavy (כבד), and their eyes (עיניים) stick together (שעע) so that they cannot see with their eyes or hear with their ears. The ultimate consequence is that they cannot turn and be healed (6:10). In contrast to most other references to the motif of the hardness of heart in the book of Isaiah, 63:17 does not make use of the words "seeing" and "hearing." This section does, however, refer to Isa 6 with the mention of the hardened heart (קשח)[39] and the consequences of the hardness of heart. The prophecy of the hardness of heart made in Isa 6:9–11 has become the reality of those who offer this prayer. Their hearts are hardened and no longer recognize the path of virtue. Because Yhwh initiated this state of judgment, the people can no longer turn and be healed (6:10b). For this reason they complain: "Why do you let us stray from your paths?" The following appeal to release the hardness of heart and return so that the people will once again be granted participation in Yhwh's saving presence can only be made to Yhwh himself. The prophet's reaction in Isa 6 implicitly shows that only Yhwh can fulfill this appeal. Thus, in Isa 6:11a he asks Yhwh עד־מתי, (Yhwh, how long?), one of the typical questions of the communal lament, "How long will this state of unavoidable judgment remain?"(6:11a). Yhwh's answer in 6:11b echoes this prayer: "Until (עד) the cities (ערים) be wasted (שאה) and the land (אדמה) be utterly desolate (שממה)." Parallel to this statement, the destruction of the holy cities and the desolation (שממה) of Jerusalem are described as the current reality of God's people in Isa 64:9–10. What

---

38. The translations follow Brevard S. Childs, *Isaiah* (OTL; Louisville: Westminster John Knox, 2001), 50.

39. The fattening (שמן) of the heart in 6:10, the sticking (טחח) of the heart in 44:18, and the hardening (קשח) of the heart in 63:17. All three verbs are unique in connection with the word "heart" in the book of Isaiah.

Yhwh had pronounced in Isa 6:11b (עד) has come true. However, only Yhwh himself can end the present state of judgment and return to his people since the repentance of the people is no longer possible due to their fatty hearts (6:11; 63:17; 64:4).

The key word שממה, which is rarely used in the book of Isaiah, opens up one further literary connection to Isa 1. It has often been noted that this key word connects Isa 1 to Isa 6, but it also connects Isa 1 to 63:7–64:11.[40] In 1:2 Yhwh's sons (בנים) whom he has taken care of (גדל) become unruly (פשעו בי), similar to Isa 63:8–10. Yhwh's chosen people, sons who do not lie (63:8), turn into a people who rebel against him (63:10, והמה מרו). Analogous to the lament in Isa 63:7–64:11, Isa 1 develops the profound entanglement of guilt/sin using the woe oracle of verses 4–9, 10–17. As in the communal lament, this results in the desolation (שממה) of the land (ארץ) and burned cities (עריכם שרפות עש, see 64:10). The connection of שרף and אש is found in only these two parts of the book of Isaiah. In 64:10 לשרפת אש is said about the temple and שממה about Yhwh's holy cities.[41] The state of judgment previously announced in the woe oracle has become reality for those who pray the communal lament. So the transition from Isa 1 to Isa 6 to Isa 63:7–64:11 can be described as follows. The announcement of the judgment becomes the unavoidable judgment that is intensified in the communal lament because it has become reality.[42] As prophesied in Isa 1:7, not only the land and the cities are desolate but also Yhwh's holy cities, Zion, Jerusalem and the temple (64:9–10). Thus communication between Yhwh and his people has been destroyed as prophesied in Isa 6. So the end of the book of Isaiah returns to its beginning. Understood in this light, it is clear that the prophecies of the beginning have become the reality of the ones offering the communal lament. With reference to Isa 6, the end of the book urges Yhwh to repeal the entanglement of guilt and to return, since after Isa 6:1–13 only the return of Yhwh could once again make his holy place accessible.

Yhwh as Creator in Isa 57:14–27

Isaiah 57:14–21 represents a text within the so-called Trito-Isaianic collection which addresses the hardness of heart issue in Isa 6 as well as the communal lament in Isa 63:7–64:11. The text is part of the composition of Isa 56:9–59:21 but is clearly elevated from its context by the imperative plural of (סלל) in the begin-

---

40. The links between Isa 1 and 6 are emphasized by Uwe Becker, *Jesaja— von der Botschaft zum Buch* (FRLANT 178; Göttingen: Vandenhoeck & Ruprecht, 1997), 182–92; and Aejmelaeus, "Der Prophet als Klageliedsänger," 48.

41. שממה is also used in Isa 17:9; 62:4 and the noun שמה in Isa 5:9; 13:9; 24:12.

42. Another aspect that connects the three texts is the terminology of sin (Isa 1:4; 6:7; 64:4–8), which however expresses–following the line of argument above–different nuances.

ning and the connection of פנה דרך. The idea of a "clearing of the way" from Isa 40:3 and Isa 62:10 also resonates within it.[43] However, unlike the famous prologue of Deutero-Isaiah, the way is meant to be cleared for the people rather than Yhwh, and unlike Isa 62:10, the theme of returning home plays no role in the text. While Isa 62:10 indicates that the people of Jerusalem clear the way for those coming home, Isa 57:14 emphasizes that the obstacles separating God's people from Yhwh should be removed. Thus, Isa 57:14–21 does not aim at the return of the exiles (like Isa 40 and Isa 62:10), but at the return of the people to their God, which would mean an "inner" homecoming. The possibility of removing the obstacles from the way is added in v. 15 with a כי sentence resonating with Isa 6.[44] Yhwh is imagined as high and exalted, as ever-living and holy who, as such, is with the contrite and humble. He will not contend and be angry forever, bent on destroying the breath he has created (v. 16). The spirit of life and the breath that Yhwh created are already faint before him. Because Yhwh's wrath has already begun to destroy his own creation, he removes the obstacles from the way between himself and his people. Therewith, Yhwh's wrath is not only directed against his people because of their guilt, but ultimately against himself as creator of the spirit of life. The guilt[45] of the people in v. 17 is then described similarly to the confession of the communal lament (Isa 64:4–6). The different aspects of the verbs in the verse refer to the conditions that have lasted into the present and have affected it. Yhwh contends (קצפתי) because of the people's guilt, and he struck them (imperfect + *waw copulativum*), hid (הסתר *infinitive absolutus*) his face and was angry (ואקצף imperfect + *waw copulativum*).[46] This correlation between guilt and wrath is presumed and, in Yhwh's perspective, leads the people to turn away and follow the ways of their hearts (שובב בדרך לבו, v. 17b). In light of this, Isa 63:17 seems to present the perspective of the praying people. They complain that Yhwh lets them stray from his path and they ask Yhwh to return. Yhwh's answer to this petition seems to be contained in Isa 57:18, which again refers back to Isa 6:9–10.[47] Yhwh sees them straying from the paths and understands the connection between the people's guilt and the divine wrath. He returns to his people and wants to lead, heal (Isa 6:10; 57:18) and comfort them. The people cannot turn around and save themselves, and their futility is rooted in the pronouncement in Isa 6:9–10. But Yhwh can return to his people and promise them healing. Thereby, the entanglement in guilt acknowledged in Isa 64:4–6

---

43. Cf. Odil Hannes Steck, *Bereitete Heimkehr: Jesaja 35 als redaktionelle Brücke zwischen dem Ersten und dem Zweiten Jesaja* (SBS 121; Stuttgart: Katholisches Bibelwerk, 1985), 66–71; and Goldenstein, *Das Gebet der Gottesknechte*, 175–179.

44. Cf. Blenkinsopp, *Isaiah 56–66*, 170.

45. The definition of בצע is given by Rainer Kessler, "Art.: Israel. II Geschichte: 4. Sozialgeschichte," *RGG*[4] 4:296–97.

46. Cf. Koenen, *Ethik und Eschatologie*, 51.

47. Cf. Blenkinsopp, *Isaiah 56–66*, 172; and Berges, *Das Buch Jesaja*, 471–472.

and addressed in the petition of Isa 63:17 that made it impossible for the people to return to find healing is abolished.[48] The reason for the breaking of the connection between guilt and wrath is not based, however, on the praying people as Yhwh's servants as in Isa 63:17, but on Yhwh's status as creator and the fallibility of his creatures. This means that the dimension of guilt is now reflected on the level of creation and becomes part of human life. At the same time the historical perspective on the relation between God and the people of Isa 6:1–11 and the communal lament is absent. While the hardness of heart in Isa 6:1–11 is the result of the people's guilt and the historical recital (Isa 63:8–10.11–14) transfers guilt to the history of Yhwh with his people, Isa 57:14–21 looks back on the members of the people as fallible creatures. By embedding the concept of hardness of heart into the larger perspective of the divine creation, the end of the hardness of heart or the renunciation of everlasting divine wrath is cast on Yhwh (Isa 57:14–21). With the repeated resonance of Isa 6, this passage projects an escape from the entanglement in guilt of Isa 63:15–17. Though Yhwh is hidden, as in Isa 6, he is also creator, and thus he will renounce his wrath forever for the sake of his creation and, ultimately, for his own sake.

The Servants of Yhwh

The concept of Yhwh as creator and the subsequent implied renunciation of divine wrath, as in Isa 57:14–21, indicate a salvific option for the praying people; however, the appeal to Yhwh to return for the sake of his servants at the end of verse 17 represents a grounds for deliverance. This means the ones who pray consider themselves Yhwh's servants with reference to the diverse and complex tradition of the *Ebed* Yhwh in Second Isaiah. Concerning this tradition, I will only mention Isa 43:8–13, because this text connects the motif of the hardness of heart and the notion of *Ebed* Yhwh with each other.[49]

Isa 43:8[50]	Isa 43:8
Bring forth[51] the <u>people</u> who have <u>eyes</u> yet are <u>blind</u>,	הוציא עם־<u>עור ועינים</u> יש

---

48. Cf. further Goldenstein, *Das Gebet der Gottesknechte*, 98, 115–16, 125, 161.

49. The servants of Yhwh as a main subject of Deutero- and Trito-Isaiah is emphasized by Joseph Blenkinsopp, "The Servant and the Servants in Isaiah and the Formation of the Book," in *Writing and Reading the Scroll of Isaiah: Studies of an Interpretative Tradition, Formation and Interpretation of the Old Testament Literature* (ed. Craig C. Broyles and Craig A. Evans; VTSup 70.1-2; Leiden: Brill, 1997), 155–75.

50. The translation follows Blenkinsopp, *Isaiah 40–55*, 222.

51. Following Qᵃ; see Werner Grimm, *Das Trostbuch Gottes: Jesaja 40–55* (Stuttgart: Calwer, 1990), 30–31; and Karl Elliger, *Jesaja 40,1–45,7* (vol. 1 of *Deuterojesaja*; BK 11.1; Neukirchen-Vluyn: Neukirchner, 1978), 306.

who have <u>ears</u> yet are <u>deaf</u>.	וחרשים ואזנים למו
Isa 43:10	**Isa 43:10**
You are my witness—Y<small>HWH</small> declares—	אתם עדי נאם־יהוה
my <u>servant</u> whom I have chosen,	<u>ועבדי</u> אשר בחרתי
that you may know me and trust me	למען תדעו ותאמינו לי
and understand that I am the One.	ותבינו כי־אני הוא

Westermann has rightly classified this text as an announcement of judgment. God's people are called to the witness box. The characterization of Israel is of major importance: she is blind but has eyes, deaf but has ears. This correlates with the statement made in Isa 6:9–10. However, this Israel is also the servant (singular) that Y<small>HWH</small> has chosen (43:10). The people should testify that there is no other God than Y<small>HWH</small> and no other redeemer (מושיע, Isa 43:11). The prophecy of judgment in Isa 6:1–11 has been fulfilled. Israel is blind although she has eyes, but at the same time she is Y<small>HWH</small>'s servant. Thus Isa 43:8–10 shows that the people have a particular relationship with Y<small>HWH</small>, and, thus, they are on the way to salvation. Just as the blind and deaf people are Y<small>HWH</small>'s servants, so is Y<small>HWH</small> the redeemer of the people. The petition and the communal lament in verse 17 refer to this ambivalence. The hearts that Y<small>HWH</small> hardened are now a reality; the people are living with the hardness of heart. However all-embracing the state of judgment is, those who pray refer to a promise that can make even this situation result in salvation—since the people can be hard of heart and the chosen servant at the same time. With their appeal, those who pray place themselves in the tradition of the servant of Y<small>HWH</small> and name themselves so (now in the plural form). Thus they are a living reminder that hardness of heart does not nullify the prophecy that promises, even in the midst of guilt, a way of salvation granted by Y<small>HWH</small>.[52]

Yet the praying people ask Y<small>HWH</small> to return not only because they are his servants but also for the sake of the tribes of his heritage. Thus another text stands behind Isa 63:17, which again refers to the tradition of the servant:

Isa 54:17[53]	**Isa 54:17**
This, then, is <u>the lot of Y<small>HWH</small>'s servants</u>,	זאת <u>נחלת עבדי יהוה</u>
their vindication from me. A word of Y<small>HWH</small>.	וצדקתם מאתי נאם־יהוה

---

52. Another text that underlies the communal lament in a way similar to Isa 43:8–10 is 42:18–19. See the detailed discussion in Goldenstein, *Das Gebet der Gottesknechte*, 156–57, 162.

53. The translation follows Blenkinsopp, *Isaiah 40–55*, 358.

The correlation between both texts lies especially in their reference to God's people or the praying people as Yhwh's *servants* (plural) and as his inheritance.[54] While the meaning of the servant alternates between addressing the people in plural and in singular (as in Isa 43:10), this text is the first one in the order of the text that uses the title in the plural.[55] At the same time, at the end of the great promise of salvation in which Zion the barren becomes the fruitful, Zion the desolate becomes the inhabited (54:1–10), Zion the abandoned becomes the prosperous (54:11–16), Zion itself becomes the place of divine salvific presence and the inheritance of Yhwh's servants. Just as in Isa 43:8–10, the reversal from devastation to salvation is promised here. The total desolation of the country as announced in Isa 6:1–11 is contrasted with the renewed salvific presence of Yhwh in Zion. For the praying people, this promise has not yet been fulfilled. They still suffer because of their distance from God (Isa 64:4–6) and its consequences as they mourn over the desolation of the holy place (Isa 64:8–11). By designating themselves as Yhwh's servants and tribes of his inheritance they remind Yhwh of his promises of salvation for the Zion. Their status also gives them confident hope in their salvation even in their situation of suffering under hardness of heart.[56]

The Hardness of Heart and the Servants of Yhwh in the Book of Isaiah

The reference to the motif of the hardness of heart in Isa 6 and the description of God's people as servants includes and connects two main lines of prophetic self-perception in First and Second Isaiah. The incorporation of the motif of the hardness of heart from Isa 6 shows the concept of guilt that is made particularly clear by the confession. Yhwh allows his people to leave the path of virtue and then hardens their heart (Isa 63:17). This state of permanent judgment mirrors the threat of judgment in Isa 6. Yhwh has denied his people his redeeming presence and thus imposed the state of the hardness of heart upon them. Nevertheless, those who pray describe themselves as servants of Yhwh, and thus they refer to a situation in which Yhwh once promised the blind people salvation.

The redactors of Isa 63:7–64:11 chose this form of prayer with its elements of lament and petition because they knew that only Yhwh could take back his judging presence as announced in Isa 6. The foundation of this is the promises

---

54. See Goldenstein, *Das Gebet der Gottesknechte*, 101.
55. See Blenkinsopp, "Servant and the Servants," 164; and Willem A.M. Beuken, "The Main Theme in Trito-Isaiah: 'The Servants of YHWH,'" *JSOT* 47 (1990): 67–76.
56. The tradition of the *Ebed* Yhwh cannot be discussed further in this paper. For the connections to the fourth song of *Ebed* Yhwh, in which the praying people identify themselves with the suffering *Ebed* without adopting the idea that the servant bears the burden of the community's transgression and iniquity, see Goldenstein, *Das Gebet der Gottesknechte*, 164–67; and Steck, *Studien zu Tritojesaja*, 238, 240.

of Deutero-Isaiah. Therefore, they used the form of penitential prayer in order to stand in the tradition of Lamentations and the communal laments of the Psalms.[57] In contrast to Lam 2, however, in which Israel is shaken by the destruction of Israel and Yhwh stands on the side of the enemies, the people praying here address Yhwh on the basis of the Isaianic theology of God as "father" in all its ambivalence (Isa 63:15–17).[58] At the same time, Isa 63:7–64:11 contains many allusions to the whole preceding book of Isaiah and in effect summarizes the book's main topics. As a result, the prayer in Isa 63:7–64:11, standing as a literary composition placed at the end of the book, cannot be understood in its depth without the context of the rest of the book of Isaiah. In this sense the communal lament embodies the theology of the whole preceding book of Isaiah and, in my opinion, can be understood as a conclusion of an earlier form of this book. This ending, however, motivated someone to add a continuation that we find in the present chapters 65 and 66.

---

57. See Richard J. Bautch, "The Psalmic Origins of Trito-Isaiah's Penitential Prayer" (in this volume): by employing expressions typical of psalmic penitence, "the composer is able to underscore both the people as sinners and God as alienated from the covenant by their sins" (92–93 above). At the same time, "[t]he lament of Isa 63–64 and the book of Lamentations set the tone for a kind of penitential piety, both public and private, both mainstream and sectarian, that came to be a characteristic feature of Jewish religious life throughout the Second Temple period" (Blenkinsopp, *Isaiah 55–66*, 266).

58. According to Emmendörfer, *Der ferne Gott*, 291–92, this refers to a temporal distance. While he dates Lam 2 during the exile, Isa 63:7–64:11 belongs to laments developed after the exile.

Ezra 9:6–15: A Penitential Prayer within Its Literary Setting

Michael W. Duggan

Introduction

The three penitential prayers in Ezra-Nehemiah (Ezra 9:6–15; Neh 1:5–11; 9:6–37) function as keys for interpreting the whole narrative from a theological perspective. The prayer of the Levites (Neh 9:6–37) has been a primary focus of past research on penitential prayers in the Persian period.[1] In this essay I want to concentrate on Ezra 9:6–15 in order to complement previous work on the Levites' prayer. The prayer of Ezra (Ezra 9:6–15) exhibits remarkable integration within its literary context. As such, this prayer is uniquely suitable for examining the contribution that context makes to the content and interpretation of a penitential psalm. I undertake such an examination through a synchronic analysis of Ezra's prayer within its narrative setting. At the same time, I provide a diachronic analysis of those elements in the prayer that reinterpret various traditions in order to address the issues that are central to Ezra-Nehemiah. I examine the relationship between Ezra's prayer and the Levites' psalm in order to identify features of penitential prayer that were significant to the author of Ezra-Nehemiah.

My analysis consists of seven parts: (1) a description of the narrative context (Ezra 7:1–10:44); (2) a literal translation of the prayer; (3) a structuring of the prayer; (4) a scrutiny of the vocabulary that establishes the prayer within the immediate context of Ezra's marriage reform; (5) a consideration of the links between the prayer and material in Nehemiah; (6) notations on the connection between the prayer and the material that precedes Ezra's reform; and (7) concluding comments on the form and content of the prayer.

---

1. Mark J. Boda, *Praying the Tradition: The Origin and Use of Tradition in Nehemiah 9* (BZAW 277; Berlin: de Gruyter, 1999); and Michael W. Duggan, *The Covenant Renewal in Ezra-Nehemiah (Neh 7:72b–10:40): An Exegetical, Literary, and Theological Study* (SBLDS 164; Atlanta: Society of Biblical Literature, 2001), 157–233.

Ezra 9:6–15 within Its Literary Setting

I have argued elsewhere that Ezra-Nehemiah is a single book that has two major divisions: Ezra 1–6 and Ezra 7–Neh 13.[2] The story of Ezra marks a new beginning following the drama of constructing and dedicating the temple (Ezra 1–6). The marriage reform and renewal of the covenant, which Ezra initiates (Ezra 7–10; Neh 7:72b–10:40), provides the communal foundation for the rebuilding of the walls and subsequent social reform under Nehemiah (Neh 1:1–7:72a; 11:1–12:43; 12:44–13:31).

The narrative of Ezra's initial work in Jerusalem consists of four parts: (1) an introduction of his background and summary of his journey (7:1–10); (2) the royal documents that constitute his commission (7:11–26); (3) his journey to Jerusalem and depositing of silver, gold, and vessels at the temple (7:27–8:36); and (4) his marriage reform (9:1–10:44).[3] The material is a mixture of third-person narrative and first-person autobiography. The narrative sections provide a framework around the autobiographical material. The narrator, at the beginning, introduces Ezra and transcribes the royal edicts (7:1–26) and, at the end, describes the process of undoing the marriages that crossed acceptable ethnic boundaries (10:1–44). Ezra provides a first-person account of his journey from Babylon to Jerusalem (7:27–8:36) and of his reaction to the news of the illicit marriages (9:1–15). Prayer provides an inclusion for the autobiographical section, which opens with Ezra's thanksgiving to God for gaining the favor of Artaxerxes (7:27–28) and concludes with his penitential prayer (9:6–15).[4]

The autobiographical account of Ezra's marriage reform focuses on the double scandals of adult Judahite men marrying young foreign women and of Judahite men arranging for their sons to marry foreigners. The third-person narrative, on the other hand, describes only the sundering of marriages that adult men have contracted with foreign women (9:2; cf. 10:2–3, 10–11). Hence these

---

2. Duggan, *Covenant Renewal*, 59–67; Sara Japhet, "Composition and Chronology in the Book of Ezra-Nehemiah," in *Second Temple Studies 2: Temple Community in the Persian Period* (ed. Tamara C. Eskenazi and Kent H. Richards; JSOTSup 175: Sheffield: JSOT Press, 1994), 208–15.

3. The book of Ezra (7:1–10:44) recounts Ezra's early work of delivering supplies to the temple and of implementing a marriage reform. Ezra resurfaces later in the book of Nehemiah in the covenant renewal (Neh 7:72b–8:18) and in the dedication of the city walls (Neh 12:27–43).

4. At some early stage in the tradition history, the Ezra material in Ezra-Nehemiah may have taken the form of an Ezra Memoir (EM) in the first person. This memoir would have described Ezra's mission in the following sequence: Ezra 7:1–26 (introduction of Ezra and his mandates: first, to transport material to the temple [7:13–20, 21–24]; second, to apply the law in Yehud [7:14, 25–26]); 7:27–8:36 (implementation of the first mandate: the transportation of the goods to temple); Neh 8:1–18 (implementation of the second mandate: the teaching of the law in the land); Ezra 9:1–10:44 (the specific application of the law: the abolition of marriages, which the law had exposed as illicit). See Duggan, *Covenant Renewal*, 6–15.

portions overlap in their shared concern about the illicitness of adult Judahite men marrying foreigners. References to particular social categories and temporal sequences bind the two sections together. The officials tell Ezra about the illicit marriages in the beginning; subsequently, Shechaniah confesses the offense and invites the marriage reform (9:1–2; cf. 10:2–4). "Those who tremble" (*hărēdîm*) at God's word or commandment are allies of Ezra in each section (9:4; cf. 10:3).[5] Ezra describes how he fasted and then knelt to pray and the narrator relates that he stood up after prayer and continued his fast through the night (9:5; cf. 10:5–6). The temporal sequence is consistent across the two sections: Ezra begins his prayer at the time of the evening sacrifice, gets up and passes the night in Jehohanan's chamber, and addresses the crowd some three days later (9:5; 10:6, 9).

Ezra's penitential prayer fits superbly into its immediate context.[6] The narrative in 10:1 picks up on the autobiography in 9:5 through a shared emphasis on Ezra praying while on the ground. Nevertheless his penitential psalm provides the required transition from biography to narrative. Most significantly, insofar as the penitential prayer focuses on the offense of marriage to non-Judahites, it provides the essential thematic bridge from the autobiographical section to the subsequent narrative (9:12, 14; cf. 9:2–3; 10:2–3, 10–11).

Translation of Ezra 9:6–15

9:6 My God,
I am too ashamed and disgraced to lift my face to you, my God;
for our iniquities abound overhead
and our great guilt to the heavens.
7 From the days of our ancestors until today,
we have been in great guilt.
and for our iniquities, we, our kings, and our priests have been given
into the power of the kings of the lands,
to the sword, to captivity, to plundering and to being shame faced today.
8 But now, for a brief moment, there is mercy from Yhwh, our God,
to leave a remnant, to give us a stake in his holy place,
to enlighten our eyes, our God, and to give us a little reviving in our servitude.
9 For we are slaves, but in our servitude, our God has not forsaken us,
but he has extended to us favor before the kings of Persia
to give us reviving,
to raise up the house of our God,

---

5. The *hărēdîm* are a significant group in the era of resettlement after the exile (Isa 66:2, 5). For a description of the *hărēdîm* and an interpretation of links between Isa 65–66 and Ezra 9–10, see Joseph Blenkinsopp, *Ezra-Nehemiah* (OTL; Philadelphia: Westminster, 1988), 69, 178–79.

6. See Hugh G. M. Williamson, *Ezra, Nehemiah* (WBC 16; Waco, Tex: Word, 1985), 128.

to reconstruct its ruins,
and to give us a wall in Judah and in Jerusalem.
¹⁰ But now, our God, what shall we say after this?
For we have forsaken your commandments,
¹¹ which you commanded through your servants the prophets, saying,
"The land, which you are entering to possess
is a land polluted with the pollution of the peoples of the lands,
with their abominations, with which they have filled it from one end to the other,
in their impurities.
¹² And now, do not give your daughters to their sons
and do not take their daughters for your sons
and do not seek their peace or prosperity forever.
In this way, you will become strong and feed on the good of the land
And you will bequeath it to your children forever."
¹³ After all that has come upon us
for our bad deeds and for our great guilt—
though you, our God, have suppressed our iniquities
and you have given us a remnant such as this—
¹⁴ shall we turn back to break your commandments
and to enter into marriage among peoples of these abominations?
Would you not rage against us until you would destroy us
so that there would be no survivor or remnant?
¹⁵ Yhwh, God of Israel,
You are righteous.
For we are left as a remnant as of today.
Here we are before you in our guilt
even when no one can stand before you on account of this.

The Structure of Ezra's Prayer

Ezra's penitential prayer takes the form of a prose psalm, which lacks the cadences that are emblematic of Hebrew poetry.[7] Nevertheless, the prayer exhibits a structure that derives from a combination of confessional appeals,

---

7. Harm W. M. van Grol ("Exegesis of the Exile—Exegesis of Scripture? Ezra 9:6–9," in *The Crisis of Israelite Religion: Transformation of Religious Tradition in Exilic and Post-Exilic Times* [ed. Bob Becking and Marjo C. A. Korpel; OtSt 42; Leiden: Brill, 1999], 32–33; and "'Indeed, Servants We Are': Ezra 9, Nehemiah 9 and 2 Chronicles 12 Compared," in Becking and Korpel, *Crisis of Israelite Religion,* 210) describes Ezra 9:6–15 as both a prayer and a sermon. In his view, the homiletic elements are: (1) Ezra's speaking of God in the third person (9:7–9); (2) the words of the prophets, spoken in the second person, presumably to Ezra's audience (9:11–12); (3) Ezra's rhetorical questions, which address his audience more than God (9:10–14; esp. 9:13–14a); and (4) the final sentence, which describes the plight of the community (9:15). For his structuring of

transitional terms, repetitions and reinforcement of themes through similes that characterize each section. The direct invocation of God introduces the first and last parts of the prayer (9:6-7, 15). Ezra's personal appeal ("my God," 9:6) at the beginning gives way to the more communal confession at the end ("YHWH, God of Israel, you are righteous," 9:15). The introductory invocation consists of two parts: Ezra's confession of guilt (אשמה, 9:6-7) and his interpretation of the present servitude to foreign overlords as divine retribution for past iniquities (9:7).[8] This bifocal emphasis in the opening confession corresponds with the twofold reference to YHWH's righteousness and the people's guilt (אשמה, 9:15) in the concluding confession.

Transitional vocabulary introduces the middle section (9:8-14) and subdivides it into three parts: "but now" (ועתה, 9:8, 10) leads into a declaration of God's mercy in the present (9:8-9) and then into a subsequent confession of sin (9:10-12), while the summarizing phrase "after all that has come upon us" (אחרי כל־הבא עלינו, 9:13) provides the transition to a rhetorical appeal for fidelity on the part of the people in the present (9:13-14).[9]

Hence the prayer exhibits the following structure:

A. Confession of the people's guilt in the past (9:6-7)
   1. The guilt of the people (9:6)
   2. Divine retribution for the people's guilt (9:7)
B. God's mercy and the people's decision in the present (9:8-14)
   1. Proclamation of divine mercy (9:8-9)
   2. Confession of present sin: trespassing the prophets' commandments (9:10-12)
   3. Decision against the sin of intermarriage (9:13-14)
C. Summary confession of God's righteousness and the people's guilt (9:15)
   1. The righteousness of YHWH seen in the remnant (9:15a)
   2. Acknowledgment of guilt (9:15b)

In terms of literary forms, Ezra's prayer contains three confessions of sin (9:6-7, 10, 15b), which are closely related to three acknowledgments of God's mercy (9:8-9, 13, 15a). Furthermore, the quotation of the prophets (9:11-12) leads into the two rhetorical questions, which underline the necessity of dissolving the marriages to foreigners (9:13-14).

---

the text as a combination of prayer and sermon, see van Grol, "Exegesis of the Exile," 33-36; and idem, "Indeed, Servants We Are," 210.

8. I read the passive voice in v. 7 ("we have been given"; נתנו אנחנו) as theological in view of both the direct address to God in the preceding verse and the primacy of divine agency in the following verse.

9. ועתה occurs also in the quotation of the prophets, where it provides the transition from their instruction (v. 11) to their commandments (v. 12).

Recurring terminology unifies the prayer and establishes the themes of each subsection. The vocative appeal to God is at the forefront of each confession ("my God" [אלהי, 2x] 9:6; "our God" [אלהינו] 9:10; "Yhwh, God of Israel" [ישראל יהוה אלהי], 9:15). Emphasis on "our guilt" at the beginning and end of the prayer further establishes the inclusion (אשמתנו, 9:6, 15). Moreover, in the Hebrew of the same verses, the expression for being too ashamed to lift "my face to you" (פני אליך, 9:6) resonates with no one being able to "stand before you" (לפניך, 9:15). Finally, references to "today" occur only in the first and last sections of the prayer (יום הזה, 9:7 [bis], 15).

Significantly, each mention of divine mercy refers to the survival of a "remnant" (פליטה, 9:8, 13, 15; cf. 9:14) as the demonstration of such mercy. This emphasis on the "remnant" provides the primary inclusion for the middle section of the prayer (9:8, 14). God's sustaining of a remnant up to the present time (9:8, 13) provides the background for the final rhetorical question, which foresees the consequence of losing the remnant should the people not dissolve the marriages to foreigners (9:14).

A fourfold repetition of the verb "to give" (נתן) with God as the subject and "us" as the indirect object provides the thread through the first subsection of the middle portion, which emphasizes God's mercy (9:8–9). God "gave" the people a "stake" (יתד) in his holy place, a "reviving" (מחיה [bis]) amid oppression, and a "wall" (גדר) in Jerusalem. Add to this the "favor" of the Persian kings, which God has "extended" (יט־עלינו חסד, 9:9) to the people, and one comprehends the dimensions of Yhwh's "mercy" (תחנה, 9:8) that opens this subsection.

The next two subsections are held together by the concern for observance of God's "commandments" (מצותיך, 9:10, 14) at the beginning and end. The quotation of the prophets exhibits the language of conquest (ירש hip'il, 9:11, 12) that coincides with a fixation on "the land" (ה]ארץ] [3x], 9:11–12). The prophets' message consists of two parts: (1) a generic description of the land as defiled by the "pollution" (נדה), "abominations" (תועבות), and "impurities" (טמאת) of the "peoples of the lands" (עמי־הארצות, 9:11); and then (2) a specific focus on the prohibition against Judahite parents arranging for their children to marry foreigners (9:12).[10] Persistent observance of this commandment would allow for successive generations to inhabit the land "forever" (עד־עולם).[11]

---

10. Harold C. Washington ("Israel's Holy Seed and the Foreign Women of Ezra-Nehemiah: A Kristevan Reading," *BibInt* 11 [2003]: 427–37) perceives a derogatory reference to the foreign women behind the relationship between the "unclean" land and the "unclean" peoples of the land (9:11, נדה; cf. Lev 12:5; 15:19; Ezek 18:6). For a sociological description of how ritual expulsion of foreign women represents a purification of the community, see David Janzen, *Witch-Hunts, Purity and Social Boundaries: The Expulsion of the Foreign Women in Ezra 9–10* (JSOTSup 350; Sheffield: Sheffield Academic Press, 2002).

11. "Forever" (עד־עולם) here stands in contrast to "for a brief moment" (כמעט־רגע) in 9:7.

Two rhetorical questions formulate the decision against intermarriage following the quotation of the prophets (9:13, 14). The first question contains three terms, which either echo the introduction or foreshadow the concluding confession: the vocative appeal to God ("our God," 9:13; cf. "My God," 9:1; "God of Israel," 9:15); "our [great] guilt" אשמתנו גדלה, 9:13, 6, 7; cf. אשמתינו, 9:15); and "our iniquities" (עוננו, 9:13; cf. עונתינו, 9:6, 7).[12] This rhetorical piece turns attention back to the initial statement of the prophets against marriage to foreigners, which is now subsumed under the category of divine "commandments" (מצותיך, 9:14a). The second rhetorical question contemplates the sanction for trespassing this commandment, that is, the loss of even the "remnant," which is the evidence of divine mercy up to the present moment (פליטה, 9:14; cf. 9:8, 13, 15).

Ezra's Prayer within the Context of Ezra's Marriage Reform (Ezra 9–10)[13]

The prophets' condemnation of mixed marriages and Ezra's rhetorical application of their words to his situation forge the primary bond between Ezra's prayer and the surrounding material (9:12a, 14a; cf. 9:1–2; 10:2–3, 10–11). However, the prayer belongs more strictly with the preceding autobiography than with the narrative that follows. The vocabulary of the prophets in Ezra's prayer (9:12a) resonates with some terms that the officials use to describe the offensive marriages (9:1–2) but has almost no association with the words of Shechaniah (10:2–4) and Ezra in the subsequent narrative (10:10–11). Note the identical vocabulary in Ezra 9:12a and 9:2a: (1) the verb "to take" (נשא); (2) the object "their daughters" (בנתיהם); and (3) the indirect object "for [their/your] sons" (בנים). Ezra's quotation of the prophets concentrates on the prohibition against parents arranging mixed marriages for their sons and daughters (9:12a). This prohibition echoes the report of the officials that some fathers had chosen foreign wives for their sons (9:2a). By way of contrast, the prophets' words do not address precisely the exist-

---

12. Neh 3:37 and 9:2 represent the only other occurrences of עון in Ezra-Nehemiah.
13. For a fine diachronic analysis of the narrative, see Yonina Dor, "The Composition of the Episode of the Foreign Women in Ezra ix–x," *VT* 53 (2003): 26–47. Dor argues that the story of Ezra's marriage reform developed from three sources that underwent two revisions. The earliest source is the "long narrative," a composition by an author close to the actual events; however, this source suffered some subsequent corruption or alteration (10:7–44). A group of separatists in a subsequent era added a short narrative focusing on Shechanaiah, which served to further highlight the ideal of absolute separation from foreigners, including divorcing of foreign wives (10:2–6). The prayer (9:6–15) was an independent source, around which the author of Ezra-Nehemiah constructed a frame (9:1–5; 10:1). This author exercised a moderating influence on the material in Ezra 10 by emphasizing the prescription against marrying foreigners, which was already in the prayer, without making any reference to sundering the marriages that people had contracted previously (9:12–14; cf. 9:2).

ing illicit marriages between adult men and foreign women, which is the exclusive preoccupation of the subsequent reform, as it had been the foremost concern of the officials' original report (10:2–3, 10–11; cf. 9:2a). In fact, there is no text in the Pentateuch that requires the dissolution of marriages to foreigners.

Nevertheless, Ezra's prayerful application of the prophets' words addresses the situation of Judahite men taking foreigners as their wives (9:14a). At the same time, however, his language for marriage differs from that of the surrounding narrative. At this point in the prayer, Ezra employs the verb חתן (*hitpaʿel*) whereas in the subsequent narrative Shechaniah, Ezra, and the narrator successively use the verb ישב (*hipʿil*) to describe the contracting of marriage to foreign women (9:14a; cf. 10:2, 10, 14, 17, 18).[14]

The language pertaining to marriage in Ezra 9:12a and 9:2a reflects Deut 7:3, whereas there are no such resonances in the vocabulary of Ezra 10.[15] Ezra's version of the prophets' admonition represents variants of the Deuteronomic text. First, Ezra 9:12a employs the plural forms of verbs, objects, and indirect objects, while

---

14. Ezra 9:14 represents the only occurrence of the verb חתן (*hitpaʿel*) in Ezra-Nehemiah. The terminology of marriage to foreign women in Ezra 10 occurs again in the narrative of Judahites marrying women of Ashdod, Ammon, and Moab, which prompts Nehemiah's marriage reform (ישב *hipʿil*, Neh 13:23, 27).

15. See Blenkinsopp, *Ezra-Nehemiah*, 175–76. Five of the eight nations listed in Ezra 9:1 derive from Deut 7:3 (Canaanites, Hittites, Perizzites, Jebusites and Amorites). Mention of Ammonites, Moabites, and Egyptians reflects the influence of Deut 23:4–9, which stipulates the enduring exclusion of Ammonites and Moabites from the community, on one hand, but the admission of Egyptians after the third generation. The Deuteronomistic Historian recalls Deut 7:1–4 in his listing the nationalities of Solomon's foreign wives (1 Kgs 11:1–2). Note also the warning against intermarriage in Exod 34:11–16, which parallels Deut 7:1–4. Tamara C. Eskenazi and Eleanore P. Judd ("Marriage to a Stranger in Ezra 9–10," in Eskenazi and Richards *Second Temple Studies 2*, 268) point out that Ezra 9:1 speaks of "abominations like" those of the Canaanites and the other ethnic groups in the land prior to the conquest (9:1, לכנעני כתועבתיהם). Hence the text does not necessarily refer to members of these eight groups. "The people of the lands," whose women had married men of the golah, could refer to any of the resident people who did not belong to those clans of Judah and Benjamin, which had returned from exile (cf. Ezra 1:5; 4:1–4). Hence the foreign women in question could be either Ammonites and Moabites (Neh 13:23) or Judahites who had remained resident in the land throughout the exile (ibid., 268–70; cf. Harold C. Washington, "The Strange Woman [אשה זרה/נכריה] of Proverbs 1–9 and Post-Exilic Judaean Society," in Eskenazi and Richards *Second Temple Studies 2*, 238). Mary Douglas ("Responding to Ezra: The Priests and the Foreign Wives," *BibInt* 10 [2002]: 6–7, 8–23) asserts that applying the nomenclature of Israel's ancient enemies serves to prejudice the reader against anyone who was not of the golah community. She notes that the Priestly tradition in the Pentateuch contains no legislation against marrying foreigners. In fact, she argues, priestly contemporaries around 400 B.C.E. tailored significant material in Numbers and Leviticus to counteract the xenophobia in Ezra-Nehemiah.

Deut 7:3 has the singulars throughout.[16] Second, while the verb "to give" (נתן) is common to both texts, the verb "to take" is not (נשא: Ezra 9:12; cf. לקח: Deut 7:3).[17] Perhaps most noteworthy, Ezra 9:12 does not contain the opening admonition of Deut 7:3, "Do not enter into marriage with them." This imperative would have fitted most appropriately with the situation of adult men (rather than their children) marrying foreign wives, which is precisely the issue that is of foremost concern in the surrounding context (Ezra 9:2 and 10:2-3, 10-11). Nevertheless, the verb "to marry" (חתן hitpa'el) of Deut 7:3 does occur within the prayer, in Ezra's rhetorical question about breaking the commandments (9:14). Hence the tradition of Deut 7:3 provides, on one hand, a unifying force between the quotation of the prophets and its application within the penitential prayer and, on the other hand, a linkage with the preceding autobiography (Ezra 9:12a, 14; cf. 2a).[18]

Distinctive vocabulary reinforces the connection between Ezra's prayer and the autobiography (9:1-5). The term "abominations" (תועבת) occurs in 9:1, 11, 14 and nowhere else—whether singular or plural—in Ezra-Nehemiah. In each case the abominations belong to the peoples of the lands.[19] Verses 1 and 11 have almost the identical expression: "peoples of the lands with their abominations."[20] Furthermore, "the God of Israel" (אלהי־ישראל) provides a genuine link insofar as the expression does not occur after 9:15 in Ezra-Nehemiah.[21]

While the vocabulary of marriages to foreigners distinguishes Ezra's prayer from the narrative that follows, other terms serve to preserve linkage between the two sections. Ezra emphasizes the people's "guilt" at the beginning and end of his prayer and returns to the theme in his subsequent address to the crowd (אשמה, 9:6, 7, 13, 15; cf. 10:10).[22] Observance of the "commandment[s]" (מצוה, 9:10, 14; cf. 10:3) bonds Ezra with the devout "ones who tremble" in reverence

---

16. Deut 7:3 literally reads, "Do not give your daughter to his son, and do not take his daughter for your son" (בתך לא־תתן לבנו ובתו לא־תקח לבנך).

17. However, the Deuteronomistic account of the Israelites' offensive marriages to foreigners in Judg 3:6 (ויקחו את־בנותיהם להם לנשים ואת־בנותיהם נתנו לבניהם) employs plurals while maintaining the verbs of Deut 7:3. For a proposal on the relationships between Ezra 9:12a, 14a and Deut 7:3, see Juha Pakkala, *Ezra the Scribe: The Development of Ezra 7–10 and Nehemiah 8* (BZAW 347; Berlin: de Gruyter, 2004), 108–10.

18. A Deuteronomistic inflection appears in Ezra 9:14b as the sanction for "marrying" foreign inhabitants (חתן hitpa'el) consists in perishing from the land (cf. Josh 23:12–13).

19. Note the expression in 9:14, "peoples of these abominations" (עמי תעבות האלה).

20. Neh 9:1: עמי האצות בתעבתים; cf. Neh 9:11: עמי האצות בתעבתים.

21. The other occurrences of אלהי־ישראל are in Ezra 1:3; 3:2; 4:1, 3; 6:21, 22; 7:6; 8:35.

22. Finally, the priests make the guilt offering for their offense when they banish their foreign wives (10:19). The six occurrences of the term אשמה in Ezra 10 account for almost one-third of the total (19) in the MT. The word occurs nowhere else in Ezra-Nehemiah.

(ḥărēdîm).²³ Ezra's concern for God's "raging" (אנף, 9:14) against the Judahites for trespassing his commands prompts the officials to carry out the marriage reform so as to abate God's "anger" (אף, 10:14).²⁴ Reference to "Judah and Jerusalem" together (9:9; cf. 10:7) and to the city and region separately ground the penitential prayer within the setting of the marriage reform (Judah: 10:7; Jerusalem: 10:7, 9). In Ezra's prayer, as in the reform, the opponents are the same: alternatively, the "peoples of the lands" (עמי הארצות, 9:11) or the "peoples of the land" (עמי הארץ, 9:2, 11). Identical grammatical conjunctions "and now" occur three times in the prayer and three times in the narrative and nowhere else in the book of Ezra (ועתה, 9:8, 10, 12; 10:2, 3, 11).²⁵ Furthermore, the expression על־זאת is a summarizing term that refers to the scandal of mixed marriages at the end of the prayer and in Shechaniah's opening statement ("on account of this," 9:15; "in spite of this" 10:2).²⁶

The literary connection between Ezra's prayer and the subsequent narrative of reform is very similar to the transition from the Levites' psalm to the people's commitment to the covenant renewal (Ezra 9:6–15; 10:1–44; cf. Neh 9:6–37; 10:1–40).²⁷ In each case the audience responds to the penitential prayer of the leader[s] by deciding to make a covenant agreement (כרת־ברית, Ezra 10:3; cf. כרת אמנה, Neh 10:1). In both cases the first-person plural pronoun carries forth from the penitential confession to the community that voices the commitment (אנחנו, Ezra 9:7, 9; 10:2, 4; Neh 9:33, 36, 37; 10:1). In each case this community becomes identified according to the social categories of priests, Levites, and the people (Ezra 10:5, 18, 23, 25 [Israel]; Neh 10:8, 9, 14 [leaders]). Moreover, in both narratives the author provides the names of individuals belonging to each category (Ezra 10:18–44; Neh 10:2–28). In both narratives mention of "our priests" in the prayer leads to highlighting them as participants in the covenant commitment (כהנינו, Ezra 9:7; cf. 10: 5, 10, 16, 18; Neh 9:32, 34; cf. 10:1, 9, 29).²⁸ Ezra's gratitude for the reestablishment of "the house of our God" contributes to the

---

23. Note that Ezra 10:3 speaks of "those who tremble at the commandment" (מצוה החרדים), whereas 9:4 refers to all who tremble at the "words" of God (בדברי אלהי[ם] חרד).

24. In Ezra-Nehemiah, the verb אנף occurs only in Ezra 9:14. The noun אף, meaning "anger," occurs only in Ezra 8:22; 10:14; and Neh 9:17.

25. The five other occurrences of ועתה in Ezra-Nehemiah are in Neh 5:5; 6:7 [bis], 9; and 9:32.

26. The term על־זאת arises again in Ezra 10:15. Outside of Ezra 9–10, it occurs only in Ezra 8:23 and Neh 13:14.

27. For the rationale behind viewing the Levites as the declaimers of the psalm, see Duggan, *Covenant Renewal*, 162.

28. The "weeping" of the "men, women, and children" in response to Ezra's prayer and gestures (Ezra 10:1) resonates subsequently with the people's "weeping" in response to his teaching the Torah and reading it to the "men, women and those who could understand" (Neh 8:2, 3, 9).

poignancy of his praying on the ground before "the house of God" (בית אלהינו, Ezra 9:9; cf. בית האלהים, Ezra 10:1). Finally, the prayerful confession to "our God" prompts the leaders to acknowledge the offenses against "our God" (אלהינו, 9:8, 9, 10, 13; cf. 10:2, 3, 14).

Ezra's Prayer and Nehemiah 1–13

Ezra's penitential prayer introduces two factors that are essential to the narrative throughout Nehemiah: (1) the protocol that Nehemiah and the Levites should voice their penitential prayers before undertaking their respective reforms (Ezra 9:6–15; Neh 1:5–11; 9:6–37); and (2) the reform of marriages (Ezra 9:12a, 14), which extends beyond the immediate marriage reform (10:1–44) first into the covenant renewal (10:31) and then into Nehemiah's corrections of the Judahites who had lapsed from the covenant (13:23–27).

Ezra's prayer shares extensive vocabulary with the Levites' psalm.[29]

Ezra			Nehemiah
9:6	לשמים	[מ]שמים	9:6 [3x], 13, 15, 23, 27, 28
9:7	מימי	מימי	9:32
9:7	אבותינו	אבותינו	9:9, 16, 32, 34, 36
9:7, 9	אנחנו	אנחנו	9:33, 36 [bis], 37
9:7, 15	היום הזה	היום הזה	9:10, 32
9:7	מלכינו	מלכינו	9:32, 34
9:7	כהנינו	כהנינו	9:32, 34
9:7	מלכי הארצות	מלכים	9:37
9:8, 10, 12	ועתה	ועתה	9:32
9:8, 15	יהוה	יהוה	9:6, 7
9:8, 9, 10, 13	אלהינו	אלהינו	9:32
9:8 [bis], 9 [bis], 13; cf. 9:7	נתן (God as subject)	נתן (God as subject)	9:8 [bis], 10, 13, 15, 20, 22, 24, 26; cf. 9:27, 30, 37
9:8	קדשו	קדשך	9:14

---

29. For a comparison between Ezra's prayer and Nehemiah's prayer (Neh 1:5–11), see Pakkala, *Ezra the Scribe*, 122–25.

Ezra			Nehemiah
9:8	להיר	להיר	9:12, 19
9:8, 9	עבדתנו	עבדתם	9:17
9:9	עבדים אנחנו	אנחנו עבדים	9:36 [bis]
9:9	לא עזבנו	לא עזבתם	9:17, 19, 31
9:9	חסד	חסד	9:17, 32
9:9	מלכי פרס	מלכי אשור	9:32
9:10, 14	מכותיך	מצותיך	9:14, 16. 29, 34
9:11	צוית	צוית	9:14
9:11	ביד עבדיך	ביד משה עבדיך	9:14
9:11	הנביאים	נביאיך	9:26, 30
9:11, 12	הארץ	הארץ	9:15, 23, 24, 36
9:11; cf. v. 12	באים לרשתה	לבוא לרשת	9:15, 23; cf. vv. 22, 24, 25
9:11	עמי הארצות	עמי הארץ	9:24, 30
9:12	אכלתם את־טוב	את־טוב ... לאכל	9:36
9:13	כל־הבא עלינו	כל־הבא עלינו	9:33
9:14	עד־כלה	לעשיתם כלה	9:31
9:15	צדיק אתה	צדיק אתה	9:8, cf. 9:33
9:15	הננו	הנה	9:36 [bis]
9:15	לפניך	לפניך	9:8

Some thirty-two expressions in Ezra's prayer recur in the Levites' psalm. Almost half of this vocabulary is central to the final portion of the Levites' psalm, which consists of a petition for mercy, a confession of sins, and a description of the people's present distress (Neh 9:32–37). The Levites provide a refined structure of Israel's history, which represents an elaboration upon Ezra's rough survey from the time of the ancestors through the era of conquest to the present day. In both prayers, long life in the land depends on overcoming the people of the land and observing the commandments, which God gave through his servants, alternatively Moses and the prophets. Ezra's singular confession to God, "You are righteous" (צדיק אתה), echoes twice in the Levites' psalm, as does his highlighting of divine favor toward the people (חסד). Each prayer concludes with an expression of anguish, but of different kinds. Ezra's final words focus on the community's guilt, while the Levites describe the people's victimization (Ezra 9:15; cf. Neh 9:37).

The Levites' psalm contains no echoes of the matters pertaining to mixed marriage, which are central to Ezra's prayer (Ezra 9:12a, 14a). Nevertheless, the opposition to mixed marriages becomes law as the first stipulation in the covenant renewal (Neh 10:31). This declaration by the people provides the closest rendering of Deut 7:3 in Ezra-Nehemiah.[30] Hence the Deuteronomic legislation links Ezra's prayer to the covenant renewal. This legislation again influences the end of the book in the language of the oath that Nehemiah administers to parents who allowed their children to marry foreigners (Neh 13:25).[31] However this oath echoes more closely Ezra's prayer than Deut 7:3.[32] Therefore Ezra's quotation of the prophets in prayer is a word that resonates from within him to become integral to the new constitution of Judah and ultimately to Nehemiah's social reform of another generation (Ezra 9:12a; Neh 10:31; 13:25).[33]

Ezra's Prayer, the Imperial Court, and the Temple (Ezra 1–8)

Elements of Ezra's prayer extend not only to the end of Ezra-Nehemiah but also back to the beginning of the book. Mention of places, edifices, institutions, opponents, and offices root the prayer within its setting following the negotiations with the imperial court, first pertaining to the construction of the temple (Ezra 1:1–6:22) and then pertaining to Ezra's mandate, journey, and deposition of goods at the temple (7:1–8:36).

Ezra's assertion that God's favor prompted the kings of Persia to allow for the reconstruction of the temple in Judah and Jerusalem (9:9) represents a summary of Ezra 1–6. Ezra's concern for "Jerusalem and Judah" recalls the initial proclamation by Cyrus that the exiles should return to these locales (9:9; 1:2–3; cf. 2:1). Ezra refers to the temple through the expression "house of God," the very term

---

30. Neh 10:31: לֹא־נִתֵּן בְּנֹתֵינוּ לְעַמֵּי הָאָרֶץ וְאֶת־בְּנֹתֵיהֶם לֹא נִקַּח לְבָנֵינוּ.
Deut 7:3: בִּתְּךָ לֹא־תִתֵּן לִבְנוֹ וּבִתּוֹ לֹא־תִקַּח לִבְנֶךָ.
31. Daniel L. Smith-Christopher ("The Mixed Marriage Crisis in Ezra 9–10 and Nehemiah 13: A Study of the Sociology of the Post-exilic Judaean Community," in Eskenazi and Richards, *Second Temple Studies 2*, 253–61) underlines a primary difference in the issues under consideration in Ezra 9–10 and Neh 13:23–31, respectively. Ezra is concerned with reforming the whole community, which consisted of the exiles who had returned to Judah, whereas Nehemiah is preoccupied with the particular marriages between temple authorities and political leaders who were outside the community.
32. Neh 13:25: אִם־תִּתְּנוּ בְנֹתֵיכֶם לִבְנֵיהֶם וְאִם־תִּשְׂאוּ מִבְּנֹתֵיהֶם לִבְנֵיכֶם לָכֶם.
Ezra 9:12a: בְּנֹתֵיכֶם אַל־תִּתְּנוּ לִבְנֵיהֶם וּבְנֹתֵיהֶם אַל־תִּשְׂאוּ לִבְנֵיכֶם.
33. For a more detailed discussion of the relationships among Deut 7:3; Ezra 9:12; Neh 9:31; and 13:25, see Duggan, *Covenant Renewal*, 271–74.

that Cyrus employs in his declaration and that the author uses throughout the narrative of its construction.³⁴ Ezra's expression, "the house of our God," identifies precisely the destiny of the ministers, the offerings, and the vessels that Ezra brought from Babylon (בית אלהינו, 8:17, 18, 25, 30, 33). The "kings of Persia" are God's agents who mandate the restoration of the temple and Jerusalem. Ezra's expression includes Cyrus, Darius, and Artaxerxes, the three monarchs whose edicts and responses to inquiries were essential to the completion of the temple and the provision of its furnishings and offerings (9:9; cf. 1:1–4; 5:13–17; 7:11–26). Ezra's succinct reference to the Persian kings complements the narrator's description of their synergy in terms of a singular decree from Cyrus, Darius, and Artaxerxes, which accounted for the successful completion of the temple (9:9; cf. 6:14).³⁵

Two products serve as metaphors that describe the progress in the reconstruction work up to the time of Ezra's arrival: "a stake in the holy place" and "a wall in Jerusalem and Judah." Both components are gifts from God (9:8, 9). However, the terms "stake" and "wall" are enigmatic. The "holy place" is the temple (מקום קדשו, 9:8; cf. Ps 24:3). The stake (יתד) is a spike that secured a tent, after the fashion that spikes made from bronze anchored the wilderness tabernacle (Exod 27:19; 38:20, 31).³⁶ Such evidence suggests that Ezra mentions the stake as an inference that the temple is a reliable anchor for the community. The wall (גדר) generally is a field fence of piled rock (Num 22:24; Isa 5:5–6). Ezekiel uses the term to designate a partition in the temple precincts (Ezek 42:7, 10). He also employs the word as a metaphor for the protection that the prophets in Jerusalem should have provided for the people but did not (13:5). For Ezra, the wall is a metaphor for the security that the patronage of the Persian monarchs has provided for the Judahites.³⁷

---

34. בית [ה]אלהים occurs 23 times in Ezra 1–6 (1:4, 7; 2:28, 68; 3:8, 9; 4:24; 5:2, 8, 13, 14, 15, 16, 17; 6:3, 5 [bis], 7, 8, 12, 16, 17, 22) and five times in Artaxerxes' letters of commission for Ezra (7:16, 17, 19, 23, 24).

35. On the centrality of Ezra 6:14 to the narrative, see Tamara C. Eskenazi, *In an Age of Prose: A Literary Approach to Ezra-Nehemiah* (SBLMS 36; Atlanta: Scholars Press, 1988), 45, 190.

36. For discussion of the term יתד, see Blenkinsopp, *Ezra-Nehemiah* 184–85; and Williamson, *Ezra, Nehemiah*, 135–36.

37. Hence the wall Ezra speaks of is not the more formal structure that Nehemiah would build later (חמה, Neh 3:13; 7:1). See Blenkinsopp, *Ezra-Nehemiah*, 184; Williamson, *Ezra, Nehemiah*, 136. Van Grol ("Exegesis of the Exile," 51–60) perceives that in Ezra 9:9 Isaian tradition echoes through the terms "stake" (יתד, Isa 33:20; 54:2); "wall," in relationship to Judah and Jerusalem (גדר, Isa 5:5; cf. 5:3 and 58:12); and "ruins" in reference to the temple (חרבות, Ezra 9:9; cf. Isa 64:10). He suggests that Ezra does not make allusions to specific texts but rather calls upon a repertoire of such Isaian material that was current in his day.

Ezra's reference to the "peoples of the lands" recalls the opponents who provoked anxiety in the Judahites who set the altar on its foundations and worked on the construction of the temple (עמי הארצות, 9:11; cf. 3:3 עמי־הארץ 4:4).

Ezra's concluding appeal to "Yhwh, God of Israel" harkens back to the title of God that Cyrus, the narrator, and the leaders associate with the temple (9:15; cf. 1:3; 4:1, 3). Furthermore, this is the name of the one whom purified residents in the land worshiped at Passover (6:21). It is also the title of God who gave Moses the Torah that Ezra studied (7:6).[38]

Finally, Ezra's concern for observance of the commandments recalls his title "the scribe of the commandments," which the narrator gave him as the recipient of Artaxerxes' letter (מצות, 9:10, 14; cf. 7:11).

Conclusion

Ezra's penitential psalm fits neatly into its setting within the Ezra-Nehemiah complex. From a formal perspective, its prose style ensures that it does not intrude into the surrounding narrative, as a poetic piece would. In terms of content, references to Jerusalem, Judah, the temple, the stake, and the wall all ground the psalm spatially and temporally within the local situation following the rebuilding of the temple. Mention of the Persian kings and the peoples of the land recall the drama of the Judahites seeing to the reconstruction of the temple by interacting with their patrons and adversaries respectively (Ezra 1–8). Ezra's fixation on the scandal of Judahites entering into marriages with other ethnic groups ties the psalm to the immediate issue of marriage reform and extends the resonances of the psalm into the covenant renewal (Neh 9:31) and Nehemiah's social reform at the end of the story (Neh 13:23–27).

The extensive vocabulary that Ezra's prayer shares with the Levites' psalm (Neh 9:6–37) gives Ezra's confession the character of a comparatively rough historical review that the Levites subsequently transform into the sophisticated structure of their poetic psalm. The formal irregularity of Ezra's prayer suggests an emotional intensity that bespeaks his immediate aversion to the mixed marriages. Ezra is struggling to initiate a reform. The Levites, by contrast, utter their penitential psalm after the people have separated themselves from the foreign inhabitants of the land (Neh 9:2). Hence their psalm resonates with the deliberation and rhythm that derive from affective unity with the people (cf. Neh 8:9–13). By way of contrast, Ezra's prayer defies systemization because it reflects a spontaneous outpouring of faith, grief, fear, hope, and judgment all tangled together.

In his penitential prayer Ezra underscores his convictions that, for the community, the time available is but a "brief moment" and so far there is only a "little

---

38. These are the only occurrences of the expression יהוה אלהי ישראל in Ezra-Nehemiah.

reviving" (Ezra 9:8). Nevertheless the moment is at hand for the "remnant" to decide for or against the survival of the golah. The destiny of Judah depends on how the Judahites respond to the traditional legislation, which prohibits mixed marriages (Deut 7:3). Continued breaking of the commandments will lead to ultimate destruction, while observance of them will allow for future generations to inherit the land forever (9:12, 14).

Form Criticism in Transition: Penitential Prayer and Lament, *Sitz im Leben* and Form

Mark J. Boda

Introduction

Over the past decade much attention has been paid to a series of prayers found in books recounting the later history of Israel, that is, the prayers of Ezra 9; Neh 1; 9; and Dan 9. Methodological approaches to these prayers have ranged from form to tradition to rhetorical criticism, each offering insights into the character of these prayers in their prewritten oral phase as well as the role of these prayers in their present literary context. The purpose of this paper is to review this recent history of scholarship and offer some resolution to areas of enduring controversy. In the end this will be a case study of the value and limitation of form criticism for the study of the Old Testament.

Form Criticism and Prayer

Form Criticism of Psalms

It is difficult to consider the study of prayer in the Old Testament without first considering the history of research on the book of Psalms.[1] The study of the Psalter prior to the nineteenth century was dominated by the study of the psalms as personal expressions of worship in particular historical contexts, an approach that by the second half of the nineteenth century had led to the dominant conclusion that most of the Psalms arose within the latter phase of Second Temple

---

1. I am indebted to the superb work on tracing parts of this history in Ronald E. Clements, *A Century of Old Testament Study* (rev. ed.; Cambridge: Lutterworth, 1983); Walter Brueggemann, *The Message of the Psalms: A Theological Commentary* (Minneapolis: Augsburg, 1984); idem, *The Psalms and the Life of Faith* (ed. Patrick D. Miller; Minneapolis: Fortress, 1995); William H. Bellinger, *Psalms: Reading and Studying the Book of Praises* (Peabody, Mass.: Hendrickson, 1990); and Harry P. Nasuti, *Defining the Sacred Songs: Genre, Tradition and the Post-critical Interpretation of the Psalms* (JSOTSup 218; Sheffield: Sheffield Academic Press, 1999).

Judaism (Maccabean era), although there was much controversy over the specific historical contexts.

Gunkel and Mowinckel

In this milieu Herman Gunkel offered a way forward.[2] Although he agreed that the psalms were largely postexilic and individual, their origins were actually preexilic and communal. The written forms now found in the Psalter represented the end product of a long oral process that was fostered in communal settings prior to the exile. Studying the Psalter as a whole and against the backdrop of ancient Near East literature through his new form-critical methodology, Gunkel highlighted various typical forms of psalms and linked these various types to corresponding settings in Israel's worship (*Sitz im Leben*). For him the major types included: hymns (also songs of Zion, enthronement psalms, Old Testament hymns outside the Psalter), communal laments, individual laments (also psalms of trust), individual psalms of thanksgiving, and royal psalms. The minor types were: pilgrimage songs, communal psalms of thanksgiving, wisdom psalms, liturgies (general, prophetic, Torah), and mixed types (thus Pss 9–10 as thanksgiving and lament).

Mowinckel, however, took Gunkel's work a step further.[3] The focus of Gunkel's study had been on the cataloguing of the elements of each type of psalm with less focus on the settings that fostered these types. Mowinckel concluded that the psalms betray their oral origins in the worship of Israel and so sought to define these worship settings more carefully through his "cult-functional" approach. Taking his lead from Gunkel's sensitivity to the broader ancient Near Eastern context, Mowinckel highlighted the key role that an Israelite form of the New Year's Enthronement festival practiced at Babylon played in the development of the Psalter with its many references to the kingship of Yhwh. Into this enthronement festival context Mowinckel put many of the hymns, royal psalms, and even some laments of the Psalter. Other psalms were linked to other aspects of the Israelite cult and even to private temple services. Mowinckel succeeded in pushing the origins and use of the psalms into the preexilic period and narrowing the life situations that gave rise to the psalms to a limited number of liturgical contexts.

After Mowinckel, however, there were serious questions over whether he had forced the psalms into the liturgical mould of a festival that is unattested in the Old Testament. Form critics continued to suggest liturgical contexts, such as

---

2. Hermann Gunkel and Joachim Begrich, *Einleitung in die Psalmen: Die Gattungen der Religiösen Lyrik Israels* (2d ed.; Göttingen: Vandenhoeck & Ruprecht, 1933).

3. Sigmund Mowinckel, *The Psalms in Israel's Worship* (2 vols.; New York: Abingdon, 1962).

Weiser with his covenant festival and Kraus with his royal Zion festival.[4] Such monolithic approaches could not take into account all the psalms in the Psalter, and form-critical analysts provided an increasing number of settings for particular psalms (e.g., Gerstenberger's liturgical sermons, Schmidt and Delekat's sacral justice forms, Seybold's private sickroom forms).[5] The problem with the search for such precise settings lay in the original problem that led to the rise of form criticism. The language of the psalms is stereotypical and generalized, making it useful for reemployment in a variety of circumstances and settings.

Westermann and Brueggemann

In the wake of this strenuous activity of form criticism, two key figures loosed the psalms from the straitjacket of speculative and global liturgical contexts. With Westermann and Brueggemann there was a clear shift to generalization of setting and to simplification of form categories.[6] For Westermann there were basically two modes of prayer: praise and lament. Lament is the basic form, and other psalm forms are derived from or are a response to lament. Like the two ends of a pendulum, prayer forms are constantly moving toward praise from lament. Brueggemann, leveraging Ricoeur's description of the human condition, that is, that humans experience life through phases of orientation, disorientation, and new orientation, simplified the typology of forms and generalized them to human experience rather than to specific liturgical contexts.

FORM CRITICISM OF PENITENTIAL PRAYER FORMS

This history of work on prayer forms in the Psalter forms the backdrop to discussion of prayers in the Old Testament outside the book of Psalms, especially those now embedded in the narratives of the Old Testament. Among the prayers embedded in the narratives recounting the later history of Israel are those found in the books of Ezra, Nehemiah, and Daniel, prayers that represent the penitential cry of the community for relief from their enduring predicament brought on by the fall of Jerusalem, the exile of the people, and the loss of national autonomy.

---

4. Artur Weiser, *The Psalms: A Commentary* (OTL; Philadelphia: Westminster, 1962); Hans-Joachim Kraus, *Psalms 1–59: A Commentary* (CC; Minneapolis: Augsburg, 1988); idem, *Psalms 60–150: A Commentary* (Minneapolis: Augsburg, 1989).

5. Erhard Gerstenberger, *Psalms: Part 1 with an Introduction to Cultic Poetry* (FOTL 14; Grand Rapids: Eerdmans, 1988); idem, *Psalms: Part 2 and Lamentations* (FOTL 14; Grand Rapids: Eerdmans, 1988);

6. Claus Westermann, *Praise and Lament in the Psalms* (Atlanta: John Knox, 1981); Brueggemann, *Message of the Psalms*.

Early Phase

In the early phase of form criticism these works embedded in the books of Ezra, Nehemiah, and Daniel were linked most often with the communal laments of the Psalter (Gunkel-Begrich, Mowinckel).[7] This link was evident, first of all, in the presence of the form-critical "elements" of lament, the most developed and intricate of all the psalmic forms. These prayers contained second-person singular address employing the vocative, request with motivation, complaint involving all three subjects (God, enemy, suppliant), descriptions of internal anguish and external predicaments, and the use of historical overviews.[8] The link between the two forms was evident, secondly, from the fact that the settings suggested for the communal laments in the Psalter by the early form critics were the same as the ones that appear in the narrative descriptions that introduce the penitential prayers.

Second Phase

In the second phase of form criticism, however, this view was reexamined as critics noticed not only the absence of a direct attack on Yhwh but also in its place an exoneration of Yhwh, justifying divine punishment of the people. There was an absence of the searching questions of "why" and "how long" that were characteristic of the communal laments. Furthermore, instead of the people's expression of innocence or the catalogue of the unrighteous deeds of the enemy, the accent was now on the confession of the sins of the people often with an intergenerational dimension. Some form critics had claimed that such confession of sin was a component of communal laments from the beginning,[9] but this was challenged by others.[10] Representative of this new phase of form criticism is Westermann with his view that the communal lament had undergone "eine tiefgehende Veränderung" that can be described as nothing short of "ihre Brechung."[11] Miller gives

---

7. Gunkel and Begrich, *Einleitung in die Psalmen*; Mowinckel, *Psalms in Israel's Worship*.

8. Mark J. Boda, *Praying the Tradition: The Origin and Use of Tradition in Nehemiah 9* (BZAW 277; Berlin: de Gruyter, 1999), 25.

9. Gunkel and Begrich, *Einleitung in die Psalmen*, 131–33; Weiser, *Psalms*, 74–76; Mowinckel, *Psalms in Israel's Worship*, 1:183.

10. Edward Lipiński, *La Liturgie Pénitentielle dans la Bible* (LD 52; Paris: Cerf, 1969), 35–36, 39–41, 71–73; Johannes Kühlewein, *Geschichte in den Psalmen* (Calwer Theologische Monographien; Stuttgart: Calwer, 1973), 33–48; Westermann, *Praise and Lament*, 171–73, 185–213; Kraus, *Psalms 1–59*, 51; idem, *Theology of the Psalms* (trans. Keith R. Crim; CC; Minneapolis: Augsburg, 1986), 97–99; Timo Veijola, "Das Klagegebet in Literatur und Leben der Exilsgeneration am Beispiel einiger Prosatexte," in *Congress Volume: Salamanca, 1983* (ed. John A. Emerton; VTSup 36; Leiden: Brill, 1985), 304–5.

11. Westermann, *Praise and Lament*, 173.

special attention to his analysis of what he calls the "Late Prose Prayers," which he admits "bear some resemblance to the community prayers for help or laments in that they are communal prayers rising out of distress and often calling God to remember the covenant promises," but he notes "they lack the strong element of complaint, the questioning of God's actions. On the contrary, the acknowledgement of God's justice is a persistent theme, and confession of sin has replaced the complaint against God."[12]

Recent Phase

Over the last decade more focused work has been conducted on these prayers, in particular by Werline and me.[13] Werline's work, which spans the entire Second Temple period, and my own, which focused on the biblical prayers, have explored the ideological roots of this shift in prayer form, identifying the key role that Deuteronomic and Priestly theology (cf. Lev 26; Deut 4; 30; 1 Kgs 8) played in the development of this prayer form in the approach and wake of the exile of the southern kingdom. This phase has seen the cataloguing of formal elements of the prayer form and identification of common rituals (*Sitz im Leben*) with which these prayers were associated. In my own work I have shown links between this prayer form and covenant ceremonies but have carefully noted that this context is not evidenced in all the prayers. Links in the end between these prayers and Zech 1:1–6 and 7:1–8:23, with their reference to the exilic fasts, suggest a liturgical context for the use of these prayers. In further work on such texts as Jer 14:1–15:4 and Lam 3, I have identified evidence for the initial stages of the transformation from communal lament to penitential prayer and suggested the theological shifts that were essential to move from "why" and "how long" to "we have sinned."[14]

In recent years, however, Bautch has questioned the distinction between communal lament and penitential prayer, although not with precision.[15] Key to his argument is the striking similarity between penitential prayer and communal

---

12. Patrick D. Miller, *They Cried to the Lord: The Form and Theology of Biblical Prayer* (Minneapolis: Fortress, 1994), 256.

13. Rodney A. Werline, *Penitential Prayer in Second Temple Judaism: The Development of a Religious Institution* (SBLEJL 13; Atlanta: Scholars Press, 1998); Boda, *Praying the Tradition*.

14. Mark J. Boda, "From Complaint to Contrition: Peering through the Liturgical Window of Jer 14,1–15,4," *ZAW* 113 (2001): 186–97; idem, "The Priceless Gain of Penitence: From Communal Lament to Penitential Prayer in the 'Exilic' Liturgy of Israel," *HBT* 25 (2003): 51–75; idem, "From Fasts to Feasts: The Literary Function of Zechariah 7–8," *CBQ* 65 (2003): 390–407; idem, "Zechariah: Master Mason or Penitential Prophet?" in *Yahwism after the Exile: Perspectives on Israelite Religion in the Persian Era* (ed. Bob Becking and Rainer Albertz; Studies in Theology and Religion; Assen: Van Gorcum, 2003), 49–69.

15. Richard J. Bautch, *Developments in Genre between Post-exilic Penitential Prayers and the Psalms of Communal Lament* (SBLAcBib; Atlanta: Society of Biblical Literature, 2003).

lament and the fact that "[a]lthough the confession of sin becomes one of the best attested prayer forms in the Second Temple Period and serves as a hallmark of postexilic piety, its predominance waxes and wanes." Bautch argued:

> Our study has shown, indeed, that disparate streams of tradition developed in the wake of the psalms of communal lament. Across the prayers of the Second Temple Period, penitence is in no way univocal. Thus it is at this point premature to conclude that the grouping of prayers constitutes a new genre or even a homogenous set. To argue for a distinct organization of the penitential prayers from the Second Temple period, one must develop 'a systematic consideration of how to classify and relate' the variety of texts within this grouping. It is now impossible to provide such a consideration with exactitude. Methodologically, it is more appropriate to define these texts as penitential prayers and to comment on features that establish a form-critical affinity to the psalms of communal lament or other genres, such as the Levitical sermon that has influenced Ezra 9:6–15.[16]

Bautch also links these prayers to what he calls the "liturgy of repentance," evidence for which is drawn from texts such as Zech 7:3, 5; 8:19; Lam 2:10–11; Jer 41:5.

Becking also has offered his perspective on these form-critical results.[17] He challenges my view that penitential prayer was in some way linked to some form of Persian period covenant ceremony, even though he does admit that I did not link this prayer tradition exclusively to this context. In light of this, Becking suggests that "it would therefore be better to assume that the *Sitz im Leben* of this genre is more psychological of character: prayers like this function in the context of a human being or a community that is wanting to settle accounts of the past in order to make a fresh start in life."[18] Becking highlights the "problematic" of *Sitz im Leben*, noting the trend in form-critical research to speak of a primary context and secondary contexts. In the case of penitential prayer, he suggests that this form "was originally at home in an individual ritual of confession of guilt,

---

16. Bautch claims that after the exile "the psalms of communal lament evince a new dominant element, the confession of sin," noting that "the genre changes substantively and *is dominated* by the penitential element newly introduced" (21). Furthermore, he argues: "Especially after the exile, the confession of sin supplants the lament as the element preparatory to the petition in a psalm of communal lament" (142) and "Through structural and lexical transformations, the penitential prayers of the Second Temple Period not only distinguish themselves from the psalms of communal lament but in certain cases later in the era reappropriate patterns that had predominated in the psalms" (159).

17. Bob Becking, "Nehemiah 9 and the Problematic Concept of Context *(Sitz im Leben)*," in *The Changing Face of Form Criticism for the Twenty-First Century* (ed. Marvin A. Sweeney and Ehud Ben Zvi; Grand Rapids: Eerdmans, 2003), 253–65.

18. Ibid., 261

but was reapplied in the context of an occasional ceremony in postexilic times."[19] Thus, while Bautch has challenged the history and type of the form, Becking has challenged the setting of the form.

THE WAY AHEAD

PENITENTIAL PRAYER AND LAMENT

Can one talk about penitential prayer as a form that has developed out of "lament" of the preexilic period? Is there really a separate form called penitential prayer,[20] or is it simply "postexilic lament"?[21]

All are in agreement that the phenomenon of penitential prayer is somehow related to the phenomenon of what we often call "lament." Some of us may have given the impression (or even believed) that there was a unified and ordered transition in prayer forms (some command *ex Cathedra*) that moved the people from the one form to the other. That is clearly incorrect. If Bautch's evidence can be embraced, there are indications of an enduring tradition of "lament" beyond the Babylonian period even if there is clearly a dominance of "penitential prayer." In my own work, I have highlighted texts in the late kingdom period and early post–fall of Jerusalem period that reveal a close association between lament and penitential prayer. At times I probably had in mind this monolithic transfer from one form to the other, but maybe it would be best to talk about a continuum of prayer expression that moves from lament on the one side to penitence on the other.

In some ways this continuum approach, rather than the "pure form" approach of earlier form critics, can be discerned in the approach of Westermann with his two basic forms of prayer speech to God: lament and praise, or, better, request and praise. Westermann was sensitive to such a continuum in his distinction between descriptive and declarative praise but not as helpful on the request side of the continuum. For this I have found Brueggemann's approach, relying on Ricoeur's typology of human experience, far more helpful, but still there is a need for further refinement by distinguishing between disorientation psalms in stage one and stage two as one moves on the continuum from request to praise.[22] The beginning of disorientation stage one may be best typified by the darkest of all psalms (Ps 88); in this stage one hears those questions that are fundamental to classic

---

19. Ibid., 262.
20. As, for example, Werline, *Penitential Prayer*, and myself.
21. As, for example, Daniel L. Smith-Christopher, *A Biblical Theology of Exile* (OBT; Minneapolis: Fortress, 2002); cf. Bautch, *Developments in Genre*.
22. For the inclusion of psalms of confidence/trust among the psalms of disorientation (contra Brueggemann), I am indebted to my former colleague Kelvin Friebel (Houghton) and his student Bryan Keough (Weyburn), the latter also prompting me to consider further stages or phases in disorientation.

lament (Why? How long?). One finds similar elements in psalms that belong to disorientation stage two (psalms of confidence, repentance): the description of a predicament, the request, the motivations (rooted in God's character, the desperation of the conditions, the fierceness of the enemy); missing, however, are those key questions, and accentuated are the elements of either human culpability or divine confidence.

Prior to the exile there is evidence of the element of penitence within the prayer forms of Israel, and these were associated with the request form that is often called lament. However, the exile represents a key moment historically and theologically for the people of Israel, and with it there is a development in the history of request prayer that is unique. Calling these forms penitential prayer recognizes the unique character of these forms within the larger prayer tradition of Israel, while reminding us of the dominance this form will exert within the liturgical life of Israel.

PENITENTIAL PRAYER AND *SITZ IM LEBEN*

Can one talk about a *Sitz im Leben* for penitential prayer? Is there one? Are there many? Or should it be spoken of in more existential terms, moving away from any fixed institution?

One reason for the oft time connection between lament and penitential prayer is the fact that they share not only formal elements but also common settings in life, that is, as understood as common social settings and liturgical institutions. Almost all agree that the penitential prayer tradition has arisen out of the setting of a regular fasting rhythm that was established throughout the exile, evidence for which can be discerned in Jer 41 and Zech 7–8. In the early Persian period such fasting continues to be the occasion for penitential prayer, even if it is linked to various liturgical events and even at times ceremonies that have a covenantal character. In the late preexilic period Jer 14:1–15:4 shows us that such liturgical settings were already incorporating a significant element of confession of sin. The book of Lamentations not only showcases some of the early forms used within such a context but also reveals the key to the shift from lament with a little confession to penitential prayer.

Whether we talk about this shift as a new form or a major transformation within an older form, one must admit that there is a difference between a prayer of request that is dominated by complaint (lament) and a prayer of request that has an absence of complaint and dominance of penitence. The shift is not one of context: in both cases the setting is identical; that is, the pray-ers are living in the wake of the fall of Jerusalem and the destruction of the state. The setting also may be the same, that is, the fasting liturgies. The shift is rather one of perspective of the pray-ers. They have moved from a place where there is ambiguity over the cause of the predicament to one where there is certainty, and that certainty is that the people now believe they are implicated and God is exonerated. This is the same for another type of prayer of request that is found in the Psalter and narrative books, the prayers of confidence, that is, those prayers in which the lament is absent and there is a dominance of confidence in God's promise to save. Both prayers of penitence and prayers of confidence would fit in what I call disorientation stage two. For both types nothing has necessarily changed in the life of the people: there is still a predicament, and human institutions and actions may even be similar. There is, however, a significant change in the perspective of the prayer. Should not then the identification of *Sitz im Leben*, even in the more generic sense, be supplemented by the identification of what we shall call: *Ausblick aufs Leben* (*Der Lebensausblick*), that is, the "outlook/perspective on life"? This may satisfy Becking's suggestion that the *Sitz im Leben* of this genre is "more psychological of character." By distinguishing between *Sitz im Leben* and *Ausblick aufs Leben*, it is easier to show that the historical circumstances and even the liturgical context may not have changed but the perspective or outlook on the circumstances has changed radically, and this is signaled by a change in form.

Evidence for the impact that a shift in *Ausblick aufs Lebens* can have on the form of prayer can be culled from the narrative traditions of prayer in the Old Testament.[23] For instance, Josh 7 showcases the use of a disorientation prayer in a key crisis in the experience of Israel. Following the climactic and miraculous victory at Jericho in Josh 6, the narrator recounts the devastating defeat at Ai in 7:1–5. In response, a distraught Joshua and his fellow elders of Israel cry to God in ritual actions and lexical stock that is appropriate for a prayer of disorientation (stage one).[24] God's response in 7:10–15 makes it clear that this form of prayer is inappropriate in this instance, revealing to the leaders that the problem lies not with the divine partner in the covenant relationship but rather with the human partner (7:10–15). The divine message proceeds to identify confession of sin as the appropriate form of communication, and it is this form that appears on the lips of Achan in 7:19–21. This narrative highlights the close relationship between form and setting, but it also reveals the role that the word of Yhwh can play in shaping the form within a setting. At the outset of Josh 7 the form is pure disorientation (stage one), a form that places responsibility for the disorientation upon God. After the word of Yhwh breaks into this setting and identifies the infidelity of the people as the cause of the disorientation, the speech form shifts considerably. Although the setting has remained constant, the speech form has shifted, and this shift is linked to a shift in *Ausblick aufs Leben* caused by the word of Yhwh.

---

23. See also Mark J. Boda, "Prayer," in *Dictionary of the Old Testament: Historical Books* (ed. Bill T. Arnold, Hugh G. M. Williamson, and Daniel G. Reid; Downers Grove: InterVarsity Press, 2005), 806–11.

24. See in 7:6–9 the use of the question "Why?" and the accompanying rituals of tearing clothes, falling on the face, placing dust on the head.

A second instance of how such a shift in *Ausblick aufs Leben* can impact form is the crisis faced by Hezekiah in 2 Kgs 18–19. Again, military defeat precipitates the crisis, in this case the incursion of the Assyrian Sennacherib into Judah. As in Josh 7, Hezekiah and his officials respond with the ritual actions reminiscent of the prayer of disorientation (stage one): tearing clothes and putting on sackcloth (2 Kgs 19:1).[25] Again as in Josh 7, the word of Yhwh breaks in, this time through the prophet Isaiah, revealing to Hezekiah God's intention to save him from the Assyrian threat (19:5–7). Although the crisis deepens following this message (19:8–13), Hezekiah returns to the temple and offers a prayer of trust (19:14–19). This is followed by an additional prophetic word of salvation (19:20–34) and in the end by the saving action of God (19:35–37). Again as in Josh 7, the setting of crisis has not changed, but a shift in *Ausblick aufs Leben* caused by the word of Yhwh has resulted in a shift in expression.

This evidence has implications for our study of penitential prayer. The legacy of the destruction of Jerusalem and the exile of the people is seen in the size of its impact on the prayer forms of Israel from this point forward. There is a fundamental shift in outlook from this point on in the history of Israel. The events of 587–586 demonstrate the truth of the prophetic warnings, and this results in a massive rearrangement of the theological outlook of the community, one that will inform Jewish prayer throughout the Second Temple period. The general *Sitz im Leben* of penitential prayer is the ad hoc moment of the cry of the people after the fall of Jerusalem, both individually and corporately. In the fading moments of the kingdom of Judah these prayers appeared to have been used in assemblies instituted to deal with a particular crisis (cf. Jer 14:1–15:4). In the wake of the fall of Jerusalem throughout the exilic and early Persian periods, the prayers would have been connected with the regular fasting schedule that arose (Jer 41; Zech 7–8). As worship in Jerusalem matured throughout the Persian period, these prayers could be used as part of ad hoc assemblies organized to deal with specific issues as a community (Ezra 9; Neh 9). There appears to be an enduring interest in the use of these prayers on the individual level, especially for those who remained in exilic contexts removed from Jerusalem, such as Nehemiah (Neh 1) and Daniel (Dan 9). Beyond the exilic fasts, there is no indication of an enduring and consistent liturgical setting for this prayer form. Thus, key to the setting of penitential prayer is that it arose from a people who had experienced the pain of the loss of state. That is the existential *Sitz im Leben*. Key, however, is the *Ausblick aufs Lebens* of these prayers, that is, that it reflects a theological perspective informed by the values of Lev 26; Deut 4; 30; and 1 Kgs 8.

---

25. His words to God are not recorded, but the tone in his request to Isaiah displays a sense of crisis (19:3). By entering into the temple, Hezekiah is depicted as following the mandate of the prayer of Solomon in 1 Kgs 8, a mandate that was to shape the response of Israel in crisis.

Form Criticism

Is form criticism still a valuable methodology today? Although I have my questions about the helpfulness of form criticism for the analysis of narrative, I do believe that form-critical analysis has enduring value for the study of Hebrew poetic and liturgical literature, in particular psalms, wisdom, prophecy, and prayer. This critical method does provide insights into the underlying historical and sociological experience of the Jewish community, reminding us that the literary remains of the Babylonian and early Persian periods are not mere figments of some group's imagination but rather reflections of the practices and ideologies of that ancient community.

At the same time, however, I think form criticism is inadequate as an all-embracing methodology. It must be supplemented by (among other methodologies) rhetorical synchronic methodologies. Such methodologies investigate the unique expression of the basic form in the particular passage and, secondly, look for the role of these form-critical units in the literary context of the book in which they are found. For the former we need to continue to pursue the path well worn by Alter, Berlin, Sternberg, among many others. [26] For the latter the way was opened long ago by the likes of von Rad, Noth, and Plöger in their work on the Former Prophets and Chronicles, and in recent years has been encouraged along by Weinfeld, Greenberg, Braun, Throntveit, and especially Balentine and Duggan.[27] It is this that will correct the inadequacy noted by Becking in his

---

26. James L. Kugel, *The Idea of Biblical Poetry: Parallelism and Its History* (New Haven: Yale University Press, 1981); Wilfred G. E. Watson, *Classical Hebrew poetry: A Guide to Its Techniques* (JSOTSup 26; Sheffield: JSOT Press, 1984); Robert Alter, *The Art of Biblical Poetry* (New York: Basic Books, 1985); Adele Berlin, *The Dynamics of Biblical Parallelism* (Bloomington: Indiana University Press, 1985); cf. Shimeon Bar-Efrat, *Narrative Art in the Bible* (JSOTSup 70; Sheffield: Almond, 1989); Yairah Amit, *Reading Biblical Narratives: Literary Criticism and the Hebrew Bible* (Minneapolis: Fortress, 2001).

27. Gerhard von Rad, "The Levitical Sermon in the Books of Chronicles," in *The Problem of the Hexateuch and Other Essays* (London: Oliver & Boyd, 1966), 267–80; Martin Noth, *The Chronicler's History* (trans. H. G. M. Williamson; JSOTSup 50; Sheffield: JSOT Press, 1987); Otto Plöger, "Reden und Gebete im deuteronomistischen und chronistischen Geschichtswerk," in *Festschrift für Günther Dehn zum 75 Geburstag* (ed. Wilhelm Schneemelcher; Neukirchen-Vluyn: Neukirchener, 1957); Moshe Weinfeld, *Deuteronomy and the Deuteronomic School* (Oxford: Clarendon, 1972); Moshe Greenberg, *Biblical Prose Prayer as a Window to the Popular Religion of Ancient Israel* (Los Angeles: University of California Press, 1983); Roddy L. Braun, *1 Chronicles* (WBC 14; Waco, Tex.: Word, 1986); Mark A. Throntveit, *When Kings Speak: Royal Speech and Royal Prayer in Chronicles* (SBLDS 93; Atlanta: Scholars Press, 1987); Samuel E. Balentine, *Prayer in the Hebrew Bible: The Drama of Divine-Human Dialogue* (OBT; Minneapolis: Fortress, 1993); Michael W. Duggan, *The Covenant Renewal in Ezra-Nehemiah (Neh 7:72b–10:40): An Exegetical, Literary, and Theological Study* (SBLDS 164; Atlanta: Society of Biblical Literature, 2001).

review of my initial work in the *Review of Biblical Literature*: "Boda pays too less attention to the dynamics of Neh. 9 as a composition, since he immediately is looking for a generic approach.... Should Neh. 9 not first be read in the context of the Book of Nehemiah? The literary context of the prayer within the narrative would reveal some meaning."[28] It appears there is still work to be done.[29]

---

28. Bob Becking, review of Mark J. Boda, *Praying the Tradition: The Origin and Use of Tradition in Nehemiah 9*, *Review of Biblical Literature* [online: http://www.bookreviews.org] (2000).

29. For initial forays in this direction, see Mark J. Boda, "Redaction in the Book of Nehemiah: A Fresh Proposal," in *(Dis)Unity of Ezra-Nehemiah* (ed. Mark J. Boda and Paul Redditt; Hebrew Bible Monographs; Sheffield: Sheffield Phoenix, forthcoming); idem, "Prayer as Rhetoric in the Book of Nehemiah," in *The Book of Nehemiah: Religion and Literature, History and Autobiography* (ed. Isaac Kalimi; London: T&T Clark, forthcoming).

Afterword

Samuel E. Balentine

Introduction

My introductory essay in this volume provides an overview of where research on penitential prayer has brought us thus far and where it might lead us in the future. My task in this "Afterword" is to offer an assessment of our collective work to date. I begin with two caveats. First, the present collection is but a first installment; the essays that will appear in subsequent volumes will surely move the discussion in new directions, which will in turn require that this interim report be revisited and no doubt revised. Second, because I have been invited to have the first and last word in this publication, the temptation is to measure these essays against my own hopes and expectations. In the interest of objectivity, I shall try not to yield to this temptation. However, given the obvious importance of penitence in the texts upon which we focus, it is prudent to confess at the outset that, in the words of Oscar Wilde, "I can resist everything except temptation" (*Lady Windermere's Fan*).

Although there is considerable diversity in these essays, their distinctive contributions may be loosely categorized and reviewed with respect to four general foci.

Texts and Methodologies

Previous scholarship on penitential prayer focused largely on a group of four prose texts: Ezra 9:6–15; Neh 1:5–11; 9:6–37; and Dan 9:4–19. These texts continue to serve as a touchstone for our work, but the present collection invites close scrutiny of other texts, both prose and poetic, especially Lev 16; 26; Isa 63:7–64:11; Jer 12:1–13; 14:1–15:4; Joel 1–2; Ps 106; and Job. Form-critical distinctions between the genres of lament and penitence and traditio-historical investigations of the prophetic, priestly, and Deuteronomic idioms in these texts continue to be important and productive. But it is also clear that other approaches, which provide fresh insights, are now emerging. Hogewood applies John Austin's philosophy of language use (*How to Do Things with Words*, 1975) to the verbal *performance* of confession in priestly texts. He compares Lev 16:20–22, which describes the rite but does not provide the words of confession, with Ezra 9:6–15, which describes both the ritual acts and the verbal utterance of confession—the "sound of repentance" (74). While the contexts and objectives of the two penitentiary rites are different, Hogewood argues that in both cases confession is an "illocutionary act" (73): to *say* confession is to *do* confession. That is, *to confess sin*, whether in accord with unfixed and unworded priestly prescriptions (Lev 16) or by participating in fixed and worded penitential liturgies (Ezra 9), is *to act differently*, with respect to both community and God. By viewing confession through the lens of speech-act theory, Hogewood identifies "ritual-critical dimensions" (71) of Second Temple penitential prayer that have both sociological and theological implications. His primary focus is on the sociological ramifications—confession's capacity to shape the behavior of the Israelite community—but the theological inferences are also clearly important. On this latter aspect, readers will profit from placing Hogewood's essay in constructive dialogue with Boda's essay on "Confession as a Theological Expression," especially his discussion of the Priestly tradition's "theology of repentance" (28–34).

The essays by Gärtner and Duggan also signal a shift in methodological approach. While not abandoning the diachronic analyses that have to date dominated the discussion of penitential prayers, both demonstrate the value of synchronic approaches for elucidating the role of these prayers within the literary context in which they are found. Gärtner's focus is on the concept of sin and guilt in the communal lament of Isa 63:7–64:11. The significance of this text, she argues, cannot be grasped fully either by isolating its form-critical units or by locating its psalmic and prophetic idioms within larger traditio-historical streams of thought. Instead, this lament develops principal features of Isianic theology. It not only responds to earlier emphases in the book (Israel's hardness of heart in 6:1–11; Yhwh as creator in 57:14–27; and the complex collection of texts on the servants of Yhwh, e.g., Isa 43:8–13); it may also have served as the "conclusion of an earlier form of the book" that "motivated someone to add a continuation that we find in the present chapters 65 and 66" (163). Duggan's literary analysis of the function of Ezra 9:6–15 within Ezra-Nehemiah, which he argues is a single book, models a similar approach. In terms of style and content, Ezra's penitential prayer develops and responds to both the beginning of the book (especially emphases on the imperial court and the temple in Ezra 1–8) and the ending narrative in Neh 1–13 (especially the shared vocabulary with the penitential prayer in Neh 9:6–37). Readers will no doubt examine the details of these essays closely, but my strong suspicion is that these approaches are a harbinger of where we are going. In this prediction, I concur with Boda, who argues that conventional diachronic methods must now be "supplemented by (among other methodologies) rhetorical synchronic methodologies" (191) that attend not only to generic forms and traditional idioms but also to the function of penitential prayers within the literary and theological contexts in which they are found.

William Morrow also pushes beyond conventional approaches, but in doing so he places a question mark over the possible move away from diachronic readings. Whereas previous research has looked to "innerbiblical developments" (116)—Deuteronomistic, priestly, and prophetic speech forms and traditions—to explain the emergence of penitential prayer in postexilic Judaism, Morrow argues that global intellectual shifts are a primary causal factor. Drawing upon the philosophy of Karl Jaspers (*Vom Ursprung und Ziel der Geschichte*, 1949), Morrow identifies the "Axial Age" (800–200 B.C.E.) as a time of social, political, religious, and intellectual transformation, not only in ancient Israel but also, for example, in Greece, Iran, China, and India. The transformation is fueled to a large degree by changing perceptions of reality. In pre-Axial civilizations, the mundane (everyday) world was a mirror image of transcendent reality; that is, both deities and mortals were believed to be guided by similar principles and common objectives. In short, cosmic justice and righteousness were human aspirations writ large. Axial Age civilizations, like Israel during the Babylonian exile, experience a sharp disjunction between transcendent ideals and on-the-ground realities of everyday life. Israel's entry into the Axial Age can be associated with the prophets, who responded to the imperial claims of Israel's overlords (the empires of the Assyrians, Babylonians, and Persians) by emphasizing a vision of God as more powerful than everyday orders, a God whose righteousness and justice can be neither thwarted nor questioned. The move toward the "suppression of the theology of lament" (116), Morrow argues, crystallizes in the book of Job (see, e.g., the arguments of the friends, especially Elihu in 37:19–24). It is reinforced and solidified with the emergence of penitential prayers, which use historical retrospectives to accent Israel's persistent disobedience to divine commandments and confessions of sin to demonstrate the only appropriate response to a righteous and just God.

As with all the essays in this volume, the details of Morrow's analysis merit close scrutiny. I believe, however, that his call to locate Israel's penitential prayers within the larger context of global political and intellectual movements is instructive. To address the issues, we will need not only to continue exploration of the development of penitential themes in postbiblical Judaism but also to broaden our investigation to other cultures, both contiguous and noncontiguous with ancient Israel. How do Israel's responses to revolutionary changes in the intellectual climate compare with those of other societies facing similar challenges? Is the displacement of lament, protest, and resistance (social, political, and religious) by confession, penitence, and surrender a response unique to Israel? Does Israel reflect, adopt, and/or adapt responses common to other cultures? Morrow suggests that as Israel's prophets and priests were responding to the challenges of the Axial Age, "Greek philosophers, the Chinese scholar-class, and Buddhist monks" (106) were also engaged in similar tasks. If these various Axial Age thinkers produced the "first true ideologies" (106) by offering comprehensive views of the world and human vocation, then where does penitential prayer fall on the spectrum of global possibilities?

The Relationship between Lament and Penitence

Two aspects of this issue emerge in these essays. The first is the ongoing discussion of genre and the form-critical distinctives that are associated with lament and penitence. The isolation of the four penitential prayers in Ezra 9; Neh 1; 9; and Dan 9 relied heavily on a clear distinction between lament and penitence. Prayers assigned to the former genre were characterized by strong articulations of complaint and protest; prayers were assigned to the latter genre if they replaced lament with confession of sin and protest with petitions for forgiveness. Some of the essays here (Rom-Shiloni, Morrow) continue to rely on this distinction; others challenge it. Bautch and Gärtner, although working from different perspectives, show that in Isa 63:7–64:11 lament (63:15–19a; 64:9–10) and confession of sin (64:4b–6, 11) play integral roles in one cohesive penitential prayer. Hayes focuses on the juxtaposition of lament and penitence in Jer 12:1–13 and Joel 1–2, again calling attention to a dynamic twofold response to catastrophic events.

These discernments strengthen those already advanced, for example, by Werline, who argued in one of the seminal works of this new generation of scholarship, that "ancient writers had no problems expressing both complaint and confession within the same text."[1] They also keep us mindful that genre distinctions are scholarly constructs. They are useful as such, but they are also limited. No genre is pure or autonomous. Instead, we should assume that a variety of complex speech forms are simultaneously available in any given society. They could be mixed and matched, coupled and integrated in ways that both preserve their distinctive modes of expression and creatively change them, as circumstances on the ground may require. In this respect, I believe Boda's comments, which reflect his own emerging perspective on the form-critical question, are instructive:

> Some of us may have given the impression (or even believed) that there was a unified and ordered transition in prayer forms (some command *ex Cathedra*) that moved people from the one form to the other. That is clearly incorrect.... [M]aybe it would be best to talk about a continuum of prayer expression that moves from lament on the one side to penitence on the other. (187)

Boda's call for a "continuum approach" provides a segue to a second issue concerning the relationship between lament and penitence. Were lament and penitence co-existent aspects within the larger prayer tradition of Israel? Boda suggests that they were, but he speaks of a development that effectively severs the two. Prior to the exile, lament is the dominant of the two prayer forms; after the exile, there is a "shift" or a "major transformation" (188) that results in the domi-

---

1. Rodney A. Werline, *Penitential Prayer in Second Temple Judaism: The Development of a Religious Institution* (SBLEJL 13; Atlanta: Scholars Press, 1998), 44. Note Bautch's citation of Werline on p. 99 in this volume.

nance of penitence. Boda describes this development toward penitential prayer as a *maturing* process (190), which suggests that lament is left behind as historical circumstances and theological perspectives render it less compatible with or useful for the pray-er's changed "outlook/perspective on life" (188–90). Other contributors take a similar view. Rom-Shiloni argues that communal laments and penitential prayers are contemporaneous responses to the crises of the Neo-Babylonian period. The advocates for penitential prayer, however, "polemicize against" (53) the dissident proponents of lament. The result? "While 'nonorthodox' voices, including the communal laments, apparently *vanished* in the course of the postexilic period, penitential prayers, their 'orthodox' counterpart, flourished" (67, emphasis added). Morrow also tracks a development away from lament toward the "domination" (101) of penitence in Israel's prayers. And he too equates the dominance of penitence with the "suppression" (116) and ultimately the "*exclusion* of the rhetoric of lament" (108, emphasis added), which in his estimation extends "throughout the Second Temple era and beyond" (117).

The articles by Gärtner, Hayes, and Bautch invite a different question. If lament and penitence were co-existent prayer forms in ancient Israel, were there historical or theological developments that effected the suppression or replacement of lament with penitence? In his contribution to this collection, Bautch reiterates and buttresses the assessment he advanced in a previous publication.[2] Although "scholars today routinely speak of the 'loss of lament'" (83), the evidence does not support such a unilateral conclusion. Lament is not lost in the postexilic period. It is in fact "regained" in penitential prayers "via the confession of sin" (90, 98). In his words,

> In postexilic writings such as Isa 63:7–64:11, one may document lament functioning as an influence that is vestigial and proximate. It is a vestigial influence in Isa 63:15–19a and Isa 64:9–10, two laments whose origins significantly predate the final form of the prayer in Trito-Isaiah. As echoes of the complaints issued by the preexilic and exilic forebears, the two laments effectively voice the pain and theological bewilderment of postexilic Jews. The religious tradition in question, postexilic Judaism, had "lost" lament only to regain it through the redaction of much earlier endeavors in theodicy. Lament is a proximate influence inasmuch as the theology of Isa 63:7–64:11 stands upon that of the psalms of lament as it is keyed by the complaints therein. The prayer, however, reverses the theological polarities of the complaint. As a result, the prayer's confessions of sin exonerate the God whom the laments would indict. Lament is indeed the penultimate point in the theological progression toward the confession of sin, and in this sense lament is a proximate influence upon the penitential prayer. (98)

---

2. Richard J. Bautch, *Developments in Genre between Post-exilic Penitential Prayers and the Psalms of Communal Lament* (SBLAcBib; Atlanta: Society of Biblical Literature, 2003).

198   SEEKING THE FAVOR OF GOD: ORIGINS

These contrasting explanations of the relationship between lament and penitence leave us at a crossroad. One fork turns us away from streets named lament to others signed confession and repentance, the other to a destination where lament and penitence are different sides of the same street. My own sense of the journey before us is that the turn toward lament *and* penitence promises the greater reward.

Theologies and Ideologies

In my initial assessment of where our future work on penitential prayer should lead us, I called attention to the need to include a theological component (16–18). This component, which was so important in previous work (see especially Claus Westermann and Walter Brueggemann), was largely missing in the new work I was reviewing at the time. I am pleased to note that the present volume addresses this issue in substantial ways. Readers will find that almost all of the essays here are probing the ideology, sociology, and theology of the God-people-world relationships that come to expression in Israel's prayers of lament and penitence.

Boda's essay on the "theological orientation" (27) of the earliest penitential prayers (Ezra 9; Neh 1; 9; Dan 9; and Ps 106) sets the compass by which we may navigate by identifying specific characteristics that mark the theologies of repentance, sin, God, people, and Scripture. Although it will not do justice to the breadth of his essay, I single out one of Boda's discernments for comment, primarily because I believe it stands in constructive tension with those of other contributors to this volume.

Boda distinguishes between the individual orientation (personal guilt and individual responsibility) that characterizes precedent prayers and the communal orientation (corporate guilt and collective responsibility) that characterizes penitential prayers. The former he associates with Deuteronomic and prophetic theological traditions (e.g., Deut 4; 30; Jer 29:10–14), which promulgate theologies of sin and repentance that are calibrated to obedience or disobedience to the Torah; the latter he associates with Priestly traditions (e.g., Lev 5; 16; 26; Num 5), which interpret personal transgression as idolatrous behavior that compounds individual infidelity to corporate guilt. In his words,

> Penitential prayer, therefore, relies heavily upon the foundational notions of corporate guilt that link the present generation of the pray-ers with the past generation of guilt. This leads to the consistent articulation of the sinfulness of Israel as something related to both past and present generations (Ezra 9:6; Neh 1:6; 9:32–37; cf. 9:2; Dan 9:5–6, 8; Ps 106:6). (38)

Boda's discussion of this point intersects with two additional theological issues. On the one hand, he argues that the Priestly theology of repentance, exemplified in the notion of compound guilt, calls for a reassessment of the "development of corporate ideology in the Hebrew Bible" (38).[3] On the other hand, Boda notes that the accent on compound guilt in penitential prayers is important for assessing the theology of God these prayers disclose. The roots of this theology can be traced to the ancient creedal characterization of God in Exod 34:6–7. In the multiple allusions to this text elsewhere in the Hebrew Bible, its accents on God's grace and God's disciplinary judgment are held in tension. In penitential prayers, however, the focus is reduced to the first part of the creed: the grace and mercy that assures God's favorable response to confession.

The suggestion that the theology of God in penitential prayers becomes reductive, accenting one divine attribute—righteousness—above all others, invites further reflection. Are there contributing sociological or political factors that explain or rationalize such theological moves? In his second contribution to this collection (181–92), Boda explores one possible answer. He suggests that the shift from lament, which accents God's justice by questioning it, to penitence, which accents God's grace by avoiding the questioning of other divine attributes, may be explained by distinguishing between the *Sitz im Leben* (setting in life) and the *Ausblick aufs Leben* ("outlook/perspective on life") of penitential prayers. The former term identifies the primary objective of form critics, who associate different prayer genres with changing sociohistorical settings in life. The latter term invites us to identify different ways of praying with the changing psychological perspectives of the pray-ers. Thus, while both lament and penitential prayers share to some extent the same historical context—the crisis of faith created by the destruction of Jerusalem and the exile to Babylon—prayers of penitence reflect a fundamental shift in the theological outlook of the community. Pray-ers "have moved from a place where there is ambiguity over the cause of the predicament to one where there is certainty, and that certainty is that people now believe they are implicated and God is exonerated" (188).

Boda's call to examine the psychological factors that bear on changing theological perspectives opens up suggestive new areas for exploration, which I trust Boda and others will continue to pursue. If we are to work on firm ground, however, we will need to develop clear methodological controls. Boda's suggestion that penitential prayers such as Ezra 9 and Neh 9 disclose how "worship in Jerusalem *matured* throughout the Persian period" (190, emphasis added) may be intended as only a loose categorization. It is nevertheless symptomatic of the issues we must consider carefully. By what objective criteria, and by whose authoritative judgment, can we evaluate some theological perspectives as more "mature" than others?

---

3. See especially his engagement with Joel Kaminsky's discussion of transgenerational retribution in *Corporate Responsibility in the Hebrew Bible* (JSOTSup 196; Sheffield: Sheffield Academic Press, 1995).

Several of these essays tie the theology of lament and penitence to the nexus of historical and political factors associated with the exilic and postexilic periods. Here again we may discern the continuing influence of previous scholarship, especially of Claus Westermann. Yet even as these recent explorations sharpen Westermann's historical schematization of prayer, they invite further questions. Both Rom-Shiloni and Morrow posit a binary opposition between the theologies of lament and penitence. The former they associate with the pious complaints of the "dissident," "nonorthodox," or "ostracized people," loosely characterized as the *vox populi*. The latter they associate with the "orthodox," "mainstream," or "new social elites," whose perspectives are represented primarily by the Deuteronomistic historians, the priests, and the prophets. Both Rom-Shiloni and Morrow envision the dominance of penitence as a victory of orthodoxy, in the wake of which lament "vanished" (67) or was excluded (108). The question this assessment invites is similar to that addressed above to Boda. By what criteria is one perspective judged orthodox, another nonorthodox? And, to return once again to the need for further analysis of the social and political contexts that inform these prayers, who has the authority to make such judgments, and whose interests do they serve?

Let me press this question a bit further with respect to both contributors. Rom-Shiloni suggests that penitential prayers express the God-people relationship with a "political metaphor" (61): they characterize God as a suzerain overlord who demands obedience but has no obligation to people, beyond judging their failures in accord with recognized requirements. Morrow argues that the Axial Age necessitates an intellectual transformation in Israel's conceptualization of the world, God, and human identity that is "under the pressure of, and partly in reaction to, imperial imagery and claims made by Israel and Judah's overlords and conquerors: the empires of Assyria, Babylon, and Persia." He continues, "The politics of empire was an impetus for the emergence of the Axial Age and the need for vision of a sufficiently transcendent order to comprehend this new international reality" (107). Both authors identify politics as a factor in shaping theology; neither, in my judgment, capitalizes fully on the importance of their observations.

Bautch contributes to the same issue in another way. He, too, recognizes that the political events that most likely background the changing accents in prayers of lament and penitence "are not without a religious dimension" (84). Further, while departing from Westermann on a number of key points, Bautch seems to concur with one of his fundamental observations concerning the changes wrought by the exile: "an Israel stripped of its sovereignty changes the way it prays" (85). Upon these insights, Bautch's exegesis of Isa 63:7–64:11 constructs an argument in support of the continuing importance of lament in postexilic Judaism. Against the prevailing consensus to date, he counters that the rhetoric of lament may have changed in the wake of the crisis of the exile, but it was not lost. As he puts it, "postexilic Judaism … 'lost' lament only to regain it through the redaction of much earlier endeavors in theodicy" (98). I believe that this assessment is correct and that it will continue to serve as an important touchstone for our future work.

That said, Bautch goes on to ask what I think is a still more important question. If lament is regained, then "to what end?" (98). He answers his own question by suggesting what I take to be another version of the argument advanced by Rom-Shiloni and Morrow. Lament survives, in mutated forms, in postexilic Judaism because it provides the necessary counter testimony to orthodox perspectives that authorize penitence, not complaint, as the appropriate response to political misfortune. Absent the nonorthodox outlet of lament, the orthodoxy of penitence would presumably have imploded. I find this observation to be instructive but counterintuitive. Lament survives, not because of its intrinsic merit, but instead because its retention validates the viability of its opposite? Perhaps. But it seems to me that we need more than one text to buttress the argument before signing off on Bautch's conclusion.

To theological issues, Hogewood's essay adds an invitation to reflect on the ethical ramifications of penitential prayer, an emphasis that thus far has not factored significantly into our work. If we are to follow his lead, then we must continue to investigate how confession as a speech act shapes the behavior of the community "in ways conducive to covenant life with Yhwh" (73). "Illocutionary acts" of penitence, Hogewood argues, are more than verbal exercises; they are ritual gestures that have the capacity to morph into ethical behavior. How we talk and relate to God in liturgical contexts has a palpable effect on how we relate to others in everyday life. In short, liturgy generates ethics. Hogewood presses the argument still further. All ritual acts, most specifically the utterance of confession, are "embedded in, integrally related to, supported by, and ... give support to specific socio-cultural contexts of which they are a part" (81).[4] He continues, "By expressing or giving voice to sin, the phenomenology of confession highlights the human capacity to practice a performance that is situational, strategic, ... and committed to reimaging the order of the world" (81).

Hogewood does little more than hint at how penitential prayers may "give support to" regnant political hegemonies. Nonetheless, he forcefully argues that confession is not only "commissive," that is, a declaration of promise or intent; it is also "behabitive" (82). In this latter sense, ritual words of confession *enact* or *embody* (more literally, *body forth*) convictions that either endorse and reinforce status quo systems of power or critique and transform them. Hogewood focuses on the ways the penitential prayer in Ezra 9:6–15 shapes Yehud's internal behavioral practices, specifically intermarriage with the people of the land, in conformity with the "law of the Lord" (Ezra 7:10). However, there is also an external reality that significantly shapes Yehud's behavior—the imperial policies

---

4. Hogewood is here quoting Frank H. Gorman, *The Ideology of Ritual: Space, Time, and Status in the Priestly Theology* (JSOTSup 91; Sheffield: Sheffield Academic Press, 1990), 14.

of the Persian king, Artaxerxes—and the text indicates that Ezra is aware of the need to respect it:

> And you, Ezra, according to the God-given wisdom you possess, appoint magistrates and judges who may judge all the people in the province Beyond the River who know the laws of your God; and you shall teach those who do not know them. All who will not obey the law of your God and the law of the king, let judgment be strictly executed on them, whether for death or for banishment or for confiscation of their goods or for imprisonment. (Ezra 7:25–26)

If confession is "practiced with a certain strategy" (81) that is situationally specific, as Hogewood argues, then should we not explore how the behaviors it commends are shaped by and for the realities of its world? Yehud is charged to obey "the law of your God *and* the law of the king." It is the "and" that invites further investigation. In the political world that lies on the other side of this conjunctive, what are the moral, ethical, and political ramifications of confessions such as "I am too ashamed and embarrassed to lift my face to you" (Ezra 9:6) or "From the days of our ancestors to this day we have been deep in guilt" (Ezra 9:7)?

Lingering Issues and Questions

I conclude with brief comments on some lingering issues, which although addressed in these essays nevertheless raise additional questions.

1. Rom-Shiloni specifically relates the theology of penitential prayers to the "trilemma of theodicy" (55): the reality of suffering vis-à-vis convictions about God's absolute goodness and God's absolute power. This is a fruitful connection that requires further exploration. The prevailing consensus, exemplified by Rom-Shiloni, typically associates the priestly tradition with a cultic or liturgical strategy that effectively silences complaint, vindicates God, and thus shifts the burden of responsibility for what is wrong to human beings. I continue to suspect that this assessment is too neat and that, as often suggested in these essays, the dialogue between priests, prophets, and other religious spokespersons who were addressing these issues cannot be simply polarized as a debate between orthodoxy and nonorthodoxy. Given the intractable persistence of theodicean questions, is it reasonable to argue that priests constructed a liturgical system designed to dismiss them as unimportant, inappropriate, or simply wrong-headed? Would such a liturgical system have enjoyed any support among people for whom questions about God and justice were existential matters of survival, not merely exercises in sacramental or theological correctness?

Hayes's analysis of the dialogue between divine laments and prophetic laments in Jer 12, for example, invites an interesting question. She rightly notes that God often appears to be "self-questioning" (123–24), thus sympathetically interacting with a lament process shared by the prophet and the people. If the prophetic tradition characterizes God as one whose anguish can best be expressed through lament, might not the priestly tradition characterize God as one whose remorse (guilt? shame? culpability?) can be authentically expressed in divine penitence? Does the biblical tradition depict God as repenting? The work by Terence Fretheim, to cite one prominent example, suggests that biblical authors probed the question in various ways.[5] I suggest that placing the penitential prayers within the wide spectrum of theodicean strategies in the Old Testament will be an important step in contextualizing and assessing their contribution to Second Temple Judaism.

2. A related issue is the emerging importance of the contribution of the book of Job to this discussion. Bautch has described Job as the "missing link" in the developments that lead from lament to penitential prayer.[6] In my introduction to this collection I seconded Bautch's initial assessment and suggested it might be strengthened by bringing Job more directly into our conversation (19–20). In locating both penitential prayers and Job within the nexus of the Axial Age (101–17), Morrow has now advanced this conversation in important ways. He wisely acknowledges that his interpretation is but one among other defensible possibilities, and with an increasing number of commentators he concurs that such a multivalent book ultimately resists definitive declarations. Morrow's reading, nevertheless, generally conforms to conventional conclusions. Job's laments and protests, though resolute and undiminished, are in the end ineffective; the three friends, who endorse the deeply entrenched wisdom of retribution theology, are in the end unable either to persuade or coerce Job to accept their side of the argument; and God, whose speeches compete with those of Elihu, ultimately refrains from offering a response that clearly endorses either the friends or Job. The conclusion of the book, such as it is, Morrow states as follows:

> God is not within our reach. By reason of his power and righteousness, God is to be feared and reverenced. The divine being has no accounts to render to human beings (37:19–24). Obviously, protests or doubts in connection with divine faithfulness or justice cannot be entertained in such a worldview. (113)

I am in general agreement with much of Morrow's analysis, but here again I continue to wonder if conventional assessments are adequate for the questions now on our radar. I do not yet have clarity on how or what Job contributes to this discussion, but I suspect that Job may well be the best case study we have for thinking about the vexed intersection between lament and penitence. I have noted a preliminary reason why this may be so in the introductory essay (20–21; see also n. 61 there). To that I now add, still by way of a preliminary rumina-

---

5. See, e.g., Terence Fretheim, "The Repentance of God: A Key to Evaluating Old Testament God-Talk," *HBT* 10 (1988): 47–70.

6. Bautch, *Developments in Genre*, 163–65.

tion, that the prologue-epilogue (1:1–2:13; 42:7–17) subtly frames Job's story with cultic (sacrificial) language. This raises the possibility that one objective of the book is to probe a critical concern conventionally associated with the priestly agenda. How can cultic rituals—such as the sacrifices Job offers for his children and for his friends (Job 1:5; 42:8)—"comfort and console" (Job 2:11; 42:11) an innocent sufferer like Job? Inside this framing question, the friends solicit Job's confession and repentance (Job 8:5–7; 11:13–20; 22:21–27). Job counters that he cannot repent of sins he has not committed (Job 6:28–30; 9:21; 10:7; 16:17; 19:6-7; and especially Job's oaths of innocence in ch. 31), which in turn threatens to nullify his place in the cult, unless its rituals can be stretched to embrace his complaints and challenges to the God it serves.[7] It may well be that the "resolution" to this conundrum is to be found where Morrow (with a majority of commentators) suggests, in the elevation of God's mysterious holiness and the suppression of Job's lament. The burden of interpretation falls on the exegesis of the divine speeches in Job 38–41 and especially Job's enigmatic response in 42:6, and here, it is safe to say, there is more than one alternative. Job may be representative of Axial Age intellectual shifts, as Morrow argues, but whether these shifts ensure the "continuing dominance" of penitence "throughout the Second Temple era and beyond" (117) remains, I believe, an open question.

3. Lastly, I want to endorse Boda's invitation to pay close attention to the "theology of scripture" (46–49). His principal concern is the theology of Torah that undergirds the penitential prayer tradition. This specific I leave to others to critique. I am, however, persuaded that Boda has tapped into a larger hermeneutical issue. With J. Newman,[8] he argues that scripture interprets scripture, which means per force that biblical prayers both preserve and solicit ongoing interpretation and exposition. By extension, I take this to mean that communities of faith learn how to pray—what wrongs to protest and what sins to confess—by immersing themselves deeply in the prayers preserved in scripture. For this journey, which will likely be shaped by both scholarly rigor and confessional imperatives, there is, as Boda concludes, "still work to be done" (192).

---

7. See further Samuel E. Balentine, "Inside the Sanctuary of Silence: The Moral/Ethical Demands of Suffering" in *Character and Ethics in the Torah* (ed. M. Daniel Carroll R. and Jacqueline E. Lapsley; Louisville: Westminster John Knox, forthcoming).

8. Judith H. Newman, *Praying by the Book: The Scripturalization of Prayer in Second Temple Judaism* (SBLEJL 14; Atlanta: Scholars Press, 1999).

Bibliography

Abrams, M. H. *A Glossary of Literary Terms*. 6th ed. Fort Worth, Tex.: Harcourt Brace College, 1993.
Achtemeier, Elizabeth. *The Community and Message of Isaiah 56-66*. Minneapolis: Fortress, 1982.
Ackroyd, Peter R. *Exile and Restoration: A Study of Hebrew Thought of the Sixth Century B.C.* Philadelphia: Westminster, 1968.
Aejmelaeus, Anneli. "Der Prophet als Klageliedsänger: Zur Funktion des Psalms Jes 63,7-64,11 in Tritojesaja." *ZAW* 107 (1995): 31-50.
Albani, Matthias. " 'Wo sollte ein Haus sein, das ihr mir bauen könntet?' (Jes 66,1). Schöpfung als Tempel JHWHs?" Pages 37-56 in *Gemeinde ohne Tempel: Zur Substituierung und Transformation des Jerusalemer Tempels und seines Kults im Alten Testament, antiken Judentum und frühen Christentum*. Edited by Beate Ego, Armin Lange, Kathrin Ehlers, and Peter Pilhofer. WUNT 118. Tübingen: Mohr Siebeck, 1999.
Albertz, Rainer. *A History of Israelite Religion in the Old Testament Period*. Old Testament Library. 2 vols. Louisville: Westminster John Knox, 1994.
———. *Persönliche Frömmigkeit und Offizielle Religion: Religionsinterner Pluralismus in Israel und Babylon*. Calwer theologische Monographien Reihe A, Bibelwissenschaft 9. Stuttgart: Calwer, 1978. Repr., Atlanta: Society of Biblical Literature, 2005.
Alt, Albrecht. "The Origins of Israelite Law." Pages 79-132 in idem, *Essays on the Old Testament and Religion*. Oxford: Blackwell, 1966.
Alter, Robert. *The Art of Biblical Poetry*. New York: Basic Books, 1985.
Amit, Yairah. *The Book of Judges: The Art of Editing*. Leiden: Brill, 1999.
———. *Reading Biblical Narratives: Literary Criticism and the Hebrew Bible*. Minneapolis: Fortress Press, 2001.
Anderson, Carl R. "The Formation of the Levitical Prayer of Nehemiah 9." Th.D. diss., Dallas Theological Seminary, 1987.
Armstrong, Karen. *A History of God: The 4,000-Year Quest of Judaism, Christianity and Islam*. New York: Ballantine, 1993.
Austin, John L. *How to Do Things with Words*. Edited by J. O. Urmson and Marina Sbisa. 2d ed. Cambridge: Harvard University Press, 1975.
———. *Philosophical Papers*. Oxford: Clarendon, 1961.

Balentine, Samuel E. "Inside the Sanctuary of Silence: The Moral/Ethical Demands of Suffering." In *Character and Ethics in the Torah*. Edited by M. Daniel Carroll R. and Jacqueline E. Lapsley. Louisville: Westminster John Knox, forthcoming.

———. "Job as Priest to the Priests." *ExAud* 18 (2003): 29–52.

———. *Leviticus*. Louisville: Westminster John Knox, 2002.

———. *Prayer in the Hebrew Bible: The Drama of Divine-Human Dialogue*. OBT. Minneapolis: Fortress, 1993.

Baltzer, Klaus. *The Covenant Formulary: In Old Testament, Jewish, and Early Christian Writings*. Philadelphia: Fortress, 1971.

Bar-Efrat, Shimeon. *Narrative Art in the Bible*. JSOTSup 70. Sheffield: Almond, 1989.

Barton, John. *Joel and Obadiah*. OTL. Louisville: Westminster John Knox, 2001.

Baumgartner, Walter. *Jeremiah's Poems of Lament*. Sheffield: Almond, 1987.

Bautch, Richard. *Developments in Genre between Post-exilic Penitential Prayers and the Psalms of Communal Lament*. SBLAcBib 7. Atlanta: Society of Biblical Literature, 2003.

Becker, Uwe. *Jesaja—von der Botschaft zum Buch*. FRLANT 178. Göttingen: Vandenhoeck & Ruprecht, 1997.

Becking, Bob. "Nehemiah 9 and the Problematic Concept of Context (*Sitz im Leben*)." Pages 253–65 in *The Changing Face of Form Criticism for the Twenty-First Century*. Edited by Marvin A. Sweeney and Ehud Ben Zvi. Grand Rapids: Eerdmans, 2003.

———. Review of Mark J. Boda, *Praying the Tradition: The Origin and Use of Tradition in Nehemiah 9*. *Review of Biblical Literature* (2000). No pages. Online: http://www.bookreviews.org/pdf/567_397.pdf.

Belfiore, Elizabeth S. *Tragic Pleasures: Aristotle on Plot and Emotion*. Princeton: Princeton University Press, 1992.

Bell, Catherine. "Performance." Pages 205–21 in *Critical Terms for Religious Studies*. Edited by Mark C. Taylor. Chicago: University of Chicago Press, 1998.

———. *Ritual Theory, Ritual Practice*. Oxford: Oxford University Press, 1992.

———. *Ritual: Perspectives and Dimensions*. Oxford: Oxford University Press, 1997.

Bellinger, William H. *Psalms: Reading and Studying the Book of Praises*. Peabody, Mass.: Hendrickson, 1990.

Berges, Ulrich. *Das Buch Jesaja. Komposition und Endgestalt*. HBS 16. Freiburg: Herder, 1998.

Berlin, Adele. *The Dynamics of Biblical Parallelism*. Bloomington: Indiana University Press, 1985.

———. "Psalms and the Literature of Exile: Psalms 137, 44, 69, and 78." Pages 65–86 in *The Book of Psalms: Composition and Reception*. Edited by Peter W. Flint and Patrick D. Miller. VTSup 99. Leiden: Brill, 2005.

Beuken, Willem A.M. *Jesaja deel III B. De Prediking van het Oude Testament*. Nijkerk: Uitgeverij G. F. Callenbach, 1989.

———. "The Main Theme in Trito-Isaiah: 'The Servants of YHWH.'" *JSOT* 47 (1990): 67–76.
Beuken, Willem A. M., and Harm W. M. van Grol. "Jeremiah 14,1–15,9: A Situation of Distress and Its Hermeneutics, Unity and Diversity of Form—Dramatic Development." Pages 297–342 in *Le livre de Jérémie: Le Prophète et son milieu, les oracles et leur transmission*. Edited by Pierre Bogaert. BETL 54. Leuven: Peeters, 1981.
Biddle, Mark. *Polyphony and Symphony in Prophetic Literature: Rereading Jeremiah 7–20*. Studies in Old Testament Interpretation 2. Macon, Ga.: Mercer University Press, 1996.
Blackman, Philip, ed. and trans. *Mishnayoth*. 6 vols. Gateshead, N.Y.: Judaica, 2000.
Blenkinsopp, Joseph. *Ezra-Nehemiah*. OTL. Philadelphia: Westminster, 1988.
———. *Isaiah 40–55: A New Translation with Introduction and Commentary*. AB 19A. New York: Doubleday, 2000.
———. *Isaiah 56–66: A New Translation with Introduction and Commentary*. AB 19B. New York: Doubleday, 2003.
———. "The Servant and the Servants in Isaiah and the Formation of the Book." Pages 155–75 in *Writing and Reading the Scroll of Isaiah: Studies of an Interpretative Tradition, Formation and Interpretation of the Old Testament Literature*. Edited by Craig C. Broyles and Craig A. Evans. VTSup 70. Leiden: Brill, 1997.
Boda, Mark J. "From Complaint to Contrition: Peering through the Liturgical Window of Jer 14,1–15,4." *ZAW* 113 (2001): 186–97.
———. "From Fasts to Feasts: The Literary Function of Zechariah 7–8." *CBQ* 65 (2003): 390–407.
———. "Prayer." Pages 806–11 in *Dictionary of the Old Testament: Historical Books*. Edited by Bill T. Arnold, Hugh G. M. Williamson, and Daniel G. Reid. Downers Grove: InterVarsity Press, 2005.
———. "Prayer as Rhetoric in the Book of Nehemiah." In *The Book of Nehemiah: Religion and Literature, History and Autobiography*. Edited by Isaac Kalimi. London: T&T Clark, forthcoming.
———. *Praying the Tradition: The Origin and Use of Tradition in Nehemiah 9*. BZAW 277. Berlin: de Gruyter, 1999.
———. "The Priceless Gain of Penitence: From Communal Lament to Penitential Prayer in the 'Exilic' Liturgy of Israel." *HBT* 25 (2003): 51–75.
———. "Reading between the Lines: Zechariah 11:4–16 in Its Literary Contexts." Pages 277–91 in *Bringing Out the Treasure: Inner Biblical Allusion and Zechariah 9–14*. Edited by Mark J. Boda and Michael H. Floyd. JSOTSup 370. Sheffield: Sheffield Academic Press, 2003.
———. "Redaction in the Book of Nehemiah: A Fresh Proposal." In *(Dis)Unity of Ezra-Nehemiah*. Edited by Mark J. Boda and Paul Redditt. Hebrew Bible Monographs. Sheffield: Sheffield Phoenix, forthcoming.

———. "Renewal in Heart, Word, and Deed: Repentance in the Torah." Pages 3–24 in *Repentance in Christian Theology*. Edited by Mark J. Boda and Gordon T. Smith. Collegeville, Minn.: Liturgical Press, 2006.
———. "Words and Meanings: ידה in Hebrew Research." *WTJ* 57 (1995): 277–97.
———. "Zechariah: Master Mason or Penitential Prophet?" Pages 49–69 in *Yahwism after the Exile: Perspectives on Israelite Religion in the Persian Era*. Edited by Bob Becking and Rainer Albertz. Studies in Theology and Religion. Assen: Van Gorcum, 2003.
Boda, Mark J., and M. H. Floyd, eds. *Bringing Out the Treasure: Inner Biblical Allusion and Zechariah 9–14*. JSOTSup 370. Sheffield: Sheffield Academic Press, 2003.
Bouzard, Walter C. *We Have Heard with Our Ears, O God: Sources of the Communal Laments in the Psalms*. SBLDS 159. Atlanta: Scholars Press, 1997.
Braun, Roddy L. *1 Chronicles*. WBC 14. Waco, Tex.: Word, 1986.
Brettler, Mark Zvi. "Predestination in Deuteronomy 30:1–10." Pages 171–88 in *Those Elusive Deuteronomists: The Phenomenon of Pan-Deuteronomism*. Edited by Linda S. Schearing and Steven L. McKenzie. JSOTSup 268. Sheffield: Sheffield Academic Press, 1999.
Brown, Andrew. *A New Companion to Greek Tragedy*. Totowa, N.J.: Barnes & Noble, 1983.
Broyles, Craig C. *The Conflict of Faith and Experience in the Psalms: A Form-Critical and Theological Study*. JSOTSup 52. Sheffield: Sheffield Academic Press, 1989.
Brueggemann, Walter. "The Costly Loss of Lament." *JSOT* 36 (1984): 57–71.
———. "The Costly Loss of Lament." Pages 98–111 in *The Psalms and the Life of Faith*. Edited by Patrick D. Miller. Minneapolis: Fortress, 1995.
———. "The Formfulness of Grief." *Int* 31 (1977): 263–75.
———. "From Hurt to Joy, from Death to Life." *Int* 28 (1974): 3–19.
———. "Jeremiah's Use of Rhetorical Questions." *JBL* 92 (1973): 358–76.
———. *The Message of the Psalms: A Theological Commentary*. Minneapolis: Augsburg, 1984.
———. "A Shape for Old Testament Theology II: Embrace of Pain." *CBQ* 47 (1985): 395–415.
———. "Theodicy in a Social Dimension." *JSOT* 33 (1985): 3–25.
———. *Theology of the Old Testament: Testimony, Dispute, Advocacy*. Minneapolis: Fortress, 1997.
Burrows, Millar, ed. *The Dead Sea Scrolls of St. Mark's Monastery*. 2 vols. New Haven: American Schools of Oriental Research, 1951.
Buss, Martin. "Potential and Actual Interactions between Speech Act Theory and Biblical Studies." *Semeia* 41 (1988): 125–34.
Carroll, Robert P. *Jeremiah*. OTL. London: SCM, 1986.
Chazon, Esther G. "4Q DibHam: Liturgy or Literature?" *RevQ* 15 (1992): 447–56.

———. "Hymns and Prayers in the Dead Sea Scrolls." Pages 244–70 in *The Dead Sea Scrolls after Fifty Years: A Comprehensive Assessment*. Edited by Peter W. Flint and James C. VanderKam. 2 vols. Leiden: Brill, 1998–99.
———. "A Liturgical Document from Qumran and Its Implications: 'Words of the Luminaries' (4QDibHam)." Ph.D. diss., Hebrew University, 1991.
———. "Prayers from Qumran and Their Historical Implications." *DSD* 1 (1994): 265–84.
———. "Prayers from Qumran: Issues and Methods." Pages 762–64 in *Society of Biblical Literature 1993 Seminar Papers*. SBLSP 32. Atlanta: Scholars Press, 1993.
Childs, Brevard S. *Isaiah*. OTL. Louisville: Westminster John Knox, 2001.
Chrostowski, Waldemar. "An Examination of Conscience by God's People as Exemplified in Neh 9,6–37." *BZ* 34 (1990): 253–61.
Clements, Ronald E. *A Century of Old Testament Study*. Rev. ed. Cambridge: Lutterworth, 1983.
———. *Jeremiah*. IBC. Atlanta: John Knox, 1988.
Clifford, Richard. "In Zion and David a New Beginning: An Interpretation of Psalm 78." Pages 121–41 in *Traditions in Transformation: Turning Points in Biblical Faith*. Edited by Baruch Halpern and Jon D. Levenson. Winona Lake, Ind.: Eisenbrauns, 1981.
———. "Narrative and Lament in Isaiah 63:7–64:11." Pages 93–102 in *To Touch the Text: Biblical and Related Studies in Honor of Joseph A. Fitzmyer*. Edited by Maurya P. Horgan and Paul J. Kobelski. New York: Crossroad, 1989.
Clines, David J. A. *Ezra, Nehemiah, Esther*. NCB. Grand Rapids: Eerdmans, 1984.
———. "Nehemiah 10 as an Example of Early Jewish Biblical Exegesis." *JSOT* 21 (1981): 111–17.
Collins, John J. *The Apocalyptic Vision of Daniel*. HSM 16. Missoula, Mont.: Scholars Press, 1977.
———. *Daniel: A Commentary on the Book of Daniel*. Hermeneia. Minneapolis: Fortress, 1993.
Condamin, Albert. *Le livre de Jérémie*. Paris: Gabalda, 1936.
Craigie, Peter C., Page H. Kelley, and Joel F. Drinkard Jr. *Jeremiah 1–25*. WBC 26. Dallas: Word, 1991.
Crenshaw, James L. "Job, Book of." *ABD* 3:863–64.
———. *Old Testament Wisdom: An Introduction*. Rev. ed. Louisville: Westminster John Knox, 1998.
———. *Prophetic Conflict: Its Effect upon Israelite Religion*. BZAW 124. Berlin: de Gruyter, 1971.
Culley, Robert E. *Oral Formulaic Language in the Biblical Psalms*. Near and Middle East Series 4. Toronto: University of Toronto Press, 1967.
Dahood, Mitchell. "Hebrew-Ugaritic Lexicography I." *Bib* 44 (1963): 289–303.
Deist, Ferdinand E. "Parallels and Reinterpretation in the Book of Joel: A Theology of the Yom Yahweh?" Pages 63–70 in *Text and Context: Old Testament*

and Semitic Studies for F. C. Fensham. Edited by Walter T. Claassen. JSOTSup 48. Sheffield: Sheffield Academic Press, 1988.

Delitzsch, Franz. *Commentar über das Buch Jesaia.* Leipzig: Dörffling & Franke, 1889.

Dentan, Robert C. "The Literary Affinities of Exodus XXXIV 6f." *VT* 13 (1963): 34–51.

Deventer, Hans van. "The End of the End, Or, What is the Deuteronomist (Still) Doing in Daniel?" Pages 62–74 in *Past, Present, Future: The Deuteronomistic History and the Prophets.* Edited by Johannes C. de Moor and Harry F. Van Rooy. OtSt. Leiden: Brill, 2000.

Dhorme, Édouard. *A Commentary on the Book of Job.* London: Nelson, 1967.

Diamond, A. R. *The Confessions of Jeremiah in Context: Scenes of Prophetic Drama.* JSOTSup 45. Sheffield: Sheffield Academic Press, 1987.

Dobbs-Allsopp, Frederick W. "Tragedy, Tradition, and Theology in the Book of Lamentations." *JSOT* 74 (1996): 29–60.

Dor, Yonina. "The Composition of the Episode of the Foreign Women in Ezra ix–x." *VT* 53 (2003): 26–47.

Douglas, Mary. *Leviticus as Literature.* Oxford: Oxford University Press, 1999.

———. *Purity and Danger: An Analysis of the Concepts of Pollution and Taboo.* London: Routledge, 1966.

———. "Responding to Ezra: The Priests and the Foreign Wives." *BibInt* 10 (2002): 1–23.

Dozeman, Thomas B. "Inner-Biblical Interpretation of Yahweh's Gracious and Compassionate Character." *JBL* 108 (1989): 207–23.

Driver, Samuel R. *The Books of Joel and Amos.* Cambridge: Cambridge University Press, 1897.

Duggan, Michael. *The Covenant Renewal in Ezra-Nehemiah (Neh 7:72b–10:40): An Exegetical, Literary, and Theological Study.* SBLDS 164. Atlanta: Society of Biblical Literature, 2001.

Easterling, Pat E. "Form and Performance." Pages 151–77 in *The Cambridge Companion to Greek Tragedy.* Edited by Pat E. Easterling. Cambridge: Cambridge University Press, 1997.

———. "Weeping, Witnessing, and the Tragic Audience: Response to Segal." Pages 173–81 in *Tragedy and the Tragic: Greek Theatre and Beyond.* Edited by M. S. Silk. Oxford: Clarendon, 1996.

Eisenstadt, S. N. "The Axial Age Breakthrough in Ancient Israel." Pages 127–34 in *The Origins and Diversity of Axial Age Civilizations.* Edited by S. N. Eisenstadt. SUNY Series in Near Eastern Studies. Albany: State University of New York Press, 1986.

———. "The Axial Age Breakthroughs—Their Characteristics and Origins." Pages 1–25 in *The Origins and Diversity of Axial Age Civilizations.* Edited by S. N. Eisenstadt. SUNY Series in Near Eastern Studies. Albany: State University of New York Press, 1986.

Elkana, Yehuda. "The Emergence of Second-Order Thinking in Classical Greece." Pages 40–64 in *The Origins and Diversity of Axial Age Civilizations*. Edited by S. N. Eisenstadt. SUNY Series in Near Eastern Studies. Albany: State University of New York Press, 1986.
Elliger, Karl. *Jesaja 40,1–45,7*. Volume 1 of *Deuterojesaja*. BKAT 11.1. Neukirchen-Vluyn: Neukirchner, 1978.
Else, Gerald F. *Introduction to Aristotle: Poetics*. Translated by Gerald F. Else. Ann Arbor: University of Michigan Press, 1970.
Emerton, John A. "Notes on Jeremiah 12,9 and on Some Suggestions of J. D. Michaelis about the Hebrew Words *naḥa, 'aᵉbrā, and jadā'*." *ZAW* 81 (1969): 182–91.
Emmendörfer, Michael. *Der ferne Gott: Eine Untersuchung der alttestamentlichen Volksklagelieder vor dem Hintergrund der mesopotamischen Literatur*. FAT 21. Tübingen: Mohr Siebeck, 1998.
Eskenazi, Tamara C. *In an Age of Prose: A Literary Approach to Ezra-Nehemiah*. SBLMS 36. Atlanta: Scholars Press, 1988.
Eskenazi, Tamara C., and Eleanore P. Judd. "Marriage to a Stranger in Ezra 9–10." Pages 266–85 in *Second Temple Studies 2: Temple and Community in the Persian Period*. Edited by Tamara C. Eskenazi and Kent H. Richards. JSOTSup 175. Sheffield: JSOT Press, 1994.
Evans, Donald D. *The Logic of Self-Involvement: A Philosophical Study of Everyday Language with Special Reference to the Christian Use of Language about God as Creator*. London: SCM, 1963.
Falk, Daniel K. "4Q393: A Communal Confession." *JJS* 45 (1994): 184–207.
———. *Daily, Sabbath, and Festival Prayers in the Dead Sea Scrolls*. STDJ 27. Leiden: Brill, 1998.
———. "Motivation for Communal Prayer in the Dead Sea Scrolls and Early Judaism." Paper presented at the Fifth Orion International Symposium—Liturgical Perspectives: Prayer and Poetry in Light of the Dead Sea Scrolls. Hebrew University of Jerusalem, 19–23 January 2000.
Fischer, Irmtraud. *Wo ist Jahwe? Das Volksklagelied Jes 63,7–64,11 als Ausdruck des Ringens um eine gebrochene Beziehung*. SBB 19. Stuttgart: Verlag Katholisches Bibelwerk, 1989.
Fishbane, Michael A. *Biblical Interpretation in Ancient Israel*. Oxford: Clarendon, 1985.
Fitzmyer, Joseph. *The Aramaic Inscriptions of Sefire*. Rome: Pontifical Biblical Institute, 1995.
Fleischer, Ezra. "On the Beginnings of Obligatory Jewish Prayer." *Tarbiz* 59 (1990): 397–444.
Fretheim, Terence. "The Earth Story in Jeremiah 12." In *The Earth Bible 1: Readings from the Perspective of Earth*. Edited by Norman C. Habel. Sheffield: Sheffield Academic Press, 2000.

———. "The Repentance of God: A Key to Evaluating Old Testament God-Talk." *HBT* 10 (1988): 47–70.

Gärtner, Judith. *Jesaja 66 und Sacharja 14 als Summe der Prophetie. Eine traditions- und redaktionsgeschichtliche Untersuchung zum Abschluss des Jesaja- und des Zwölfprophetenbuches.* WMANT 114. Neukirchen-Vluyn: Neukirchener, 2006.

Gauchet, Marcel. *The Disenchantment of the World: A Political History of Religion.* New French Thought. Princeton: Princeton University Press, 1997.

Gerstenberger, Erhard. *Der bittende Mensch: Bittritual und Klagelied des Einzelnen im Alten Testament.* WMANT 51. Neukirchen-Vluyn: Neukirchener, 1981.

———. *Psalms: Part 1 with an Introduction to Cultic Poetry.* FOTL 14. Grand Rapids: Eerdmans, 1988.

———. *Psalms: Part 2 and Lamentations.* FOTL 14. Grand Rapids: Eerdmans, 1988.

Gilbert, Maurice. "La place de la loi dans la prière de Néhémie 9." Pages 307–16 in *De la Tôrah au Messie.* Edited by Maurice Carrez, Joseph Doré, and Pierre Grelot. Paris: Desclée, 1981.

Girard René. *Job, the Victim of His People.* London: Athlone, 1987.

Goldenstein, Johannes. *Das Gebet der Gottesknechte. Jesaja 63,7–64,11 im Jesajabuch.* WMANT 92. Neukirchen-Vluyn: Neukirchner, 2001.

Goldingay, John. *Daniel.* Word Biblical Themes. Dallas: Word, 1989.

Goodhill, Simon. "The Audience of Athenian Tragedy." Pages 54–68 in *The Cambridge Companion to Greek Tragedy.* Edited by Pat E. Easterling. Cambridge: Cambridge University Press, 1997.

Gorman, Frank H. *Divine Presence and Community: A Commentary on the Book of Leviticus.* International Theological Commentary. Grand Rapids: Eerdmans, 1997.

———. *The Ideology of Ritual: Space, Time, and Status in the Priestly Theology.* JSOTSup 91. Sheffield: Sheffield Academic Press, 1990.

Gottwald, Norman K. *The Hebrew Bible: A Socio-Literary Introduction.* Philadelphia: Fortress, 1985.

———. "Tragedy and Comedy in the Latter Prophets." *Semeia* 32 (1984): 83–96.

Gould, John. "Tragedy and Collective Experience." Pages 217–43 in *Tragedy and the Tragic: Greek Theatre and Beyond.* Edited by M. S. Silk. Oxford: Oxford University Press, 1996.

Grabbe, Lester L. *Ezra-Nehemiah.* Old Testament Readings. London: Routledge, 1998.

———. *Leviticus.* Old Testament Guides. Sheffield: Sheffield Academic Press, 1993.

Green, Ronald M. "Theodicy." *ER* 14:430–41.

Greenberg, Moshe. *Biblical Prose Prayer as a Window to the Popular Religion of Ancient Israel.* The Taubman Lectures in Jewish Studies, Sixth Series. Berkeley and Los Angeles: University of California Press, 1983.

———. *Ezekiel 1-20*. AB 22. Garden City, N.Y.: Doubleday, 1983.
———. *Ezekiel 21-37*. AB 22A. New York: Doubleday, 1997.
———. *Lectures on Prayer*. Jerusalem: Academon, 1983.
Grimm, Werner. *Das Trostbuch Gottes. Jesaja 40-55*. Stuttgart: Calwer, 1990.
Grol, Harm W. M. van. "Exegesis of the Exile—Exegesis of Scripture? Ezra 9:6-9." Pages 31-61 in *Intertextuality in Ugarit and Israel: Papers Read at the Tenth Joint Meeting of the Society for Old Testament Study and Het Oudtestamentisch Werkgezelschap in Nederland en Belgie (Held at Oxford, 1997)*. Edited by Johannes C. de Moor. OtSt 40. Leiden: Brill, 1998.
———. " 'Indeed, Servants We Are': Ezra 9, Nehemiah 9 and 2 Chronicles 12 Compared." Pages 209-27 in *The Crisis of Israelite Religion: Transformation of Religious Tradition in Exilic and Post-Exilic Times*. Edited by Bob Becking and Marjo C. A. Korpel. Leiden: Brill, 1999.
———. "Schuld und Scham: Die Verwurzelung von Esra 9,6-7 in der Tradition." *EstBib* 55 (1997): 29-52.
Groß, Walter. "Jes 64,4: 'Siehe, du hast gezürnt, und dann haben wir gesündigt.' Zu 2000 Jahren problematischer Redaktion zweier brisanter Sätze." Pages 163-73 in *Schriftauslegung in der Schrift*. Edited by Reinhard G. Kratz, Konrad Schmidt, and Thomas Krüger. BZAW 300. Berlin: de Gruyter, 2000.
———. "Wer soll YHWH verehren? Der Streit um die Aufgabe und die Identität Israels in der Spannung zwischen Abgrenzung und Öffnung." Pages 11-33 in *Kirche in der Zeit*. Edited by Hermann J. Vogt and C. Steiling. Munich: Wewel, 1990.
Gunkel, Hermann, and Joachim Begrich. *Einleitung in die Psalmen: Die Gattungen der religösen Lyrick Israels*. Göttingen: Vandenhoeck & Ruprecht, 1933.
———. *The Psalms: A Form-Critical Introduction*. Facet Books Biblical Series 19. Philadelphia: Fortress, 1967.
Gutmann, Joseph. "The Strange History of the Kapporet Ritual." *ZAW* 112 (2000): 624-26.
Haar, Murray J. "The God-Israel Relationship in the Community Lament Psalms." Ph.D. diss., Union Theological Seminary, 1985.
Halpern, Baruch. "Jerusalem and the Lineages in the Seventh Century BCE: Kinship and the Rise of Individual Moral Liability." Pages 11-107 in *Law and Ideology in Monarchic Israel*. Edited by Baruch Halpern and Deborah W. Hobson. JSOTSup 124. Sheffield: JSOT Press, 1991.
Hartenstein, Friedhelm. *Die Unzugänglichkeit Gottes im Heiligtum: Jesaja 6 und der Wohnort JHWHs in der Jerusalemer Kulttraditon*. WMANT 75. Neukirchen-Vluyn: Neukirchner, 1997.
Hartley, John E. "From Lament to Oath. A Study of Progression in the Speeches of Job." Pages 79-100 in *The Book of Job*. Edited by Willem A. M. Beuken. Leuven: Leuven University Press, 1994.
Hayes, Katherine M. *"The Earth Mourns": Prophetic Metaphor and Oral Aesthetic*. SBLAcBib 8. Atlanta: Society of Biblical Literature, 2002.

Heinemann, Joseph. *Prayer in the Talmud: Forms and Patterns*. SJ 9. Berlin: de Gruyter, 1977.
Herbert, Arthur S. *The Book of Isaiah Chapters 40–66*. CBC. Cambridge: Cambridge University Press, 1975.
Hermisson, Hans-Jürgen. *Jesaja 45,8–49,13*. Vol. 2 of *Deuterojesaja*. BKAT 11.2. Neukirchen-Vluyn: Neukirchner, 2003.
Hiebert, Theodore. "Joel." *ABD* 3:873–880.
Hillers, Delbert R. *Treaty Curses and the Old Testament Prophets*. 2d ed. BibOr 16. Rome: Pontifical Biblical Institute, 1964.
Hoffman, Yair. *A Blemished Perfection: The Book of Job in Context*. JSOTSup 213. Sheffield: Sheffield Academic Press, 1996.
Holladay, William L. *Jeremiah*. Hermeneia. 2 vols. Philadelphia: Fortress, 1986–89.
Holmgren, Fredrick C. "Faithful Abraham and the ʿamānâ Covenant, Nehemiah 9,6–10,1." *ZAW* 104 (1992): 249–54.
Jakobson, Lea. "The Individual's Suffering in Psalms and in Mesopotamian Narratives" [Hebrew]. *Beth Mikra* 168 (2001): 33–55.
Janzen, David. *Witch Hunts, Purity and Social Boundaries: The Expulsion of the Foreign Women in Ezra 9–10*. JSOTSup 350. Sheffield: Sheffield Academic Press, 2002.
Japhet, Sara. "Composition and Chronology in the Book of Ezra-Nehemiah." Pages 208–15 in *Second Temple Studies 2: Temple Community in the Persian Period*. Edited by Tamara C. Eskenazi and Kent H. Richards. JSOTSup 175. Sheffield: JSOT Press, 1994.
Jaspers, Karl. *Vom Ursprung und Ziel der Geschichte*. Zürich: Artemis, 1949.
Jeremias, Jörg. "Joel/Joelbuch." *TRE* 17:91–97.
Joüon, Paul, and T. Muraoka. *A Grammar of Biblical Hebrew*. Rome: Pontifical Biblical Institute, 1991 [1923].
Kaminsky, Joel S. *Corporate Responsibility in the Hebrew Bible*. JSOTSup 196. Sheffield: Sheffield Academic Press, 1995.
———. "Joshua 7: A Reassessment of Israelite Conceptions of Corporate Punishment." Pages 315–46 in *The Pitcher Is Broken: Memorial Essays for Gösta W. Ahlström*. Edited by Steven W. Holloway and Lowell K. Handy. Sheffield: Sheffield Academic Press, 1995.
———. "The Sins of the Fathers: A Theological Investigation of the Biblical Tension between Corporate and Individualized Retribution." *Judaism* 46 (1997): 319–32.
Kaufmann, Yehezkel. *The Religion of Israel*. Chicago: University of Chicago Press, 1960.
Kessler, Rainer. "Art.: Israel. II Geschichte: 4. Sozialgeschichte." *RGG*[4] 4:296–97 in *Religion in Geschichte und Gegenwart*. 4th ed. 8 vols. Edited by Kurt Galling. Tübingen: Mohr Siebeck, 2001.
———. "Das kollektive Schuldbekenntnis im Alten Testament." *EvT* 56 (1996): 29–43.

Kiesow, Klaus. *Exodustexte im Jesajabuch: Literarkritische und motivgeschichtliche Analysen.* OBO 24. Göttingen: Vandenhoeck & Ruprecht, 1979.
Kiuchi, Nobuyoshi. *The Purification Offering in the Priestly Literature: Its Meaning and Function.* JSOTSup 56. Sheffield: Sheffield Academic Press, 1987.
Klawans, Jonathan. *Impurity and Sin in Ancient Judaism.* Oxford: Oxford University Press, 2000.
Klopfenstein, Martin A. "שקר." *TLOT* 3:1399–1405.
Knierim, Rolf. "מרה." *TLOT* 2:687–88.
Knohl, Israel. "Axial Transformations within Ancient Israelite Priesthood." Pages 213–21 in *Axial Civilizations and World History.* Edited by Johann P. Árnason, S. N. Eisenstadt, and Björn Wittrock. Jerusalem Studies in Religion and Culture 4. Leiden: Brill, 2005.
———. "Between Voice and Silence: The Relationship between Prayer and the Temple Cult." *JBL* 115 (1996): 17–30.
———. *The Sanctuary of Silence: The Priestly Torah and the Holiness School.* Minneapolis: Fortress, 1995.
Knoppers, Gary N. "Prayer and Propaganda: Solomon's Dedication of the Temple and the Deuteronomist's Program." *CBQ* 57 (1995): 229–54.
Koch, Klaus. "חטא." *TDOT* 4:309–19.
Koenen, Klaus. *Ethik und Eschatologie im Tritojesajabuch: Eine literarkritische und redaktionsgeschichtliche Studie.* WMANT 62. Neukirchen-Vluyn: Neukirchner, 1990.
Kraemer, David. *Responses to Suffering in Classical Rabbinic Literature.* New York: Oxford University Press, 1995.
Kraus, Hans-Joachim. *Psalms 1–59: A Commentary.* Translated by Hilton C. Oswald. CC. Minneapolis: Augsburg, 1988.
———. *Psalms 60–150: A Commentary.* Translated by Hilton C. Oswald. CC. Minneapolis: Augsburg, 1989.
———. *Theology of the Psalms.* Translated by Keith R. Crim. CC. Minneapolis: Augsburg, 1986.
Kugel, James L. *The Idea of Biblical Poetry: Parallelism and Its History.* New Haven: Yale University Press, 1981.
Kühlewein, Johannes. *Geschichte in den Psalmen.* Calwer Theologische Monographien. Stuttgart: Calwer, 1973.
Lacocque, Andre. "The Liturgical Prayer in Daniel 9." *HUCA* 47 (1976): 119–42.
Lambert, David. "Reconsidering the 'Penitence' in 'Penitential Prayer.'" Paper delivered at the Annual Meeting of the Society of Biblical Literature. Philadelphia, 20 November 2005.
Lanser, Susan S. "(Feminist) Criticism in the Garden: Inferring Genesis 2–3." *Semeia* 41 (1988): 67–84.
Lau, Wolfgang. *Schriftgelehrte Prophetie in Jes 56–66: Eine Untersuchung zu den literarischen Bezügen in den letzten elf Kapiteln des Jesajabuches.* BZAW 225. Berlin: de Gruyter, 1994.

Laytner, Anson. *Arguing with God: A Jewish Tradition*. Northvale, N.J.: Aronson, 1990.
Lee, Bernon P. Y. "Reading Law and Narrative: The Method and Function of Abstraction." Ph.D. diss., University of St. Michael's College, University of Toronto, 2003.
Levine, Baruch A. *Leviticus*. JPS Torah Commentary. Philadelphia: Jewish Publication Society, 1989.
Liebreich, Leon J. "The Impact of Nehemiah 9:5–37 on the Liturgy of the Synagogue." *HUCA* 32 (1961): 227–37.
Lipiński, Edward. *La Liturgie pénitentielle dans la Bible*. LD 52. Paris: Cerf, 1969.
Lundbom, Jack R. *Jeremiah 1–20*. AB 21A. New York: Doubleday, 1999.
Machinist, Peter. "On Self-Consciousness in Mesopotamia." Pages 183–202 in *The Origins and Diversity of Axial Age Civilizations*. Edited by S. N. Eisenstadt. SUNY Series in Near Eastern Studies. Albany: State University of New York Press, 1986.
Mandolfo, Carleen. *God in the Dock: Dialogic Tension in the Psalms of Communal Lament*. JSOTSup 357. London: Sheffield Academic Press, 2002.
Matties, Gordon. *Ezekiel 18 and the Rhetoric of Moral Discourse*. SBLDS 126. Atlanta: Scholars Press, 1990.
McConville, J. Gordon. "I Kings VIII 46–53 and the Deuteronomic Hope." *VT* 42 (1992): 67–79.
———. *Judgment and Promise: An Interpretation of the Book of Jeremiah*. Winona Lake, Ind.: Eisenbrauns, 1993.
McDonough, Sheila. "Orthodoxy and Heterodoxy." *ER* 11:124–29.
McKane, William. *Jeremiah*. Vol. 1. Edinburgh: T&T Clark, 1986.
Milgrom, Jacob. *Cult and Conscience: The Asham and the Priestly Doctrine of Repentance*. SJLA 18. Leiden: Brill, 1976.
———. "Further on the Expiatory Sacrifices." *JBL* 115 (1996): 511–14.
———. *Leviticus 1–16: A New Translation with Introduction and Commentary*. AB 3. New York: Doubleday, 1991.
———. *Leviticus 23–27: A New Translation with Introduction and Commentary*. AB 3B. New York: Doubleday, 2001.
———. *Numbers*. JPS Torah Commentary. Philadelphia: Jewish Publication Society, 1990.
———. "Priestly Doctrine of Repentance." *RB* 82 (1975): 186–205.
Miller, Patrick D. *They Cried to the Lord: The Form and Theology of Biblical Prayer*. Minneapolis: Fortress, 1994.
Moore, Carey A. "Daniel, Additions to." *ABD* 2:18–28.
Morrow, William S. "Comfort for Jerusalem: The Second Isaiah as Counselor to Refugees." *BTB* 34 (2004): 80–86.
———. "Consolation, Rejection, and Repentance in Job 42:6." *JBL* 105 (1986): 223–25.

———. "The Limits of Lament. The Fate of Late Second Temple Community Complaint Prayer in the Light of Rev 6:9–11." Paper presented at the annual meeting of the Canadian Society of Biblical Studies. Halifax, NS, 31 May 2003.
———. "Post-Traumatic Stress Disorder and Vicarious Atonement in the Second Isaiah." Pages 163–87 in vol 1 of *Psychology and the Bible: A New Way to Read the Scriptures*. Edited by J. Harold Ellens and Wayne G. Rollins. 4 vols. Westport, Conn.: Greenwood-Praeger, 2004.
———. *Protest against God: The Eclipse of a Biblical Tradition*. Sheffield: Sheffield Phoenix, 2006.
Mowinckel, Sigmund. *Psalmenstudien*. 6 vols. Kristiana: Dybwad, 1921–24.
———. *The Psalms in Israel's Worship*. Translated by D. R. Ap-Thomas. 2 vols. New York: Abingdon, 1962.
Myers, Jacob M. *Ezra-Nehemiah*. AB 14. Garden City, N.Y.: Doubleday, 1965.
Nasuti, Harry P. *Defining the Sacred Songs: Genre, Tradition and the Post-Critical Interpretation of the Psalms*. JSOTSup 218. Sheffield: Sheffield Academic Press, 1999.
Neusner, Jacob. *The Idea of Purity in Ancient Judaism*. Leiden: Brill, 1973.
Newman, Judith H. "Nehemiah 9 and the Scripturalization of Prayer in the Second Temple Period. Pages 112–23 in *The Function of Scripture in Early Jewish and Christian Tradition*. Edited by Craig A. Evans and James A. Sanders. JSNTSup 154. Sheffield: Sheffield Academic Press, 1998.
———. *Praying by the Book: The Scripturalization of Prayer in Second Temple Judaism*. SBLEJL 14. Atlanta: Scholars Press, 1999.
Newsom, Carol A. "Angels, Old Testament." *ABD* 1:248–53.
———. "Cultural Politics and the Reading of Job." *BibInt* 1 (1993): 119–38.
———. "Job." Pages 130–36 in *The Women's Bible Commentary*. Edited by Carol A. Newsom and Sharon H. Ringe. Louisville: Westminster John Knox, 1992.
Nitzan, Bilhah. *Qumran Prayer and Religious Poetry*. Leiden: Brill, 1994.
Noth, Martin. *The Chronicler's History*. Translated by Hugh G. M. Williamson. JSOTSup 50. Sheffield: JSOT Press, 1987.
O'Connor, Kathleen M. *The Confessions of Jeremiah: Their Interpretation and Role in Chapters 1–25*. SBLDS 94. Atlanta: Scholars Press, 1984.
Oeming, Manfred. " 'See, We Are Serving Today' (Nehemiah 9:36): Nehemiah 9 as a Theological Interpretation of the Persian Period." Pages 571–88 in *Judah and Judeans in the Achaemenid Period*. Edited by Oded Lipschits and Manfred Oeming. Winona Lake, Ind.: Eisenbrauns, 2006.
Olyan, Saul. *Biblical Mourning: Ritual and Social Dimensions*. Oxford: Oxford University Press, 2004.
Oorschott, Jürgen van. *Von Babel zum Zion. Eine literarkritische und redaktionsgeschichtliche Untersuchung*. BZAW 206. Berlin: de Gruyter, 1993.
Oswalt, John. *The Book of Isaiah: Chapters 40–66*. NICOT. Grand Rapids: Eerdmans, 1998.

Overholt, Thomas W. "Jeremiah 2 and the Problem of 'Audience Reaction.'" *CBQ* 41 (1979): 262–73.

Pakkala, Juha. *Ezra the Scribe: The Development of Ezra 7–10 and Nehemiah 8*. BZAW 347. Berlin: de Gruyter, 2004.

Parpola, Simo, and Kazuko Watanabe. *Neo-Assyrian Treaties and Loyalty Oaths*. SAA 2. Helsinki: Helsinki University Press, 1989.

Paul, Shalom M. "Adoption Formulae: A Study of Cuneiform and Biblical Legal Clauses." *Maarav* 2.2 (1979–80): 173–85.

Perdue, Leo G. *Wisdom and Creation: The Theology of Wisdom Literature*. Nashville: Abingdon, 1994.

———. *Wisdom in Revolt: Metaphorical Theology in the Book of Job*. JSOTSup 112. Sheffield: JSOT Press, 1991.

Petersen, John E. "Priestly Materials in Joshua 13–22: A Return to the Hexateuch?" *HAR* 4 (1980): 131–46.

Plöger, Otto. "Reden und Gebete im deuteronomistischen und chronistischen Geschichtswerk." Pages 35–49 in *Festschrift für Günther Dehn zum 75 Geburstag*. Edited by Wilhelm Schneemelcher. Neukirchen-Vluyn: Neukirchener, 1957.

Polk, Timothy. *The Prophetic Persona: Jeremiah and the Language of the Self*. JSOTSup 32. Sheffield: JSOT Press, 1984.

Porten, Bezalel. *Archives from Elephantine: The Life of an Ancient Jewish Military Colony*. Berkeley and Los Angeles: University of California Press, 1968.

Preus, James S. *From Shadow to Promise: Old Testament Interpretation from Augustine to the Young Luther*. Cambridge: Harvard University Press, 1969.

Pröbstl, Volker. *Nehemia 9, Psalm 106 und Psalm 136 und die Rezeption des Pentateuchs*. Göttingen: Cuvillier, 1997.

von Rad, Gerhard. "The Form of the Hexateuch." Pages 1–78 in idem, *The Problem of the Hexateuch and Other Essays*. Translated by E. W. Trueman Dicken Edinburgh: Oliver & Boyd, 1963.

———. *Gesammelte Studien zum Alten Testament*. Munich: Kaiser, 1958.

———. "The Levitical Sermon in I and II Chronicles." Pages 267–80 in idem, *The Problem of the Hexateuch and Other Essays*. Translated by E. W. Trueman Dicken. New York: McGraw-Hill, 1966.

———. *Old Testament Theology*. Translated by D. M. G. Stalker. 2 vols. New York: Harper & Row, 1965.

———. *The Problem of the Hexateuch and Other Essays*. London: Oliver & Boyd, 1966.

Redditt, Paul L. "Daniel 9: Its Structure and Meaning." *CBQ* 62 (2000): 236–49.

Reif, Stefan. *Judaism and Hebrew Prayer: New Perspectives on Jewish Liturgical History*. Cambridge: Cambridge University Press, 1993.

Rendtorff, Rolf. "Nehemiah 9: An Important Witness of Theological Reflection." Pages 111–17 in *Tehillah le-Moshe: Biblical and Judaic Studies in Honor of*

Moshe Greenberg. Edited by Mordechai Cogan, Barry L. Eichler, and Jeffrey H. Tigay. Winona Lake, Ind.: Eisenbrauns, 1997.

Reventlow, Henning G. *Gebet im Alten Testament*. Stuttgart: Kohlhammer, 1986.

Roberts, J. J. M. "The Motif of the Weeping God in Jeremiah and Its Background in the Lament Tradition of the Ancient Near East." Pages 132–42 in *The Bible and the Ancient Near East: Collected Essays*. Edited by J. J. M. Roberts. Winona Lake, Ind.: Eisenbrauns, 2002.

Rodriguez, Angel M. "Leviticus 16: Its Literary Structure." *AUSS* 34 (1996): 269–86.

Rom-Shiloni, Dalit. "God in Times of Destruction and Exiles: Theology and Ideology in the Prophetical Literature and in the Poetry of the First Half of the Sixth Century B.C.E." Ph.D. diss., Hebrew University of Jerusalem, 2001.

———. "Psalm 44: The Powers of Protest." Paper presented at the Psalms Section at the Annual Meeting of the Society of Biblical Literature. Philadelphia, 21 November 2005.

Roskes, David G. *The Literature of Destruction: Jewish Responses to Catastrophe*. Philadelphia: Jewish Publication Society, 1989.

Ross, James F. "Job 33:14–30: The Phenomenology of Lament." *JBL* 94 (1975): 38–46.

Said, Edward W. "Reflections on Exile." Pages 173–86 in *Reflections on Exile and Other Essays*. Cambridge: Harvard University Press, 2000.

Sakenfeld, Katharine D. *Faithfulness in Action: Loyalty in Biblical Perspective*. OBT 16. Philadelphia: Fortress, 1985.

Saydon, Paul P. "Sin-Offering and Trespass-Offering." *CBQ* 8 (1946): 393–98.

Scharbert, Josef. "Formgeschichte und Exegese von Ex 34,6f und seiner Parallelen." *Bib* 38 (1959): 130–50.

Schenker, Adrian. "Interprétations récentes et dimensions spécifiques du sacrifice ḥaṭṭāʾt." *Bib* 75 (1994): 59–70.

Schoors, Anton. *I Am God Your Savior: A Form-Critical Study of the Main Genres in Is. Xl–LV*. VTSup 24. Leiden: Brill, 1973.

Schuller, Eileen M. "Penitential Prayer in Second Temple Judaism: A Research Survey." Paper presented at the Annual Meeting of the Society of Biblical Literature. San Antonio, 21 November 2004.

Schwienhorst, Ludger. "מרה." *TDOT* 9:5–9.

Scullion, John J. "God in the OT." *ABD* 2:1042–43.

Searle, John R. *Speech Acts: An Essay in the Philosophy of Language*. London: Cambridge University Press, 1969.

Segal, Charles. "Catharsis, Audience, and Closure in Greek Tragedy." Pages 149–72 in *Tragedy and the Tragic: Greek Theatre and Beyond*. Edited by M. S. Silk. Oxford: Clarendon, 1996.

Seitz, Christopher R. "Job: Full Structure, Movement and Interpretation." *Int* 43 (1989): 5–17.

———. "The Place of the Reader in Jeremiah." Pages 67–75 in *Reading the Book of Jeremiah: A Search for Coherence*. Edited by Martin Kessler. Winona Lake, Ind.: Eisenbrauns, 2004.

Silk, M. S. "Tragic Language: The Greek Tragedians and Shakespeare." Pages 458–96 in *Tragedy and the Tragic: Greek Theatre and Beyond*. Edited by M. S. Silk. Oxford: Clarendon, 1996.

Smith, Mark S. "Jeremiah IX, 9—A Divine Lament." *VT* 37 (1987): 97–99.

———. *The Laments of Jeremiah and Their Contexts*. SBLMS 42. Atlanta: Scholars Press, 1990.

Smith, Morton. *Palestinian Parties and Politics That Shaped the Old Testament*. London: SCM, 1987.

Smith-Christopher, Daniel L. *A Biblical Theology of Exile*. OBT. Minneapolis: Fortress, 2002.

———. "The Mixed Marriage Crisis in Ezra 9–10 and Nehemiah 13: A Study of the Sociology of Post-exilic Judaean Community." Pages 243–65 in *Second Temple Studies 2: Temple and Community in the Persian Period*. Edited by Tamara C. Eskenazi and Kent H. Richards. JSOTSup 175. Sheffield: JSOT Press, 1994.

Steck, Odil H. *Bereitete Heimkehr: Jesaja 35 als redaktionelle Brücke zwischen dem Ersten und dem Zweiten Jesaja*. Stuttgarter Bibelstudien 121. Stuttgart: Verlag Katholisches Bibelwerk, 1985.

———. *Israel und das gewaltsame Geschick im Alten Testament*. Neukirchen-Vluyn: Neukirchener, 1967.

———. "Der neue Himmel und die neue Erde: Beobachtungen zur Rezeption von Gen 1–3 in Jes 65,16b–25." Pages 349–65 in *Studies in the Book of Isaiah: Festschrift Willem A. M. Beuken*. Edited by Jacques van Ruiten and M. Vervenne. BETL 132. Leuven: Leuven University Press, 1997.

———. *Studien zu Tritojesaja*. BZAW 203. Berlin: de Gruyter, 1991.

Stone, Michael E. "Eschatology, Remythologization, and Cosmic Aporia." Pages 241–51 in *The Origins and Diversity of Axial Age Civilizations*. Edited by S. N. Eisenstadt. SUNY Series in Near Eastern Studies. Albany: State University of New York Press, 1986.

Thiselton, Anthony. "The Supposed Power of Words in Biblical Writings." *JTS* 25 (1974): 283–99.

Thompson, Michael E. W. *I Have Heard Your Prayer: The Old Testament and Prayer*. Peterborough: Epworth, 1996.

Throntveit, Mark A. *When Kings Speak: Royal Speech and Royal Prayer in Chronicles*. SBLDS 93. Atlanta: Scholars Press, 1987.

Tigay, Jeffrey H. *Deuteronomy*. JPS Torah Commentary. Philadelphia: Jewish Publication Society, 1996.

Towner, W. Sibley. "Retributional Theology in the Apocalyptic Setting." *USQR* 26 (1971): 203–14.

Uffenheimer, Benjamin. "Myth and Reality in Ancient Israel." Pages 135–68 in *The Origins and Diversity of Axial Age Civilizations*. Edited by S. N. Eisenstadt. SUNY Series in Near Eastern Studies. Albany: State University of New York Press, 1986.
Veijola, Timo. "Das Klagegebet in Literatur und Leben der Exilsgeneration am Beispiel einiger Prosatexte." Pages 304–05 in *Congress Volume: Salamanca, 1983*. Edited by John A. Emerton. VTSup 36. Leiden: Brill, 1985.
Venter, Pieter. M. "Bybelse Teologie en skuldbelydenis." *HvTSt* 55 (1999): 533–62.
———. "Die aard van die geloofsgemeenskap in Nehemiah 9 (Afrikaans)." *HvTSt* 51 (1995): 720–31.
———. "Intertekstualiteit, kontekstualiteit en Daniël 9." *In die Skriflig* 31 (1997): 327–46.
Vickers, Brian. *Towards Greek Tragedy*. London: Longman, 1973.
Villanueva, Frederico G., Jr. "Confession of Sins or Petition for Forgiveness: A Study of the Nature of the Prayers in Nehemiah 1, 9, Daniel 9, and Ezra 9." Masters thesis, Asia Graduate School of Theology, 2002.
Washington, Harold C. "Israel's Holy Seed and the Foreign Women of Ezra-Nehemiah: A Kristevan Reading," *BibInt* 11 (2003): 427–37.
———. "The Strange Woman [אשה זרה/נכריה] of Proverbs 1–9 and Post-Exilic Judean Society." Pages 217–42 in *Second Temple Studies 2: Temple and Community in the Persian Period*. Edited by Tamara C. Eskenazi and Kent H. Richards. JSOTSup 175. Sheffield: JSOT Press, 1994.
Watson, Wilfred G. E. *Classical Hebrew Poetry: A Guide to Its Techniques*. JSOTSup 26. Sheffield: JSOT Press, 1984.
Weinfeld, Moshe. "בְּרִית." *TDOT* 2:252–79.
———. *Deuteronomy and the Deuteronomic School*. Oxford: Clarendon, 1972.
———. "Prayer and Liturgical Practice in the Qumran Sect." Pages 241–58 in *The Dead Sea Scrolls: Forty Years of Research*. Edited by Devorah Dimant and Uriel Rappaport. Leiden: Brill, 1992.
———. "The Prayers for Knowledge, Repentance and Forgiveness in the 'Eighteen Benedictions'—Qumran Parallels, Biblical Antecedents and Basic Characteristics." *Tarbiz* 48 (1979): 186–200.
———. "The Protest against Imperialism in Ancient Israelite Prophecy." Pages 178–81 in *The Origins and Diversity of Axial Age Civilizations*. Edited by S. N. Eisenstadt. SUNY Series in Near Eastern Studies. Albany: State University of New York Press, 1986.
Weiser, Artur. *The Psalms: A Commentary*. Translated by Herbert Hartwell. OTL. Philadelphia: Westminster, 1962.
Wenham, Gordon J. *The Book of Leviticus*. NICOT. Grand Rapids: Eerdmans, 1979.
Werline, Rodney A. "Defining Penitential Prayer." Paper presented at the Annual Meeting of the Society of Biblical Literature. Atlanta, 22 November 2003.

———. *Penitential Prayer in Second Temple Judaism: The Development of a Religious Institution*. SBLEJL 13. Atlanta: Scholars Press, 1998.

———. "Prayer, Politics, and Social Vision in Daniel 9." In *The Development of Penitential Prayer in Second Temple Judaism*. Volume 2 of *Seeking the Favor of God*. Edited by Mark J. Boda, Daniel K. Falk, and Rodney A. Werline. SBLEJL. Atlanta: Society of Biblical Literature, forthcoming.

Westermann, Claus. *Das Buch Jesaja. Kapitel 40–66*. 5th ed. ATD 19. Göttingen: Vandenhoeck & Ruprecht, 1986.

———. *Elements of Old Testament Theology*. Atlanta: John Knox, 1982.

———. *Die Klagelieder: Forschungsgeschichte und Auslegung*. Neukirchen-Vluyn: Neukirchener, 1990.

———. *Isaiah 40–66*. OTL. Philadelphia: Westminster, 1969.

———. *Lamentations: Issues and Interpretation*. Translated by Charles Muenchow. Minneapolis: Fortress, 1994.

———. *Praise and Lament in the Psalms*. Atlanta: John Knox, 1981.

———. *The Psalms: Structure, Content and Message*. Minneapolis: Augsburg, 1980.

———. "Struktur und Geschichte der Klage im Alten Testament." *ZAW* 66 (1954): 44–80.

Whybray, R. Norman. *Isaiah 40–66*. NCB. Grand Rapids: Eerdmans, 1981.

Williamson, Hugh G. M. *Ezra, Nehemiah*. WBC 16. Waco, Tex.: Word, 1985.

———. "Isaiah 63:7–64:11: Exilic Lament or Post-exilic Protest?" *ZAW* 102 (1990): 48–58.

———. "Laments at the Destroyed Temple." *BRev* 6.4 (1990): 12–17.

Willis, John T. "Dialogue between Prophet and Audience as a Rhetorical Device in the Book of Jeremiah." *JSOT* 33 (1985): 63–82.

Wilson, Gerald H. "The Prayer of Daniel 9: Reflection on Jeremiah 29." *JSOT* 48 (1990): 91–99.

Wolff, Hans W. *Joel and Amos*. Hermeneia. Philadelphia: Fortress, 1977.

Wright, George E. *God Who Acts*. Studies in Biblical Theology 1.8. London: SCM, 1952.

Young, Edward. *The Book of Isaiah*. 3 vols. Grand Rapids: Eerdmans, 1965–72.

Zahavi-Ely, Naama. "Multiple Speaking Voices in the Book of Jeremiah: A Survey of a Poetic Convention and Its Effects." Paper delivered at the Annual Meeting of the Society of Biblical Literature. Philadelphia, 19 November 2005.

Contributors

Samuel E. Balentine, Ph.D. (Oxford), Professor of Old Testament, Union Theological Seminary-Presbyterian School of Christian Education, Richmond, Virginia, U.S.A.

Richard J. Bautch, Ph.D. (Notre Dame), Associate Professor of Religious Studies, St. Edward's University, Austin, Texas, U.S.A.

Mark J. Boda, Ph.D. (Cambridge), Professor of Old Testament, McMaster Divinity College, Professor, Faculty of Theology, McMaster University, Hamilton, Ontario, Canada.

Michael W. Duggan, Ph.D. (Catholic University of America), Associate Professor of Religious Studies and Theology, St. Mary's College, Calgary, Alberta, Canada.

Daniel K. Falk, Ph.D. (Cambridge), Associate Professor of Ancient Judaism and Biblical Studies, University of Oregon, Eugene, Oregon, U.S.A.

Judith Gärtner, Ph.D. (Marburg), Wissenschaftliche Mitarbeiterin, Institute of Protestant Theology, University of Hamburg, Germany.

Katherine M. Hayes, Ph.D. (Catholic University of America), Professor of Old Testament, Seminary of the Immaculate Conception, Huntington, New York, U.S.A.

Jay C. Hogewood, Ph.D. (Texas Christian University), Senior Pastor, University Baptist Church, Baton Rouge, Louisiana, U.S.A.

William S. Morrow, Ph.D. (Toronto), Associate Professor of Hebrew and Hebrew Scriptures, Queen's Theological College and the Department of Religious Studies, Queen's University, Kingston Ontario, Canada.

Dalit Rom-Shiloni, Ph.D. (Hebrew University), Visiting Assistant Professor of Biblical Studies at the University of Chicago Divinity School, Chicago, Illinois,

U.S.A., at Tel Aviv University, Tel Aviv, Israel, and at the Rothberg International School of the Hebrew University of Jerusalem, Israel.

Rodney A. Werline, Ph.D. (Iowa), Senior Minister, First Christian Church (Disciples of Christ), Greensboro, North Carolina, U.S.A.

Ancient Sources Index

Old Testament/Hebrew Bible

Exodus
5:22	85
5:22–23	4
9:27	54 n. 19
10:16–17	54 n. 19
15:15	96
15:23	146 n. 5
17:3	4
18:10	4
27:19	178
32–34	24
33–34	41
33:19	41
34	39
34:6	24, 41
34:6–7	41, 199
34:7	35
34:11–16	172 n. 15
34:14	88
38:20	178
38:31	178

Leviticus
4	37 n. 70
4:3	37 n. 70
4:13	37 n. 70
5	71, 198
5:5	10, 18, 78
5:1–4	30
5:1–6	30
5:5	69
5:14–19	29
5:20–26	29
12:5	170 n. 10

14:10	29
14:21–25	29
15:19	170 n. 10
16	20, 31, 32, 32, 70, 71, 72, 74, 80, 81, 193, 198
16:20–22	69, 72, 74, 75, 78, 80, 194
16:20–34	74
16:21	10, 18, 30, 31, 31 n. 53, 33, 69, 79 n. 23
18	115
18:24–30	47 n. 110, 52 n. 6, 62
18:26–30	116
20:5	37 n. 70
22:14–16	29
24	20 n. 60
25	57 n. 31
26	12, 18, 19, 23, 28, 33, 34, 36, 38, 52 n. 6, 54 n. 17, 57 n. 31, 59, 71, 185, 190, 193, 198
26:9	58
26:11–13	58
26:12	204
26:13	58
26:14	47 n. 111
26:15	60 n. 39, 61
26:18	33
26:21	33
26:24	33
26:27–30	30
26:28	33
26:36	44
26:39	44
26:40	74, 80 n. 26
26:39–40	35, 39, 78

ANCIENT SOURCES INDEX

Leviticus (continued)
26:39–42	60, 63
26:40	30, 69
26:39–40	28, 30
26:39–42	24
26:40	10, 18
26:40–45	16
26:44	60 n. 38
26:44–45	61
26:45	61 n. 42

Numbers
5	71, 198
5:5	10
5:6–8	29
5:6	29, 30
5:7	18, 69
5:21	47
6:12	29
11:11	4
14:8	41
14:13–19	42 n. 90
15:30	30
15:30–31	35
16:31–33	37 n. 70
19	142
20:1	146 n. 5
22:24	178
22:31	112
26:10–11	37 n. 70

Deuteronomy
4	5, 22, 27, 185, 190, 198
4:10	88 n. 21
4:25–31	47 n. 111
4:26	88
4:27	47 n. 111, 52 n. 4
4:27–29	62
4:28–30	47
4:29–31	60, 63
5:2	58
5:3	58
5:9	88
5:9–10	36
5:26	88 n. 21
6:2	58, 88 n. 21

6:13	88 n. 21
6:15	88
6:17	58
6:24	88 n. 21
7:1	47 n. 110
7:1–3	47 n. 110, 82, 115, 173, 180
7:1–4	172 n. 15
7:3	47 n. 110, 172, 177
7:6	47 n. 109
7:9	42 n. 92
7:9–10	36
7:12	42 n. 92
7:21	42 n. 92
8:6	88 n. 21
9:7	5
9:12	88, 180
9:14	180
9:16	88
9:29	52 n. 4, 62
10:12	88 n. 21
10:17	42 n. 92
10:20	88 n. 21
11:8	47 n. 110
11:16	37 n. 70
11:28	88
12:11	52 n. 4
13:5	88 n. 21
14:2	47 n. 109
14:21	47 n. 109
14:23	88 n. 21
17:19	88 n. 21
18:9	47 n. 110
21:3–7	115
21:18–21	91 n. 34
23:4	47
23:4–7	62
23:4–9	172 n. 15
23:6	47 n. 110
24	38
24:16	36, 36
26:17	58
26:17–19	58
26:19	47 n. 109
27	15
28	59
28:9	47 n. 109
28:20	60 n. 39

ANCIENT SOURCES INDEX 227

28:31	60 n. 39	**2 Samuel**	
28:58	42 n. 92, 88 n. 21	7	37 n. 72
28:64	47 n. 111	15:31	4
29:12	58	21	38
29:20–29	47		
30	5, 22, 27, 28, 33 n. 59, 185, 190, 198	**1 Kings**	
30:1–4	47 n. 111	8	185, 190
30:1–5	47 n. 111	8:23	42 n. 92
30:1–6	141	11:1–2	172
30:1–10	60, 63, 141 n. 95		
30:2	52 n. 4	**2 Kings**	
30:2–5	62	8:19	37 n. 72
30:4	52 n. 4	14:5–6	36
31:6	60 n. 40	17:7–23	57 n. 31
31:8	60 n. 40	17:15	60 n. 39
31:12	88 n. 21	17:19	58
31:13	88 n. 21	17:20	60
31:16	60 n. 39	18–19	190
31:20	60 n. 40, 62 n. 46	19:1	190
31:29	88	20:16–18	37 n. 72
32	91 n. 35	21	59
32:6	88 n. 19	21:16	47 n. 110
32:16	88	21:10–15	36
32:21	88	21:10–16	39
		22:17	60 n. 39
Joshua		23:7	60 n. 30
6	189	23:26–27	36, 39, 59
7	12, 13, 23, 28, 35, 38, 55 n. 23, 189, 190	24:1–4	59
		24:2–4	36
7:7	85	24:3–4	39
7:7–9	4	24:20	59
22:20	35		
23:12–13	173 n. 18	**2 Chronicles**	
24:16	60 n. 39	12	26 n. 27, 168 n. 7
Judges		**Ezra**	
2:1	112	1–6	166
3:6	173 n. 17	1–8	177, 194
6:13	4, 85	1:1–4	178, 179
6:22	4	1:1–6:22	177
10:10	60 n. 39, 114	1:2–3	177
10:13	60 n. 39	1:3	173, 179
10:15	114	1:5	172 n. 15
13:6	112	2:1	177
15:18	4	3:2	173
21:3	4	3:3	179
		4:1	173, 179

Ezra (continued)

4:1–4	172 n. 15
4:3	179
4:4	179
5:13–17	178
6:20	173
6:21	173, 179
7–10	166
7:1–10	166
7:1–8:36	177
7:1–10:44	165, 166
7:6	173, 179
7:7–28	166
7:10	201
7:11	179
7:11–26	166, 178
7:25–26	202
8:17	178
8:18	178
8:25	178
8:30	178
8:33	178
8:35	173
9	12, 13, 16, 17, 18 n. 51, 25, 26, 33, 43, 45, 46, 52 n. 8, 54, 62, 63, 72, 74 n. 13, 80, 104, 107, 114, 115 n. 70, 116, 128, 181,190, 194, 196, 199
9–10	13, 31 n. 49, 32, 70, 71, 72, 74, 77, 80
9:1	171, 172 n. 15, 173
9:1–2	45, 167, 171
9:1–5	173
9:1–10:44	166
9:2	79, 166, 171, 172, 173, 174
9:2–3	167
9:3	174
9:4	167, 174
9:5	167, 174
9:6	9, 38, 45 n. 103, 78, 79, 173, 198, 202
9:6–7	169
9:6–7	39
9:6–14	51
9:6–15	1, 8, 25, 53 n. 7, 77, 79, 101, 165 166, 174, 175, 186, 193, 194, 201
9:6–10:1	74
9:7	9, 41, 44, 62, 63, 78, 169, 173, 174, 201
9:7–13	113
9:8	44, 45 n. 103, 115, 169, 171, 175, 176, 178, 180
9:8–9	41, 44
9:8–10	64
9:9	63, 64, 174, 175, 176, 177, 178, 179
9:10	45 n. 103, 169, 173, 175, 176, 179
9:10–11	113
9:10–12	47, 52 n. 6, 62, 169
9:11	28, 46, 115, 173, 174, 11
9:11–12	62, 169
9:11–14	35
9:12	44, 167, 171, 172, 174, 175, 176, 177, 180
9:13	9, 44, 45 n. 103, 61, 63, 78, 83 n. 1, 116, 169, 171, 173, 175, 176
9:13–14	46, 64, 169
9:14	43, 44, 46, 167, 171, 172, 173, 174, 175, 176, 177, 179, 180
9:15	9, 13, 43, 44, 45, 61, 63, 83 n. 1, 113, 169, 171, 173, 174, 175, 176, 177
9:18	174
9:23	174
9:25	174
10:1	8, 10, 32, 69, 77, 167, 174, 175
10:1–11	74
10:1–44	174
10:2	172, 174, 175
10:2–3	166, 167, 171, 172, 173
10:2–4	167, 171
10:3	167, 173, 174, 175
10:4	174
10:5–6	167
10:7	174
10:9	167
10:10	172, 174
10:10–11	166, 167, 171, 172, 173
10:11	74, 174
10:14	172, 175
10:15	174
10:16	174
10:17	172
10:18	172, 174
10:18–44	174
10:19	29, 31 n. 49, 173

10:31	175	9:7	48, 62 n. 45, 175
		9:7–8	54 n. 18, 61, 62
Nehemiah		9:8	13, 43, 44, 45, 63, 175
1	16, 26, 28, 44, 46, 47, 54, 62 n. 45, 71, 80, 114, 181, 190, 196, 198	9:9	89, 90 n. 27, 175
		9:10	175
1:1–7:72	166	9:11	173 n. 20
1–13	175, 194	9:9–11	54 n. 18
1:3	44	9:12	176
1:5	42, 44, 61, 63, 113	9:12–21	54 n. 18
1:5–11	1, 8, 51, 101, 165, 175, 193	9:13	38, 175
1:6	8, 32, 38, 61, 69, 74, 198	9:13–14	62
1:6–7	9	9:14	62, 113, 175, 176
1:6–11	54 n. 15	9:15	44, 115, 175, 176
1:7	46, 113	9:16	175, 176
1:7–9	113	9:16–18	9
1:8	32, 46	9:17	9, 41 n. 89, 45, 63, 64, 174 n. 24, 176
1:8–9	44, 62		
1:8–10	52 n. 4, 62	9:17–18	24, 48
1:9	28, 44, 78	9:18	35
1:10	41, 61	9:19	9, 41 n. 89, 63, 64, 176
1:11	44	9:22	54 n. 18, 175, 176
3:13	178 n. 37	9:23	44, 48, 175, 176
3:37	171 n. 12	9:24	44, 175, 176
5:5	174 n. 25	9:25	44, 62 n. 46, 176
6:7	174 n. 25	9:26	28, 35, 46, 62 n. 46, 78, 175
7:1	178 n. 37	9:26–31	54 n. 18
7:72–8:18	166 n. 3	9:27	9, 41 n. 89, 43, 44 n. 101, 63, 175
7:72–10:40	25, 166	9:28	175
8:1–18	166 n. 4	9:27–28	89, 90 n. 27
8:2	174 n. 28	9:27–29	63
8:3	174 n. 28	9:27–30	44
8:9	174 n. 28	9:28	9, 43
8:9–13	179	9:29	28, 48, 78, 176
9	9, 11, 12, 14, 15, 16, 17, 18 n. 51, 19, 22, 23, 24, 25, 38, 39, 40, 42, 45, 46, 48, 49, 54, 61, 62, 64, 65, 66, 71, 80, 89, 90 n. 27, 104, 114, 168 n. 7, 181, 190, 192, 196, 198, 199	9:29–30	46
		9:30	28, 43, 63, 176
		9:30–31	44
		9:31	9, 41 n. 89, 44, 31, 63, 64, 176, 177 n. 33, 179
9:1	173 n. 20	9:32	42, 44, 45 n. 103, 61, 63, 113, 174, 175, 176
9:1–10:1	63 n. 49		
9:2	32, 45, 69, 74, 9:2, 198	9:32–37	38, 176, 198
9:3	32, 69, 74	9:33	13, 19, 41 n. 89, 43, 63, 83 n. 1, 105, 113, 174, 175, 176
9:5–37	101, 105, 115, 167, 174, 193		
9:6	54 n. 18, 128 n. 46, 175	9:34	46, 174, 175, 176
9:6–31	113	9:35	28, 41 n. 89, 78
9:6–37	1, 8, 20, 51, 52 n. 7, 64 n. 52, 67 n. 59, 175, 179, 194	9:35–37	44, 45
		9:36	174, 175, 176

Nehemiah (continued)		29–31	109, 110
9:36–37	54 n. 15	31:5–22	109
9:37	44, 174, 175, 177	32:6–9	111
10	47 n. 110	32:12–22	111
10:1	174	32–37	111
10:1–40	174	33:12–22	112
10:2–28	174	33:23–26	112
10:8	174	34:21–30	112
10:9	174	35:1–8	112
10:14	174	37:19–24	195
10:29	174	38–41	204
10:31	177	38–42	109, 111
11:1–12:43	166	42:6	204
12:27–43	166 n. 3	42:11	204
12:44–13:31	166	42:7–17	204
13:1–3	47		
13:14	174 n. 26	**Psalms**	
13:23	172	1:3–4	94
13:23–27	47, 179	6	2
13:23–31	177 n. 13	6:1	4 n. 11
13:25	177	6:4	126 n. 39
13:27	172	7:4–6	109
		7:14	127 n. 42
Job		9–10	102, 182
1:1–2:13	204	9:11	60 n. 38
1–27	110	10:1	84
2:11	204	13:2	95 n. 55
3–27	109	17:3–5	109
6:28–30	109, 204	22:10	109
8:5–7	204	22:25	95 n. 55
9:21	204	24:3	178
10:7	204	26:2	127 n. 42
10:8–12	109	26:2–7	109
11:13–20	204	27:9	4 n. 11, 95 n. 55
16:17	204	27:12	4 n. 11
16:16–17	109	28:1	4 n. 11
19:6–7	204	31	113
22:21–27	204	32	2
23:10–12	109	32:1–2	2 n. 3
27:2–6	109	32:5	54 n. 19
28	111	35:13	31
28:12	111	36:3	93
28:13	111	38	2
28:16–19	111	38:1	4 n. 11
28:20	111	38:19	2
28:20–22	111	38:21	4 n. 11
28:28	111	39:10–11	4 n. 11

39:11	4 n. 11	78:32	94, 98
39:12	4 n. 11	78:32–39	94 n. 46
44	53 n. 11, 57 n. 31, 64, 95, 97, 102	78:39	95
44:2–4	113	78:40	91
44:2–9	58	78:56	91
44:9	4 n. 10, 85	78:65	95 n. 52
44:10	60	79	52 n. 9, 53 n. 11, 57 n. 31, 64, 96, 97, 102
44:10–17	58, 59		
44:12–13	84	79:1–4	59, 84 n. 2
44:18	92, 98	79:5	59
44:18–23	59	79:6	95, 98
44:23–24	4 n. 9	79:8	98
44:24	59, 95, 98	79:8–9	54, 59, 96, 102
44:24–25	59, 84	79:9	98
44:24–27	58	79:13	59
44:25	60	79:15	59
51	2, 3, 5 n. 12, 54 n. 19	79:20	59
51:4	2 n. 3	79:79	94
51:11	4 n. 11	80	53 n. 11, 57 n. 31, 80, 95, 97, 102
55:1	4 n. 11	80:2–3	59
56:6	146 n. 5	80:4	4 n. 9
58:2–5	84	80:5	59, 126 n. 39
60	102	80:5–7	84 n. 2
60:8–10	113	80:9–12	58, 113
60:10	4 n. 10	80:13	59
60:3–5	84 n. 2	80:15–20	58
60:12	84 n. 2	80:18	95
66:10	85	80:19	59, 95, 98
69:8	95 n. 55	80:20	60
69:17	4 n. 11	82:2	126 n. 39
71:9	4 n. 11	83	102
74	52 n. 9, 74 n. 11, 55, 57 n. 31, 59, 64	83:10–13	113
74:1	4 n. 9, 59, 60	85	102
74:2	113	86:15	41
74:1–15	59	87:40	146 n. 5
74:4–11	84 n. 2	88	187
74:10	126 n. 39	88:15	95 n. 55
74:12–17	58	89	52 n. 9, 53 n. 11, 57 n. 31, 59, 102
75:1	95	89:4	58
75:9	4 n. 9	89:6–19	58
77	55, 57 n. 31, 77, 102	89:20–38	58, 113
77:8	60	89:31–34	54
77:8–10	59	89:34	91 n. 34, 98
78	91	89:38	4 n. 10, 85
78:1–4	91 n. 35	89:39	60
78:8	91	89:39–40	59
78:17	91	89:39–46	59, 84 n. 2

Psalms (continued)

Reference	Page
89:41–43	59
89:46	4 n. 9
89:47	84
90:8	54 n. 19
90:13	126 n. 39
94	102
94:1–11	127 n. 41
94:3	126 n. 39
94:8–11	129
94:14	60 n. 38
99:6	95 n. 51
102	2
102:2	4 n. 11
102:3	95 n. 55
103:8	41
103:10–11	63 n. 48
103:10–14	54 n. 19
105	49 n. 105
105:1	95 n. 51
106	12, 22, 24, 26, 39, 40, 45, 46, 48, 49, 57 n. 31, 65, 91, 102 n. 8, 193, 198
106:1	41 n. 89
106:4	41 n. 89
106:6	38, 54 n. 19
106:7	41 n. 89, 91
106:8	40
106:19–20	35
106:28	35
106:33	91
106:34–39	58
106:35–39	35
106:41–43	44
106:43	91
106:45	41 n. 89
106:45–46	44
106:47	44
108:11	4 n. 10
109:1	4 n. 11
111:4	41
116:4	95 n. 51
116:13	95 n. 51
116:17	95 n. 51
123	55
130	2, 3 n. 5
130:7	2 n. 3
135	22
136	49
137	53 n. 11, 55, 59, 64
137:7–9	58
143	2
143:2	2 n. 3
143:7	4 n. 11, 95 n. 55
145:8	41

Isaiah

Reference	Page
1	158
1:4	158 n. 42
1:7	158
1:19	47 n. 110, 52 n. 6
1:30	94 n. 49
2:2–4	154
3:12	88
5:5–6	178
5:9	158 n. 41
6	154, 157, 159, 162
6:1–3	107
6:1–11	151, 156, 160, 161, 162
6:1–13	154 n. 30, 158
6:4	154
6:7	158 n. 42
6:9–10	159, 161
6:9–11	157
6:10	157, 159
6:11	157, 158
8:17	95 n. 54
9:15	88
11:11	154 n. 32
13:9	158 n. 41
17:9	158 n. 41
18:17	54 n. 19
19:5–7	190
19:8–13	190
19:14–19	190
19:20–34	190
19:35–37	190
24:4	127
24:12	158 n. 41
26:14	84 n. 2
26:17–18	84 n. 2
33:9	127
33:20	178 n. 37
34:4	94 n. 49
40–55	107, 109

40:2	141 n. 96	62:10	159
40:3	159	63–64	26 n. 28, 107
40:5	154	63:5–19	98
40:12–18	108	63:7	98
40:28	153 n. 26	63:7–10	87 n. 18, 91
41:17	60 n. 40	63:7–14	86, 92 n. 39, 113
42:5–9	153 n. 26	63:8	92, 98
42:13–16	95 n. 52	63:8–10	158, 160
42:14	151 n. 19	63:9	147 n. 6
42:16	60 n. 40	63:10	92
43:1–10	161	63:11	147 n. 6
43:8	160	63:11–14	160
43:8–10	161, 162	63:15–17	163
43:8–13	160194	63:15–19	87, 89
43:8–19	153	63:7–64:11	1, 12, 19, 20, 24, 25, 40, 52
43:10	162		n. 9, 67 n. 59, 83, 86, 91, 93 n. 41, 97,
43:11	161		98, 99, 102, 145, 146, 152, 156, 158,
43:18–19	153		162, 163, 193, 194, 196, 197, 200
45:7–8	153 n. 26	63:15–17	157, 160
45:12	153 n. 26	63:15–19	197
45:15–25	107	63:16	147 n. 6
45:18	153 n. 26	63:17	88, 151, 157, 159, 160, 161, 162
45:20	154 n. 31	63:19–64:4	86
46:3	88 n. 19	64:1	148 n. 12
49:14	60 n. 40	65:1–7	154
49:15	88 n. 19	64:2	148 n. 12
51:9–11	95 n. 52	64:3–4	148
54:2	178 n. 37	64:4	9, 93
54:6	60 n. 38	64:4–5	102
54:6–8	60 n. 40	64:4–6	86, 93, 96, 148, 159, 162
54:8	95 n. 54	64:4–8	158 n. 42
54:17	161	64:5	93, 94, 95, 98
56–66	146	64:6	9, 93, 95, 97, 98
56:9–59:21	158	64:7	156
57:14	159	64:8	9, 96, 97
57:14–21	158, 159, 160	64:8–11	162
57:18	159	64:9–10	157, 197
58:3	1 n. 9, 31	64:10	156
58:10	31	64:11	151
59	114 n. 61	63:8–11	147 n. 9
59:1–15	97 n. 52	63:15	156
59:9–16	114	63:15–17	151
59:12	9	63:17	156
60:4	155	63:19	151
60:9	155	64:9–10	86, 89, 98
62:1	151 n. 19	54:10	158
62:4	158 n. 41	64:11	86

Isaiah (continued)

64:12	1 n. 9
64:44	147 n. 6
65–66	154, 156
65:1–7	151, 152
65:1–12	152
65:8	152
65:8–10	152
65:8–11	152
65:8–12	151
65:13–25	153
65:16	153
65:16–25	153
65:19–25	153
66	154, 155, 156
66:1–4	151 n. 20
66:1–24	154
66:2	154
66:13	88 n. 19
66:17	151 n. 20, 153
66:18–21	154
66:18–23	154
66:23	154

Jeremiah

1–12	120, 121, 122, 123, 124, 125, 127, 138, 140, 142
1:16	60
2:3	29
2:4–37	122
2:6	57 n. 31
2:8	57 n. 31
2:13	125
2:19	125
2:23	125
2:32	125
2:34–35	125
3:1–5	75 n. 31
3:4	57 n. 32, 88 n. 19
3:19	88 n. 19
3:12–13	60
3:14–18	60
3:19–25	60
3:21	125
3:22	126 n. 36
3:22–25	114, 139
4:5	122 n. 15
4:5–6:30	126 n. 36
4:8	122 n. 15, 123 n. 25, 125
4:9	124 n. 31
4:13	125
4:14	129 n. 50
4:15–16	124 n. 30
4:16–17	122 n. 14
4:19–21	125
4:19–22	122 n. 13, 124 n. 31
4:21	129 n. 50
4:22	125
4:23–26	142
4:28	127
4:30	60 n. 39
4:31	125
5:1–5	124 n. 31
5:2	127
5:3	125
5:3–6	130 n. 57
5:7–8	60 n. 39, 125
5:9	123
5:10	131 n. 62
5:12	125
5:15–17	125
5:19	60 n. 39
5:23–24	125
5:29	123
6:4	125
6:4–5	124 n. 30, 124 n. 31
6:9	131 n. 62
6:10	125
6:11	60 n. 39
6:15	125
6:16–17	125
6:19	60 n. 39
6:22–30	124
6:24	123 n. 26
6:24–25	125
6:24–26	122 n. 15
6:26	125
6:27	124 n. 28
7–20	119, 125
7:23	58 n. 35
7:16	124 n. 28
7:29	60 n. 39, 125
8:4–5	123 n. 21
8:5–6	125

8:8	125	12:7	60 n. 39, 130
8:9	60 n. 39	12:7–13	126, 129 n. 52, 130 n. 54, 131
8:11–12	125	12:8	131 n. 61
8:13	94 n. 49	12:9	130
8:14–15	123 n. 26, 125	12:10	131
8:14–17	124 n. 31	12:10–13	130
8:1–9:1	124 n. 29	12:11	127, 131, 132
8:18–9:2	122 n. 13, 125	12:13	129 n. 47
8:19–20	125	12:14	131 n. 60
8:23	140	13:15–17	123 n. 23
9:1	141	14	139
9:2	141	14–15	26 n. 28, 107
9:3	141	14:1–15:4	19, 23, 185, 188, 190, 193
9:8	123	14:2–6	84 n. 2
9:9	122 n. 13	14:7	9, 139
9:9–10	125	14:7–9	60
9:12	60 n. 39	14:8	4 n. 9, 139
9:16–18	122 n. 14	14:8–9	139
9:17	125, 140	14:10–12	140
9:17–20	124 n. 29	14:17–18	123 n. 23, 140
9:18	123 n, 26, 125, 142	14:19	4 n. 9
9:19	125	14:19–21	140 n. 92
9:20	123 n. 25, 125	14:20	9, 139
9:24	141	14:21	59
10:17–25	124 n. 31	14:22	139, 140
10:19–20	125	14:26	114 n. 63
10:22	124 n. 30	15:1–4	19, 140
10:23–25	125	15:4	36
10:25	84 n. 2	15:5–9	123 n. 23, 140
11–20	119	17:10	127 n. 42
11:1–14	59	18:1–12	36
11:2	58	19:4	60 n. 39
11:3	58	20:12	127 n. 42
11:4	58 n. 35	21:2	56, 59
11:6	58	22:9	60 n. 39
11:14	124 n. 28	23	56
11:20	127 n. 42	23:10	127, 128 n. 43, 129
12	202	23:33	60 n. 39
12:1	63 n. 47, 127	24:7	58 n. 35
12:1–3	143	25:11	140
12:1–4	127, 129 n. 47, 131	26:7	56
12:1–6	121, 126 n. 39, 129 n. 52, 131	28	56
12:1–13	120, 124, 125, 126, 132, 134, 138, 193, 196	29	33 n. 56, 56
		29:10–14	12, 23, 27, 198
12:2	127	29:12	23 n. 9
12:3	127	29:12–14	140
12:4	128, 129, 130	30:1	141 n. 95

236   ANCIENT SOURCES INDEX

Jeremiah (continued)
30:22	58 n. 35
31	38
31:1	58 n. 35
31:9	57 n. 32
31:18	84 n. 2
31:29–31	36
31:31–34	141 n. 95
31:33	58 n. 35
31:37	60
32	40 n. 85
32:16–25	24
32:17–26	40 n. 84
32:18	42 n. 92
32:17–25	49 n. 119, 52 n. 9
32:18–19	36
32:30–31	36
32:38	58 n. 35
33:5	95 n. 54
33:24	60
33:24–27	60
34:13	58
36:7	27 n. 32
37:3	56
41	188, 190
41:5	186
41:9	95 n. 56
49:23	96

Ezekiel
1:22–28	107
5:6	60 n. 39
8–11	60
8:12	60
9:9	60
11:19–20	61
11:20	58 n. 35
13	56
14:3	9
14:11	58 n. 35
16	57 n. 32
16:1–4	57 n. 32
16:47	47 n. 110
16:62	58
18	12, 13, 37 n. 18, 38
18:6	170 n. 10
18:21–32	60
20:1–8	57 n. 31
20:5–38	59
20:13	60 n. 39
20:16	60 n. 39
20:21	58
20:24	60 n. 39
20:32	57 n. 31
23	57 n. 32
27:10–25	154 n. 32
34:25	58
36:16–32	141
36:26–27	61
36:28	58 n. 35
37:23	58 n. 35
37:27	58 n. 35
38:1	154 n. 32
39:23	95 n. 54
39:24	95 n. 54
39:29	95 n. 54
42:7	178
42:10	178
47:12	94 n. 49

Daniel
9	5, 12, 15, 16, 17, 26, 32, 33, 46, 54, 62, 63, 65, 71, 104, 114, 128 n. 46, 190, 196
9:1	141
9:1–19	141
9:3	141
9:3–9	54 n. 15
9:4	8, 9, 10, 32, 42, 44, 61, 63, 69, 74, 113
9:4–19	1, 8, 51, 64 n. 52, 79 n. 23, 101, 193
9:4–21	33
9:5	9, 46, 62
9:5–6	38, 198
9:6	28, 46, 62
9:6–11	54 n. 15
9:7	9, 32, 43, 44, 62 n. 45, 63, 83 n. 1, 113
9:7–15	113
9:8	44, 46, 62
9:9	41 n. 89, 45 n. 103, 61, 62 n. 45, 63, 80
9:10	28, 45 n. 103, 46, 61, 62 n. 45, 113

ANCIENT SOURCES INDEX

9:10–11	62	1:20	136
9:11	43, 46	2	121, 134, 137
9:11–13	47	2:1	136
9:12–14	63	2:1–11	136, 143 n. 104
9:13	28, 41 n. 89, 44, 62 n. 45, 78	2:2–3	136
9:14	9, 13, 43, 46, 61, 113	2:5	136
9:15	41, 44, 45 n. 103, 61, 62 n. 45	2:12	136
9:16	9, 13, 43, 61, 62, 63 n. 47, 115	2:12–13	136
9:16–17	44	2:12–17	136, 137
9:17	45 n. 103, 61	2:18	137
9:17–18	41 n. 89	2:18–27	137
9:18	9, 13, 45 n. 103	2:13	41
9:19	45	2:14	136, 137 n. 84
9:20	8, 10, 32, 69, 74	2:15	136
9:22–23	32		

Hosea

		Amos	
4:1–3	129 n. 28	1:2	127, 128 n. 23
4:6	60 n. 38	2:4	88
4:12	88	5:21	60 n. 28
9:15	131	**Jonah**	
14:1–2	27 n. 32	4:2	41

Joel

		Micah	
1	121, 129 n. 52, 134, 137	3:4	95 n. 54
1–2	120, 134, 135, 138, 140, 142, 143, 193, 196	3:5	88
1:2	135	**Nahum**	
1:2–3	135	1:3	41
1:2–4	134 n. 76		
1:2–2:17	134 n. 77	**Habakkuk**	
1:4–7	136	1:13	4 n. 9
1:5	136		
1:5–14	134 n. 76	**Haggai**	
1:5–20	136, 137 n. 81	2:13–14	94
1:8	136		
1:9	136	**Zechariah**	
1:10	127, 128 n. 43	1–8	23, 52
1:11	128 n. 43	1:1–6	185
1:12	128 n. 43	1:1–6:7	14, 24
1:13	136	7–8	188, 190
1:14	136	7:1–8:23	14, 24, 185
1:15	136	7:3	186
1:18–20	84	7:5	186
1:19	136	8:19	186

Apocryphal/Deuterocanonical Texts

Tobit
- 3:1–6 — 9

Judith
- 9:2–14 — 12, 102

Additions to Esther
- 13:9–17 — 102
- 14:3–9 — 102
- 14:6–7 — 105 n. 24

Wisdom of Solomon
- 4:7–9 — 112

Baruch
- 1:15 — 113
- 1:15–3:8 — 5, 9, 15, 101, 141

Prayer of Azariah
- 3–22 — 102, 103 n. 14
- 4–9 — 113
- 9 — 105 n. 24
- 12 — 115

1 Esdras
- 3:28–36 — 103 n. 15
- 5:28 — 103 n. 15
- 6:55–69 — 103 n. 15
- 8:73–90 — 5, 9, 101 n. 4
- 8:87 — 115

3 Maccabees
- 2:2–20 — 12, 102, 103 n. 12, 204
- 3:1–20 — 9
- 6:2–15 — 103 n. 12

New Testament

Acts
- 16 — 17

Romans
- 3:4 — 2 n. 3
- 3:20 — 2 n. 3
- 3:24 — 2 n. 3
- 4:7–8 — 2 n. 3

Pseudepigraphal and Rabbinic Texts

1 Enoch
- 85–90 — 15
- 84:2–6 — 103
- 93:1–10; 91:11–17 — 15

2 Baruch
- 3:1–9 — 103 n. 15

m. Yoma
- 6:2 — 75

Psalms of Solomon
- 1 — 102 n. 6
- 2 — 101, 102 n. 6
- 2:3 — 115
- 2:13 — 115
- 2:15–16 — 113
- 2:15–18 — 105 n. 24
- 8 — 102 n. 6
- 8:7 — 105 n. 24
- 8:11–12 — 115
- 8:22 — 115
- 9 — 5, 9, 102 n. 6
- 9:2 — 113

Hebrew Words Index

אבל	128, 129, 131, 135	לקח	173
אמנה	174	מאס	60
אף	174	מוג	95, 96
אפק	147, 150, 151	מחיה	170
אָשָׁם	28, 29, 30, 32, 34, 78, 79	מַעַל	29, 30, 32, 33, 34, 35, 80
אַשְׁמָה	35, 169, 170, 173	מצוה	170, 173
בדל	45, 78	מָרַד	34
בוש	129, 130	מָרָה	34, 91, 92, 146, 158
בלה	94	מתעורר	95
ברא	153	נבט	150
ברית	174	נדה	170
בשר	155	נטש	60, 130
גדר	170, 178	נשא	171, 173
גזרה	82	נתן	170, 173
דָּרַשׁ	47	סלל	158
הִתְוַדָּה	8, 10, 28, 30, 31, 32, 34, 69, 70, 71, 73, 78, 80	סתר	159
		עֲבָדוּת	45
ועתה	169, 174	עָוֹן	33, 34, 42, 93, 94, 150
זכר	147, 153	עזאזל	75, 80
זנח	60	עזב	60, 130
זעק	136	עמי הארצות/הארץ	170, 174, 179
חדש	153	עצב	91, 92, 146
חטא	29, 35, 93, 94, 126, 139	ערג	136
חַטָּאת	33, 42	פְּלֵיטָה	44, 170
חֶסֶד	45, 63, 170	פלל	23
חרדים	167, 174	פנה	159
חשה	151, 152	פֶּשַׁע	33, 34, 42, 158
חתן	172, 173	צַדִּיק	13, 43, 63, 176
טחח	157	צְדָקָה	9
טמא	94	קנאה	88
טֻמְאָה	32, 170	קצף	150, 159
יבש	127, 128, 129, 135, 136	קרא	23, 136, 151
ירש	44, 170	קשח	157
ישב	172	רַחוּם	9
יתד	178	ריב	127
כבד	157	רָשָׁע	34
כֻּפֶּר	33	שאר	43, 44

שְׁאֵרִית	44	שעע	157
שׁוּב	28, 78, 125, 141, 159	שקר	91, 92
שכח	60	שׂרף	158
שמה	130, 131	תועבות	170, 173
שממה	130, 131, 158	תחנה	170
שמע	23	תעה	88

Modern Authors Index

Abrams, M. H. 121 n. 10
Achtemeier, Elizabeth 87 n. 18
Ackroyd, Peter. R. 54 n. 14, 90, 90 n. 31
Adorno, Theodor 18
Aejmelaeus, Anneli 145 n. 1, 146 n. 3
Albani, Matthias 154 n. 29
Albertz, Rainer 23 n. 13, 25, 89 n. 26, 103 n. 18, 104 nn. 21–22, 108 n. 42, 109 n. 45, 185 n. 14
Alt, Albrecht 10 n. 27
Alter, Robert 191, 191 n. 26
Amit, Yairah 89 n. 29, 191 n. 26
Anderson, Carl R. 27 n. 33
Armstrong, Karen 107 n. 30
Austin, John L. 70, 70 n. 2, 71 n. 4, 72 n. 8, 73, 73 nn. 9–10, 74 n. 11, 81 n. 27
Balentine, Samuel E. 1 n. 1, 8 n. 23, 9 n. 24, 20 n. 61, 21, 21 nn. 1–2, 26, 27, 27 n. 29, 29 n. 33, 30, 30 n. 46, 31 nn. 51 and 53, 39, 39 n. 79, 42 n. 92, 42 n. 95, 43, 43 n. 98, 51 n. 1, 54, 54 nn. 15–16, 57 n. 30, 71, 71 n. 6, 74 n. 12, 80 n. 26, 101 nn. 1–2, 113 n. 58, 114 n. 65, 191, 191 n. 27, 204 n. 7
Baltzer, Klaus 10 n. 27
Bar-Efrat, Shimeon 191 n. 26
Barton, John 134 n. 77, 137 n. 81
Baumgartner, Walter 126 n. 38, 127 n. 39
Bautch, Richard J. 11, 11 n. 31, 12, 12 n. 35, 13, 13 n. 37, 16, 18 n. 51, 19, 20, 20 nn. 57–58, 25, 25 nn. 20–25, 26 n. 26, 28 n. 35, 34 n. 60, 43 n. 96, 47 n. 109, 48 n. 112, 52 nn. 6–7 and 9, 53 nn. 11–12, 54, 54 n. 16, 55 n. 23, 65 nn. 53–54, 66 nn. 57 and 59, 87 n. 17, 89 n. 25, 102 n. 8, 103 n. 18, 104 n. 19, 105, 105 n. 23, 107, 107 n. 34, 108 n. 38, 116 n. 72, 163 n. 57, 185, 185 n. 15, 186, 186 n. 16, 187, 187 n. 21, 196, 197, 197 n. 2, 200, 201, 203, 203 n. 6

Becker, Uwe 158 n. 40
Becking, Bob 23 n. 13, 26 n. 27, 168 n. 7, 185 n. 14, 186, 186 nn. 17–18, 187, 187 n. 19, 191, 192 n. 28
Belfiore, Elizabeth S. 120 n. 9
Bell, Catherine 81 n. 27
Bellinger, William H. 81 n. 1
Berges, Ulrich 152 n. 21, 159 n. 47
Berlin, Adele 11 n. 31, 23 n. 10, 51 n. 3, 56 n. 28, 64 n. 51, 80 n. 26, 102 n. 8, 103 n. 16, 146 nn. 2–3, 149 n. 14, 153 n. 26, 165 n. 1, 173 n. 17, 184 n. 8, 191, 191 n. 26
Beuken, Willem A. M. 109 n. 43, 120 n. 5, 121 n. 12, 140 nn. 92–94, 145 n. 1, 149 n. 13, 153 n. 27, 162 n. 55
Biddle, Mark 119, 120 n. 5, 121 nn. 11–12, 122 n. 13, 123 nn. 23–24, 124 n. 27, 125, 125 nn. 32 and 34, 126 nn. 36–37, 138 n. 85, 139 nn. 89 and 91
Blackman, Philip 75 n. 14
Blenkinsopp, Joseph 47, 47 n. 11, 79 n. 23, 87 n. 18, 147 n. 8, 149 n. 16, 150 n. 17, 152 n. 22, 153 nn. 23 and 25, 154 nn. 28 and 31–32, 155 nn. 34–35, 159 nn. 44 and 47, 160 nn. 49–50, 161 n. 53, 162 n. 55, 163 n. 57, 167 n. 5, 172 n. 15, 178 nn. 36–37
Boda, Mark J., 11, 11 n. 31, 12, 13, 13 nn. 38–39, 14, 14 n. 40, 16, 18, 19, 19 nn. 55–56, 23 nn. 10–13, 26 n. 28, 27 nn. 31 and 33, 28 nn. 34–35, 32 n. 55, 33 nn. 57–58, 34 n. 61, 38 n. 77, 40 n. 83, 41 n. 89, 43 n. 96, 46 nn. 105–6, 48 n. 116, 49

Boda, Mark J. (continued)
n. 119, 51, 51 n. 3, 52 nn. 4–9, 53 nn. 12 and 14, 54 n. 17, 55 nn. 21 and 23, 62 nn. 44 and 46, 63 n. 49, 64 n. 52, 65 n. 54, 67 n. 61, 69 n. 10, 71 n. 7, 77 n. 18, 78, 78 n. 19, 80 n. 26, 88 n. 22, 102 n. 8, 103 n. 18, 107, 107 n. 33, 115, 115 nn. 69 and 71, 128 n. 46, 137 nn. 82 and 86, 139 n. 90, 140 n. 92, 165 n. 1, 184 n. 8, 185 nn. 13–14, 189 n. 23, 192, 192 nn. 28–29, 194, 196, 197, 198, 199, 200, 204

Bouzard, Walter C.   53 n. 11, 54 n. 15, 55 n. 20
Braun, Roddy L.   191, 191 n. 27
Brettler, Marc Zvi   141 n. 95
Brown, Andrew   120 n. 9, 10
Broyles, Craig C.   53 n. 13, 160 n. 49
Brueggemann, Walter   6, 6 n. 20, 7, 7 n. 21, 8, 16, 39 n. 80, 83 n. 1, 85, 86, 86 nn. 9–13, 99 n. 65, 120 n. 5, 122 n. 17, 181 n. 1, 183, 183 n. 6, 187 n. 22, 198
Burrows, Millar   94 n. 48, 95 n. 58
Buss, Martin   70 n. 3
Carroll, Robert P.   114 n. 63, 204 n. 7
Chazon, Esther G.   12 n. 34, 102 n. 7
Childs, Brevard S.   157 n. 38
Chrostowski, Waldemar   54 n. 18, 64 n. 52
Clements, Ronald E.   130 n. 55, 181 n. 1
Clifford, Richard   92 n. 39, 94 n. 46
Clines, David J. A.   47, 47 nn. 110–11
Collins, John J.   9 n. 25
Condamin, Albert   130 n. 56
Craigie, Peter C.   130 n. 56
Crenshaw, James L.   56 n. 28, 108 nn. 40–41
Culley, Robert E.   67 n. 62
Dahood, Mitchell   95 n. 56
Deist, Ferdinand E.   134 n. 77, 137 n. 81
Delitzsch, Franz   93, 93 n. 44
Dentan, Robert C.   41 n. 87
Deventer, Hans van   26 n. n. 27, 32 n. 56
Dhorme, Édouard   113 n. 57
Diamond, A. R.   119, 119 n. 3, 126 n. 39, 127 n. 41, 129 nn. 47 and 49
Dobbs-Allsopp, Frederick W.   132 n. 66
Dor, Yonina   171 n. 13

Douglas, Mary 20 n. 60, 81 n. 27, 172 n. 15
Dozeman, Thomas B.   41 n. 87
Driver, Samuel R.   136 n. 81, 137 n. 84
Duggan, Michael   25 nn. 18–19, 90 n. 27, 165, 165 n. 1, 166 nn. 2 and 4, 174 n. 27, 177 n. 33, 191, 191 n. 27, 194
Easterling, Pat E.   120 n. 9, 123 n. 22, 132 n. 64, 133, 133 nn. 68–70 and 73, 134 n. 74, 143 n. 106
Eisenstadt, S. N.   106, 106 nn. 26–28, 107 nn. 29 and 31, 108 n. 35, 113 n. 59, 114 n. 66, 115 n. 68
Elkana, Yehuda   114 n. 66
Ellinger, Karl   160 n. 51
Else, Gerald F.   120 n. 10
Emerton, John   130 n. 53, 184 n. 10
Emmendörfer, Michael   145 n. 1, 146, 146 nn. 4–5, 147 nn. 7–10, 148 n. 11, 163 n. 58
Eskenazi, Tamara C.   79 nn. 23–24, 166 n. 2, 172 n. 15, 177 n. 31, 178 n. 35
Evans, Donald D.   24 n. 14, 70 n. 2, 73 n. 10, 160 n. 49
Falk, Daniel K.   11, 11 n. 31, 15, 15 nn. 42–44, 16, 19, 24, 24 n. 17, 27 n. 32, 28, 28 n. 35, 29 n. 36, 31, 51 n. 2, 71 n. 7
Fischer, Irmtraud   145, 145 n. 1, 146 n. 2, 147 n. 8, 148 n. 11, 149 n. 16
Fishbane, Michael   41 n. 87
Fitzmyer, Joseph   92 nn. 38–39
Fleischer, Ezra   12 n. 34
Fretheim, Terence   121 n. 12, 122 n. 14, 203, 203 n. 5
Gärtner, Judith   145, 194, 196, 197
Gauchet, Marcel   107 n. 32
Gerstenberger, Erhard   109, 109 n. 44, 110 n. 47, 112 n. 56, 183 n. 5
Gilbert, Maurice   46 n. 104
Girard, René   108 n. 41
Goldenstein, Johannes   145 n. 1, 146, 146 n. 3, 147 n. 9, 148 n. 12, 150 n. 18, 151 n. 18, 159 n. 43, 160 n. 48, 161 n. 52, 162 nn. 54 and 56
Goldingay, John   33 n. 57
Goodhill, Simon   133 n. 68
Gorman, Frank H.   32 n. 54, 81 n. 27, 201 n. 4

MODERN AUTHORS INDEX

Gottwald, Norman K.   114 n. 60, 132 n. 65, 137 n. 83
Gould, John   132, 132 nn. 64 and 66–67, 134 n. 75
Grabbe, Lester L.   78 n. 20, 79 n. 24
Green, Ronald M.   55, 55 n. 24
Greenberg, Moshe   26 n. 27, 27 n. 33, 37 n. 70, 54 n. 19, 55 n. 22, 61 n. 41, 63 n. 47, 74 n. 12, 76, 76 nn. 15–16, 77 n. 17, 114 n. 63, 191, 191 n. 27
Grimm, Werner   160 n. 51
Grol, Harm W. M. van   26 n. 27, 46 n. 107, 47 n. 108, 52 n. 8, 120 n. 5, 121 n. 12, 140 n. 92, 140 n. 93, 168 n. 7, 169 n. 7
Groß, Walter   149 n. 14, 155 n. 36
Gunkel, Hermann   3, 3 n. 5, 6, 7, 9, 10, 39 n. 80, 84, 84 n. 3, 86, 86 n. 15, 182, 182 n. 2, 184, 184 nn. 7 and 9
Gutmann, Joseph   32 n. 55
Haar, Murray J.   104 n. 20
Halpern, Baruch   36 n. 69, 37 n. 70, 38 nn. 75 and 77, 94 n. 46
Hartenstein, Friedhelm   154 n. 30, 156, 156 n. 37
Hartley, John E.   109 n. 43
Hayes, Katherine M.   119, 128 n. 45, 130 n. 53, 134 n. 77, 196, 197
Heinemann, Joseph   103 n. 16
Herbert, Arthur S.   91 n. 35, 96 n. 61
Hermisson, Hans-Jürgen   154 n. 31
Hiebert, Theodore   136 n. 79
Hillers, Delbert R.   59 n. 36
Hoffmann, Yair   111 nn. 50–51
Holladay, William L.   114 n. 63, 122 nn. 12–13, 126 nn. 35–36 and 39, 127 n. 39, 130 n. 55
Holmgren, Fredrick C.   61 n. 43, 66 n. 56
Jakobson, Lea   110 n. 47
Janzen, David   170 n. 10
Japhet, Sara   166 n. 2
Jaspers, Karl   101, 106, 106 n. 25, 195
Jeremias, Joachim   134 n. 48, 137 n. 81
Joüon, Paul   96 n. 60
Kaminsky, Joel S.   35 n. 66, 37, 37 nn. 70–74, 38, 38 nn. 75–76 and 78
Kaufmann, Yehezkel   10 n. 26
Kessler, Rainer   26 n. 27, 121 n. 11, 159 n. 45
Kiesow, Klaus   153 n. n. 25
Kiuchi, Nobuyoshi   29 n. 40, 78, 78 nn. 20–21
Klawans, Jonathan   33 n. 58, 79 n. 22
Klopfenstein, Martin A.   92 n. 37
Knierim, Rolf   91 n. 34
Knohl, Israel   20 n. 60, 74 n. 13, 115 nn. 67–68
Knoppers, Gary N.   33 n. 50
Koch, Klaus   93 n. 42
Koenen, Klaus   145, 145 n. 1, 146 n. 2, 147, 152 nn. 20–21, 155 n. 35, 159 n. 46
Kraemer, David   103 n. 16
Kraus, Hans-Joachim   183, 183 n. 4, 184 n. 10
Kugel, James L.   191 n. 26
Kühlewein, Johannes   184 n. 10
Lacocque, Andre   10 n. 30, 52 nn. 4 and 8, 64 n. 52
Lambert, David   141 n. 95
Lanser, Susan S.   70 n. 3
Lau, Wolfgang   145, 146 n. 2, 150 n. 18, 152 n. 20
Laytner, Anson   103 nn. 16–17
Lee, Bernon P. Y.   48 n. 113
Levine, Baruch A.   30 n. 43, 31 nn. 50 and 52, 32 n. 54
Liebreich, Leon J.   9, 10, 10 n. 26
Lipiński, Edward   10, 10 n. 29, 184 n. 10
Lundbom, Jack R.   126 n. 35, 127 n. 39
Machinist, Peter   106 n. 28
Mandolfo, Carleen   99, 99 nn. 65–66
Matties, Gordon   38 n. 75
McConville, J. Gordon   33 n. 59, 121 n. 11, 126 n. 36
McDonough, Sheila   56, 56 n. 26
McKane, William   126 n. 35, 130 nn. 54–55
Milgrom, Jacob   18, 18 n. 52, 19, 19 nn. 53–54, 24, 28–29, 29 nn. 36 and 39–41, 30, 30 nn. 43–44 and 47, 31, 31 n. 49, 32 n. 54, 35, 35 nn. 63 and 65, 36, 36 nn. 67–68, 37 n. 70, 41 nn. 42–43, 42 n. 90, 47, 47 n. 104, 58 n. 33, 61 n. 42, 69 n. 1, 77 n. 18, 78, 78 nn. 20–21, 79, 79 n. 22

Miller, Patrick D.   8 n. 23, 21, 22 nn.
   3–4, 27, 27 nn. 30 and 33, 34 n. 62, 41
   n. 89, 42 n. 92, 43 n. 97, 64 n. 51, 74 n.
   12, 86 n. 9, 113 n. 58, 181 n. 1, 184, 185
   n. 12
Moore, Carey A.   101 n. 5
Morrow, William S. 101, 103 n. 15, 108 nn.
   37 and 39, 110 n. 39, 195–97, 200–201,
   203–4
Mowinckel, Sigmund   3, 3 n. 6, 10, 53 n.
   13, 86, 86 n. 16, 87 n. 18, 182, 182 n. 3,
   184, 184 n. 7, 184 n. 9
Myers, Jacob M   52 n. 8
Nasuti, Harry P.   2 n. 2, 7, 7 n. 22, 8, 17,
   181 n. 1
Neusner, Jacob   94, 94 n. 47
Newman, Judith H.   11, 11 n. 31, 16, 24,
   24 nn. 14–16, 33, 33 n. 59, 41 n. 89, 42,
   42 nn. 90–91, 48, 48 n. 114, 49 n. 117
   and 119, 51 n. 2, 204, 204 n. 8
Newsom, Carol A.   109 n. 46, 110 n. 110,
   48, 112 n. 55
Nitzan, Bilhah   12 n. 34
Noth, Martin   191, 191 n. 27
Oeming, Manfred   26 n. 27, 27 n. 29, 39,
   39 n. 82, 44 n. 101, 45 n. 102
Olyan, Saul   128, 128 n. 46, 134 n. 77, 142,
   142 nn. 98–102, 143
O'Connor, Kathleen M.   119 n. 3, 121 n.12
Oorschott, Jürgen van   153 n. 26
Oswalt, John   93 n. 44
Overholt, Thomas W.   120 n. 5
Pakkala, Juha   173 n. 17, 175 n. 29
Parpola, Simo   58 n. 34
Paul, Shalom M.   57 n. 32
Perdue, Leo G.   108 n. 41, 111 n. 50, 112 n.
   53
Petersen, John E.   38 n. 77
Plöger, Otto   8 n. 23, 191, 191 n. 27
Polk, Timothy   122 n. 14
Porten, Bezalel   90, 90 nn. 28–29
Preus, James S.   3 n. 4
Pröbstl, Volker   12 n. 36, 22, 22 n. 6, 48 n.
   115, 49
Rad, Gerhard von   10 n. 27, 16, 37, 39, 39
   n. 81, 40, 40 n. 6, 72 n. 8, 119, 119 nn.
   1–2, 122 n. 14, 191, 191 n. 27

Reddit, Paul L.   26 nn. 27–28, 33 n. 57,
   192 n. 29
Reif, Stefan   12 n. 34, 21
Rendtorff, Rolf   26 n. 27, 63 n. 47
Reventlow, Henning G.   8 n. 23
Roberts, J. J. M.   122 nn. 13–14, 123 n. 23
Rodriguez, Angel M.   31 n. 51, 32 n. 55
Rom-Shiloni, Dalit 51, 53 nn. 10–11, 56 n.
   27, 57 n. 29 and 32, 59 n. 37, 71 n. 7, 74
   n. 12, 85 nn. 6–7, 196–97, 200–202
Roskes, David G.   103 n. 17
Ross, James F.   112 n. 54
Said, Edward W.   17, 17 n. 49, 18, 18 n. 50
Sakenfeld, Katharine D.   41 n. 88, 42 n. 92
Saydon, Paul P.   29 n. 37
Scharbert, Josef   37, 41 n. 87, 42 n. 92
Schenker, Adrian   29 n. 40
Schoors, Anton   114 nn. 61–62
Schuller, Eileen M.   71 n. 5
Schwienhorst, L.udger   91 n. 34, 92 n. 36
Scullion, John J.   108 nn. 35–36
Searle, John R.   70 n. 2, 81 n. 27
Segal, Charles   120 n. 9, 133, 133 nn. 71–
   73, 143, 143 n. 105
Seitz, Christopher R.   111 n. 103, 121 n.
   11, 139 n. 89, 143 n. 103
Silk, M. S.   120 n. 9, 121, 121 n. 10, 132
Smith, Gordon T.   27 n. 31
Smith, Mark S.   119 n. 3, 123 n. 23, 126 n.
   39, 127 nn. 39–40, 129 nn. 51–52
Smith, Morton   88 n. 23
Smith-Christopher, Daniel   17, 17 nn.
   45–48, 177 n. 31, 187 n. 21
Steck, Odil H.   10, 10 n. 28, 13, 146, 146 n.
   3, 150 n. 18, 152 n. 21, 153 n. 27, 154 n.
   31, 155 n. 33, 159 n. 43, 162 n. 56
Stone, Michael E.   113 n. 59
Thiselton, Anthony   72 n. 8
Thompson, Michael E.   22, 22 n. 5
Throntveit, Mark A.   191, 191 n. 27
Tigay, Jeffrey H.   26 n. 27, 35–36, 37 n. 72,
   63 n. 47
Towner, W. Sibley   8, 8 n. 23, 54 n. 23, 54,
   54 n. 18
Uffenheimer, Benjamin   108 n. 35
Veijola, Timo   184 n. 10
Venter, Pieter M   26 n. 27, 33 n. 56

Vickers, Brian 120 n. 10,
Villanueva, Frederico G., Jr. 26 n. 28
Washington, Harold C. 170 n.10, 172 n. 15
Watson, Wilfred G. E. 191 n. 26
Weinfeld, Moshe 8 n. 23, 12 n. 34, 21, 21 n. 2, 37 n. 72, 42, 42 nn. 92–93, 46 n. 105, 57 nn. 31–32, 88, 88 n. 20, 89, 89 n. 26, 107 n. 31, 191, 191 n. 27
Weiser, Artur 91 n. 35, 95 n. 53, 183, 183 n. 4, 184 n. 9
Wenham, Gordon J. 30 n. 43, 31 n. 52, 32 n. 54
Werline, Rodney A. 11, 11 nn. 31–32, 12–14, 14 n. 41, 15, 16, 22, 22 n. 7, 23, 23 n. 9, 24, 27, 27 n. 31, 28 n. 35, 29 n. 36, 33 n. 59, 46 n. n. 107, 47, 48 n. 112, 51 nn. 2–3, 52 nn. 4 and 6, 67 n. 60, 70 n. 4, 78 n. 19, 98–99, 99 nn. 63–64, 101 nn. 1–2, 102 nn. 6–8, 107, 107 n. 34, 114 n. 64, 115 nn. 67 and 70, 141 n. 97, 185, 185 n. 13, 187 n. 20, 196, 196 n. 1

Westermann, Claus 3, 4 nn. 7–8, 4 n. 11, 5, 5 nn. 12–16, 6, 6 nn. 17–19, 7, 8, 9, 13, 14, 16, 18, 39 n. 80, 53, 53 n. 13, 55, 55 n. 23, 64, 64 n. 50, 67, 83 n. 1, 85, 85 nn. 4 and 8, 86, 90 n. 30, 101 nn. 3–4, 102, 102 nn. 6 and 8, 102 n. 10, 103 nn. 12–14, 105, 105 n. 24, 114 n. 61, 145 n. 1, 155 n. 35, 161, 183, 183 n. 6, 184 nn. 10–11, 187, 198, 200
Whybray, R. Norman 94 n. 44,
Williamson, Hugh G. M. 47 nn. 110–11, 64 n. 52, 89 n. 25, 167 n. 6, 178 nn. 36–37, 189 n. 23, 191 n. 27
Willis, John T. 120 n. 5, 121 n. 12, 126 n. 36, 140 n. 92
Wilson, Gerald H. 33 n. 56
Wolf, Hans W. 134 nn. 76–77, 136 n. 81
Wright, George E. 41 n. 86
Young, Edeward 3 n. 4, 94 n. 45
Zahavi-Ely, Naama 122, 122 n. 16, 124 n. 27, 126 n. 38, 139 n. 89

Subject Index

Adorno, Theodor 18
allegorical interpretation 2
Amos 13, 19
Aristotle 120
Artaxerxes 178, 179, 202
ashes 10
Atonement, Day of 15, 20, 31, 32, 33, 41, 69, 74–77, 80, 81, 82
Augustine 2
autobiography 166, 167, 171, 173
Axial age 101–17, 195, 200, 203–4
Cassiodorus 2
character credo 24, 38–39, 41, 42, 199
Christian prayer 6
complaint 4, 53, 55, 63, 65, 83, 84, 85, 102, 104, 105, 108, 110, 185, 188
confession of sin 1, 2, 4, 5, 8, 15, 16, 20, 30, 31, 35, 36, 54–55, 58, 61, 63, 65, 66, 69–82, 85, 87, 90–97, 98, 99, 101, 102, 105, 114, 139, 145, 148–49, 151, 159, 169, 170, 174, 176, 184, 185, 186, 188, 194, 196, 204
contrition 2, 82, 101
covenant 10, 13, 15, 16, 28, 29, 30, 34, 38, 42, 43, 45, 46, 47, 57, 58, 59, 60, 62, 63, 65, 87, 105, 166, 174, 175, 177, 183, 185
credo (short historical) 39–40
cult-functional approach 182
Cyrus 178, 179
Darius I 178
Deuteronomic tradition 8, 9, 10, 12, 13, 14, 16, 17, 18, 22, 23, 24, 25, 26, 27, 28, 33, 34, 38, 39, 42, 44, 45, 47, 49, 51, 52, 56, 57, 58, 60, 62, 64, 67, 88, 89, 92, 99, 115, 116, 172, 177, 185, 193, 195, 198, 200
diachronic analysis 165, 194

divorce 169, 170
earth, personification 119–43
Elephantine texts 90
eschatology 153, 154, 156
exile 5, 8, 9, 17, 24, 26, 30, 31, 33, 40, 44, 47, 53, 56, 59, 60, 63, 80, 83, 97, 104, 109, 183, 188, 195, 199, 200
exilic fasting. *See* fasting
Ezekiel, Ezekielian tradition 12, 13, 19, 36–37, 39, 51, 52, 56, 60
Ezra (person) 165–180, 202
fasting 10, 31, 185, 188, 190
Feast of Weeks 15
foreigners, separation from 44, 45, 74, 179
form criticism 6, 7, 11, 16, 23, 86, 145, 181–92, 193–98
Gerichtsdoxologie 13
God
 character 39–43
 mercy, grace 9, 41–42, 43, 44, 45, 54, 56, 63, 87, 89, 97, 101, 169, 171, 199
 discipline 43, 44, 45, 63, 155, 198
 forgiveness 56
 glory (*kabod*) 154, 155, 156
 justice 3, 6, 9, 15, 54, 56, 63, 85, 101, 105, 127
 omnipotence 56, 139
 omnipresence 56
 omniscience 56
 righteousness, righteous 43, 63, 85, 103, 104, 113, 169, 176, 199
 sovereignty 113
 transcendence 107, 108, 111, 116
 wrath 2, 38, 59, 84, 92, 96, 97, 123, 149, 152, 160, 174
Greek tragedy 119–43

guilt, guilty 29, 39, 76, 78, 80, 91, 143, 150, 155, 158, 159, 161, 169, 170, 171, 173, 177, 198
Haggai 14, 52
hardness of heart 156–63
hermeneutics 48, 71–72, 82, 204
historiography 17
Holiness Code 33, 64
Holocaust 7
humility 31
hymns 3
idolatry 30, 35, 45, 198
innerbiblical allusion/exegesis. *See* intertextuality
intermarriage 44, 47, 74, 77, 79, 165–79, 201
intertextuality 11, 12, 22, 47, 49, 52
Isaiah, Isaianic tradition 145–63
Jeremiah, Jeremianic tradition 33, 36, 39, 52, 56, 60, 119–143
Jaspers, Karl 101–17, 195
Jewish liturgy 10
Job, book of 19–20, 101–17, 203–4
lament 119–43, 195, 196
    divine 119, 127, 129, 130, 202
    communal 1, 3, 5, 6, 7, 11, 14, 17, 19, 20, 44, 52, 53, 54, 55, 57, 58, 59, 60, 61, 63, 64, 65, 66, 67, 68, 83–99, 101–17, 120, 121, 134–43, 145–63, 181–92, 193, 193–97
    communal: stages/development 4, 85–86, 181–83, 196, 197, 199, 200, 201
    individual 3, 112
    loss of 6, 7, 83–99, 101–17
Lamentations, book of 56, 57, 188
land 44, 45, 58, 60, 62, 66, 176, 180
Latter Prophets 24
Levitical circles 10, 13
literary criticism 25, 165–80, 192, 194
Luther, Martin 2
Micah 13, 19
Moses 28, 44, 62, 179
mourning rituals 128, 129, 130, 142
narrative criticism. *See* literary criticism
nations, judgment/pilgrimage of 154, 155
Nehemiah (person) 166, 177
New Year's festival 182

oath, oath violation 29, 30, 35, 177
original sin 2
Passover, Feast of 179
penitence. *See* repentance
penitential prayer
    definition 11
    genre elements 8–11
    institutionalization 12, 14–16, 18, 23
penitential psalms 3
people, theology of 43–45
performative utterance 69–82, 194, 201
political, political metaphor 15, 17, 61, 86, 106, 200
prayer replacing sacrifice 14
prayer times, set 14
prayers, prose 4, 5, 8
Priestly doctrine of repentance 24, 28–29, 33
Priestly tradition 10, 12, 13, 14, 16, 18, 19, 20, 22, 23, 24, 25, 26, 28, 29, 32, 33, 34, 35, 36, 38, 39, 47, 49, 51, 52, 56, 57, 60, 62, 64, 67, 69–82, 115, 116, 185, 193, 194, 195, 198
prophetic drama 119–43
prophetic liturgy 23, 112
prophets, prophetic tradition 9, 18, 24, 25, 27, 28, 46, 49, 52, 56, 58, 61, 62, 64, 65, 67, 107, 119, 169, 171, 193, 195, 203
    Persian period 49
prose prayers. *See* prayers, prose
Psalms 56, 57, 181–83, 189
Qumran 15, 16, 19
    festival prayers 15
rabbinic literature 12
reconciliation 18
redaction criticism 145, 146, 150, 151, 162–63
Reformation 2
remnant 43, 44, 155, 170, 171
repentance 2, 27–34, 63, 71, 102
restoration 45, 60, 155, 158, 159
retribution 109, 169
    collective, compound 35, 36, 37, 38, 39, 42
rhetorical criticism. *See literary* criticism
Rib 13
Ricoeur, Paul 183, 187

ritual criticism	69–82, 194
ritual theory	69–82
royal psalms	3
foyal Zion festival	183
Sabbath	76, 155
sackcloth	10, 31, 123, 190
sacrifice	28–29, 30, 31, 32, 82
scripturalization, Scripture	11, 16, 24, 46–49, 113–16, 204
Servant(s) of YHWH	145–63
seven deadly sins	2
seven penitential prayers (Christianity)	2
seventy years	33
shame	17, 79, 142, 170
sin	34–39, 54, 59, 61, 62–63, 65, 69–82, 85, 90–98, 169, 171
deliberate	30, 31, 35, 79
intergenerational/intragenerational	35, 36, 37, 38, 39, 42, 59, 66, 80, 152, 199
involuntary	30, 79
Sitz im Leben	3, 4, 7, 13, 182, 186, 188, 189, 190, 199
sociology	8, 17, 18, 72, 75, 76, 85, 86, 106, 194
speech act theory	69–82, 193
suffering	6, 31, 59, 109, 110, 112
suzerainty treaty, suzerain	57–58
synagogue	9
synchronic analysis/methodologies	165, 191, 194
temple	14, 31, 44, 105, 108, 150, 151, 154, 156, 158, 166, 174, 175, 177, 178, 179, 190, 194
theodicy	55–56, 86, 89, 101–17, 202–3
Torah, law	28, 34, 45, 46–49, 62, 113–14, 170, 171, 179, 201, 204
tradition criticism	11, 16, 23, 24, 27, 46, 48, 151, 165, 193, 194
wisdom tradition	19–20, 101–17, 203–204
Zechariah, Zecharian tradition	14, 24, 52
Zion, Daughter Zion	24, 124, 125, 126, 158, 162

www.ingramcontent.com/pod-product-compliance
Lightning Source LLC
Chambersburg PA
CBHW032003220426
43664CB00005B/123